THE CHRISTIAN WRITERS
MARKET GUIDE

2026

THE CHRISTIAN WRITERS
MARKET GUIDE

2026

Your Comprehensive Resource for Getting Published

STEVE LAUBE

CWI CHRISTIAN
WRITERS
INSTITUTE

THE CHRISTIAN WRITERS MARKET GUIDE 2026

ISBN: 978-162-184-2521 (paperback)
       978-162-184-2538 (ebook)

Cover design by Hannah Linder (*hannahlinderdesigns.com*)
Typesetting by Jamie Foley (*jamiefoley.com*)
Edited by Lin Johnson (*wordprocommunications.com*)

Printed in the United States of America.

Visit The Christian Writers Institute at *www.ChristianWritersInstitute.com*.

E-mail: *admin@christianwritersmarketguide.com*

TABLE OF CONTENTS

Foreword by Jerry B. Jenkins vii
Introduction by Steve Laube ix
How to Use This Book xi

PART 1: TRADITIONAL BOOK PUBLISHERS 1

1. Traditional Book Publishers 3
2. Book Anthology Series 79

PART 2: INDEPENDENT BOOK PUBLISHING 83

3. Independent Book Publishers 85
4. Design and Production Services 107
5. Distribution Services 125

PART 3: PERIODICAL PUBLISHERS 127

6. Topics and Types 129
7. Adult Markets 137
8. Teen/Young Adult Markets 187
9. Children's Markets 195
10. Writers Markets 205

PART 4: SPECIALTY MARKETS 211

11. Devotional Booklets and Websites 213
12. Drama 225
13. Gifts and Greeting Cards 229
14. Tracts 233

15. Bible Curriculum 235

16. Miscellaneous 237

PART 5: SUPPORT FOR WRITERS 241

17. Literary Agents 243

18. Writers Conferences and Seminars 257

19. Writers Organizations and Groups 277

20. Editorial Services 313

21. Publicity and Marketing Services 381

22. Legal and Accounting Services 291

23. Speaking Services 393

24. Writing Education Resources 397

25. Contests and Awards 411

Denominational Publishers 431

Publishing Lingo 435

Index 447

Notes 461

FOREWORD

WHAT A TREASURE TROVE YOU HOLD IN YOUR HANDS—OR SEE ON YOUR SCREEN! And what a bargain!

Normally, I wouldn't write something so commercial; but if you're reading this, you've already invested in it, so I don't have to sell you on it.

I invest in guides like this every year, without fail. I believe writers are either stagnating or they're lifelong learners, growing in their skills. And *The Christian Writers Market Guide* is a nonnegotiable asset to that end.

Why do I still do this, after writing over 200 published books? Couldn't I just coast at this point?

Sure I could, and so could you. But I want to finish well. Two-thirds of my published works have been novels, so that means the remaining titles have been nonfiction books of all stripes. Where else could I go to keep up with what's happening in the marketplace in both broad genres?

I'm not the first and won't be the last to hammer home that the publishing landscape is roiling with change as never before. We all wonder where it will land, but I also think we realize it may never settle again. With the miracles of technology we see every day, we have to strap in and hang on for a tumultuous ride.

Never has it been easier to find a publishing solution. I'm an enthusiastic proponent of traditional publishing, urging every hopeful author to exhaust all efforts to get paid for being published, rather than paying even a dime to be printed.

But I'm also a realist and know how stacked against you the odds are these days. There's hardly an excuse for *not* getting your manuscript published nowadays. You're more likely to self-publish than not, so do yourself a favor:

Immerse yourself in this guide and learn everything you need to know about all the available options. It's still writing done well and stories well told that rise in the marketplace, so set yourself apart in the sea of competition and produce the absolute best work of which you're capable.

That you've chosen the *Christian* market guide tells me something. You have a message, something to say, a mission to accomplish. Welcome to the journey! I urge you to strive for excellence. Don't hide behind excuses or explanations that begin, "It's okay for a Christian book . . ."

Because we have access to a power source the rest of the market lacks, we should be leading the way in quality writing. Settle for nothing less.

— Jerry B. Jenkins
www.JerryJenkins.com

INTRODUCTION

WRITING IS A SERIOUS BUSINESS. It is also a serious calling. The privilege of having your words influence other people's thinking or inspiring their spirit is a gift from God. A number of publication opportunities for great writing from great authors exist. Traditional methods for publication remain, but the diversity of online opportunities are seemingly endless. In addition, independent-publication options have made it easier to see your byline on a book, on a blog post, or in an online magazine.

Since many Christian bookstores have closed, it may seem like the Christian publishing industry is shrinking; but it is not. It is simply changing. Therefore, you must research more effectively to find the best places for your work. The problem with online search engines is the immense number of results you receive. Then the results depend on that site's search-engine optimization and those who have paid to have their sites show at the top. *The Christian Writers Market Guide* has curated the information for you. Now you can find what is targeted specifically for the Christian market and your areas of interest.

One of the biggest mistakes a writer can make is to ignore the guidelines of an agent, an editor, or a publishing house. In the past, some publications dropped their listings in this guide because writers failed to follow the instructions in it. Editors are looking for writers who understand their periodicals or publishing houses and their unique approaches to the marketplace. This book will help you be such a writer. With a little time and effort, you can meet an editor's expectations, distinguish yourself as a professional, and sell what you write.

If you can, I recommend you attend a writers conference, whether in person or online. (We have many listed inside.) It is good to meet new people and become familiar with the best teachers in the industry. If you cannot get to a conference, consider exploring the courses available online at *ChristianWritersInstitute.com*. There are almost 50 to choose from, and you can enjoy them at any time on any device.

If this is the first time you've used this guide, read the "How to Use This Book" section. If you run into an unfamiliar term, look it up in the "Publishing Lingo" section in back and learn the terminology.

Please be aware that the information in this guide is provided by the companies or individuals through online questionnaires and email inquiries, as well as their websites and writers guidelines. The companies or individuals do not pay to be listed in this guide. The entries are not endorsed by me or The Christian Writers Institute. We make every attempt to verify the accuracy of the information provided. The entries are for information only. Any transaction(s) between a user of the information and the individuals or companies listed is strictly between those parties.

May God bless your writing journey. We are on a mission to change the world, word by word. To that end, strive for excellence and make your work compelling and insightful. Great writing is still in demand. But it must be targeted, crafted, critiqued, edited, polished, and proofread until it shines.

My thanks go to Lin Johnson whose invaluable work makes this all possible. She keeps tabs throughout the year on market changes, so every listing is accurate to the best of our information at the time of publication. (Our online version of this guide, *ChristianWritersMarketGuide.com*, is updated regularly during the year.) As the editor-administrator of the online and print editions, she is the genius behind the details. In addition, I would also like to acknowledge my wife, Lisa. Her love, support, and encouragement have been incalculable. We make a great team!

Steve Laube
President Emeritus
The Christian Writers Institute
and
President
The Steve Laube Agency
24 W. Camelback Rd. A-635
Phoenix, AZ 85013
www.christianwritersinstitute.com
www.stevelaube.com

To update a listing or to be added to the next edition or online, go to *christianwritersmarketguide.com*. Click on the Get Listed tab, and fill out the form.

For direct-sales questions, email the publisher:
admin@christianwritersinstitute.com.

For books and courses on the writing craft, visit The Christian Writers Institute:
www.christianwritersinstitute.com.

HOW TO USE THIS BOOK

THE CHRISTIAN WRITERS MARKET GUIDE 2026 IS DESIGNED to make it easier for you to sell your writing. It will serve you well if you use it as a springboard to become thoroughly familiar with the markets best suited to your writing style and areas of interest and expertise.

As you look through this guide, you may run into words in the listings that you are not familiar with. If so, check "Publishing Lingo" at the back of the book.

GETTING ACQUAINTED WITH THIS BOOK

Start by getting acquainted with the setup of this guide.

Book Publishers

Part 1 lists traditional book publishers and anthology series with information about what they are looking for. Notice that many houses accept manuscripts only from agents or through meeting with their editors at a writers conference. If you need a literary agent, check the agent listings in chapter 17.

Independent Book Publishing

Since independent book publishing is a viable option today, Part 2 provides resources to help you. Chapter 3 lists independent book publishers, many of which provide all the services you need as packages or à la carte options. If you decide to publish on your own, chapters 4 and 5 list design, production, and distribution services. You'll also want to hire a professional editor and proofreader, so see chapter 20 for help in this area.

Periodical Publishers

Part 3 lists periodical—magazine, journal, newspaper, and newsletter—publishers. Chapter 6 will help you find markets by topics (e.g., marriage, evangelism) and types (e.g., how-to, poetry, personal experience). Although these lists are not comprehensive, they provide a shortcut for finding appropriate markets for your ideas.

Cross-referencing may be helpful. For example, if you have an idea for a how-to article on parenting, look at the lists in both the how-to and parenting categories. Also, don't overlook writing on the same topic for different periodicals, such as money management for a general adult magazine, a teen magazine, a women's newsletter, and a magazine for leaders. Each would require a different slant, but you would get more mileage from one idea.

Specialty Markets

In Part 4, you'll find nonbook, nonperiodical markets like devotionals and drama. Here you can explore types of writing you may not have thought about but can provide a steady writing income.

Support for Writers

As a writer, you'll need support to keep going. Part 5 provides information for various kinds of support.

One of the best ways to get published today is to meet editors at writers conferences. Check out chapter 18 for a conference or seminar near you or perhaps in a location you'd like to visit. Before deciding which conference to attend, check the websites for who is on faculty, what houses are represented, and what classes are offered that can help you grow your craft and writing business. You may also want to factor in the size of the conference. Don't be afraid to stretch outside your comfort zone.

For ongoing support and feedback on your manuscripts, join a writers group. Chapter 19 lists groups by state and internationally. If you can't find one near you, consider starting one or join an online group.

Since editors and literary agents are looking for polished manuscripts, you may want to hire a professional editor. See chapter 20 for people who offer a variety of editorial services, including coaching.

Whether you publish your book with a royalty house or go the independent route, you'll need to do most, if not all, of the promotion. If you want to hire a specialist with contacts, check out chapter 21, "Publicity and Marketing Services." And if you need accounting or legal help, check out chapter 22.

One way to promote your message and your books is through speaking. If you need help in this area—and most writers do—see chapter 23, "Speaking Services." There you will find organizations and conferences that train speakers and/or connect them with groups looking for speakers.

Since writers who stagnate don't get published, check out chapter 24 for education resources to help you improve your writing style, write different types of manuscripts, and learn the business of writing and publishing. You'll find a variety of free and paid resources, including podcasts and classes.

Entering a writing contest can boost your sales, supplement your writing income, lead to publication, and sometimes give you valuable feedback on your writing. Check out chapter 25 for a list of contests and awards by genre. Many of them are not Christian oriented, but you can enter manuscripts with a Christian worldview.

USING THIS BOOK

Once you get acquainted with this guide, start using it. After you identify potential markets for your ideas and/or manuscripts, read their writers guidelines. If these are available on the website, the URL is included. Otherwise, email or send (with a SASE) for a copy. Also study at least one sample copy of a periodical (information to obtain one is given in most listings) or the book publisher's website to see if your idea truly fits there. Never send a manuscript without doing this market study.

Above all, keep in mind that this guide is only a starting point for your research and change is the one constant in the publishing industry. It is impossible for any market guide to be 100 percent accurate since editors move around, publications and publishing houses close, and new ones open. But this guide is an essential tool for getting published in the Christian market and making an impact on God's Kingdom with your words.

PART 1

TRADITIONAL BOOK PUBLISHERS

1

TRADITIONAL BOOK PUBLISHERS

Before submitting your query letter or book proposal, it's critical that you read and follow a publisher's guidelines exactly. In many cases, the guidelines are available on the website and a direct link is given in the entry. If you do not have a literary agent—and even if you do—check out a publisher thoroughly before signing a contract.

> **Note**: Not all the imprints listed in entries below are in this book, and some may be in separate entries here or in other sections.

1517 MEDIA
Augsburg Fortress, Beaming Books, Broadleaf Books, Fortress Press

ABINGDON PRESS
810 12th Ave. S, Nashville, TN 37203 | 615-749-6000
www.abingdonpress.com
Constance Stella, senior acquisitions editor
> **Denomination:** United Methodist
> **Parent company:** United Methodist Publishing House
> **Mission statement:** to provide the best, most effective religious publications available
> **Submissions:** Publishes 120 titles per year; receives 2,000 submissions annually. First-time authors: fewer than 5%. Submit proposal with sample chapters on the website. Bible: CEB.
> **Types and topics:** Christian living/spirituality, leadership, theology, academic

Royalty: minimum 7.5%

Types of books: ebook, hardcover, paperback

Guidelines: *www.abingdonpress.com/submissions*

Tip: "We're focusing on material to help pastors and other leaders do their jobs, and focusing more squarely on Methodist and other mainline leaders, churches, readers."

ABUNDANCE BOOKS LLC

1001 2nd St. #1001, Kalamazoo, MI 49001 | 616-648-1795

books@abundance-books.com | *abundance-books.com*

Jenn DaFoe-Turner, acquisition editor

Mission statement: to develop emerging authors and publish works that inspire, instruct, and encourage

Submissions: Publishes 25 titles per year; receives 500 submissions annually. First-time authors: 50%. Length: 60,000 words. Agent not required. Email proposal with complete manuscript or sample chapters. Responds in four weeks.

Types and topics: Christian living/spirituality, self-help, Bible studies, children, devotionals, fiction, memoir, middle grade

Royalty: 30–40%; advance sometimes, $500–1,000

Types of books: audiobook, ebook, hardcover, offset paperback, POD

Guidelines: *abundance-books.com/authors-2*

Tip: "Submit a full proposal."

AMBASSADOR INTERNATIONAL

411 University Ridge, Ste. B14, Greenville, SC 29601 | 864-751-4844

publisher@emeraldhouse.com | *www.ambassador-international.com*

Katie Cruice Smith, senior editor

Mission statement: to magnify Jesus while promoting His gospel through the written word

Submissions: Publishes 50 titles per year; receives 750 submissions annually. First-time authors: 50%. Length: minimum 144 pages. Submit proposal with sample chapters on the website. Responds in one month. Bible: KJV, NIV, ESV, NKJV, NASB.

Types and topics: biography, business, Christian living/spirituality, finances, theology, Bible studies, children, devotionals, fiction, teen/YA

Royalty: 15–20%, 25% for ebooks; no advance

Types of books: ebook, hardcover, paperback

Guidelines: *ambassador-international.com/get-published/submission-guidelines*

Tip: "We're most open to a book which has a clearly defined market and the author's total commitment to the project. We do well with first-time authors. We have full international coverage. Many of our titles sell globally."

AMG PUBLISHERS

6615 Standifer Gap Rd., Chattanooga, TN 37421 | 423-894-6060
amandaj@amginternational.org | *www.amgpublishers.com*
Amanda Jenkins, acquisitions and sales manager

Parent company: AMG International

Mission statement: to meet people's deepest needs, spiritual and physical, while inspiring hope, restoring lives, and transforming communities in Jesus' name

Submissions: Publishes 10 titles per year; receives 300 submissions annually. First-time authors: 50%. Length: minimum 150 pages. Agent not required. Email proposal with sample chapters, or submit through *ChristianBookProposals.com*. Responds in six months. Bible: NASB, ESV, NIV, KJV, CSB.

Types and topics: Bible characters, Bible study, Christian living/spirituality, self-help, spiritual growth, women's issues, Bible studies, devotionals

Royalty: starts at 14%; advance sometimes

Types of books: ebook, offset paperback, POD

Imprints: AMG (reference, Bible studies, Bibles, devotionals), Living Ink (YA fiction), God and Country Press (military/history devotionals)

Guidelines: *amgpublishers.com/index.php/author-guidelines*

Tip: "Looking for good, biblical content that does not offer a personal or denominational slant."

ANCIENT FAITH PUBLISHING

PO Box 3027, Munster, IN 46321 | 800-967-7377
marcij@ancientfaith.com | *ancientfaith.com/publishing*
Marci Rae Johnson, managing editor
Jane Meyer, children's book editor, jmeyer@ancientfaith.com

Denomination: Eastern Orthodox

Parent company: Ancient Faith Ministries, Inc.

Mission statement: to carry out the Great Commission of Jesus Christ through accessible and excellently crafted publications and creative media that educate, edify, and evangelize, leading to a living experience of God through His Holy Orthodox Church

Submissions: Publishes 14–18 titles per year; receives 50

submissions annually. First-time authors: 25%. Length: depends on book. Email proposal with complete manuscript. No agents. Responds in 6–12 weeks. Bible: NKJV.

Types and topics: Christian living/spirituality, church year, prayer, worship, academic, adult, children, devotionals, YA

Royalty: 6–12%; advance sometimes

First print run: 2,000–5,000

Types of books: audiobook, ebook, hardcover, offset paperback, POD

Imprints: Ancient Faith Kids (children)

Guidelines: *ww.ancientfaith.com/documents/12/Author_Submission_Guidelines_REV03-2025.pdf*

Tip: "We are looking for high-quality books from experienced writers. Submitting a full manuscript in lieu of sample chapters is viewed as a plus."

ANEKO PRESS

PO Box 652, Abbotsford, WI 54405 | 715-223-3013
jeremiah@lspbooks.com | *www.anekopress.com*
Jeremiah Zeiset, president

Parent company: Life Sentence Publishing, Inc.

Mission statement: to publish books for ministry

Submissions: Niche is publishing ministry-related books. Publishes 20 titles per year; receives 50 submissions annually. First-time authors: 20%. Length: 30,000–100,000 words. Submit proposal with complete manuscript on the website. Responds in two weeks. Bible: KJV, ESV, NKJV.

Types and topics: Christian living/spirituality

Royalty: 30%; no advance

First print run: 1,000–5,000

Types of books: audiobook, ebook, hardcover, offset paperback

Guidelines: *anekopress.com/write-for-us*

Tip: "The majority of our authors are in ministry as missionaries or other similar ministries."

ANGLICAN HOUSE PUBLISHERS

info@anglicanhousepublishers.org | *anglicanhousepublishers.org*
Rev. Ben Jefferies, liturgical book developer

Denomination: Anglican

Mission statement: to publish Bible-centered Anglican authors and satisfy the liturgical publishing needs of the church and to promote spiritual formation and showcase the Anglican Way of being a Christian

Submissions: Email proposal with sample chapters. Responds in three months minimum.
Types and topics: denomination, discipleship, ministry
Types of books: ebook, paperback
Guidelines: *anglicanhousepublishers.org/submissions*

ASHBERRY LANE

13607 Bedford Rd. NE, Cumberland, MD 21502 | 866-245-2211
r.white@whitefire-publishing.com | *AshberryLane.com*
Roseanna White, senior fiction editor
Parent company: WhiteFire Publishing
Mission statement: to publish heartfelt stories of faith
Submissions: Publishes 5-10 titles per year; receives 50 submissions annually. First-time authors: 10%. Length: 60,000-110,000 words. Email proposal with sample chapters. Responds in three months.
Types and topics: fiction: historical romance, romance, romantic suspense
Royalty: 50% for ebooks, 10% of retail for print; advance sometimes, $500-2,000
Type of books: POD
Guidelines: *ashberrylane.com/submissions*
Tip: "Please be familiar with our titles and mission."

ASPIRE PRESS

Tyndale House Publishers, 351 Executive Dr., Carol Stream, IL 60088 | 855-277-9400
LynnettePennings@tyndale.com | *www.hendricksonpublishers.com/lp/hr-aspire-press*
Lynnette Pennings, managing editor
Parent company: Rose Publishing/Tyndale House Publishers
Mission statement: to provide counseling for Christian living
Types and topics: Christian living/spirituality, counseling
Tip: Publishes books that are "compassionate in their approach and rich with Scripture," giving "godly insight and counsel for those personally struggling and for believers who have a heart to minister and encourage others." Need credentials in helping others.

AUGSBURG FORTRESS

PO Box 1209, Minneapolis, MN 55440-1209 | 800-328-4648
afsubmissions@augsburgfortress.org | *www.augsburgfortress.org*
Suzanne Burke, publisher, congregational resources

Denomination: Evangelical Lutheran Church in America
Parent company: 1517 Media
Mission statement: to develop engaging resources for Lutheran congregations
Submissions: Email proposal with sample chapters or a query. Responds in 60 days, only if it fits publishing needs.
Types and topics: Bible study, Christian living/spirituality, leadership, worship
Guidelines: *ms.augsburgfortress.org/downloads/Submission%20 Guidelines.pdf*

AVE MARIA PRESS

PO Box 428, Notre Dame, IN 46556 | 800-282-1865, ext. 1
submissions@mail.avemariapress.com | *www.avemariapress.com*
Josh Noem, editorial director
Katie Meads, acquisitions editor
> **Denomination:** Catholic
> **Mission statement:** to serve the spiritual and educational needs of individuals, groups, and the Church as a whole
> **Submissions:** Publishes 40 titles per year; receives 350 submissions annually. First-time authors: 30%. Length: 20,000–60,000 words. Email or mail proposal with sample chapters. Responds in three to four weeks. Bible: RSV2CE, NABRE.
> **Types and topics:** Advent, Christian living/spirituality, death and dying, evangelism, faith formation, family, grief, healing, marriage, ministry, parenting, prayer, theology, curriculum, ministry resources, small group study guides
> **Royalty:** 10%; advance, at least $1,000
> **Types of books:** ebook, hardcover, offset paperback
> **Guidelines:** *www.avemariapress.com/manuscript-submissions*
> **Tip:** "Our most successful books identify and address a specific felt-need for a potential reader. We are eager to work with authors who have robust platforms and direct connections to their potential readers."

B&H KIDS

200 Powell Pl., Ste. 100, Brentwood, TN 37027-7707 | 615-251-2000
www.bhpublishinggroup.com/categories/kids
Lauren Groves, acquisitions editor
> **Denomination:** Southern Baptist
> **Parent company:** B&H Publishing/Lifeway Christian Resources
> **Mission statement:** to help kids develop a lifelong relationship with

Jesus and to empower parents and church leaders to guide the spiritual growth of the next generation

Submissions: Any book for children or teens with a Christian message. Themes include but are not limited to adventure, attributes of God, Bible-story retellings, biblical virtues, church, community, diversity and inclusion, family, relationships, friendships, prayer, emotions, and theology. Publishes 18–24 titles per year; receives hundreds of submissions annually. First-time authors: 10–20%. Length: depends on age group. Agent only. Responds in one to three months. Bible: CSB.

Types and topics: Bible stories, board books, children, devotionals, fiction, first-chapter, middle grade, nonfiction, picture books, teen/YA

Royalty: 18–22%; advance

Types of books: audiobook, board books, ebook, hardcover, offset paperback, picture books

Guidelines: available via email

Tip: "We are a conservative Christian publishing house that publishes Protestant authors. Note that illustrations for children's books are not necessary or suggested."

B&H PUBLISHING GROUP

200 Powell Pl., Ste. 100, Brentwood, TN 37027-7707 | 615-251-2000
www.bhpublishinggroup.com
Mary Wiley, acquisitions editor, trade books
Logan Pyron, acquisitions editor, academic
Ashley Gorman, acquisitions and development editor, women's
Kristen Padilla, acquisitions editor, academic

Denomination: Southern Baptist

Parent company: LifeWay Christian Resources

Mission statement: to provide Bible-centered content that impacts hearts and minds, inspiring people in their lifelong relationship with Jesus Christ, because every word matters

Submissions: Publishes 90 titles per year; receives thousands of submissions annually. First-time authors: 10%. Agent only. Responds in two to three months. Bible: CSB.

Types and topics: Bible study, Christian living/spirituality, church growth, evangelism, leadership, marriage, parenting, theology, women, worship, academic, Bible reference/commentaries, children

Royalty: advance

Types of books: ebook, hardcover, offset paperback

Imprints: B&H Publishing (trade books), B&H Kids (children), B&H Academic (textbooks), Holman Bibles

Guidelines: not available

Tip: "Be informed that the market in general is very crowded with the book you might want to write. Do the research before submitting."

BAAL HAMON PUBLISHERS

244 Fifth Ave., Ste. T279, New York, NY 10001 | 646-233-4017
submissions@baalhamon.com | www.baalhamonpublishers.com
Temitope Oyetomi, managing and acquisitions editor

Parent company: Joy and Truth Christian Ministry

Mission statement: to be a global leader in publishing, distinguished by superlative production and distribution and an unwavering commitment to truth and integrity

Submissions: Publishes 30 titles per year; receives 90 submissions annually. First-time authors: 60%. Length: 50,000–70,000 words. Agent not required. Email proposal with sample chapters. Responds in one to two weeks. Bible: ESV.

Types and topics: Christian living/spirituality, counseling, health, marriage, parenting, self-help, biography, devotionals; fiction: most genres except fantasy, science fiction, and apocalyptic

Royalty: 60%; advance sometimes

First print run: hardcover, 1,000; paperback, 3,000

Types of books: ebook, hardcover, offset paperback, POD

Guidelines: *www.baalhamonpublishers.com/guidelines.html*

Tip: "Include a good analysis of similar books in the market and why yours will be better than most."

BAKER ACADEMIC

6030 E. Fulton Rd., Ada, MI 49301 | 616-676-9185
submissions@bakeracademic.com | bakeracademic.com
Robert Hosack, senior acquisitions editor
Anna Moseley Gissing, senior acquisitions editor
Brandy Scritchfield, acquisitions editor
Dustyn Elizabeth Keepers, acquisitions editor
Kristen Padilla, acquisitions editor

Parent company: Baker Publishing Group

Mission statement: to publish books that are notable for their inherent quality and deemed essential reading by students and scholars

Submissions: Publishes 50 titles per year, first-time authors: 20%. Agent preferred. Submit through *ChristianBookProposals.com*, or email proposal with sample chapters. Responds in 10 days.

Types and topics: Bible, Christian education, counseling, evangelism, leadership, ministry, missions, preaching, religion, spiritual formation, theology, worship, academic, professional

Royalty: 12–24%; advance, $500–15,000

Types of books: ebook, hardcover, offset paperback

Guidelines: *bakeracademic.com/pages/submit-a-proposal*

Tip: "Baker Academic welcomes book proposals from prospective authors holding relevant academic credentials (which usually means a PhD or similar degree in the field of the proposed book and a teaching position at a recognized institution of higher learning)."

BAKER BOOKS

6030 E. Fulton Rd., Ada, MI 49301 | 616-676-9185
bakerpublishinggroup.com/bakerbooks
Eddie Larow, acquisitions editor
Brian Vos, editorial director

Parent company: Baker Publishing Group

Mission statement: to build up the body of Christ through books that are relevant, intelligent, and engaging

Types and topics: apologetics, Christian living/spirituality, culture, discipleship, leadership, marriage, ministry, parenting, theology

Types of books: ebook, hardcover, offset paperback

Guidelines: *bakerpublishinggroup.com/contact/submission-policy*

BAKER PUBLISHING GROUP

Baker Academic, Baker Books, Bethany House, Brazos Press, Chosen, Lexham Press, Revell, Seed and Sparrow

BANNER OF TRUTH

610 Alexander Spring Rd., Carlisle, PA 17015 | 717-249-5747
info@banneroftruth.co.uk | *banneroftruth.org*
Ian Thompson, manager of North American operations

Types and topics: biography, Christian living/spirituality, church life, history, ministry, theology, children, commentaries, devotionals

Types of books: ebook, hardcover, offset paperback

Guidelines: *banneroftruth.org/us/about/contact-us/submit-a-manuscript*

Tip: "What makes a Banner book? It must be a book worthy of publication irrespective of its likely commercial success; it must pass theological and doctrinal scrutiny; it must promote practical Christian living; it most likely has enduring application and will be as relevant in 100 years as it is today; it must be well written and carefully edited; it must be well produced."

BARBOUR PUBLISHING, INC.

PO Box 719, Uhrichsville, OH 44683 | 740-922-6045
submissions@barbourbooks.com | *www.barbourbooks.com*
Annie Tipton, senior acquisitions editor, nonfiction
Paul Muckley, senior acquisitions editor, Bible and reference
Rebecca Germany, senior editor and acquisitions, fiction

Mission statement: to inspire the world with the life-changing message of the Bible

Types and topics: Christian classics, Christian living/spirituality, activities and puzzles, Bible reference/commentaries, Bible stories, children, devotionals, journals, planners, puzzles/quizzes; fiction: Amish, contemporary, historical, romance, suspense/thriller

Types of books: ebook, offset paperback

Imprints: Barbour Books (nonfiction), Barbour Fiction (novels), Barbour Reference, DayMaker (planners), Barbour Young Adult (nonfiction, devotionals), Barbour Kidz (children), Barbour Español (Spanish speaking), Barbour Bibles

Guidelines: *www.barbourbooks.com/frequently-asked-questions*

Tip: "To be considered, any proposal must (1) demonstrate a conservative, evangelical Christian worldview, and (2) speak to broad segments of the evangelical Christian market."

BEAMING BOOKS

510 Marquette Ave., Minneapolis, MN 55403 | 800-960-9705
www.beamingbooks.com
Naomi Krueger, senior acquisitions editor
Elizabeth Schleisman, acquisitions editor

Denomination: Evangelical Lutheran Church in America

Parent Company: 1517 Media

Submissions: Publishes 24 titles per year; receives 250 submissions annually. Board books for ages birth-3, picture books for ages 3–8, activity books for ages 3–8, early-reader and first-chapter books for ages 5–9, nonfiction books for ages 5–9 and 8–12, fiction for ages 8–12, activity books for families, devotionals for children ages 0–12 and families. First-time authors: 50%. Length: 500 words for picture books. Only agent or conference contact. Responds in three months. Bible: NIV, CEB.

Types and topics: activities and puzzles, children, devotionals, fiction, nonfiction

Royalty: advance

Types of books: board books, picture books, hardcover, paperback

Guidelines: *www.beamingbooks.com/info/submissions*
Tip: "We are most interested in picture books intended for a progressive Christian audience that take fresh, unexpected takes on familiar biblical or theological concepts."

BETHANY HOUSE PUBLISHERS

7808 Creekridge Cir., Ste. 250, Bloomington, MN 55439 | 952-829-2500
bakerpublishinggroup.com/bethanyhouse
Andy McGuire, editorial director
David Long, nonfiction acquisitions editor
Jeff Braun, nonfiction acquisitions editor
Jennifer Dukes Lee, nonfiction and children's acquisitions editor
Jessica Sharpe, senior fiction acquisitions editor
Rochelle Gloege, fiction acquisitions editor
  Parent company: Baker Publishing Group
  Mission statement: to publish high-quality writings that represent historical Christianity and serve the diverse interests and concerns of evangelical readers
  Submissions: Publishes 75–85 titles per year. Only agent or *ChristianBookProposals.com*. Bible: NIV.
  Types and topics: Christian living/spirituality, family, prayer, relationships, theology, devotionals; fiction: Amish, biblical, contemporary, fantasy, historical, Regency, romance, romantic suspense
  Royalty: varies; advance
  Types of books: ebook, hardcover, offset paperback
  Guidelines: *bakerpublishinggroup.com/contact/submission-policy*
  Tip: "The best opportunities for new authors come via literary agencies, conferences, writing communities, and author referrals. Get connected."

BOLD VISION BOOKS

PO Box 2011, Friendswood, TX 77549-2011 | 281-797-3920
boldvisionbooks@gmail.com | *www.boldvisionbooks.com*
Larry J. Leech, editor in chief
  Mission statement: to publish compelling, creative, and beautiful books to change the world and further the message of Christ through the written word
  Submissions: Publishes five titles per year; receives 250 submissions annually. First-time authors: 85%. Length: 50,000–60,000 words. Only agent or conference contact. Responds in six months. Bible: any but no more than five per book.
  Types and topics: Christian living/spirituality, devotionals

Royalty: 25%; advance sometimes, $1,000–5,000
Types of books: ebook, hardcover, offset paperback, POD
Guidelines: not available
Tip: "Give us a fresh approach to a time-honored concept. Build your platform through ministry, not numbers."

BRAZOS PRESS
6030 E. Fulton Rd., Ada, MI 49301 | 616-676-9185
submissions@brazospress.com | *bakerpublishinggroup.com/pages/ brazos-press*
Katelyn Beaty, editorial director and acquisitions
Robert Hosack, senior acquisitions editor
Grace P. Cho, senior acquisitions editor
   Parent company: Baker Publishing Group
   Mission statement: to draw upon the riches of the Christian story to deepen our understanding of God's world and inspire faithful reflection and engagement
   Submissions: Publishes books that creatively draw on the riches of our catholic Christian heritage to deepen our understanding of God's creation and inspire faithful reflection and engagement. Authors typically hold advanced degrees and have established publishing platforms. Agent preferred. Email proposal with sample chapters. Responds in 10 days.
   Types and topics: nonfiction
   Royalty: 12–24%; advance, $500-15,000
   Types of books: audiobook, ebook, hardcover, offset paperback, POD
   Guidelines: *bakerpublishinggroup.com/brazospress/submitting-a-proposal*
   Tip: "We welcome book proposals from scholars, church leaders, activists, artists, and writers who have something to say and can write with both skill and passion, demonstrating that serious writing can also be lively and compelling."

BRIMSTONE FICTION
1440 W. Taylor St., Ste. 449, Chicago, IL 60607 | 224-339-4159
rowena.brimstonefiction@gmail.com | *www.brimstonefiction.com*
Rowena Kuo, CEO and executive editor
   Submissions: Publishes 8–12 titles per year; receives 60 submissions annually. First-time authors: 60%. Length: 60,000–100,000 words. Agent or conference contact preferred. Email proposal with sample chapters or complete manuscript. Responds in six to eight weeks. Bible: NIV.

Types and topics: fiction: adventure, fantasy, historical, romantic suspense, science fiction, speculative, teen/YA, time travel, women's

Royalty: 30% of profits; no advance

Types of books: ebook, POD

Tip: "We welcome new and multipublished authors and/or authors with or without agents. If you have a good story, come and meet us at writers conferences or through our website."

BROADLEAF BOOKS

PO Box 1209, Minneapolis, MN 55440-1209 | 800-328-4648
submissions@broadleafbooks.com | *www.broadleafbooks.com*
Valerie Weaver-Zercher, senior acquisitions editor
Lisa Kloskin, acquisitions editor

Denomination: Evangelical Lutheran Church in America

Parent company: 1517 Media

Mission statement: to inspire transformation in readers and their communities to foster a more open, just, and compassionate world

Submissions: Agent preferred. Email proposal with sample chapters. Responds only if interested.

Types and topics: Christian living/spirituality, culture, social justice

Guidelines: *www.broadleafbooks.com/info/submissions*

Tip: "Please note that we receive a large volume of proposals. You will receive a response only if we see your proposal as a potential fit for our program."

BROADSTREET PUBLISHING GROUP

8646 Eagle Creek Cir., Ste. 210, Savage, MN 55378 | 855-935-2000
proposals@broadstreetpublishing.com | *www.broadstreetpublishing.com*
Tim Payne, editorial director

Submissions: Publishes 100+ titles per year. Agent preferred. Email proposal with sample chapters.

Types and topics: Bible promises, biography, Christian living/ spirituality, children, coloring books, devotionals, fiction, journals

Imprints: Belle City Gifts (journals and planners), Broadstreet Kids (children)

Guidelines: *broadstreetpublishing.com/contact*

CALLA PRESS PUBLISHING

1495 Timbercreek Dr., Stephenville, TX 76401 | 972-971-8745
callapresspublishing@gmail.com | *www.callapresspublishing.com*
Samantha Cabrera, founder, publisher

Madison Aichele, executive director, madison.callapresspublishing@gmail.com

Denomination: Christian Reformed

Mission statement: to spread the gospel truth through pure, lovely, and noble books

Submissions: Publishes 10 titles per year; receives 200 submissions annually. Currently requires fully illustrated children's picture books. Periodically closes to submissions, so check the website to see if it is open. First-time authors: 75%. Length: 50,000 words. Prefers agent or conference contact. Submit through *ChristianBookProposals.com*, or email proposal with complete manuscript or sample chapters or a query. Responds in five to eight months. Bible: ESV, NLT.

Types and topics: Christian living/spirituality, children, devotionals, fiction, teen/YA

Royalty: 20%; no advance

First print run: 300–500

Types of books: ebook, hardcover, offset paperback, POD

Guidelines: *www.callapresspublishing.com/book-submissions*

Tip: "The work must be polished grammatically, be biblically sound, and preferably be in the active voice."

CASCADE BOOKS

199 W. 8th Ave., Ste. 3, Eugene, OR 97401 | 541-344-1528
proposal@wipfandstock.com | *wipfandstock.com/search-results-grid/
?imprint=cascade-books*
Michael Thomson, acquisitions and development editor

Parent company: Wipf and Stock

Submissions: Agent not required. Email proposal with sample chapters. Responds in one to two months.

Types and topics: religion, theology

Types of books: ebook, POD

Guidelines: *wipfandstock.com/submitting-a-proposal*

CASCADIA PUBLISHING HOUSE

126 Klingerman Rd., Telford, PA 18969
editor@CascadiaPublishingHouse.com | *CascadiaPublishingHouse.com*
Michael A. King, publisher and editor

Submissions: Looking for creative, thought-provoking, Anabaptist-related material.

Types and topics: nonfiction

Imprints: DreamSeeker Books

Guidelines: *www.cascadiapublishinghouse.com/submit.htm*

Tip: "All Cascadia books receive rigorous evaluation and some form of peer or consultant review."

CASTLE QUAY BOOKS

3798 Hamilton Key, West Palm Beach, FL 33411 | 416-573-3249
lwillard@rogers.com | castlequaybooks.com
Marina Hofman, acquisitions editor

Parent company: Castle Quay Communications, Inc.

Mission statement: to advance the Canadian and American Christian writing community, with the purpose of developing and publishing inspirational, balanced, moral, quality titles by both established and new authors, promoting quality messages that will inform, challenge, inspire, and uplift all readers

Submissions: Publishes 12 titles per year; receives 30 submissions annually. First-time authors: 30%. Length: 40,000 words. Agent not required. Submit through *ChristianBookProposals.com,* or email proposal with sample chapters or a query. Responds in five weeks. Bible: ESV.

Types and topics: biography, business, Christian living/spirituality, culture, family, finances, history, leadership, politics, self-help, social justice, teaching, academic, children, devotionals, fiction, gift, memoir, teen/YA

Royalty: 10–15%; advance sometimes

First print run: 1,000

Types of books: audiobook, ebook, hardcover, offset paperback, POD

Guidelines: *castlequaybooks.com/pages/submitting-a-manuscript*

Tip: "Be brief."

CATHOLIC BOOK PUBLISHING CORP.

77 W. End Rd., Totowa, NJ 07572 | 877-228-2665
info@catholicbookpublishing.com | www.catholicbookpublishing.com
Anthony Buono, editor

Denomination: Catholic

Submissions: No agents. No simultaneous submissions. Mail query first. Responds in two to three months.

Types and topics: Christian living/spirituality, liturgy, prayer

Royalty: flat fee; no advance

Imprint: Resurrection Press (popular nonfiction)

Guidelines: *catholicbookpublishing.com/pages/faq*

CELEBRATE LIT PUBLISHERS

35459 Stockton St., Beaumont, CA 92223 | 909-520-8603
celebratelitpublishing@celebratelit.com | *www.celebratelitpublishing.com*
Denise Barela, commissioning editor
Sandra Barela, owner

Mission statement: to encourage you and change your life

Submissions: Publishes 20–30 titles per year; receives 100 submissions annually. First-time authors: 80%. Length: 70,000 words. Agent not required. Email proposal with complete manuscript. Responds in eight weeks. Bible: ESV.

Types and topics: Bible study, Christian living/spirituality, self-help, memoir; fiction: Amish, children, contemporary, fantasy, historical, mystery, suspense, teen/YA

Royalty: 70%; no advance

Guidelines: *www.celebratelitpublishing.com/submit-a-manuscript*

Tip: "Include a solid marketing plan."

CF4K

Geanies House, Fearn, Tain, Ross-shire IV20 1TW, Scotland, UK | 01862-871011
Catherine.Mackenzie@christianfocus.com | *www.christianfocus.com/en-gb/imprints/cf4kids*
Catherine Mackenzie, children's editor

Parent company: Christian Focus Publications

Mission statement: to help children find out about God and get them enthusiastic about reading the Bible, now and later in their lives

Submissions: Email or mail proposal with sample chapters. Responds in three to six months.

Types and topics: Christian living/spirituality, Bible stories, biography, crafts, devotionals, game books, puzzles and activities

Types of books: hardcover, paperback

Guidelines: *www.christianfocus.com/en-gb/about/submissions/childrens-guidelines*

Tip: "Read our website please. Don't send us stuff we don't publish."

CHALICE PRESS

11939 Manchester Rd. #110, Des Pares, MO 63131
submissions@chalicepress.com | *chalicepress.com*

Denomination: Disciples of Christ

Parent company: Christian Board of Publication

Submissions: Publishes 12 titles per year; receives hundreds of submissions annually. Email query first.

Types and topics: contemporary issues, leadership, social justice, spiritual maturity, church resources; fiction: contemporary, historical after 1800

Guidelines: *chalicepress.com/pages/write-for-us*

Tip: "Every Chalice contract begins with an 'Affirmation of Diversity': The Christian Board of Publication and its imprints affirm the faith and gifts of persons regardless of race, color, religion, gender, national origin, age, disability, sexual orientation, or gender expression and will not publish material that opposes this affirmation."

CHARISMA HOUSE

600 Rinehart Rd., Lake Mary, FL 32746 | 407-333-0600
Debbie.Marrie@CharismaMedia.com | *www.charismahouse.com*
Debbie Marrie, VP of acquisitions and content development

Denomination: Charismatic/Pentecostal

Parent company: Charisma Media/Plus Communications, Inc.

Mission statement: to inspire people to encounter the power of the Holy Spirit

Submissions: Publishes 50–60 titles per year; receives 150–200 submissions annually. First-time authors: fewer than 10%. Length: 50,000–60,000 words/224–256 pages. Agent preferred. Email proposal with sample chapters. Responds in one month. Bible: MEV.

Types and topics: Christian living/spirituality, end-times prophecy, fitness, health, spiritual warfare

Royalty: 16–25%; advance sometimes

Types of books: audiobook, ebook, hardcover, offset paperback, POD

Imprints: Siloam (natural health remedies), FrontLine (current events, end-time prophecy)

Guidelines: via email

Tip: "Three key areas we evaluate are the concept, the writing quality, and the author's platform."

CHOSEN

7808 Creekridge Cir., Ste. 250, Bloomington, MN 55439 | 952-829-2500
bakerpublishinggroup.com/chosen
Kim Bangs, editorial director
Luverta Reames, acquisition editor

Denomination: Charismatic

Parent company: Baker Publishing Group

Mission statement: to publish books that highlight the active work of the Holy Spirit

Submissions: Publishes 24 titles per year; receives 100 submissions annually. First-time authors: 75%. Length: 50,000–53,000 words. Only agent or conference contact. Bible: any.

Types and topics: Charismatic, nonfiction

Royalty: varies; advance sometimes

Types of books: audiobook, ebook, hardcover, offset paperback

Guidelines: not available

Tip: "Build relationships and platform."

CHRISM PRESS

13607 Bedford Rd. NE, Cumberland, MD 21502 | 301-876-4876
submissions@chrismpress.com | *www.chrismpress.com*
Karen Ullo, editor
Rhonda Ortiz, editor
Marisa Stokely, editor
William Gonch, editor

Denomination: Catholic, Orthodox Christian

Parent company: WhiteFire Publishing

Mission statement: to publish stories informed by Catholic and Orthodox Christianity that may not be able to find a home in either mainstream secular or Christian (evangelical) presses

Submissions: Publishes 6–12 titles per year; receives 50 submissions annually. First-time authors: 25%. Length: 60,000–120,000 words. Email query first. Responds in three months.

Types and topics: fiction: all genres, adult, teen/YA

Royalty: 50% for ebooks, 10% for print; advance sometimes

Types of books: audiobook, ebook, POD

Guidelines: *www.chrismpress.com/submissions*

Tip: "We are acquiring adult and young-adult fiction that reflects a Catholic or Orthodox Christian worldview and appeals to Catholic and/or Orthodox readers. Please read our submissions guidelines and FAQ."

CHRISTIAN FOCUS PUBLICATIONS

Geanies House, Fearn, Tain, Ross-shire IV20 1TW, Scotland, UK | 01862-871011
submissions@christianfocus.com | *www.christianfocus.com*
Willie Mackenzie, director of publishing
Catherine Mackenzie, children's editor, Catherine.Mackenzie@christianfocus.com

Types and topics: Christian living/spirituality, theology, academic, biography, children, commentaries

Types of books: hardcover, paperback

Imprints: Christian Focus (popular adult titles), CF4K (children), Mentor (serious readers), Christian Heritage (classic writings from the past)

Guidelines: *www.christianfocus.com/en-us/about/submissions/adult-guidelines*

Tip: "Read our website please. Don't send us stuff we don't publish."

CHURCH PUBLISHING INCORPORATED

19 E. 34th St., New York, NY 10016 | 800-242-1918

astuart@cpg.org | www.churchpublishing.org

Airié Stuart, senior VP and publisher

Fiona Hallowell, executive editor

Denomination: Episcopal

Types and topics: Bible study, biography, Christian living/spirituality, finances, leadership, prayer, retirement, social justice, theology, worship, academic

Types of books: audiobook, ebook, hardcover, paperback

Imprints: Morehouse Publishing (lay readers), Seabury Books (scholarly readers)

Guidelines: *www.churchpublishing.org/manuscriptsubmission*

Tip: "CPI's core publishing program is structured around *The Book of Common Prayer; The Hymnal 1982*; and the specialized books and resources used in the liturgy, faith formation, governance, life, and mission of the Episcopal Church."

CKN CHRISTIAN PUBLISHING

cknchristianpublishing.com

Mike Bray, CEO

Parent company: Wolfpack Publishing

Mission statement: to publish books that will help readers to rise and develop their understanding of God's Word and to apply it more abundantly to their lives

Submissions: Submit through the website form. Responds in three months or not interested.

Types and topics: fiction: Amish, historical, mystery, post-apocalyptic, romance, science fiction, thriller, westerns

Royalty: up to 35% retail

Types of books: ebook, POD

Guidelines: *cknchristianpublishing.com/christian-manuscript-submissions*

Tip: "We are dedicated to bringing readers wholesome novels that ensure there's something for everyone to read. No sexually explicit scenes, graphically violent descriptions, or streams of profanity."

CLC PUBLICATIONS

PO Box 1449, Fort Washington, PA 19034 | 215-542-1242
submissions@clcpublications.com | *www.clcpublications.com*
James Bock, acquisitions editor
David E. Fessenden, editorial coordinator

Parent company: CLC Ministries International

Mission statement: to produce books for the deeper life

Submissions: Publishes 12–15 titles per year; receives 100 submissions annually. First-time authors: 50%. Length: 35,000–75,000 words. Agent not required but preferred. Email proposal with sample chapters, or submit through the website form. Responds in six weeks. Bible: ESV.

Types and topics: Christian living/spirituality, adult

Royalty: 12–14%; advance sometimes

Types of books: audiobook, ebook, hardcover, offset paperback, POD

Guidelines: *www.clcpublications.com/about/prospective-authors-submissions*

Tip: "Demonstrate a thorough engagement with Scripture, and not simply proof-texting."

COLLEGE PRESS PUBLISHING

1307 W. 20th St., Joplin, MO 64804 | 417-623-6280
collpressjoplin@gmail.com | *www.collegepress.com*
Karl Halverson, executive director

Denomination: Church of Christ

Submissions: Email or mail query. Responds in two to three months.

Types and topics: apologetics, biography, Christian living/spirituality, academic, Bible reference/commentaries, Bible studies

Guidelines: *www.collegepress.com/pages/for-authors*

CONVERGENT BOOKS

1745 Broadway, New York, NY 10019 | 212-366-2724
dreed@penguinrandomhouse.com | *www.randomhousebooks.com/imprint/convergent-books*
Derek Reed, editorial director

Mathew Burdette, editor and acquisitions

Parent company: Penguin Random House

Mission statement: to seek out diverse viewpoints and honest conversations that shed light on the defining challenges facing people of faith today; to help readers ask important questions, find paths forward in disagreement, and shape the way faith is expressed in the modern world

Submissions: Publishes 12-16 titles per year; receives 100-150 submissions annually. First-time authors: 10%. Length: 204-300 pages/45,000-65,000 words. Agent only. Responds in a few weeks to two months. Bible: NIV, ESV.

Types and topics: Christian living/spirituality, deconstruction/reconstruction of faith, friendship, marriage, memoir/personal narrative, parenting, self-help, social issues, social justice, wellness, essays, memoir, poetry

Royalty: 10-15%; advance, $10,000 to high six figures

Types of books: audiobook, ebook, hardcover, offset paperback

Guidelines: not available

Tip: "Have a good agent and a good platform."

CREATIVE COMMUNICATIONS FOR THE PARISH

1564 Fencorp Dr., Fenton, MO 63026 | 800-325-9414
submissions@creativecommunications.com |
 catholic.creativecommunications.com

Denomination: Catholic

Parent Company: Bayard, Inc.

Mission statement: to communicate the gospel of Jesus to the whole body of Christ through new and innovative worship and devotional materials that can be used and distributed by churches and schools to encourage faith and evangelize

Submissions: Email or mail proposal with sample chapters or complete manuscript. Responds in 10 weeks.

Types and topics: Christian living/spirituality, ministry, prayer, sacraments, worship, children, devotionals, ministry resources, puzzles and activities, teen/YA

Types of books: ebook, paperback

Guidelines: *catholic.creativecommunications.com/Pages/Item/7341/ Submissions.aspx*

CROSSLINK PUBLISHING

1601 Mt. Rushmore Rd., Ste. 3288, Rapid City, SD 57701 | 888-697-4851
publisher@crosslink.org | www.crosslinkpublishing.com
Rick Bates, managing editor

Parent company: CrossLink Ministries

Submissions: Publishes 35 titles per year; receives 500 submissions annually. First-time authors: 85%. Length: 12,000–60,000 words. Submit on the website. Responds in one week.

Types and topics: Christian living/spirituality, Bible studies, children, devotionals, fiction

Royalty: 16%, 20% over 5,000 sold; no advance

First print run: 2,000

Types of books: ebook, offset paperback

Imprint: New Harbor Press

Guidelines: *www.crosslinkpublishing.com/submit-a-manuscript*

Tip: "We are particularly interested in providing books that help Christians succeed in their daily walk (inspirational, devotional, small groups, etc.)."

CROSSRIVER MEDIA GROUP

1185 W. 7th St., Colby, KS 67701 | 785-462-0400
submissions@crossrivermedia.com | www.crossrivermedia.com
Tamara Clymer, publisher

Mission statement: to empower women to embrace a bold, fearless faith through life-changing books and resources

Submissions: Publishes four to eight titles per year; receives 60–75 submissions annually. First-time authors: 30–40%. Length: 50,000–80,000 words. Agent or conference contact preferred. Email proposal with sample chapters. Responds in 12–16 weeks. Bible: any except NIV.

Types and topics: Bible study, Christian living/spirituality, family, inspirational, marriage; fiction: biblical, contemporary, end times, historical, mystery, romance

Royalty: 8–12%; no advance

Types of books: ebook, hardcover, POD

Guidelines: *www.crossrivermedia.com/guidelines*

Tip: "Be as complete and thorough as possible when describing your marketing plan and platform."

CROSSWAY

1300 Crescent St., Wheaton, IL 60187 | 630-682-4300
submissions@crossway.org | www.crossway.org
Todd Augustine, senior acquisitions editor
Samuel James, associate acquisitions editor
Champ Thornton, children's book acquisitions

Parent company: Good News Publishers

Mission statement: to publish books that combine the truth of God's Word with a passion to live it out, with unique and compelling Christian content

Submissions: Publishes 120 titles per year; receives 1,500 submissions annually. First-time authors: 1%. Length: 30,000–40,000 words. Agent not required. Email query first. Responds in six weeks if proposal is requested. Bible: ESV.

Types and topics: Bible study, Christian living/spirituality, contemporary issues, spiritual growth, worldview, academic, Bible reference/commentaries, devotionals

Royalty: varies; advance

Types of books: audiobook, ebook, hardcover, offset paperback

Guidelines: *www.crossway.org/submissions*

Tip: "Be sure your query clearly represents what your book is about and why you are qualified to write the book."

CSS PUBLISHING COMPANY, INC.

5450 N. Dixie Hwy., Lima, OH 45807-9559 | 419-227-1818
editor@csspub.com | www.csspub.com
David Runk, publisher

Mission statement: to provide lectionary-based preaching and worship resources

Submissions: Publishes 10–20 titles per year; receives 30 submissions annually. First-time authors: 50%. Length: 30,000–35,000 words. Agent not required. Email or mail complete manuscript. Responds in six months. Bible: NRSV.

Types and topics: Christian education, counseling, funerals, illustrations, ministry, preaching, stewardship, weddings, worship, drama, sermons

Royalty: 6%, $35–40 per sermon in a collection; no advance

Types of books: ebook, POD

Imprint: Fairway Press (self-publishing)

Guidelines: *store.csspub.com/page.php?Custom%20Pages=10*

Tip: "See our guidelines on our website."

D6 FAMILY MINISTRY

114 Bush Rd., Nashville, TN 37217 | 615-361-1221
books@d6family.com | D6family.com
Danny Conn, director of editorial and strategic projects

Denomination: Free Will Baptist
Parent company: National Association of Free Will Baptists
Mission statement: to build disciples through church and home
Submissions: Publishes 8–12 titles per year; receives 20–30 submissions annually. First-time authors: 30%. Length: 30,000–90,000 words. Agent not required. Conference contact a plus. Email proposal with sample chapters. Responds in three months. Bible: any.
Types and topics: discipleship, family ministry, academic
Royalty: 15–20%; advance sometimes, $250–500
First print run: 2,000
Types of books: audiobook, ebook, offset paperback
Imprints: D6 Family (family ministry, generational discipleship), Randall House (theology, Free Will Baptist history), Randall House Academic (family ministry textbooks)
Guidelines: *rhpweb.s3.amazonaws.com/Book-Proposal-Guide.pdf*
Tip: "Our audience is primarily theologically conservative evangelicals with interests in family ministry and discipleship."

DAVID C COOK

4050 Lee Vance Dr., Colorado Springs, CO 80918 | 719-536-0100
www.davidccook.org
Michael Covington, VP of publishing and acquisitions, pastors, leaders
Susan McPherson, acquisitions, women
Luke McKinnon, acquisitions editor, apologetics and worldview
Laura Derico, acquisitions, children

Mission statement: to equip the Church with Christ-centered resources for making and teaching disciples
Submissions: Publishes 40 titles per year; receives 1,200 submissions annually. First-time authors: 10%. Length: 45,000–50,000 words. Agent or conference contact only. Responds in one month.
Types and topics: Christian living/spirituality, discipleship, family, leadership, marriage, men, parenting, women, Bible reference/commentaries, Bible studies, church resources, devotionals, teen/YA
Royalty: 12–22%; advance
Types of books: ebook, hardcover, offset paperback, POD
Imprints: Esther Press (women), Group (church resources)
Guidelines: *davidccook.org/submissions-and-writer-guidelines*

Tip: "We look for significant platform, excellent writing, and relevant content."

DOVE CHRISTIAN PUBLISHERS

PO Box 611, Bladensburg, MD 20710 | 240-342-3293
editorial@dovechristianpublishers.com | *www.dovechristianpublishers.com*
Raenita Wiggins, acquisitions editor

Parent company: Kingdom Christian Enterprises

Mission statement: to glorify Jesus Christ and build the Kingdom of God through the written word, while entertaining, edifying, encouraging, and exhorting the body of Christ

Submissions: Publishes 10 titles per year; receives 300 submissions annually. Requires professional copyedit before submitting. First-time authors: 95%. Length: minimum 32,000 words. Agent not required. Submit proposal with sample chapters on website only. Responds in four to six weeks or not interested. Bible: NIV.

Types and topics: Christian living/spirituality, church life, discipleship, ministry, prayer, Bible studies, children, devotionals; fiction: fantasy, historical, humor, mystery, romance, science fiction, suspense/thriller

Royalty: 10–25%; no advance

Types of books: ebook, hardcover, POD

Guidelines: *www.dovechristianpublishers.com/publish-with-us*

Tip: "Author should establish a platform and familiarize themselves with book marketing and promotion prior to submission."

EERDMANS BOOKS FOR YOUNG READERS

2006 44th St. SE, Grand Rapids, MI 49508 | 800-253-7521
ebyrsubmissions@eerdmans.com | *www.eerdmans.com/youngreaders*
Kathleen Merz, editorial director
Courtney Zonnefeld, assistant editor

Parent company: Wm. B. Eerdmans Publishing Co.

Mission statement: to engage young minds with books—books that are honest, wise, and hopeful; books that delight us with their storyline, characters, or good humor; books that inform, inspire, and entertain

Submissions: Publishes 18–20 titles per year; receives 1,500 submissions annually. First-time authors: 5–10%. Length: picture books, 1,000 words; middle-grade books, 15,000–30,000 words. Agent preferred. Email proposal with complete manuscript or sample chapters. Responds in four months only if interested.

Types and topics: animals, history, multicultural, nature, social issues, board books, middle grade, picture books
Royalty: advance
Types of books: audiobook, ebook, hardcover, paperback
Guidelines: *www.eerdmans.com/youngreaders/submission-guidelines*
Tip: "We are currently looking for manuscripts appropriate for our Spectacular STEAM for Curious Readers and Stories from Latin America series." Also looking for "stories featuring diverse stories and experiences, including those related to race, ethnicity, and culture; gender and sexuality; (dis)ability and neurodiversity; age and community."

EERDMANS, WM. B. PUBLISHING CO.

2006 44th St. SE, Grand Rapids, MI 49508 | 800-253-7521
submissions@eerdmans.com | *www.eerdmans.com*
Trevor Thompson, senior acquisitions editor
Lisa Ann Cockrel, acquisitions editor

Submissions: Publishes 100 titles per year. Agent not required. Email proposal with complete manuscript or sample chapters. Responds in eight weeks.
Types and topics: biography, Christian living/spirituality, contemporary issues, ethics, history, ministry, theology, academic, Bible reference/commentaries
Royalty: advance
Imprint: Eerdmans Books for Young Readers (children and teens)
Guidelines: *www.eerdmans.com/submissions*
Tip: "Eerdmans publishes excellent books by well-qualified authors in biblical and theological studies and in religious approaches to philosophy, history, art, literature, ethics, and contemporary social and cultural issues. Target readerships range from academic to semipopular. We are publishing a growing number of books in Christian life, spirituality, and ministry."

ELK LAKE PUBLISHING, INC.

35 Dogwood Dr., Plymouth, MA 02360-3166 | 508-746-1734
Deb@ElkLakePublishingInc.com | *ElkLakePublishingInc.com*
Deb Haggerty, publisher and editor in chief
Cristel Phelps, managing editor, fiction, cristeledits@gmail.com
Judy Hagey, managing editor, nonfiction, judy@judyhagey.com

Mission statement: to encourage and empower authors to publish their works in the most professional manner possible

Submissions: Publishes 60–100 titles per year; receives 300 submissions annually. First-time authors: 80%. Length: 80,000–100,000 words. Agent not required. Conference contact a plus. Email proposal with sample chapters. Responds in two weeks. Bible: NASB, ESV.

Types and topics: Christian living/spirituality, adult, fiction, middle grade, YA

Royalty: 40%; no advance

Types of books: audiobook, ebook, POD

Guidelines: *elklakepublishinginc.com Submissions Tab*

Tip: "Send a well-written cover letter and know the types of books we publish."

EMANATE BOOKS

PO Box 141000, Nashville, TN 37214-1000 | 615-889-9000
www.thomasnelson.com/emanatebooks
Janene MacIvor, senior editor

Parent company: Thomas Nelson Publishers/HarperCollins Christian Publishing

Mission statement: to reflect the work of the Holy Spirit, feed His church, and help a new generation hear from God and grow in their spiritual journey

Types and topics: Charismatic, Christian classics

Types of books: audiobook, ebook, hardcover, offset paperback

ENCLAVE PUBLISHING

24 W. Camelback Rd. A-635, Phoenix, AZ 85013
acquisitions@enclavepublishing.com | *www.enclavepublishing.com*
Steve Laube, publisher and acquisitions editor

Parent company: Oasis Family Media

Mission statement: to publish out-of-this-world stories that are informed by a coherent theology

Submissions: Publishes 12–18 titles per year; receives 200 submissions annually. First-time authors: 20–30%. Length: 80,000–140,000 words. Author referral, conference contact, or proposal with sample chapters on the website. Responds in 60–90 days.

Types and topics: fiction: allegory, fantasy, science fiction, speculative, supernatural

Royalty: industry standard; no advance

First print run: 2,000–5,000

Types of books: audiobook, ebook, hardcover, offset paperback

Imprint: Enclave Escape (YA)

Guidelines: *www.enclavepublishing.com/guidelines*

Tip: "Keep word count above 80,000 words and below 140,000. Too often we are sent books that are either far too short or extremely long."

END GAME PRESS

PO Box 206, Nesbit, MS 38651 | 901-590-6584

submissions@endgamepress.com | *www.endgamepress.com*

Victoria Duerstock, founder

Michelle Medlock Adams, executive editor, Wren & Bear Books

Edwina Perkins, executive editor and acquisitions, Harambee Press

Mission statement: to leverage all of its resources to make the greatest positive impact possible by holding a high standard for the books it publishes in both design and quality, while also making the experience a good one for each of the authors in the End Game Press family

Submissions: Publishes 20 titles per year; receives 300 submissions annually. First-time authors: 25%. Length: depends on the genre. Agent only. Responds in two to three months. Bible: any. Also publishes general-market books.

Types and topics: Christian living/spirituality, faith, marriage, parenting, prayer, fiction

Royalty: 20–25%; advance

Types of books: audiobook, ebook, hardcover, paperback

Imprints: Wren and Bear Books (children and YA), Harambee Press (ethnic/BIPOC), Li'l Liberty (children with focus on Americana), Fusion (hybrid publishing)

Guidelines: *www.endgamepress.com/submissions*

Tip: Currently closed for submissions; check the website for updates.

EXEGETICA PUBLISHING

PO Box 241, Fort Walton Beach, FL 32549 | 816-269-8505

editor@exegeticapublishing.com | *www.exegeticapublishing.com*

Mission statement: to encourage Christians and non-Christians alike to engage with the Bible, to understand the world around them, and to "taste and see that the Lord is good," as Psalm 34:8 exhorts

Submissions: Publishes 10 titles per year; receives 30 submissions annually. First-time authors: 10%. Length: 200–300 pages. Email proposal with sample chapters. Responds in two to four weeks. Bible: NASB, NKJV, ESV.

Types and topics: Bible, Christian living/spirituality, theology, academic, nonfiction

Royalty: 10%; no advance
Types of books: ebook, offset paperback
Imprint: Grace Acres Press (trade nonfiction)
Guidelines: *exegeticapublishing.com/submit-a-proposal*
Tip: "Follow submission guidelines with solid biblical resources."

EXPANSE BOOKS

15 Lucky Ln., Morrilton, AR 72110 | 501-289-9319
expansebooks@gmail.com | *expansebooks.pub*
Erin R. Howard, managing editor
Parent company: Scrivenings Press LLC
Mission statement: to spread God's word through our writing
Submissions: Publishes three titles per year; receives 100 submissions annually. First-time authors: 30%. Length: 60,000–90,000 words. Only conference contact. Responds in four to six weeks. Bible: any.
Types and topics: fiction: YA, dystopian, fairy tales, fantasy, magical realism, speculative, time travel
Royalty: 12%, 50% ebook, 40% pages read in Kindle Unlimited; no advance
Types of books: ebook, hardcover, POD
Guidelines: *expansebooks.pub/submissions*
Tip: "If you've ever pitched a speculative proposal to a 'normal' publisher and watched the 'What are they talking about?' expression stream across their face, well, we've been there, too. At Expanse Books, we don't just publish speculative fiction, we read it. We write it. We love it. We get it."

FAITHWORDS

830 Crescent Centre Dr., Franklin, TN 37067 | 615-221-0996
www.faithwords.com
Beth Adams, editorial director
Marissa Arrigoni, acquisitions
Parent company: Hachette Book Group
Types and topics: apologetics, Bible study, Christian living/spirituality, culture, marriage, memoir/personal narrative, parenting, social issues, theology
Royalty: minimum 10%; advance
Types of books: ebook, hardcover, offset paperback
Tip: "Have a clear, well-written proposal and a solid platform."

FIRST STEPS PUBLISHING

PO Box 571, Gleneden Beach, OR 97388 | 541-961-7641
submissions@firststepspublishing.com | *www.FirstStepsPublishing.com*
RJ McRoberts, submissions editor

Mission statement: to help new authors build a strong publishing foundation through professional design, support, and guidance

Submissions: Publishes 5–15 titles per year; receives 30 submissions annually. First-time authors: 90%. Length: 50,000–100,000 words. Agent not required. Query first through the website form. Responds in 8–12 weeks, although reply is not guaranteed. Bible: NAS, NKJ, NIV. Also publishes general-market fiction.

Types and topics: children; fiction: middle grade, new adult, YA, contemporary, fantasy, historical, mystery, romance, science fiction, suspense/thriller

Royalty: 15–30%; no advance

Types of books: audiobook, ebook, hardcover, POD

Imprints: White Parrot Press (children's picture books and early readers), WestWind Press (middle grade and YA), Soul Fire Press (teen/YA fiction), Christopher Matthews Publishing (new adult and adult hybrid publishing)

Guidelines: *www.FirstStepsPublishing.com/get-published*

Tip: "Show us you know your audience. A clear genre, solid story arc, and polished writing will always rise to the top."

FLYAWAY BOOKS

100 Witherspoon St., Louisville, KY 40202-1396
submissions@flyawaybooks.com | *www.flyawaybooks.com*
Jessica Miller Kelley, senior acquisitions editor

Denomination: Presbyterian

Parent company: Westminster John Knox Press/Presbyterian Publishing Corporation

Submissions: Currently closed to submissions; check the website for updates. Email proposal with complete manuscript. Responds in six weeks or not interested.

Types and topics: picture books

Types of books: hardcover, paperback, picture books

Guidelines: *www.flyawaybooks.com/submissions*

Tip: "Flyaway Books embraces diversity, inclusivity, compassion, care for each other, and care for our world. Many of our books explore social justice and other contemporary issues. Some retell familiar religious stories in new ways, while others carry universal themes appealing to those with any, or no, religious background."

FOCUS ON THE FAMILY

8605 Explorer Dr., Colorado Springs, CO 80995 | 719-531-5181
www.focusonthefamily.com
Larry Weeden, editor in chief

Submissions: Only agent, *ChristianBookProposals.com,* and Writer's Edge.
Types and topics: family, marriage, parenting, children
Types of books: ebook, hardcover, offset paperback
Tip: "We're looking for proposals that exhibit great content and good writing, hopefully combined with a strong author platform. And we're always looking for good children's books." Books are published by Tyndale House Publishers.

FORTRESS PRESS

PO Box 1209, Minneapolis, MN 55440-1209
giffordl@fortresspress.com | *www.fortresspress.com*
Laura Gifford, editor-in-chief
Yvonne D. Hawkins, acquisitions editor, pastoral care and counseling, social justice, womanism, and the practices of the church; hawkinsy@fortresspress.com
Bethany Dickerson, managing editor and acquisitions, theology, culture, literature, religious history, and biblical studies; dickersonb@fortresspress.com
Kathleen Gallagher Elkins, acquisitions editor, biblical studies, ancient Judaism and Christianity, interreligious dialogue, feminist studies in religion; gallagherelkinsk@fortresspress.com
Adam Bursi, associate acquisitions editor, late ancient and medieval Christianity, Judaism, Islam, interreligious dialogue and comparison; religious studies; bursia@fortresspress.com

Denomination: Evangelical Lutheran Church in America
Parent company: 1517 Media
Types and topics: Bible study, Christian living/spirituality, counseling, culture, ethics, history, leadership, ministry, philosophy, social justice, theology, academic, Bible reference/commentaries
Types of books: hardcover, offset paperback
Guidelines: *www.fortresspress.com/info/submissions*

FORWARD MOVEMENT

412 Sycamore St., Cincinnati, OH 45202-4110 | 800-543-1813
sgunn@forwardmovement.org | *www.forwardmovement.org*
Scott Gunn, executive director
Richelle Thompson, managing editor

Denomination: Anglican, Episcopal
Mission statement: to offer resources that strengthen and support

discipleship and evangelism

Submissions: Submit proposal with sample chapters on the website form. Responds in four to eight weeks.

Types and topics: Bible study, discipleship, evangelism, leadership, prayer

Types of books: ebook, offset paperback

Guidelines: *forwardmovement.org/submissions*

Tip: "While many of our resources are targeted for an Episcopal/ Anglican audience, we also offer some materials for a broader reach."

THE FOUNDRY PUBLISHING

PO Box 419527, Kansas City, MO 64141 | 800-877-0700

RMcFarland@thefoundrypublishing.com | *www.thefoundrypublishing.com*

René McFarland, submissions editor

Bonnie Perry, editorial director

Denomination: Nazarene, Wesleyan

Mission statement: to empower people with life-changing ways to engage in the mission of God

Submissions: Length: 45,000–60,000 words. Email proposal with sample chapters. Responds in eight weeks.

Types and topics: Christian living/spirituality, ministry

Guidelines: *www.thefoundrypublishing.com/f-a-qs.html*

Tip: "Because we are a denominational publisher of holiness literature, our books reflect an evangelical Wesleyan stance in accord with the Church of the Nazarene. We seek practical as well as serious treatments of issues of faith consistent with the Wesleyan tradition."

THE GOOD BOOK COMPANY

1805 Sardis Rd. N, Ste. 102, Charlotte, NC 28270 | 866-244-2165

submissions@thegoodbook.com | *www.thegoodbook.com*

Tim Thornborough, publishing director

Carl Laferton, senior editor

Mission statement: to promote, encourage, and equip people to serve our Lord and Master Jesus Christ

Types and topics: Bible study, Christian living/spirituality, evangelism, activity books, Bible stories, board books, devotionals, picture books, teen/YA

Types of books: ebook, paperback

Guidelines: *www.thegoodbook.com/authors*

Tip: "Our aim with all our resources is to get people directly interacting with the Bible. So we expect our authors to facilitate that process, rather than just commenting on their own view of what the Bible says. A primary question we ask of any resource submitted to us is: Does it handle the Bible well (i.e., taking note of the context of each passage), and is it helping people understand its message?"

GOOD BOOKS

307 W. 36th St., 11th Floor, New York, NY 10018 | 212-643-6816
agehring@skyhorsepublishing.com | *www.goodbooks.com*
Abigail Gehring, associate publisher and editorial director

Parent company: Skyhorse Publishing
Submissions: Publishes 30 titles per year; receives 200 submissions annually. First-time authors: 15%. Length: varies. Email proposal with sample chapters. Bible: KJV, ESV.
Types and topics: Christian living/spirituality, house and home, activity books, devotionals, fiction
Royalty: varies; advance sometimes
Types of books: audiobook, ebook, hardcover, offset paperback
Guidelines: *skyhorsepublishing.com/good-books/submissions*
Tip: "Include information on your author platform as well as any marketing ideas or plans."

GRACE ACRES PRESS

PO Box 22, Larkspur, CO 80118 | 303-681-9995
Anne@graceacrespress.com | *www.GraceAcresPress.com*
Anne R. Fenske, publisher

Parent company: Exegetica Publishing
Mission statement: to grow your faith one page at a time
Submissions: Publishes six titles per year; receives 20 submissions annually. First-time authors: 75%. Length: 100–300 pages. Email query first. Responds in one month. Bible: NKJV, NIV.
Types and topics: Bible study, biography, discipleship, evangelism, missions
Royalty: 10–15%; no advance
First print run: 500–2,000
Types of books: ebook, hardcover, offset paperback, POD
Guidelines: available via email
Tip: "Explain your contribution as a copartner in marketing your book."

GRACE BELL PUBLISHING

Unit 3/22-24 Strathwyn St., Brendale, Queensland 4500, Australia
submissions@gracebellpublishing.com.au | *gracebellpublishing.com.au*

Mission statement: to publish books of light for the whole family

Submissions: Publishes five titles per year. Length: picture books, fewer than 1,000 words, 24- or 32-page spreads. Submit by email. Responds in four months. Bible: NIV, NLT, ESV.

Types and topics: fiction, picture books, teen/YA

Royalty: 10%; picture books, 5%; advance sometimes

Types of books: audiobook, ebook, hardcover, offset paperback

Guidelines: *gracebellpublishing.com.au/pages/submissions*

Tip: "Find the gaps in the market."

GRACE PUBLISHING

PO Box 1233, Broken Arrow, OK 74013-1233 | 918-346-7960
editorial@grace-publishing.com | *www.grace-publishing.com*
Terri Kalfas, editor and acquisitions

Parent company: The Jomaga Group

Mission statement: to develop and distribute biblically based resources that challenge, encourage, teach, equip, and entertain Christians young and old in their personal journeys

Submissions: Publishes four to six titles per year. First-time authors: varies. Length: 30,000–40,000 words; fiction, 40,000–125,000 words. Agent not required Conference contact a plus. Email or mail query. No simultaneous submissions. Responds in three months. Bible: any.

Types and topics: Christian living/spirituality, anthologies, Bible studies, devotionals, fiction, homeschooling, memoir, ministry resources

Royalty: varies; no advance

Types of books: POD

Guidelines: *grace-publishing.com/manuscript-submission*

Tip: "Write tight; know your subject; don't take Scripture verses out of context."

GUIDEPOSTS

100 Reserve Rd., Ste. E200, Danbury, CT 06810 | 800-431-2344
bookeditors@guideposts.org | *guideposts.org*
Joanna Kennedy, senior managing editor, nonfiction
Jane Haertel, senior managing editor, fiction, Fictionsubmissions@guideposts.org

Parent company: Guideposts

Mission statement: to foster connections anchored in faith by providing inspirational content so that people can grow and thrive by practicing hope and positivity in their daily lives

Submissions: Publishes 20–30 titles per year; receives 50 submissions annually. Length: 65,000–75,000. Agent preferred. Conference contact a plus. Email proposal with sample chapters or a query. Responds in one to three months for nonfiction, two to four weeks for fiction. Bible: NIV.

Types and topics: Advent, Christian living/spirituality, Christmas, Easter, Lent, memoir/personal narrative, older adults, prayer, recovery, devotionals; fiction: biblical, cozy mystery, general, historical romance, romantic suspense

Royalty: varies; advance sometimes

Types of books: audiobook, ebook, hardcover, offset paperback

Guidelines: nonfiction, *guideposts.org/tell-us-your-story/call-for-submissions;* fiction, not available

Tip: "Please note that we do not review or accept unsolicited book manuscripts.

"Guideposts fiction books are primarily part of long-running series created by Guideposts and written by a team of authors. Guideposts does not usually accept unsolicited proposals or manuscripts except through an agent, and we prefer authors who have an established publication track record. When authors are needed on a work-for-hire basis, we issue a call for proposals. Email *Fictionsubmissions@guideposts.org* to be added to the call list."

Guideposts publishes three annual devotional books per year— *Walking in Grace* (formerly *Daily Guideposts*), *Mornings with Jesus*, and *All God's Creatures*—written by a roster of writers. To be considered as an assignment writer, follow the audition guidelines at *guideposts.org/tell-us-your-story/call-for-submissions.*

HARAMBEE PRESS

PO Box 206, Nesbit, MS 38651 | 901-590-6584
submissions@endgamepress.com | *www.endgamepress.com/harambee-press*
Edwina Perkins, acquisitions editor

Parent company: End Game Press

Mission statement: to raise up the ethnic voice; and to give a place for BIPOC authors to communicate, through publication, with each other and the world

Submissions: Currently closed to submissions; check website for updates. Agent not required. Email proposal with sample chapters. Responds in two to three months. Bible: any.

Types and topics: fiction, nonfiction

Types of books: ebook, paperback

Guidelines: *www.endgamepress.com/submissions*

Tip: "We are looking for writers who want to express the diversity of their culture and writers who have stories or life lessons, whether through fiction or nonfiction. Authors should carry a message of hope and redemption."

HARBOURLIGHT BOOKS

PO Box 1738, Aztec, NM 87410
www.pelicanbookgroup.com
Nicola Martinez, editor-in-chief

Parent company: Pelican Book Group

Mission statement: to publish quality books that reflect the salvation and love offered by Jesus Christ

Submissions: Length: 25,000–80,000 words. Submit proposal with sample chapters on the website. Responds in three to four months. Bible: NIV, NAB.

Types and topics: fiction: adventure, crime, family saga, mystery, suspense, westerns, women's

Royalty: 40% on download, 7% on print; advance sometimes

Types of books: audiobook, ebook, hardcover, offset paperback, POD

Guidelines: *tinyurl.com/22zruzzw*

HARPERCHRISTIAN RESOURCES

501 Nelson Pl., Nashville, TN 37214
harperchristianresources.com

Parent company: HarperCollins Christian Publishing

Mission statement: to equip people to understand the Scriptures, cultivate spiritual growth, and live an inspired faith with Bible study and video resources from today's most trusted voices

Types and topics: Bible studies, ministry programs, small group study guides

Types of books: offset paperback, video

HARPERONE

353 Sacramento St. #500, San Francisco, CA 94111-3653 | 415-477-4400
harperone.com
Nina Shield, VP, editorial director

Parent company: HarperCollins Publishing

Mission statement: to publish books for the world we want to live in—books that represent a broad and diverse collection of voices, cultures, and perspectives

Submissions: Publishes 75 titles per year; receives 10,000 submissions annually. First-time authors: 5%. Length: 160–256 pages. Agent only. Responds in three months.

Types and topics: autobiography, biography, Christian living/spirituality, self-help, memoir

Royalty: 7.5–15%, advance

Types of books: ebook, hardcover, offset paperback

Tip: Theologically liberal.

HARVEST HOUSE PUBLISHERS

PO Box 41210, Eugene, OR 97404-0322 | 800-547-8979
harvesthousepublishers.com
Audrey Greeson, acquisitions editor, nonfiction
Ruth Samsel, senior acquisitions editor, gift books
Kyle Hatfield, senior acquisitions editor, children and family
Emma Saisslin, associate trade editor and acquisitions, nonfiction

Mission statement: to glorify God by providing high-quality books and products that affirm biblical values, help people grow spiritually strong, and proclaim Jesus Christ as the answer to every human need

Types and topics: Christian living/spirituality, family, relationships, Bible reference/commentaries, Bible studies, children, fiction, gift

Types of books: board books, ebook, hardcover, paperback

Imprint: Harvest Kids (children)

HENDRICKSON PUBLISHERS

Tyndale House Publishers, 351 Executive Dr., Carol Stream, IL 60188 | 800-358-3111
roberthand@tyndale.com | *www.hendricksonpublishers.com*
Patricia Anders, editorial director
Hannah Terenzoni, publishing director, academic acquisitions

Parent company: Tyndale House Publishers

Mission statement: to meet the publication needs of the religious studies academic community worldwide and to produce thoughtful books for thoughtful Christians

Submissions: Publishes 16 titles per year; receives 50–100 submissions annually. First-time authors: 40%. Length: trade, 75-000–100,000 words; academic, 100,000–200,000 words. Only agent, *ChristianBookProposals.com*, or conference contact. Responds in two to three months.

Types and topics: archaeology, biblical studies, church history, ministry, theology, academic, Bible reference/commentaries, biblical studies, language studies

Royalty: 12–14%; advance

Types of books: ebook, hardcover, offset paperback

Imprints: Hendrickson Academic (textbooks, reference), Hendrickson Bibles (Bibles)

Tip: "Please be sure to look at our website to see what kind of books we publish."

INCUBATOR PUBLISHING

PO Box 108, Benton, AR 72018 | 501-821-4976
tara@incubatorpublishing.com | *www.IncubatorPublishing.com*
Tara Johnson, acquisitions editor, author development

Parent company: Incubator Creative Group

Mission statement: to champion transformational Christian fiction—stories that not only entertain but spark spiritual growth and healing

Submissions: Publishes 20–30 titles per year; receives 50–100 submissions annually. First-time authors: 90%. Length: varies by genre. Agent not required. Responds in one week.

Types and topics: fiction: children, historical, historical romance, humor, mystery, speculative, suspense/thriller, teen/YA

Royalty: negotiable; advance sometimes

Types of books: audiobook, ebook, hardcover, offset paperback

Tip: "We are looking for authors who are teachable, passionate about God and people, and who are willing to write from their most vulnerable places to illustrate God's redemptive power. Incubator Publishing works hand in hand with our author development division to hone your craft. We believe your story goes beyond the book and has the ability to transform lives.

"We invite a select group of authors into a *transformational publishing experience*. We help you write redemptive, emotionally honest fiction, develop meaningful follow-up resources that serve readers, extend your novel character's life beyond the novel to continue a relationship with the reader, build a small publishing enterprise around your books supported by Incubator, earn a sustainable income without needing to be 'famous.'"

INTERVARSITY PRESS

1001 Warrenville Rd., Ste. 300, Lisle, IL 60532 | 630-734-4000
mail@ivpress.com | *ivpress.com*
Kelli Trujillo, acquisitions editor, IVP

Al Hsu, associate editorial director, trade and acquisitions
Ted Olsen, editorial director, trade books, IVP trade and media
Elissa Schauer, executive editor, IVP Kids and IVP Bible Studies
Jon Boyd, editorial director, academic and acquisitions

Parent company: InterVarsity Christian Fellowship

Mission statement: to create and publish resources that deepen lives in Christ to engage the university, the church, and the world

Submissions: Publishes 120 titles per year; receives 1,000–1,500 submissions annually. First-time authors: 20%. Length: 30,000–100,000 words. Only agent or conference contact. Responds in three months. Bible: NIV.

Types and topics: biblical studies, church leadership, counseling, culture, diverse/global perspectives, ministry, psychology, spiritual formation, theology, academic, Bible reference/commentaries, Bible studies, children

Royalty: 15–18%; trade, 10–15% academic; advance

Types of books: audiobook, ebook, hardcover, offset paperback, POD

Imprints: IVP (church, culture, ministry, discipleship), IVP Academic (undergraduate and graduate students, professors, scholars), IVP Formatio (spiritual formation), IVP Bible Studies (study guides), IVP Kids (children), IVP Español (Spanish)

Guidelines: available via email

Tip: "We accept submissions only from agents or from authors who have had direct contact with an editor."

INVITE PRESS

5700 W. Plano Pkwy., Ste. 1600, Plano, TX 75093 | 214-291-8094
lwagner@inviteresources.com | *www.inviteresources.com*
Lori Wagner, content editor

Denomination: Wesleyan/Arminian

Parent company: St. Andrew Methodist Church, Plano, Texas

Mission statement: to share the promise of Christ's New Creation

Submissions: Publishes 22–26 titles per year; receives 40 submissions annually. First-time authors: 30%. Length: 20,000–50,000 words. Agent not required. Email proposal with complete manuscript or sample chapters. Responds in two to four weeks. Bible: no preference.

Types and topics: Bible study, Christian living/spirituality, theology, academic, devotionals

Royalty: 8–15%; no advance

Types of books: ebook, hardcover, offset paperback, POD

Imprints: Invite Press (trade books), Invite Academic (focus on the academy)

Guidelines: *www.inviteresources.com/editorial-standards*

Tip: "We are about accessible ideas, presented in an engaging and relatable fashion. This is not to say we want fluff; in fact, we desire books with academic rigor and theological reasoning, but without the difficult writing. We are not interested in boring books. We want our books to be approachable and helpful resources that speak to today's issues."

IRON STREAM MEDIA

100 Missionary Ridge, Birmingham, AL 35242 | 888-811-9934
submissions@ironstreammedia.com | *www.ironstreammedia.com*
Dr. John Herring, publisher

Submissions: Publishes 20–25 titles per year; receives 150 submissions annually. First-time authors: 30%. Length: 50,000–90,000 words. Only agent or conference contact. Responds in three months. Bible: NASB.

Types and topics: Christian living/spirituality, family, leadership, memoir/personal narrative, parenting, relationships, women, Bible studies, devotionals; fiction: romance, romantic suspense, speculative, suspense, westerns

Royalty: escalating; advance

Types of books: audiobook, ebook, offset paperback, POD

Imprints: Iron Stream (nonfiction), Iron Stream Fiction (novels), Iron Stream Kids (board and picture books, Bible storybooks), Brookstone Publishing Group (independent publishing)

Guidelines: *ironstreammedia.com/resources/submission-process*

Tip: "Focus on hook, comps, and marketing sections in book proposal. Also, provide a great list of influencers."

JOURNEYFORTH

1430 Wade Hampton Blvd., Greenville, SC 29609 | 864-546-4600
journeyforth@bjupress.com | *journeyforth.com*
Charlotte Bradley, acquisitions editor

Parent company: BJU Press

Mission statement: to publish stories that will inspire young minds, shape character, instill a biblical worldview, and promote academic success by developing proficient readers and critical thinkers

Submissions: Publishes one to four titles per year; receives 50–100 submissions annually. First-time authors: 45%. Length: ages 6–8,

8,000–10,000 words; ages 9–12, 30,000–40,000 words; ages 12 and up, 40,000–60,000 words. Agent not required. Email or mail proposal with sample chapters. Responds in six to eight months. Bible: KJV, NKJV, ESV, NASB.

Types and topics: Bible study, Christian living/spirituality, youth biography, youth fiction, Bible studies, first-chapter, middle grade, teen/YA; fiction: adventure, biblical, contemporary, fantasy, folktales, historical, mystery, westerns

Royalty: 10–15%; advance sometimes

Types of books: ebook, offset paperback

Guidelines: *www.bjupresshomeschool.com/journeyforth-writers-guidelines*

Tip: "We are particularly interested in acquiring contemporary fiction for all ages, chapter books for beginning readers, and YA fiction. Our market is not open to stories that include profanity or minced oaths, magic or witchcraft, time travel, and characters who engage in unscriptural activities without a biblical consequence. We are not currently accepting picture book, short story, poetry, curriculum, memoir, adult fiction, or adult nonfiction manuscripts."

JUDSON PRESS

1075 First Ave., King of Prussia, PA 19406 | 800-458-3766
acquisitions@judsonpress.com | *www.judsonpress.com*
Rachael Lawrence, associate publisher

Denomination: American Baptist

Parent company: American Baptist Home Mission Societies

Mission statement: to produce Christ-centered leadership resources for the transformation of individuals, congregations, communities, and cultures

Submissions: Publishes 12 titles per year; receives 300 submissions annually. First-time authors: 25%. Length: 128–244 pages. Email or mail proposal with sample chapters or a query. Responds in three to six months. Bible: NRSV.

Types and topics: Christian education, Christian living/spirituality, discipleship, history, ministry, church resources, devotionals, ministry resources

Royalty: 10–15%; advance sometimes

First print run: 2,500

Types of books: ebook, offset paperback, POD

Guidelines: *www.judsonpress.com/Pages/Info/For-Authors.aspx*

Tip: "Most open to practical books that are unique and compelling, for a clearly defined niche audience. Theologically and socially we are a moderate publisher. And we like to see a detailed marketing plan from an author committed to partnering with us."

KREGEL PUBLICATIONS

2450 Oak Industrial Dr. NE, Grand Rapids, MI 49505 | 616-451-4775
KPacquisitions@kregel.com | *www.kregel.com*
Rachel Kirsch, senior managing editor
Russ Meek, senior academic editor

Mission statement: to develop and distribute—with integrity and excellence—trusted, biblically based resources that lead individuals to know and serve Jesus Christ

Types and topics: Bible study, biography, Christian living/ spirituality, church life, contemporary issues, discipleship, family, marriage, ministry, parenting, theology, women, Bible reference/ commentaries, Bible studies, children, devotionals, teen/YA, fiction: historical, romance, romantic suspense, teen/YA

Types of books: ebook, hardcover, paperback

LEAFWOOD PUBLISHERS

1694 Campus Ct., ACU Box 29138, Abilene, TX 79699 | 325-674-2720
jason.fikes@acu.edu | *www.leafwoodpublishers.com*
Jason Fikes, director

Denomination: Church of Christ

Parent company: Abilene Christian University

Mission statement: to inspire fresh and deeper conversations about faith and life one book at a time

Submissions: Publishes 20 titles per year; receives 200 submissions annually. First-time authors: 40%. Length: minimum 30,000 words. Agent preferred. Submit through *ChristianBookProposals.com,* or submit proposal with sample chapters on the website. Responds in at least six months. Bible: NIV.

Types and topics: Bible studies, Christian living/spirituality, ministry, spiritual formation, spiritual growth, theology, women's interests

Royalty: negotiated based on experience; advance, based on experience

First print run: 1,500

Types of books: ebook, hardcover, offset paperback

Guidelines: *store.acupressbooks.com/pages/author-resources*

Tip: "We enhance diverse and innovative authors (neurotypicals and those who are more atypical, age, gender, race, Christian tradition). Our audience is university based (Christian higher education) and lay people. Fresh conversations require innovation, creativity, love, courage, humility, gentleness, hospitality, freedom, and grace. We talk a lot about being practical. Practical means 'Will this book inspire fresh and deep conversations about faith and life?'"

LEXHAM PRESS

PO Box 759, Bellingham, WA 98227
thains@lexhampress.com | *www.lexhampress.com*
Todd Hains, associate publisher, acquisitions and development
> **Parent company:** Baker Publishing Group
> **Mission statement:** to increase biblical literacy, thoughtful Christian reflection, and faithful action around the world by publishing a range of Bible study materials, scholarly works, and pastoral resources
> **Submissions:** Submit proposal with sample chapters on the website. Responds in eight weeks or not interested. Publishes innovative resources for Logos Bible Software.
> **Types and topics:** Bible study, ministry, theology, academic, Bible reference/commentaries, children
> **Types of books:** ebook, hardcover, paperback
> **Guidelines:** *www.lexhampress.com/manuscript-submission*

LIGHTHOUSE PUBLISHING

228 Freedom Pkwy., Hoschton, GA 30548 | 770-709-2268
info@lighthousechristianpublishing.com | *lighthousechristianpublishing.com*
Sylvia Charvet, editor
> **Denomination:** Catholic
> **Parent company:** Lighthouse Christian Publishing and eMedia
> **Mission statement:** to spread the gospel of Jesus Christ through various kinds of media
> **Submissions:** Publishes 30 titles per year; receives 120 submissions annually. First-time authors: 50%. Length: children, 20 pages; fiction, 300 pages. Agent not required. Submit to *ChristianBookProposals. com*, email proposal with complete manuscript, or submit to Writers Edge. Responds in six to eight weeks. Bible: any version accepted by the Catholic Church.
> **Types and topics:** all topics, children, devotionals, nonfiction; fiction: fantasy, futuristic, general, historical, romance
> **Royalty:** 50%; advance sometimes, $500-1,000
> **Types of books:** audiobook, ebook, hardcover, POD, video
> **Imprint:** Lone Oak Publishing (general market)

Guidelines: available via email

Tip: Looking for "poignant and concise summaries. Works that will truly benefit the reader, through Christian education and inspiration."

LIGUORI PUBLICATIONS

1 Liguori Dr., Liguori, MO 63057-9999 | 800-325-9521
manuscript_submission@liguori.org | *www.liguori.org*

Denomination: Catholic

Mission statement: to be the leading provider of Roman Catholic publications for every stage of faith and life in an ever-changing world

Submissions: No simultaneous submissions. Email proposal with sample chapters. Responds in 8–12 weeks.

Types and topics: sacraments, saints, Bible studies, biography, devotionals

Guidelines: *www.liguori.org/submit-your-manuscript*

LITURGICAL PRESS

PO Box 7500, Collegeville, MN 56321-7500
submissions@litpress.org | *www.litpress.org*
Therese Ratliff, director

Denomination: Catholic

Mission statement: to cultivate and amplify texts and voices that deepen the faith and knowledge of a richly diverse Church

Submissions: Submit proposal with complete manuscript or sample chapters on the website. Responds in six weeks.

Types and topics: Bible, liturgy, prayer, theology

Guidelines: *www.litpress.org/Authors/submit_manuscript*

LOVE INSPIRED

195 Broadway, 24th floor, New York, NY 10007 | 212-207-7900
www.LoveInspired.com
Tina James, executive editor, Love Inspired Suspense
Melissa Endlich, senior editor
Shana Asaro, editor

Parent company: Harlequin/HarperCollins Publishers

Mission statement: to uplift and inspire through stories

Submissions: Publishes 144 titles per year; receives 500–1,000 submissions annually. First-time authors: 15%. Length: 55,000 words. Agent not required. Submit complete manuscript on the website. Responds in three months. Bible: KJV.

Types and topics: fiction: romance, romantic suspense

Royalty: on retail; advance

Types of books: ebook, mass market paperback
Imprints: Love Inspired (contemporary romance), Love Inspired
   Suspense (contemporary romantic suspense)
Guidelines: *harlequin.submittable.com/submit*
Tip: "We're looking for compelling stories with engaging characters, a
   sustained conflict, and an emotionally satisfying romance."

LOYOLA PRESS

8770 W. Bryn Mawr Ave., Chicago, IL 60631-3515 | 773-281-1818
submissions@loyolapress.com | *www.loyolapress.com*
Gary Jansen, director and executive editor, acquisitions
   Denomination: Catholic
   Mission statement: to create books and multimedia products that
      facilitate transformative experiences of God so that people of all
      ages can lead holy and purposeful lives with and for others
   Submissions: Publishes 8–10 titles per year; receives 1,000+
      submissions annually. Length: 25,000–75,000 words or 150–300
      pages. Email or mail query. Responds in 8–10 weeks. Bible: NRSV
      (Catholic Edition).
   Types and topics: Catholicism, Christian living/spirituality
   Royalty: advance
   Types of books: paperback
   Guidelines: *www.loyolapress.com/general/submissions*
   Tip: "Looking for books and authors that help make Catholic faith
      relevant and offer practical tools for the well-lived spiritual life."

MOODY PUBLISHERS

820 N. LaSalle Blvd., Chicago, IL 60610 | 800-678-8812
submissions@moody.edu | *www.moodypublishers.com*
Trillia Newbell, acquisitions director
John Hinkley, acquisitions editor, marriage, family, parenting, workplace,
   church
Catherine Strode Parks, acquisitions editor, issues, Christian life,
   middle grade
Erin Davis, acquisitions editor
Drew Dyck, acquisitions editor
   Parent company: Moody Bible Institute
   Mission statement: to resource the church's work of discipling all
      people
   Submissions: Publishes 50 titles per year; receives thousands of
      submissions annually. First-time authors: 20%. Length: depends

on genre. Agent not required but preferred. Conference contact a plus. Email proposal with sample chapters. Responds in six weeks.

Types and topics: Christian living/spirituality, counseling, leadership, women, Bible studies, devotionals, middle grade

Royalty: advance

Types of books: audiobook, ebook, hardcover, offset paperback

Guidelines: *www.moodypublishers.com/About/faq/submitting-proposals*

Tip: "Please review our website to see the latest books to help determine what we are looking for."

MOUNTAIN BROOK FIRE

submissions@fire.mountainbrookink.com | fire.mountainbrookink.com
Alyssa Roat, managing editor

Parent company: Mountain Brook Ink

Mission statement: to publish quality worldbuilding, spellbinding plots, and high-stakes adventures with a whole lot of heart for middle grade, young adult, and adult audiences

Submissions: Length: middle grade, 50,000–65,000 words; YA, 75,000–100,000 words; adult, 80,000–120,000 words. Agent not required. Email. Responds in two months. Bible: KJV, NKJV, NIV.

Types and topics: adult, middle grade, YA fiction: fantasy, science fiction, speculative, steampunk, superhero, supernatural

Royalty: 30–40%; advance, $25

Types of books: audiobook, ebook, POD

Guidelines: *fire.mountainbrookink.com/submission-guidelines*

Tip: "Manuscripts need not be explicitly 'Christian'; we are equally happy with general market. However, we're looking for fiction that is clean. Books having a Christian worldview without having a faith thread will work as well."

MOUNTAIN BROOK INK

submissions@mountainbrookink.com | www.mountainbrookink.com
Miralee Ferrell, publisher and lead acquisitions editor

Mission statement: to publish fiction you can believe in that embodies restoration and/or renewal

Submissions: Publishes 12 titles per year; receives 50+ submissions annually. First-time authors: 75%. Length: minimum 75,000 words. Email proposal with sample chapters or a query. Responds in two months. Bible: KJV, NKJV, NIV.

Types and topics: fiction: biblical, contemporary, historical, mystery,

romance, romantic suspense, suspense/thriller, women's
Royalty: 30–40%; advance, $25
Types of books: audiobook, ebook, POD
Imprints: Mountain Brook Fire (speculative fiction)
Guidelines: *mountainbrookink.com/submission-guidelines-for-inquiries*
Tip: "Send the best work you've done, preferably that's been edited so it shines."

MT ZION RIDGE PRESS

295 Gum Springs Rd. NW, Georgetown, TN 37336 | 423-458-4256
mtzionridgepress@gmail.com | *mtzionridgepress.com*
Tamera Lynn Kraft, managing editor
Mission statement: to publish Christian fiction off the beaten path and Christian nonfiction for those who want to go deeper in their faith
Submissions: Publishes 12–15 titles per year; receives 30 submissions annually. First-time authors: 70%. Length: 60,000–100,000 words. Agent not required. Conference contact a plus. Email query first. Responds in three months. Bible: NIV, NKJV, ESV, NLT, KJV.
Types and topics: Christian living/spirituality, Bible studies, devotionals; fiction: fantasy, historical, mystery, romance, romantic suspense, science fiction, speculative, suspense/thriller, teen/YA, westerns, women's
Royalty: 30%; no advance
Types of books: audiobook, ebook, offset paperback, POD
Guidelines: *www.mtzionridgepress.com/about*
Tip: "Submit stellar writing."

MY HEALTHY CHURCH

1445 N. Boonville Ave., Springfield, MO 65802 | 417-831-8000
newproducts@ag.org | *www.myhealthychurch.com*
Denomination: Assemblies of God
Parent company: Gospel Publishing House
Mission statement: to equip believers and church leaders who seek a healthy, Spirit-empowered life
Submissions: Agent only. Responds in 60–90 days.
Types and topics: Christian living/spirituality, church leadership, discipleship, leadership, ministry, academic, Bible studies, church resources
Types of books: ebook, hardcover, paperback
Guidelines: *myhealthychurch.com/store/startcat.cfm?cat=tWRITGUID*
Tip: "The content of all our books and resources must be compatible with the beliefs and purposes of the Assemblies of God."

NAVPRESS

3820 N. 30th St., Colorado Springs, CO 80904
inquiries@navpress.com | www.navpress.com
Caitlyn Carlson, senior acquisitions editor
Deborah Gonzalez, acquisitions and developmental editor

Parent company: The Navigators

Mission statement: to support readers as they know Christ, make Him known, and help others do the same

Submissions: Publishes 20 titles per year; receives 1,000 submissions annually. First-time authors: 40%. Length: 40,000 words. Only agent or current author referral. Responds in two months.

Types and topics: Christian living/spirituality, discipleship, leadership, practical theology, prayer, spiritual growth, women, Bible studies

Royalty: 16–22%; advance

Guidelines: *www.navpress.com/faq*

Tip: "Proposals with strong discipleship elements are preferred. Authors should have a ministry platform that supports their discipleship elements. NavPress does not accept unsolicited manuscripts."

NELSON BOOKS

PO Box 141000, Nashville, TN 37214-1000 | 615-889-9000
www.thomasnelson.com/nelsonbooks
Hanha Parham acquisitions editor

Parent company: Thomas Nelson Publishers/HarperCollins Christian Publishing

Mission statement: to publish biblically informed books from a Christian perspective that enhance the spiritual and personal growth of our readers

Submissions: Agent only.

Types and topics: biography, business, Christian living/spirituality, leadership, spiritual growth, devotionals

Types of books: audiobook, ebook, hardcover, offset paperback

Guidelines: not available

NEW GROWTH PRESS

PO Box 4485, Greensboro, NC 27404 | 336-378-7775
submissions@newgrowthpress.com | www.newgrowthpress.com
Rush Witt, acquisitions editor and manager
Brad Byrd, director of acquisitions and strategic partnerships

Mission statement: to reach every church and home with gospel-centered resources that point to Jesus and help every person grow closer to Christ

Submissions: Email proposal with sample chapters. Responds in six weeks or not interested.

Types and topics: Christian living/spirituality, counseling, family, parenting, relationships, Bible studies, children, devotionals, fiction, teen/YA

Types of books: audiobook, ebook, paperback

Guidelines: *newgrowthpress.com/manuscript-submissions*

Tip: "Manuscript submissions must follow the downloadable, standard New Growth Press template."

NEW LEAF PUBLISHING GROUP

3142 Highway 103 N, Green Forest, AR 72638 | 870-438-5288
submissions@nlpg.com | www.nlpg.com
Laura Welch, editor-in-chief

Mission statement: to impact eternity by glorifying God and advancing His Kingdom through faith-building education and apologetics resources

Submissions: Publishes 35–40 titles per year; receives hundreds of submissions annually. Email proposal with sample chapters. Responds in three months or not interested.

Types and topics: apologetics, Christian education, Christian living/spirituality, church leadership, church life, creation, discipleship, homeschool and Christian school curriculum, relationships, stewardship, gift, reference

Types of books: audiobook, ebook, hardcover, offset paperback

Imprints: New Leaf Press (families and ministries), Master Books (creation based for all audiences), Attic Books (classics)

Guidelines: *www.nlpg.com/submissions*

Tip: "We seek unique, high-quality manuscripts that are well-written and deliver a meaningful, positive message to readers. Our authors should be able to clearly and effectively communicate their ideas—both in writing and speaking—and leverage online media to engage their audience."

NORTHWESTERN PUBLISHING HOUSE

N16W23379 Stone Ridge Dr., Waukesha, WI 53188-1108 | 800-662-6022
submissions@nph.wels.net | online.nph.net
John Braun

Denomination: Wisconsin Evangelical Lutheran Synod

Mission statement: to deliver biblically sound, Christ-centered resources within the Wisconsin Evangelical Lutheran Synod and beyond

Submissions: Email or mail proposal with sample chapters. No simultaneous submissions. Responds in two months.

Types and topics: family, history, theology, Bible reference/commentaries, devotionals

Types of books: ebook, hardcover, paperback

Guidelines: *online.nph.net/manuscript-submission*

Tip: "We are always looking for new and exciting Bible-based materials to publish!"

OLIVIA KIMBRELL PRESS

PO Box 4452, Winchester, KY 40392 | 859-577-1071
submissions@oliviakimbrellpress.com | *oliviakimbrellpress.com*
Gregg Bridgeman, editor-in-chief

Mission statement: to uplift fellow believers and encourage seekers in this fallen world

Submissions: Publishes 10–20 titles per year; receives 80–100 submissions annually. First-time authors: 10%. Length: 80,000 words maximum. Agent preferred. Conference contact a plus. Email or mail proposal with sample chapters. No simultaneous submissions. Responds in two months. Bible: KJV, NKJV. Specializes in true-to-life, meaningful Christian fiction and nonfiction titles intended to uplift the heart and engage the mind. Primary focus on "Roman Road" small-group guides or reader's guides to accompany nonfiction and fiction, and fiction stories of suspense, intrigue, or family sagas with an inspirational or romantic theme.

Types and topics: Christian living/spirituality, health, marriage, devotionals, teen/YA; fiction: fantasy, romance, romantic suspense, science fiction, suspense/thriller

Royalty: 50%; advance sometimes, $300-2,000

Types of books: audiobook, ebook, hardcover, POD

Imprints: Sign of the Whale (biblical & speculative fiction), House of Bread (nutrition)

Guidelines: *oliviakimbrellpress.com*

Tip: "No westerns."

OUR DAILY BREAD PUBLISHING

3000 Kraft Ave. SE, Grand Rapids, MI 49507 | 616-974-2210
submissions@ODBM.org | *ourdailybreadpublishing.org*
Dawn Anderson, executive editor and acquisitions
Katara Patton, executive editor, VOICES
Joel Armstrong, content editor and acquisitions for general audiences

Parent company: Our Daily Bread Ministries

Mission statement: to make the wisdom of the Bible understandable and accessible to all

Submissions: Publishes 36 titles per year; receives 150 submissions annually. First-time authors: 10%. Length: 35,000–55,000 words. Agent preferred. Conference contact a plus. Responds in three months. Bible: NIV, NASB, NET, NLT, ESV.

Types and topics: Bible study, Christian living/spirituality, men, pop reference, prayer, self-help, social issues, theology, women's interests, children, devotionals, teen/YA

Royalty: 14–18%; advance

First print run: 3,000–50,000

Types of books: audiobook, ebook, hardcover, offset paperback

Imprints: VOICES (primarily African Americans)

Guidelines: not available

Tip: "We look for strong, Bible-grounded content with practical application for everyday living. If the text does not interact with Scripture, we probably won't be interested. Most of our devotional content is written inhouse and we only acquire very strong devotionals with clear, contextual biblical exposition and application for specific audiences and/or felt needs."

OUR SUNDAY VISITOR, INC.

200 Noll Plaza, Huntington, IN 46750-4303 | 260-356-8400
www.osv.com
Scott Richert, publisher

Denomination: Catholic

Mission statement: to help Catholics fulfill their calling to discipleship, strengthen their relationship with Christ, deepen their commitment to the Church, and contribute to its growth and vitality in the world

Submissions: Publishes 30–40 titles per year; receives 500 submissions annually. First-time authors: 10%. No simultaneous submissions. Query first on the website. Responds in 8–10 weeks. Actively seeking submissions for children: board books for infants and toddlers, picture books for younger readers (ages 3–6), short chapter books for middle-grade readers (ages 7–10), and works of interest to tweens and young teens.

Types and topics: apologetics, biography, Christian living/spirituality, church life, culture, evangelism, family, history, marriage, ministry, parenting, prayer, children, devotionals, prayer guides

Royalty: 10–12%; advance, $1,500

Types of books: board books, ebook, hardcover, paperback, picture books

Imprint: OSV Kids (children and teens)

Guidelines: *osv.submittable.com/submit*

Tip: "All books published must relate to the Catholic Church; unique books aimed at our audience. Give as much background information as possible on author qualification, why the topic was chosen, and unique aspects of the project. Follow our guidelines. We are expanding our religious-education product line and programs."

P&R PUBLISHING

1102 Marble Hill Rd., PO Box 817, Phillipsburg, NJ 08865 | 908-454-0505
acquisitions@prpbooks.com | *www.prpbooks.com*
Joy Woo, acquisitions and development editor
David Almack, director of acquisitions
Melissa Craig, children's editor

Denomination: Reformed

Mission statement: to publish excellent books that promote biblical understanding and godly living as summarized in the Westminster Confession of Faith and Catechisms

Submissions: Publishes 35–40 titles per year; receives 300 submissions annually. First-time authors: 10%. Length: 150–200 pages. Agent not required. Email proposal with sample chapters. Responds in three months. Bible: ESV.

Types and topics: Christian living/spirituality, counseling, family, marriage, theology, women, academic, children, church resources, devotionals, teen/YA

Royalty: 12–14%; advance

First print run: 3,000–5,000

Types of books: audiobook, ebook, hardcover, offset paperback

Guidelines: *www.prpbooks.com/manuscript-submissions*

Tip: "We are looking for content from a Reformed theological perspective."

PACIFIC PRESS

1350 N. Kings Rd., Nampa, ID 83687 | 208-465-2569
booksubmissions@pacificpress.com | *www.pacificpress.com*
Scott Cady, acquisitions editor

Denomination: Seventh-Day Adventist

Parent company: Seventh-day Adventist Church

Mission statement: to provide readers with a wide variety of books that connect them with God and help them develop a relationship with Him; provide information about God, His character, and His ways; and encourage and uplift them in the struggles of life

Submissions: Publishes 35–40 titles per year; receives 500 submissions annually. First-time authors: 5%. Length: 40,000–90,000 words/128–320 pages. Email query first. Responds in one to three weeks.

Types and topics: Bible study, biography, Christian living/spirituality, contemporary issues, health, history, marriage, memoir/personal narrative, parenting, prayer, theology, children; fiction: end times, historical

Royalty: 12–16%; advance, $1,500

Types of books: ebook, hardcover, paperback, picture books

Guidelines: *www.pacificpress.com/authors___artists/books*

Tip: "Most open to spirituality, inspirational, and Christian living. Our website has the most up-to-date information, including samples of recent publications. For more information, see *www.adventistbookcenter.com*. Do not send full manuscript unless we request it after reviewing your proposal."

PARACLETE PRESS

PO Box 1568, Orleans, MA 02653-1568 | 508-255-4685
submissions@paracletepress.com | *www.paracletepress.com*
Lillian Miao, director and acquisitions

Denomination: Catholic, Protestant

Submissions: Publishes 40 titles per year. Agent only. Responds in one month.

Types and topics: Advent/Christmas picture books, Christian living/spirituality, grief, Lent/Easter picture books, prayer, children; fiction: contemporary, fantasy, horror, science fiction

Imprint: Raven (fiction)

Guidelines: *www.paracletepress.com/pages/submission-guidelines*

PARAKLESIS PRESS

113 Winn Ct., Waleska, GA 30183 | 404-274-8615
submissions@paraklesispress.com | *ParaklesisPress.com*
Sally Apokedak, publisher

Denomination: Presbyterian

Mission statement: to publish books leaning to right of center that are meant to delight children but also to incite them to learn more about God and His creation

Submissions: Publishes six titles per year; receives 50 submissions annually. First-time authors: 50%. Length: picture books, to 800 words; middle-grade novels, to 60,000 words; YA novels, to 100,000 words. Agent not required. Email proposal with complete manuscript. Responds in four months; feel free to send a follow-up email monthly. Bible: ESV.

Types and topics: Bible studies, biography, science, children, devotionals, picture books, no paranormal or gay and lesbian

Royalty: picture books, 20%; novels, 40%

First print run: 1,000

Types of books: ebook, hardcover, POD

Guidelines: *paraklesispress.com/submit-to-us*

Tip: "We've got a lot of picture books lined up, so your best chance to break in now would be with a chapter book, a middle-grade novel, or a YA novel. I'm open to devotionals and Bible studies written from a Calvinistic perspective."

PARSONS PUBLISHING HOUSE

PO Box 410063, Melbourne, FL 32941 | 850-867-3061
info@parsonspublishinghouse.com | *www.parsonspublishinghouse.com*
Diane Parsons, chief editor

Mission statement: to produce books that are biblically accurate, unequivocal, and with an authentic message that glorifies God and exemplifies His victorious and loving nature

Submissions: Publishes two to six titles per year; receives 30 submissions annually. First-time authors: 60%. Length: 140+ pages. Email query first. No agents. Bible: NKJV, KJV, NLT, and many others.

Types and topics: Christian living/spirituality, counseling, marriage, prayer, spiritual growth, adult

Royalty: 10%; no advance

Types of books: ebook, hardcover, offset paperback, POD

Guidelines: not available

Tip: "Tell us your Christian testimony and how you serve the Lord now. Then, give us an overview of your book."

PAULINE BOOKS & MEDIA

50 Saint Paul's Ave., Boston, MA 02130-3491 | 617-522-8911
editorial@paulinemedia.com | *pauline.org*
   Denomination: Catholic
   Parent company: Daughters of St. Paul
   Mission statement: to be a trusted provider of excellent Catholic content that nurtures families and individuals to integrate their faith with their everyday lives
   Submissions: Publishes 25 titles per year; receives 300 submissions annually. First-time authors: 12%. Agent not required. Email or mail proposal with sample chapters. Responds in six to eight weeks. Bible: NRSV.
   Types and topics: Christian living/spirituality, evangelism, family, prayer, spiritual formation, theology, board books, devotionals, fiction, first-chapter, graphic novels, middle grade, picture books, teen/YA
   Royalty: 5–10%; advance
   Types of books: ebook, hardcover, offset paperback
   Guidelines: *pauline.org/publishing/#submissionguidelines*

PAULIST PRESS

997 Macarthur Blvd., Mahwah, NJ 07430-9990
submissions@paulistpress.com | *www.paulistpress.com*
Paul McMahon, editorial director
Donna Crilly, senior academic editor
   Denomination: Catholic
   Mission statement: to publish quality materials that bring the good news of the Gospel to Catholics and people of other religious traditions; support dialogue and welcome good scholarship and religious wisdom from all sources across denominational boundaries; foster religious values and wholeness in society, especially through materials promoting healing, reconciliation, and personal growth
   Submissions: Email or mail proposal with sample chapters. Responds in six to eight weeks.
   Types and topics: academic, children, nonfiction
   Types of books: ebook, paperback
   Guidelines: *www.paulistpress.com/Pages/Center/auth_res_0.aspx*

THE PILGRIM PRESS

1300 E. 9th St. #1100, Cleveland, OH 44114 | 216-736-3875
proposals@thepilgrimpress.com | *thepilgrimpress.com*
Kathryn Martin, acquisitions editor

    Denomination: United Church of Christ

    Parent company: United Church of Christ

    Mission statement: to publish books that nurture spiritual growth, cultivate religious leadership, and provoke the soul for the sake of a just world

    Submissions: Email proposal with sample chapters. Reviewed on a quarterly basis.

    Types and topics: Christian living/spirituality, leadership, prayer, preaching, theology, Bible studies, biography, memoir, ministry resources

    Types of books: ebook, paperback

    Guidelines: *thepilgrimpress.com/pages/acquisitions*

    Tip: "We do not publish Christian fiction or anti-LGBTQ commentaries."

PRAYERSHOP PUBLISHING

11969 E. Davis Ave., Brazil, IN 47834 | 812-238-5504
jon@prayershop.org | *prayershop.org*
Jonathan Graf, publisher

    Parent company: Church Prayer Leaders Network

    Mission statement: to take readers deeper in their prayer relationship with Jesus Christ and help churches become houses of prayer by discipling and equipping individuals in the aspects of prayer

    Submissions: Publishes four to six titles per year; receives 15 submissions annually. First-time authors: 15%. Length: maximum 35,000 words. Agent not required. Email proposal with sample chapters. Responds in six weeks. Bible: NIV.

    Types and topics: prayer, children, prayer guides, teen/YA

    Royalty: 10–15%; no advance

    First print run: 3,500

    Types of books: audiobook, ebook, offset paperback, POD

    Guidelines: *www.prayerleader.com/prayershop-publishing/submissions*

    Tip: "We love books that can be used for a 21-day, 30-day, or 40-day prayer initiative by a congregation. We look most seriously at authors who have an audience, whether online or through speaking, or authors who will buy a quantity of books from the first press run."

PRISM BOOK GROUP

PO Box 1738, Aztec, NM 87410
customer@pelicanbookgroup.com | *www.prismbookgroup.com*

Jacqueline Hopper, acquisitions editor, jhopper@prismbookgroup.com
Paula Mowery, acquisitions editor, pmowery@prismbookgroup.com

Parent company: Pelican Book Group

Mission statement: to publish quality books that reflect the salvation and love offered by Jesus Christ

Submissions: Length: 25,000–80,000 words. Query first on the website. Responds in three to four months. Bible: NIV, NAB.

Types and topics: fiction: contemporary, fantasy, historical, mystery, romance, romantic suspense, science fiction, suspense/thriller, teen/YA

Royalty: 40% download, 7% print; advance sometimes

Types of books: ebook, POD

Imprints: Prism Lux (Christian), Prism CW (clean and wholesome)

Guidelines: *pelicanbookgroup.com/ec/index.php?main_page=page&id=76*

Tip: "Our books offer clean and compelling reads for the discerning reader. We will not publish graphic language or content and look for well-written, emotionally charged stories, intense plots, and captivating characters."

PURE AMORE

PO Box 1738, Aztec, NM 87410
customer@pelicanbookgroup.com | *pelicanbookgroup.com*
Nicola Martinez, editor-in-chief

Parent company: Pelican Book Group

Mission statement: to publish quality books that reflect the salvation and love offered by Jesus Christ

Submissions: Length: 40,000–45,000 words. Submit proposal with sample chapters on the website. Responds in one to four months. Only contemporary Christian romance. Pure Amore romances are sweet in tone and in conflict. These stories are the emotionally driven tales of youthful Christians between the ages of 21 and 33 who are striving to live their faith in a world where Christ-centered choices may not fully be understood.

Types and topics: fiction: romance

Royalty: 40% download, 7% print; advance sometimes

Types of books: ebook, POD

Guidelines: *pelicanbookgroup.com/ec/index.php?main_page=page&id=69*

Tip: "Pure Amore romances emphasize the beauty in chastity, so physical interactions, such as kissing or hugging, should focus on the characters' emotions, rather than heightened sexual desire;

and scenes of physical intimacy should be integral to the plot and/or emotional development of the character or relationship."

REFORMED FREE PUBLISHING ASSOCIATION

1894 Georgetown Center Dr., Jenison, MI 49428 | 616-457-5970
marco@rfpa.org | *rfpa.org*
Marco Barone, book coordinator
Olivia Huizinga, children's book coordinator, olivia@rfpa.org
   Denomination: Reformed
   Mission statement: to glorify God by making accessible to the broadest possible audience material that testifies to the truth of Scripture as understood and developed in the Reformed tradition
   Submissions: Publishes eight titles per year; receives 25 submissions annually. First-time authors: 30–40%. Length: adults, 250+ pages; teens, 100+ pages; children's, 50+ pages. Agent not required. Conference contact a plus. Submit proposal with complete manuscript or sample chapters on the website form. Responds in three months. Bible: AKJV.
   Types and topics: Bible studies, biography, Christian living/spirituality, church history, dating, marriage, academic, Bible reference/ commentaries, Bible studies, biography, children, curriculum, devotionals, teen/YA
   Royalty: 15%; no advance
   First print run: 1,000
   Types of books: audiobook, ebook, hardcover, offset paperback, POD
   Guidelines: available via email
   Tip: "Potential authors must subscribe to the creeds and confessions of the Dutch Reformed tradition (Heidelberg Catechism, Canons of Dordt, Belgic Confession). We schedule our releases more than a year in advance, so we don't publish anything immediately. We welcome questions about proposals and submissions!"

RESOURCE PUBLICATIONS

199 W. 8th Ave., Ste. 3, Eugene, OR 97401 | 541-344-1528
proposal@wipfandstock.com | *wipfandstock.com/search-results/*
   ?imprint=resource-publications
Michael Thomson, acquisitions and development editor
   Parent company: Wipf and Stock
   Submissions: Email proposal with sample chapters. Responds in one to two months.
   Types and topics: biography, fiction, poetry, sermons

Types of books: ebook, POD
Guidelines: *wipfandstock.com/submitting-a-proposal*

RESURRECTION PRESS

77 West End Rd., Totowa, NJ 07572 | 973-890-2400
info@catholicbookpublishing.com | *www.catholicbookpublishing.com*
Anthony Buono, editor

Denomination: Catholic
Parent company: Catholic Book Publishing Corp.
Submissions: Mail proposal with sample chapters. Responds in four to six weeks.
Types and topics: Christian living/spirituality, healing, ministry, prayer
Royalty: negotiable; no advance
Guidelines: *catholicbookpublishing.com/pages/faq*

REVELL

6030 E. Fulton Rd., Ada, MI 49301 | 616-676-9185
bakerpublishinggroup.com/revell
Andrea Doering, editorial director
Kelsey Bowen, senior acquisitions editor
Grace Cho, senior acquisitions editor
Rachel McRae, executive and acquisitions editor

Parent company: Baker Publishing Group
Mission statement: to publish practical books that will help bring the Christian faith to everyday life
Types and topics: apologetics, Bible study, biography, Christian living/spirituality, church life, culture, family, marriage, memoir/personal narrative, children, fiction, teen/YA
Types of books: ebook, hardcover, mass market paperback, offset paperback

ROSE PUBLISHING

351 Executive Dr., Carol Stream, IL 60188 | 855-2779400
lpennings@tyndale.com | *www.tyndale.com/rose-publishing*
Lynette Pennings, managing editor

Parent company: Tyndale House Publishers
Mission statement: to make the Bible and its teachings easy to understand
Types and topics: Bible study helps, Bible reference/commentaries, wall charts
Types of books: hardcover, paperback, PDF download

ROSEKIDZ

351 Executive Dr., Carol Stream, IL 60188 | 855-2779400
kmcgraw@tyndale.com | *www.tyndale.com/kids-and-teens*
Karen McGraw, senior acquisitions editor

Parent company: Tyndale House Publishers
Mission statement: to help kids grow closer to God in a hands-on way
Types and topics: activities and puzzles, children, crafts, devotionals, fiction
Types of books: board books, hardcover, offset paperback, PDF download

SCRIVENINGS PRESS

PO Box 847, Morrilton, AR 72110 | 501-289-9319
heather@scriveningspress.com | *scriveningspress.com*
Heather Greer, managing editor
Erin R. Howard (for speculative submissions only), expansebooks@gmail.com

Mission statement: to publish great books our readers will love and to
help our authors build their careers
Submissions: Publishes 40 titles per year; receives 120 submissions
annually. First-time authors: 20%. Length: 60,000–90,000 words.
Only agent or conference contact. Submit proposal with sample
chapters on the website form. Responds in 8–12 weeks. Bible: any.
Types and topics: devotionals, fiction, middle-grade fiction, writing craft,
YA fiction, no horror
Royalty: paperback, 12%; Kindle, 50%; Kindle Unlimited pages read,
40%; no advance
Types of books: ebook, POD
Imprints: Scrivenings Press (general fiction), Expanse Books (speculative
fiction), ScrivKids (upper middle grade), ScrivInspire (devotionals),
ScrivCraft (writing craft), ScrivSPA (self-publishing assistance)
Guidelines: *scriveningspress.com/submissions*
Tip: "Polish your manuscript before submitting it. It's a good idea to read
it out loud and correct any errors. Get feedback from beta readers.
And read widely in your genre, as well as outside your genre, to keep
up with trends in the Christian publishing industry."

SEED AND SPARROW

6030 E. Fulton Rd., Ada, MI 49301 | 616-676-9185
bakerpublishinggroup.com
Jennifer Dukes Lee, acquisitions

Parent company: Baker Publishing Group
Submissions: Agent only.
Types and topics: children

SMYTH & HELWYS BOOKS

6316 Peake Rd., Macon, GA 31210-3960 | 478-757-0564
books@helwys.com | *www.helwys.com*
Leslie Andres, editor

Mission statement: to contribute to the life and ministry of the church and provide a bridge between the church and the academy

Submissions: Email or mail proposal with sample chapters. Responds in several weeks.

Types and topics: Bible study, Christian living/spirituality, leadership, ministry

Types of books: ebook, hardcover, paperback

Guidelines: *www.helwys.com/submit-a-manuscript*

THOMAS NELSON AND ZONDERVAN GIFT

PO Box 141000, Nashville, TN 37214-1000 | 615-889-9000
www.thomasnelson.com/gift; www.zondervan.com/gift
Adria Haley, senior acquisitions editor
Gini Wietecha, senior acquisitions editor

Parent company: Thomas Nelson Publishers and Zondervan/ HarperCollins Christian Publishing

Mission statement: to inspire the world by meeting the needs of people with content that promotes biblical principles and honors Jesus Christ

Types and topics: devotionals, gift

Types of books: ebook, hardcover, offset paperback

Guidelines: not available

Tip: "A gift book is designed to be shared. It's a beautiful keepsake that makes an ideal gift, a way to mark a special occasion or holiday, a message of the heart; and it usually satisfies a strong felt need. Gift books are as much an experience as a collection of words to be read."

THOMAS NELSON PUBLISHERS

Emanate Books, Grupo Nelson, Nelson Books, Thomas Nelson TNZ Fiction, Thomas Nelson and Zondervan Gift, Tommy Nelson, W Publishing

THOMAS NELSON TNZ FICTION

PO Box 141000, Nashville, TN 37214-1000 | 615-889-9000
laura.wheeler@harpercollins.com | *www.tnzfiction.com*
Laura Wheeler, senior acquisitions editor
Becky Monds, editorial director

Kimberly Carlton, acquisitions editor

Parent company: Thomas Nelson/HarperCollins Christian Publishing

Mission statement: to inspire the world by meeting the needs of people with content that promotes biblical principles and honors Jesus Christ

Submissions: Length: 70,000–90,000 words. Agent only.

Types and topics: fiction: Amish, contemporary, historical, humor, mystery, romance, southern, suspense/thriller, teen/YA

Royalty: advance

Types of books: audiobook, ebook, hardcover, offset paperback, POD

Guidelines: not available

Tip: "What we are looking for: great writers who are passionate about their stories, a willingness to work hard and engage with readers—coupled with a true love of readers—a unique angle on or a unique connection to their story matter, a great attitude."

TOMMY NELSON

PO Box 141000, Nashville, TN 37214-1000 | 615-889-9000
www.tommynelson.com
Bri Gallagher, acquisitions editor

Parent company: Thomas Nelson Publishers/HarperCollins Christian Publishing

Mission statement: to expand children's imaginations and nurture their faith while pointing them to a personal relationship with God

Types and topics: Bible storybooks, board books, devotionals, first-chapter, middle grade, picture books

Types of books: board books, ebook, hardcover, offset paperback, picture books

THE TRINITY FOUNDATION

PO Box 68, Unicoi, TN 37692 | 423-743-0199
tjtrinityfound@aol.com | *www.trinityfoundation.org*
Thomas W. Juodaitis, president

Mission statement: to promote the Christian religion

Submissions: Publishes two to three titles per year; receives five submissions annually. First-time authors: 10%. Length: 150–200 pages. Agent not required. Email or mail proposal with sample chapters. Responds in two weeks. Bible: KJV, NKJV.

Types and topics: apologetics, philosophy, theology

Royalty: flat fee, $2,000 for theology books; no advance

First print run: 1,000

Types of books: ebook, hardcover, offset paperback
Guidelines: available via email
Tip: "Look at our content on our website, and see if your material is a good fit."

TULIP PUBLISHING

PO Box 3150, Lansvale, NSW 2166, Australia | +61 2 9055 2195
submissions@tulippublishing.com.au | tulippublishing.com.au
Brett Lee-Price, general manager and editor-in-chief
Denomination: Reformed
Mission statement: to equip the saints—pastors, students, and everyday believers alike—with biblically faithful and theologically robust resources that edify the mind, stir the heart, and strengthen the church
Submissions: Submissions deadline for the 2027-28 publishing schedule is May 15. Publishes four titles per year; receives 20 submissions annually. First-time authors: 40%. Length: 250-350 pages. Email proposal with sample chapters. Responds in two to three months. Bible: ESV.
Types and topics: Christian living/spirituality, theology
Royalty: 30-40%; no advance
First print run: 1,000
Types of books: ebook, hardcover, offset paperback
Guidelines: *tulippublishing.com.au/about/submissions*
Tip: "Be concise and succinct in your proposal; have your manuscript read and proofed by others, like family or friends, before submission."

TWENTY-THIRD PUBLICATIONS

977 Hartford Tpke., Waterford, CT 06385 | 800-321-0411
resources@twentythirdpublications.com | twentythirdpublications.com
Denomination: Catholic
Parent Company: Bayard, Inc.
Mission statement: to provide lifelong faith formation through wholistic catechesis at all stages of faith development
Types and topics: Christian living/spirituality, Christmas, Easter, prayer, Bible studies, catechetical resources, children, church resources, devotionals, puzzles and activities, teen/YA
Types of books: ebook, paperback
Guidelines: *twentythirdpublications.com/pages/submissions*

TYNDALE HOUSE PUBLISHERS

351 Executive Dr., Carol Stream, IL 60188 | 630-668-8300
www.tyndale.com
Kara Leonino, associate director of acquisitions and curriculum, nonfiction
Stephanie Broene, acquisitions director, fiction
Elizabeth Jackson, senior acquisitions editor, fiction
Jillian Schlossberg, acquisitions manager, nonfiction
Jeff Gissing, acquisitions director, Bibles
Mindy Ferguson, senior acquisitions editor, Bibles

Mission statement: to help readers discover the life-giving truths of God's Word

Submissions: Publishes 100+ titles per year. First-time authors: 5%. Length: fiction, 75,000–100,000. Only agent, author referral, *ChristianBookProposals.com*, conference contact. Responds in three to six months. Bible: NLT.

Types and topics: biography, Christian living/spirituality, counseling, family, finances, leadership, marriage, memoir/personal narrative, parenting, children, devotionals, teen/YA; fiction: biblical, contemporary, historical, mystery, romance, suspense/thriller

Types of books: audiobook, ebook, hardcover, offset paperback

Imprints: Tyndale Kids (children), Wander (YA), Tyndale Español (Spanish), Tyndale Refresh (health and wellness), Tyndale Elevate (Christian worldview topics and apologetics), Tyndale Momentum (nonfiction), Hendrickson Publishers (nonfiction), Rose Publishing (Bible study helps), RoseKidz (children), Aspire (counseling)

TYNDALE KIDS

351 Executive Dr., Carol Stream, IL 60188 | 630-668-8300
kidsandwandersubmissions@tyndale.com | *www.tyndale.com/kids-and-teens*
Talla Messina, acquisitions editor

Parent company: Tyndale House Publishers

Mission statement: to bring kids and families closer to God through publishing books with excellent content, creative formats, and outstanding design

Submissions: Publishes 10–15 titles per year; receives 300–400 submissions annually. First-time authors: 5%. Length: varies according to the age group. Only agent, *ChristianBookProposals.com*, conference contact. Responds in two to three months. Bible: NLT.

Types and topics: activities and puzzles, Bible stories, board books, coloring books, crafts, devotionals, fiction, first-chapter, game books, middle grade, picture books, teen/YA

Royalty: 10–24%; advance varies according to platform, previous sales history, and uniqueness of proposal

Types of books: audiobook, ebook, hardcover, offset paperback, POD

Imprints: Wander (YA fiction and nonfiction), RoseKidz (children's and teachers resources)

Guidelines: not available

Tip: "Looking for a solid, well-written proposal; strong platform; excellent writing."

UPPER ROOM BOOKS

1908 Grand Ave., Nashville, TN 37212 | 800-972-0433
proposals@upperroom.org | upperroombooks.com
Michael S. Stephens, editorial director

Denomination: United Methodist

Parent company: The Upper Room

Mission statement: to encourage prayer and daily disciplines that help people create daily life with God

Submissions: Publishes 12 titles per year; receives 50 submissions annually. First-time authors: 50%. Length: 112–248 pages. Mail proposal with sample chapters. Responds only if interested. Bible: NRSV.

Types and topics: Christian living/spirituality, culture, healing, leadership, Lent, relationships, spiritual formation, stewardship, church resources, devotionals, worship resources

Royalty: 10–15%; advance sometimes

Types of books: audiobook, ebook, hardcover, offset paperback, POD

Imprints: Fresh Air Books (spiritually curious people interested in the relevance of faith in our culture), Discipleship Resources (leadership and stewardship resources)

Guidelines: *upperroombooks.com/submissions*

Tip: "Upper Room Books encourage the use of inclusive language in reference to God and humanity."

W PUBLISHING

PO Box 141000, Nashville, TN 37214-1000 | 615-889-9000
www.thomasnelson.com/wpublishing
Kyle Olund, senior acquisitions editor
Lisa-Jo Baker, senior acquisitions editor

Parent company: Thomas Nelson Publishers/HarperCollins Christian Publishing

Types and topics: Christian living/spirituality, memoir/personal narrative

Types of books: audiobook, ebook, hardcover, offset paperback

Guidelines: not available

Tip: "W prides itself on the ability to provide authors a nurturing, faith-friendly, boutique style publishing experience."

WARNER PRESS

2902 Enterprise Dr., Anderson, IN 46013 | 765-644-7721
editors@warnerpress.org | *www.warnerpress.org*
Julie Campbell, product and acquisitions editor

> **Denomination:** Church of God
>
> **Mission statement:** to equip the church, to advance the Kingdom, and to give hope to future generations
>
> **Submissions:** Publishes three to five titles per year; receives 50+ submissions annually. First-time authors: 50%. Email complete manuscript. Responds in six to eight weeks. Bible: KJV, NIV, ESV, NKJV.
>
> **Types and topics:** Bible studies, small group resources, small group study guides
>
> **Royalty:** based on the author and type of book; advance sometimes
>
> **Types of books:** ebook, offset paperback
>
> **Guidelines:** *www.warnerpress.org/submission-guidelines*
>
> **Tip:** "Do your research, and visit our website to view what we already produce."

WATERBROOK & MULTNOMAH

10807 New Allegiance Dr. #500, Colorado Springs, CO 80921 | 719-590-4999
info@waterbrookmultnomah.com | *www.waterbrookmultnomah.com*
Jamie Lapeyrolerie, acquisitions editor
Sara Rubio, executive editor, children's
Bunmi Ishola, children's senior editor and acquisitions
Drew Dixon, executive editor and acquisitions
Will Anderson, senior editor and acquisitions

> **Parent company:** PRH Christian Publishing Group
>
> **Submissions:** Publishes 60 titles per year; receives 300 submissions annually. First-time authors: 15%. Length: 208–400 pages. Agent only. Responds in one to two months.
>
> **Types and topics:** Christian living/spirituality, home and lifestyle, memoir/personal narrative, relationships, spiritual growth, Bible studies, children, devotionals; fiction: Amish, historical, romantic suspense
>
> **Royalty:** advance
>
> **Types of books:** audiobook, ebook, hardcover, offset paperback, POD
>
> **Imprint:** Ink & Willow (gifts)

Tip: "We recommend working with an agent whose clientele aligns with your strengths as a writer."

WATERSHED BOOKS

PO Box 1738, Aztec, NM 87410
customer@pelicanbookgroup.com | *www.pelicanbookgroup.com*
Nicola Martinez, editor-in-chief
 Parent company: Pelican Book Group
 Mission statement: to publish quality books that reflect the salvation and love offered by Jesus Christ
 Submissions: Length: 25,000–65,000 words. Submit proposal with sample chapters on the website. Responds in three to four months. Bible: NIV, NAB. Interested in series ideas.
 Types and topics: fiction: teen/YA, adventure, coming-of-age, crime, mystery, romance, science fiction, supernatural, suspense, westerns
 Royalty: 40% on download, 7% on print; advance sometimes
 Types of books: ebook, POD
 Guidelines: *pelicanbookgroup.com/ec/index.php?main_ page=page&id=60*
 Tip: "We want to see something other than dystopian."

WESTMINSTER JOHN KNOX PRESS

100 Witherspoon St., Louisville, KY 40202-1396
submissions@wjkbooks.com | *www.wjkbooks.com*
Jessica Miller Kelley, senior acquisitions editor
 Denomination: Presbyterian
 Parent company: Presbyterian Publishing Corporation
 Submissions: Publishes 60 titles per year. Email proposal with sample chapters. Responds in two to three months.
 Types and topics: Bible study, culture, ethics, ministry, theology, worship, academic
 Types of books: ebook, hardcover, offset paperback
 Imprints: Flyaway Books (children), Geneva Press (Presbyterian Church USA)
 Guidelines: *www.wjkbooks.com/author-relations*

WHITAKER HOUSE

1030 Hunt Valley Cir., New Kensington, PA 15068 | 724-334-7000
www.whitakerhouse.com
Amy Bartlett, managing and acquisitions editor
Chip MacGregor, executive editor and acquisitions

Denomination: Charismatic/Pentecostal

Parent company: Whitaker Corporation

Mission statement: to advance God's Kingdom by publishing biblically focused authors who proclaim the power of the gospel and minister to the spiritual needs of people around the world

Submissions: Publishes 75–100 titles per year; receives 200 submissions annually. First-time authors: 30%. Length: 50,000–80,000 words. Submit only if requested by house representative or from a recognized source. Responds in one to six months. Bible: KJV.

Types and topics: Charismatic, Christian living/spirituality, children, devotionals, fiction

Royalty: 15–18%; advance sometimes

Types of books: audiobook, board books, ebook, hardcover, offset paperback, POD

Imprint: Whitaker Playhouse (parents of young children)

Guidelines: *s3.amazonaws.com/whitaker-house-s3/wp-content/uploads/20190828134818/WhitakerHouse-Book-Submission-Guidelines.pdf*

Tip: "Follow the questions and suggestions on our submission guidelines."

WHITE ROSE PUBLISHING

PO Box 1738, Aztec, NM 87410

customer@pelicanbookgroup.com | *www.pelicanbookgroup.com*

Nicola Martinez, editor-in-chief

Parent company: Pelican Book Group

Mission statement: to publish quality books that reflect the salvation and love offered by Jesus Christ

Submissions: Length: short stories, 10,000–20,000 words; novelettes, 20,000–35,000 words; novellas, 35,000–60,000 words; novels, 60,000–80,000 words. Submit proposal with sample chapters on the website. Responds in three to four months. Bible: NIV, NAB.

Types and topics: fiction: romance

Royalty: 40% on download, 7% on print; advance sometimes

Types of books: ebook, POD

Guidelines: *pelicanbookgroup.com/ec/index.php?main_page=page&id=58*

Tip: "The setting for White Rose books can be contemporary, historical or futuristic. They can be straight romances or include other factors, such as mystery, suspense, or supernatural elements, etc.; however, an element of faith must be present in all White Rose stories—without becoming overbearing or preachy. Please specify in your proposal if your story includes elements beyond simple romance."

WHITECROWN PUBLISHING

13607 Bedford Rd. NE, Cumberland, MD 21502 | 866-245-2211
marisa@whitecrownpublishing.com | *www.whitecrownpublishing.com*
Marisa Stokley, associate publisher
Janelle Leonard, managing editor, janelle@whitecrownpublishing.com

Parent company: WhiteFire Publishing Group

Mission statement: to meld faith and royal fiction in romantic tales that will appeal to teens and adults and encourage them to embrace being daughters of the King

Submissions: Publishes 6–12 titles per year; receives 100 submissions annually. First-time authors: 25%. Length: 60,000–110,000 words. Agent not required. Email proposal with sample chapters. Responds in three months. Bible: KJV for historicals.

Types and topics: fiction: royal romance, royalty

Royalty: print, 10% on retail; ebooks, 50% on net; advance sometimes depending on sales history

Types of books: audiobook, ebook, hardcover, offset paperback, POD

Guidelines: *whitecrownpublishing.com/submissions*

Tip: "We're looking for stories that include royalty as one of the primary elements, which appeal to lovers of 'princess stories' but also offer depth and faith."

WHITEFIRE PUBLISHING

13607 Bedford Rd. NE, Cumberland, MD 21502 | 866-245-2211
r.white@whitefire-publishing.com | *www.whitefire-publishing.com*
Roseanna White, managing editor

Mission statement: to publish books that shine the light of God into the darkness and embrace the motto of "Where Spirit Meets the Page"

Submissions: Publishes 24 titles per year; receives 200 submissions annually. First-time authors: 20%. Length: 60,000–100,000 words. Email query first. Responds in three months. Bible: KJV for historicals.

Types and topics: nonfiction: all topics; fiction: contemporary, general, historical, romance, suspense, women's

Royalty: 50% on ebooks, 10% on print; advance, $1,500–2,000

Types of books: audiobook, ebook, POD

Imprints: WhiteSpark (young readers), Ashberry Lane (romance), WhiteFire (nonfiction and fiction), Chrism Press (Catholic and Orthodox fiction) WhiteCrown (royal romance)

Guidelines: *whitefire-publishing.com/submissions*

Tip: "Familiarize yourself with our titles and mission."

WHITESPARK PUBLISHING

13607 Bedford Rd. NE, Cumberland, MD 21502 | 866-245-2211
r.white@whitefire-publishing.com | *www.whitefire-publishing.com*
Roseanna White, managing editor
> **Parent company:** WhiteFire Publishing
> **Mission statement:** to engender a love of reading in kids with faith-based books
> **Submissions:** Publishes 5–10 titles per year; receives 100 submissions annually. First-time authors: 10%. Email query first. Responds in three months.
> **Types and topics:** all topics, middle grade, picture books, YA
> **Royalty:** 50% on ebooks, 10% on print; advance sometimes, $200–1,000
> **Types of books:** audiobook, ebook, POD
> **Guidelines:** *whitespark-publishing.com/submissions*
> **Tip:** "Come with fresh ideas on how to reach the young readership."

WILD HEART BOOKS

14250 Hwy. 55 W, Blacksburg, SC 29702 | 704-363-0360
submissions@mistymbeller.com | *wildheartbooks.org*
Denise Weimer, acquisitions and editorial liaison
> **Parent company:** Misty M. Beller Books, Inc.
> **Mission statement:** to provide the kind of exciting historical stories readers love, complete with heroes to make them swoon, strong heroines, and inspirational messages to encourage their faith
> **Submissions:** Publishes 30 titles per year; receives 50 submissions annually. First-time authors: 20%. Length: 60,000–80,000 words. Agent not required. Conference contact a plus. Email proposal with complete manuscript or sample chapters. Responds in one week. Bible: KJV.
> **Types and topics:** fiction: historical romance
> **Royalty:** 35–45%; no advance
> **Types of books:** audiobook, ebook, paperback
> **Guidelines:** *www.wildheartbooks.org/submissions.html*
> **Tip:** "We are currently open to submissions from new and established authors, including authors who wish to relaunch their back-list titles. We prefer series instead of standalones."

WILLIAM CAREY PUBLISHING

10 W. Dry Creek Cir., Littleton, CO 80120 | 720-372-7036
submissions@WCLBooks.com | *www.missionbooks.org*

Vivian Doub, publishing manager

Parent company: Frontier Ventures

Mission statement: to edify, equip, and empower disciples of Jesus to make disciples of Jesus and prompt breakthrough among unreached peoples

Submissions: Email query first. Responds in three to six months.

Types and topics: biography, ethnography, missions, academic

Types of books: ebook, paperback

Guidelines: *missionbooks.org/pages/submission-guidelines*

Tip: "We want our books to sound like the intelligent conversation you have with friends over dinner. You may site statistics and research (like you might reference an article in a reputable source), but you are sharing it in the context of a story that makes the research matter to real people doing Kingdom work."

WINGED PUBLICATIONS

PO Box 8047, Surprise, AZ 85374 | 623-910-4279
cynthiahickey@outlook.com | *www.wingedpublications.com*
Cynthia Hickey, CEO/president
Gina Welborn, acquisitions editor
Christina Rich, acquisitions editor
Patty Smith Hall, acquisitions editor

Submissions: Publishes 50 titles per year. First-time authors: 25%. Length: minimum 20,000 words. Conference contact a plus. Email proposal with sample chapters. Responds in two weeks. Bible: NIV.

Types and topics: self-help, devotionals; fiction: humor, dystopian, fantasy, historical romance, mystery, romance, romantic suspense, science fiction, suspense/thriller, teen/YA, women's

Royalty: 60%; no advance

Types of books: ebook, POD

Imprints: Soaring Beyond (nonfiction), Aisling Books (fantasy, dystopian, science fiction), Jurnee Books (young adult, middle grade), Gordian Books (mystery, suspense, thriller), Forget Me Not Romances (contemporary and historical romances), Take Me Away Books (noninspirational)

Guidelines: *wingedpublications.com/what-were-looking-for*

Tip: "Send the cleanest proposal you can."

WIPF AND STOCK PUBLISHERS

199 W. 8th Ave., Ste. 3, Eugene, OR 97401-2960 | 541-344-1528
rodney@wipfandstock.com | *www.wipfandstock.com*

Rodney Clapp, editor

>**Submissions:** Publishes 500+ in all imprint titles per year. Email proposal with sample chapters. Responds in two months.
>
>**Types and topics:** Bible, church history, ethics, history, ministry, philosophy, theology, academic
>
>**Types of books:** ebook, offset paperback
>
>**Imprints:** Resource Publications (leaders, pastors, educators), Cascade Books (academic)
>
>**Guidelines:** *wipfandstock.com/submitting-a-proposal*
>
>**Tip:** "It is your responsibility to submit a manuscript that has been fully copyedited by a professional copy editor."

WORDCRAFTS PRESS

912 E. Lincoln, Tullahoma, TN 37388 | 615-397-8376
wordcraftspress@gmail.com | *wordcrafts.net*
Mike Parker, publisher

>**Parent company:** WordCrafts LLC
>
>**Mission statement:** to produce fiction and nonfiction books that encourage, uplift, and inspire the human spirit, above all to tell stories
>
>**Submissions:** Publishes 24–36 titles per year; receives 150+ submissions annually. First-time authors: 50%. Length: maximum 400 pages. Agent not required. Email query first. Responds in six weeks. Bible: NIV, but open to any legitimate, broadly recognized version.
>
>**Types and topics:** all topics, Christian living/spirituality, devotionals; nonfiction; fiction: biblical, fantasy, historical, mystery, romance, science fiction, women's, middle grade, YA
>
>**Royalty:** around 25%; no advance
>
>**Types of books:** audiobook, ebook, hardcover, POD
>
>**Guidelines:** *wordcrafts.net/write-for-us*
>
>**Tip:** "Tell a great story."

WORTHY KIDS

830 Crescent Centre Dr., Franklin, TN 37067 | 615-221-0996
www.hachettebookgroup.com/imprint/worthykids
Peggy Schaefer, associate publisher and acquisitions

>**Parent company:** Worthy Publishing/Hachette Book Group
>
>**Mission statement:** to create books that are much more than just words and pictures—they're an opportunity for a moment of joy between a child and his or her loved one
>
>**Submissions:** Publishes 30–35 titles per year; receives 200 submissions annually. First-time authors: fewer than 10%. Length: maximum 200

words for board books, 600 words for picture books. Agent only. Responds in one month. Bible: NLT.

Types and topics: holidays, board books, first-chapter, middle grade, picture books

Royalty: varies; advance sometimes

First print run: 10,000

Types of books: audiobook, board books, ebook, hardcover, offset paperback, picture books

Tip: "Carefully study the types of books our house has published; and submit proposals that show an understanding of the marketplace, include recent competitive titles, and identify what sets your book apart."

WORTHY PUBLISHING

830 Crescent Centre Dr., Franklin, TN 37067 | 615-932-7600
www.worthypublishing.com
Beth Adams. editorial director
Giancarlo Montemayor, senior acquisitions editor

Parent company: Hachette Book Group

Mission statement: to publish books that combine faith, creativity, and culture while establishing the next generation of voices who believe that living faith can transform the world

Submissions: Publishes 36 titles per year. Agent only.

Types and topics: biography, Christian living/spirituality, contemporary issues, culture, leadership, marriage, parenting, relationships, social justice, spiritual growth, devotionals, fiction, gift

Types of books: audiobook, ebook, hardcover, paperback

Imprints: Worthy Books (broad spectrum of genres), Worthy Kids (children), Ellie Claire (gifts)

YWAM PUBLISHING

PO Box 55787, Seattle, WA 98155 | 800-922-2143
books@ywampublishing.com | *www.ywampublishing.com*
Tom Bragg, publisher

Parent company: Youth With A Mission

Mission statement: to encourage Christians to make a difference in a needy world

Submissions: Email proposal with sample chapters. Responds only if interested.

Types and topics: Christian living/spirituality, evangelism, family, leadership, missions, prayer, relationships, Bible studies, biography, devotionals

Types of books: audiobook, ebook, paperback
Guidelines: *www.ywampublishing.com/topic.aspx?name=submission*

ZONDERVAN

Editorial Vida, Zonderkidz, Zondervan Academic, Zondervan Books, Thomas Nelson and Zondervan Gift, Zondervan Reflective

ZONDERKIDZ

3900 Sparks Dr. SE, Grand Rapids, MI 49546
ZonderkidzSubmissions@harpercollins.com | *www.zonderkidz.com*
Katherine Easter, acquisitions editor
Katherine Jacobs, senior acquisitions editor, katherine.jacobs@harpercollins.com

Parent company: Zondervan/HarperCollins Christian Publishing
Mission statement: to inspire young lives through imaginative, innovative, and educational resources that represent a Christian worldview and build up God's children and teens
Submissions: Publishes 30–40 titles per year; receives hundreds of submissions annually. First-time authors: varies. Length: varies. Agent only. Response time varies. Bible: NIV.
Types and topics: children, teen/YA, fiction, nonfiction
Royalty: varies; advance
Types of books: audiobook, board books, ebook, hardcover, paperback, picture books
Guidelines: available via mail
Tip: "Look at our backlist to get a feel for what we publish."

ZONDERVAN ACADEMIC

3900 Sparks Dr. SE, Grand Rapids, MI 49512 | 616-698-6900
submissions@zondervan.com | *www.zondervanacademic.com*
Katya Covrett, VP and publisher

Parent company: Zondervan/HarperCollins Christian Publishing
Mission statement: to reflect the breadth and diversity—both theological and global—within evangelical scholarship while maintaining our commitment to the heart of orthodox Christianity
Submissions: Email query. Responds in six weeks or not interested. Bible: NIV.
Types and topics: academic, Bible reference/commentaries
Types of books: ebook, hardcover, offset paperback
Guidelines: *zondervanacademic.com/publishing-with-us*

ZONDERVAN BOOKS

PO Box 141000, Nashville, TN 37214 | 615-889-9000
www.zondervan.com
Andrea Palpant Dilley, senior acquisitions editor
Keren Baltzer, associate publisher and acquisitions

Parent company: Zondervan/HarperCollins Christian Publishing

Submissions: Publishes 120 titles per year. Agent only. Bible: NIV.

Types and topics: biography, Christian living/spirituality, church life, contemporary issues, family, finances, marriage, ministry, Bible reference/commentaries

Types of books: audiobook, ebook, hardcover, offset paperback

ZONDERVAN REFLECTIVE

3900 Sparks Dr. SE, Grand Rapids, MI 49512 | 616-698-6900
submissions@zondervan.com | *www.zondervan.com/zondervanreflective*
Kyle Rohane, senior acquisitions editor
Dale Williams, acquisitions editor

Parent company: Zondervan/HarperCollins Christian Publishing

Mission statement: to provide guidance and inspiration for effective leadership in business and ministry

Submissions: Email query. Responds in six weeks or not interested. Bible: NIV.

Types and topics: contemporary issues, culture, leadership, ministry

Types of books: ebook, hardcover, offset paperback

Guidelines: *www.zondervan.com/about-us/manuscript-submissions*

Tip: "The authors are expected to have demonstrable expertise on the subject being addressed."

2

BOOK ANTHOLOGY SERIES

ANGELS IN OUR LIVES

100 Reserve Rd., Ste. E200, Danbury, CT 06810 | 800-431-2344

angels@guideposts.org | guideposts.org

Joanna Kennedy, senior managing editor

> **Parent company:** Guideposts
>
> **Purpose statement:** to explore the ways God moves in people's lives—and the truly angelic result—to strengthen their faith and encourage them to see signs of God's presence in the world around them and seek ways they, too, can be an angel to others
>
> **Submissions:** Email query first. Responds in one to three months. Accepts various numbers per year.
>
> **Type of manuscripts:** personal experience
>
> **Topics/upcoming books:** ongoing series
>
> **Length:** 750–1,500 words
>
> **Rights:** all
>
> **Payment:** $250, on acceptance
>
> **Guidelines:** *guideposts.org/tell-us-your-story/call-for-submissions*
>
> **Tip:** "We are looking for stories that clearly show how God intervenes in our lives through others, events, visions, objects, and animals. While the moment can be wrapped in an everyday or commonplace experience, the result should be the realization that whatever happened did so only because God sent a helper."

CHICKEN SOUP FOR THE SOUL

PO Box 700, Cos Cob, CT 06807-0700

www.chickensoup.com

Amy Newmark, publisher and editor-in-chief

> **Parent company:** Chicken Soup for the Soul Publishing LLC
>
> **Purpose statement:** to share happiness, inspiration, and hope
>
> **Submissions:** Submit complete manuscript on the website form. If

no response by two months before the book's on-sale date, not interested. Accepts 101 manuscripts per book per year. Accepts submissions from children and teens.

Types of manuscripts: personal experience, poetry, theme-related

Topics/upcoming books: *www.chickensoup.com/story-submissions/possible-book-topics*

Length: 1,200 words maximum

Rights: nonexclusive

Payment: $250 plus 10 copies of the book, one month after publication

Guidelines: *www.chickensoup.com/story-submissions/story-guidelines*

Tip: "The most powerful stories are about people extending themselves, or performing an act of love, service or courage for another person."

DIVINE MOMENTS

PO Box 1233, Broken Arrow, OK 74013-1233 | 918-346-7960

terri@grace-publishing.com | *grace-publishing.com*

Terri Kalfas, compiler and editor

Parent company: Grace Publishing/The Jomaga Group LLC

Purpose statement: to show the possibility of changing someone's life, heart, or mind

Submissions: Email complete manuscript as attachment. Responds in one to three months. Accepts 200 manuscripts per year.

Types of manuscripts: fiction, personal experience, poetry, theme-related

Topics/upcoming books: *Christmas 2026, Divine Detours, Questionable Moments, Unexpected Kindness, Patriotic Moments, Hopefilled Moments*

Length: 250–2,000 words

Rights: first, reprint with info on where and when previously published

Payment: copy of book; royalties are donated to Samaritan's Purse

Guidelines: *grace-publishing.com/manuscript-submission/divine-moments-guidelines*

Tip: "Submit work that is in line with the book theme."

JESUS CAN BOOK SERIES

1314 S. 1st St. #128, Milwaukee, WI 53204

jcbssubmissions@gmail.com | *christianwriterscollective.com*

Nyla Kay Wilkerson, editing supervisor

Parent company: Christian Writers Collective LLC

Purpose statement: to spread the gospel far and wide and to help fund the God-given dreams of our writers

Submissions: Email manuscript as attachment or on website form. Responds in one to two weeks; contact after three weeks if no reply yet. Accepts around 300 manuscripts per year. Bible: KJV.

Types of manuscripts: testimony, theme-related

Topics/upcoming books: *Jesus Can ... Love You Through Your Pain, Jesus Can ... Reconcile Your Relationships, Jesus Can ... Deal With Your Emotions, Jesus Can ... Build Your Faith, Jesus Can ... Renew Your Hope*

Length: 500–750 words

Rights: all

Payment: beginning up to three months after publication, 1% of profit for up to two years after publication date

Guidelines: *christianwriterscollective.com/share-your-story-1*

Tip: "Write like you talk. We don't want you to sound like a professional writer. We want you to sound like a regular person, having a conversation with another regular person. Your personal salvation testimony is always your first submission to a Jesus Can book. After your testimony is published, you may write an article that relates to the title of the book you want us to consider publishing it in."

LIFE REPURPOSED

michelle@faithcreativitylife.com | *www.faithcreativitylife.com*
Michelle Rayburn, publisher and editor-in-chief

Parent company: Faith Creativity Life Books

Purpose statement: to help readers find hope in the trashy stuff of life

Submissions: Submit complete manuscript on the website form. Responds in two weeks to two months. Accepts: 60–100 manuscripts per year. Bible: NLT.

Types of manuscripts: devotions, fiction, humorous, personal experience, poetry, theme-related

Topics/upcoming books: *resilience, gardening*

Length: 300–1800 words

Rights: first, reprint with info on where and when previously published

Payment: copies of book

Guidelines: *www.faithcreativitylife.com*

Tip: "Pieces should be encouraging and uplifting, inspiring readers by showing how the writer found hope through their own struggle. They should be faith-based but not preachy. Writers should show vulnerability and authenticity as well as creativity. Humor is a plus!"

TOO AMAZING FOR COINCIDENCE

100 Reserve Rd. Ste. E200, Danbury, CT 06810 | 800-431-2344

TooAmazing@guideposts.org | *guideposts.org*

Joanna Kennedy, senior managing editor

Parent company: Guideposts

Purpose statement: to explore everyday miracles—times when God intervenes to point us in the right direction, to save us from dangerous situations, to provide hope in moments of hopelessness, to lead us to healing and reconciliation

Submissions: Email query first. Responds in two to three months. Accepts various number per year.

Type of manuscripts: personal experience

Length: 75–2,000 words

Rights: all

Payment: $250, on acceptance

Guidelines: *guideposts.org/tell-us-your-story/call-for-submissions*

Tip: "We often think of miracles as earth-shattering events that happen to other people. But sometimes there are moments where a coincidence is too perfect, where everything comes together at just the right time or in just the right way, that they can only be God's hand at work. These little gifts are reminders that He is always with us."

PART 2

INDEPENDENT BOOK PUBLISHING

3

INDEPENDENT BOOK PUBLISHERS

PUBLISHING A BOOK YOURSELF NO LONGER CARRIES THE STIGMA self-publishing has had in the past—if you do it right. Even some well-published writers are now hybrid authors, with independently published books alongside their royalty books. Others have built their readerships with traditional publishers, then moved to independent publishing where it is possible to make more money per sale.

Independent book publishers require the author to pay for part of the publishing costs or to buy a certain number of books. They call themselves by a variety of names, such as book packager, cooperative publisher, self-publisher, hybrid publisher, custom publisher, subsidy publisher, or simply someone who helps authors get their books printed. Services vary from including different levels of editing and proofreading to printing your manuscript as is.

Whenever you pay for any part of the production of your book, you are entering into a nontraditional relationship. Some independent publishers also offer a form of royalty publishing, so be sure you understand the contract you receive before signing it.

Some independent publishers will publish any book, as long as the author is willing to pay for it. Others are as selective about what they publish as a royalty publisher. Some independent publishers will do as much promotion as a royalty publisher—for a fee. Others do none at all.

If you are unsuccessful in placing your book with a royalty publisher but feel strongly about seeing it published, an independent publisher can make printing your book easier and often less expensive than doing it yourself. POD, as opposed to a print run of 1,000 books or more, could save you upfront money, although the price per copy is higher. Having your manuscript produced only as an ebook is also a less-expensive option.

Entries in this chapter are for information only, not an endorsement of publishers. For every complaint about a publisher, several other authors may sing the praises of it. Before you sign with any company, get more than one bid to determine whether the terms you are offered are competitive.

A legitimate independent publisher will provide a list of former clients as references. Also buy a couple of the publisher's previous books to check the quality of the work: covers, bindings, typesetting, etc. See if the books currently are available through any of the major online retailers.

Get answers before committing yourself. You may also want someone in the book-publishing industry to review your contract before you sign it. Some experts listed in the "Editorial Services" chapter review contracts.

If you decide not to use an independent publisher but do the work yourself, at least hire an editor, proofreader, cover designer, and interior typesetter-designer. The "Editorial Services" and "Design and Production Services" chapters will help you locate professionals with skills in these areas, as well as printing companies. Plus the "Distribution Services" and "Publicity and Marketing Services" chapters can help you solve one of the biggest problems of independent publishing: getting your books to readers.

ABOVE THE SUN MEDIA

330 S. 3rd St., Cottage Grove, OR 97424 | 541-954-9479
team@abovethesun.org | abovethesun.org
Jesse Rivas, owner

> **Types:** audiobooks, ebooks, gift books, offset paperback
> **Services:** à la carte options, author websites, design, manuscript evaluation, marketing, packages of services, proofreading, substantive editing
> **Production time:** one to six months
> **Number of books published per year:** two to five
> **Tip:** "For nonfiction, start with telling the stories before teaching. For fiction, make sure you understand the character's main lie they believe, their flaw, and what they need to do to overcome the final battle."

AMPELOS PRESS

951 Anders Rd., Lansdale, PA 19446 | 267-436-2503
mbagnull@aol.com | writehisanswer.com/ampelospress
Marlene Bagnull, publisher

> **Types:** ebooks, POD
> **Services:** copyediting, design, manuscript evaluation, proofreading, substantive editing

Production time: six months
Number of books published per year: two
Tip: "Especially interested in issues fiction and nonfiction, as well as books about missions and the needs of children. Author pays a one-time fee, maintains all rights, and receives 100% royalty from Amazon KDP."

BELIEVERS BOOK SERVICES

2329 Farragut Ave., Colorado Springs, CO 80907 | 719-641-7862
dave@believersbookservices.com | believersbookservices.com
Dave Sheets, owner

Types: ebooks, gift books, hardcover, paperback, picture books, POD
Services: à la carte options, author websites, copyediting, design, distribution, manuscript evaluation, packages of services, proofreading, substantive editing
Production time: three months
Number of books published per year: 45–50
Tip: "Start thinking about strategy for publishing, marketing, and launching as soon as possible in the process. This strategy process will help produce a stronger book."

BK ROYSTON PUBLISHING

PO Box 4321, Jeffersonville, IN 47131 | 502-694-2143
bkroystonpublishing@gmail.com | www.bkroystonpublishing.com
Julia A. Royston, CEO

Types: audiobooks, ebooks, hardcover, picture books, POD
Services: à la carte options, author websites, copyediting, design, manuscript evaluation, marketing, online bookstore, packages of services, promotional materials, proofreading, substantive editing
Production time: four to six months
Number of books published per year: 50
Tip: Be sure "you are intimately connected and passionate about the message and your why this book now is clear."

BOOKBABY

7905 N. Crescent Blvd., Pennsauken, NJ 08110 | 877-961-6878
info@bookbaby.com | www.bookbaby.com

Types: audiobooks, comic books, ebooks, gift books, hardcover, offset paperback, picture books, POD
Services: copyediting, design, distribution, manuscript evaluation,

online bookstore, proofreading, social-media ads, substantive editing

Production time: varies

Tip: "When you work with BookBaby, you'll have every resource you need, such as book-cover design, editing, ebook creation, audiobook creation, and marketing services, all in one place! Plus, we also have our own storefront, BookBaby Bookshop."

BRIDGE LOGOS, INC.

14260 W. Newberry Rd. #409, Newberry, FL 32669 | 800-444-4484
swooldridge@bridgelogos.com | *www.bridgelogos.com*
Peggy Hildebrand, acquisitions editor

Types: audiobooks, ebooks, hardcover, paperback

Services: copyediting, design, distribution, proofreading, royalty contract, substantive editing

Production time: 12–18 months

Number of books published per year: 40

Tip: Traditional house that requires new Bridge Logos authors and authors with no established marketing platform to purchase 1,000–3,000 books at a discount. Start by emailing proposal and manuscript. "Looking for well-written, timely books that are aimed at the needs of people and that glorify God. Have a great message, a well-written manuscript, and a specific plan and willingness to market your book. Looking for previously published authors with an active ministry who are experts on their subject."

BROWN CHRISTIAN PRESS

16250 Knoll Trail Dr., Ste. 205, Dallas, TX 75248 | 972-381-0009
publishing@brownbooks.com | *www.brownbooks.com/brown-christian-press*

Types: audiobooks, ebooks, gift books, hardcover, paperback

Services: copyediting, design, distribution, ghostwriting, indexing, marketing, proofreading, substantive editing

Production time: six months

Tip: "We are a relationship publisher and work with our authors from beginning to end in the journey of publishing."

CALLED WRITERS CHRISTIAN PUBLISHING

1900 Rice Mine Rd. N. 401, Tuscaloosa, AL 35406 | 205-872-4509
shannon@calledwriters.com | *CalledWriters.com*
Shannon McKinney, relationship builder

Types: offset paperback, POD

Services: à la carte options, copyediting, design, manuscript evaluation, marketing, packages of services, proofreading, royalty contract, substantive editing

Production time: six months

Number of books published per year: two

Tip: "God will open the right doors for you at the right time. Don't give up."

CAPTIVATE PRESS

3001 Shelley Lynn Dr., Arnold, MO 63010 | 636-633-7846
captivatepress@gmail.com | *captivatepress.site*
Isabella Witt

Types: ebooks, gift books, hardcover, offset paperback

Services: design, distribution, marketing, proofreading, royalty contract, substantive editing

Production time: one year

Number of books published per year: 20–30

Tip: "Make sure you submit your best work. There is a lot of competition, and we only choose the work that we like the best."

CHRISTIAN FAITH PUBLISHING

832 Park Ave., Meadville, PA 16335 | 800-955-3794
Chris@christianfaithpublishing.com | *www.Christianfaithpublishing.com*
Chris Rutherford, president

Types: ebooks, hardcover, offset paperback, POD

Services: à la carte options, copyediting, design, distribution, indexing, manuscript evaluation, marketing, packages of services, promotional materials, royalty contract

Production time: 8–10 months

Number of books published per year: 1,200

Tip: "Be mindful of the fact that it is quite challenging to publish a book and have commercial success."

CLM PUBLISHING

PO Box 1217, Grand Cayman, Cayman Islands KY-11108 | 345-926-2507
production@clmpublishing.com | *www.clmpublishing.com*

Types: ebooks, gift books, hardcover, offset paperback, picture books, POD

Services: copyediting, design, distribution, illustrations, indexing, manuscript evaluation, marketing, online bookstore, proofreading, substantive editing

Production time: three to six months
Number of books published per year: eight
Tip: "Be willing to do some marketing."

CLOVERCROFT PUBLISHING GROUP

307 Verde Meadow Dr., Franklin, TN 37067 | 615-538-8557
shane@clovercroftpublishing.com | *clovercroftpublishing.com*
Shane Crabtree, COO

> **Types:** audiobooks, ebooks, gift books, hardcover, offset paperback, picture books, POD
> **Services:** à la carte options, author websites, coaching, copyediting, design, distribution, indexing, international rights, manuscript evaluation, marketing, online bookstore, packages of services, promotional materials, proofreading, royalty contract, substantive editing
> **Production time:** four to six months
> **Number of books published per year:** 25
> **Tip:** "Start planning your marketing early!"

COLEMAN JONES PRESS

13155 Noel Rd., Ste. 910, Dallas, TX 75240 | 561-720-5772
colemanjonespress.us
Tracee and Ross Jones, owners

> **Types:** audiobooks, curriculum, ebooks, hardcover, picture books, POD
> **Services:** author websites, design, distribution, marketing, packages of services, promotional materials
> **Production time:** three to six months
> **Tip:** "Write for the sake of getting the gospel out, not for the money. When choosing a cover or illustrator, make sure your design looks like something that is in major retail stores."

COVENANT BOOKS

830 Park Ave., Ste. 125, Meadville, PA 16335 | 843-507-8373
contact@covenantbooks.com | *www.covenantbooks.com*
Denice Hunter, president

> **Types:** ebooks, hardcover, offset paperback, POD
> **Services:** à la carte options, copyediting, design, distribution, marketing, online bookstore, packages of services, royalty contract
> **Production time:** six months
> **Tip:** "Publishing a book can be a fun and enlightening process. Take your time, and choose a publisher you feel comfortable with."

CREATIVE ENTERPRISES STUDIO

1507 Shirley Way, Ste. A, Bedford, TX 76022-6737 | 817-312-7393
AcreativeShop@aol.com | www.creativeenterprisesltd.com
Mary Hollingsworth, president and publisher

Types: audiobooks, ebooks, gift books, hardcover, offset paperback, picture books
Services: à la carte options, author websites, copyediting, design, distribution, indexing, manuscript evaluation, marketing, promotional materials, proofreading, substantive editing, translation into 17 languages, copyright permissions
Production time: depends on type and length of book
Number of books published per year: 7–10
Tip: "Contact us by email first, please. Then we'll set a phone appointment."

CREDO HOUSE PUBLISHERS

2200 Boyd Ct. NE, Grand Rapids, MI 49525-6714
publish@credocommunications.net | www.credohousepublishers.com
Timothy J. Beals, publisher

Type: offset paperback
Services: à la carte options, author websites, copyediting, design, distribution, indexing, manuscript evaluation, marketing, online bookstore, packages of services, promotional materials, proofreading, substantive editing
Production time: three months
Number of books published per year: 30
Tip: "Come prepared. Be persistent. Get published."

DEEP RIVER BOOKS LLC

PO Box 310, Sisters, OR 97759 | 541-549-1139
andy@deepriverbooks.com | www.deepriverbooks.com
Andy Carmichael, publisher

Types: audiobooks, ebooks, hardcover, offset paperback, POD
Services: copyediting, design, distribution, manuscript evaluation, marketing, online bookstore, packages of services, promotional materials, royalty contract, substantive editing
Production time: 9–14 months
Number of books published per year: 30–35
Tip: "Check our website on how we work with authors before you submit."

DEEPER REVELATION BOOKS

PO Box 4260, Cleveland, TN 37320-4260 | 423-478-2843
pastormikeshreve@gmail.com | *deeperrevelationbooks.org*
Mike Shreve, CEO

> **Types:** ebooks, gift books, hardcover, offset paperback, POD
> **Services:** à la carte options, author websites, copyediting, design, distribution, indexing, manuscript evaluation, marketing, online bookstore, promotional materials, proofreading, substantive editing
> **Production time:** three to six months
> **Number of books published per year:** 25–30
> **Tip:** "The root of the word *authority* is the word *author*. When you emerge as a reputable author on a specific subject, in the minds of the public, you are an authority in that area."

DESCENDANT PUBLISHING

PO Box 29, Byron Center, MI 49315 | 616-290-7829
contact@descendantpublishing.com | *www.descendantpublishing.com*
Troy Hooker, managing editor

> **Types:** audiobooks, curriculum, ebooks, POD
> **Services:** coaching, copyediting, design, distribution, marketing, online bookstore, packages of services, proofreading, royalty contract
> **Tip:** "We can walk you through the process one step at a time, helping you to bring your story to market at a fraction of the cost."

DESTINY IMAGE PUBLISHERS

167 Walnut Bottom Rd., Shippensburg, PA 17257 | 717-532-3040
manuscripts@norimediagroup.com | *norimediagroup.com/pages/publish-with-us*

> **Types:** ebooks, paperback
> **Services:** copyediting, design, manuscript evaluation, marketing, proofreading, substantive editing
> **Production time:** one year
> **Tip:** Traditional publisher that requires prepurchase of 500–3,000 copies. "Focuses on Spirit-empowered themes: supernatural God encounters, healing/deliverance, prophecy and prophetic ministry, gifts of the Holy Spirit, prayer and intercession, the presence and glory of God, and dreams/dream interpretation."

EABOOKS PUBLISHING

1136 W. Winged Foot Cir., Winter Springs, FL 32708 | 407-712-3431
Cheri@eabookspublishing.com | *www.eabookspublishing.com*

Cheri Cowell, founder

Types: audiobooks, ebooks, gift books, hardcover, picture books, POD

Services: author websites, copyediting, design, distribution, illustrating, manuscript evaluation, marketing, packages of services, proofreading, substantive editing

Production time: six months

Number of books published per year: 45

Tip: "Know your target market/audience, and follow your passion."

eBOOK CONVERSION AND LISTING SERVICES

PO Box 57, Glenwood, MD 21738 | 443-280-5077

sales@taegais.com | ebooklistingservices.com

Amy Deardon, CEO

Types: audiobooks, ebooks, POD

Services: à la carte options, design, distribution, marketing, packages of services, promotional materials

Production time: one to three months

Number of books published per year: 20

Tip: "We empower independent authors to become successful. Unlike most other independent publishers, we set you up so you are the publisher, rather than publishing through the independent company. You can create your own publishing company name and logo, and we help you with that. You remain fully in charge of all decisions, rights, and profits from start to forever. Once your book is published, you can buy as few or as many books as you want at the lowest printer's price (a 200-page book costs less than $3.50); and books are delivered in a week or two through Amazon. We also have additional packages that can list your book with the Library of Congress and help you rank higher on Amazon's search engines so readers can actually find your book and buy it. We provide you with ownership of your book and work with you to make that succeed."

ELECTRIC MOON PUBLISHING

13518 Heritage Dr., Bonner Springs, KS 66012 | 913-827-2225

info@emoonpublishing.com | emoonpublishing.com

Douglas West, publisher

Types: audiobooks, ebooks, gift books, hardcover, offset paperback, picture books, POD

Services: à la carte options, author websites, book trailer, copyediting, design, distribution, indexing, manuscript evaluation, marketing, packages of services, promotional materials, proofreading, royalty contract, substantive editing

Production time: 8–10 months

Number of books published per year: 8–12

Tip: "Feel free to ask questions of the services and publishing models offered. We are here to help and would enjoy an initial conversation with you."

EMBOLDEN MEDIA GROUP

PO Box 953607, Lake Mary, FL 32795-3607

jevon.bolden@emboldenmediagroup.com | *emboldenmediagroup.com/ book-publishing*

Types: ebooks, POD

Services: à la carte options, copyediting, design, distribution, manuscript evaluation, marketing, packages of services, proofreading, substantive editing

Tip: "Our Elite Publishing Package allows you to let your message get the polish it needs so that it reaches deep into the hearts of your readers by putting it through Embolden Media Group's complete book publishing editorial and production process. If you choose to partner with us in getting your book into the hands of readers who need it most, you will be taken through the full editorial and production process common in most traditional publishing houses—from start to finish. If you would rather skip or omit any step in the process, à la carte services are available. Your book must be fully written and complete before you embark on any of our Get Published Packages."

ENCOURAGE PUBLISHING

1116 Creekview Cir., New Albany, IN 47150 | 812-987-6148

leslie@encouragebooks.com | *encouragepublishing.com*

Leslie Turner, publisher

Types: audiobooks, ebooks, gift books, hardcover, offset paperback, picture books, POD

Services: copyediting, design, distribution, manuscript evaluation, marketing, online bookstore, packages of services, promotional materials, proofreading, royalty contract, substantive editing

Production time: 14 months

Number of books published per year: 5–10

Tip: "Mission statement required (see guidelines at *encouragepublishing.com/ books*)."

FAIRWAY PRESS

5450 N. Dixie Hwy., Lima, OH 45807-9559 | 419-227-1818
david@csspub.com | *www.fairwaypress.com*
David Runk, president

Types: ebooks, offset paperback, POD
Services: copyediting, design, manuscript evaluation, proofreading, substantive editing
Production time: 6–12 months
Number of books published per year: 10–20
Tip: "Provide a summary of each chapter along with the full manuscript. Include a table of contents. Don't use hard returns except at the end of paragraphs."

FIESTA PUBLISHING

PO Box 44984, Phoenix, AZ 85014 | 602-795-5868
julie@fiestapublishing.com | *www.fiestapublishing.com*
Julie Castro, owner

Types: ebooks, offset paperback, POD
Services: à la carte options, copyediting, manuscript evaluation, packages of services
Production time: six to eight weeks, depending on readiness of the manuscript
Number of books published per year: two to four
Tip: "Be open to suggestions."

FUSION HYBRID PUBLISHING

PO Box 206, Nesbit, MS 38651 | 901-590-6584
victoria@endgamepress.com | *www.endgamepress.com/fusion*

Types: audiobooks, ebooks, gospel tracts, hardcover, offset paperback, picture books, POD
Services: à la carte options, copyediting, design, distribution, indexing, manuscript evaluation, marketing, online bookstore, packages of services, promotional materials, proofreading, substantive editing
Production time: 6–12 months
Number of books published per year: three to four
Tip: "Fusion is a great option for those who are excited to get to market faster than traditional houses and have a great audience already."

GOODWILL MEDIA SERVICES CORP.

105 Macclamrock Ct., Cary, NC 27518 | 347-247-2106
goodwillmediaservices.sofia@gmail.com | *goodwillmediaservices.com*
Sofia Delgado, author relations consultant

> **Types:** audiobooks, ebooks, gift books, hardcover, offset paperback, picture books, POD
> **Services:** à la carte options, author websites, coaching, copyediting, design, distribution, indexing, manuscript evaluation, marketing, online bookstore, packages of services, promotional materials, proofreading, substantive editing
> **Production time:** three months
> **Number of books published per year:** 25+
> **Tip:** "Don't settle for limitations. Break free from the constraints of traditional publishing and experience the freedom of self-publishing. With our support, you can chart your own course as a Christian author."

HARRISON HOUSE

167 Walnut Bottom Rd., Shippensburg, PA 17257 | 717-532-3040
manuscripts@norimediagroup.com | *norimediagroup.com/pages/publish-with-us*

> **Types:** ebooks, paperback
> **Services:** copyediting, design, manuscript evaluation, marketing, proofreading, substantive editing, royalty contracts
> **Production time:** one year
> **Tip:** Traditional publisher that requires prepurchase of 500–3,000 copies.

HONEYCOMB HOUSE PUBLISHING

315 3rd St., New Cumberland, PA 17070 | 215-767-9600
dave@fessendens.net | *www.davefessenden.com/honeycomb-house-publishing-llc*
David Fessenden, publisher

> **Type:** POD
> **Services:** à la carte options, author websites, copyediting, design, distribution, manuscript evaluation, marketing, packages of services, promotional materials, proofreading, substantive editing
> **Production time:** three to six months
> **Number of books published per year:** one or two
> **Tip:** "Prepare a book proposal even if you plan to self-publish/subsidy publish."

ILLUMIFY MEDIA

10488 Centennial Rd., Ste. 511, Littleton, CO 80127 | 303-523-4813

mklassen@illumifymedia.com | *www.illumifymedia.com*

Michael J. Klassen, president

Types: ebook, hardcover, POD

Services: à la carte options, author websites, copyediting, design, distribution, manuscript evaluation, marketing, proofreading, substantive editing

Production time: three months once the manuscript goes to copyediting

Books per year: 60

Tip: "Transcendent books change the world. We publish books that are transcendent in quality—which build a platform of credibility and authority so you can share your transcendent message."

IMMORTALISE

PO Box 656, Noarlunga Centre, SA 5168, Australia

toastercide@gmail.com | *www.immortalise.com.au*

Ben Morton, editor

Types: ebooks, hardcover, offset paperback, picture books

Services: à la carte options, copyediting, design, manuscript evaluation, online bookstore, proofreading, substantive editing

Production time: varies

Tip: "All our services are optional, and there is no cost for enquiries. We will publish any book so long as the content is not likely to get anyone sued."

INSCRIPT BOOKS

PO Box 611, Bladensburg, MD 20710

admin@dovechristianpublishers.com | *www.inscriptpublishing.com*

Allison Kelsey, editorial director

Types: ebooks, hardcover, offset paperback, POD

Services: à la carte options, copyediting, design, distribution, manuscript evaluation, marketing, packages of services, proofreading, royalty contract, substantive editing

Production time: six to eight weeks

Number of books published per year: 12

Tip: "Full submission requirements, qualifications, and online forms are listed on our website. For consideration, please follow them carefully. We do not accept snail-mail submissions. We do not accept email submissions apart from the forms on our website."

JOMAGA HOUSE

PO Box 1233, Broken Arrow, OK 74013-1233 | 918-346-7960
terri@grace-publishing.com | *www.grace-publishing.com*
Terri Kalfas, editor

> **Types:** ebooks, hardcover, offset paperback, picture books, POD
> **Services:** à la carte options, copyediting, design, distribution, manuscript evaluation, online bookstore, proofreading, royalty contract, substantive editing
> **Production time:** two to three months from receipt of approved manuscript
> **Number of books published per year:** five
> **Tip:** "Books published for children through adults. Various genres accepted, including nonfiction, memoirs, and family genealogy."

LAKE DRIVE BOOKS

6757 Cascade Rd. SE #162, Grand Rapids, MI 49546 | 616-737-1480
david.morris@lakedrivebooks.com | *lakedrivebooks.com*
David Morris, publisher

> **Types:** audiobooks, ebooks, hardcover, offset paperback, POD
> **Services:** distribution, marketing
> **Production time:** one year
> **Number of books published per year:** eight
> **Tip:** "See our website to understand our publishing and if you would be a fit. Submissions must be in book-proposal form. There's a template on the website."

LONDON LANE DESIGNS

35 London Ln., Sharpsburg, GA 30277 | 770-710-3137
londonlanedesigns@gmail.com | *LondonLaneDesigns.com*
Gloria Erickson, owner and lead designer

> **Types:** ebooks, hardcover, POD
> **Services:** à la carte options, design
> **Production time:** two to four weeks with fully edited manuscript
> **Number of books published per year:** varies
> **Tip:** "Do your research. Some publishers are very expensive and will retain the rights to your book. Good independent publishers will publish your book, and you keep complete control over rights and design. London Lane Designs will work with you to create the book of your dreams, and you will keep control."

MORGAN JAMES PUBLISHING

5 Penn Plaza, 23rd Floor, New York City, NY 10001 | 516-900-5711
terry@morganjamespublishing.com | *www.morganjamespublishing.com*
W. Terry Whalin, acquisitions editor

Types: audiobooks, ebooks, offset paperback, picture books, POD

Services: design, distribution, manuscript evaluation, marketing, online bookstore, proofreading, royalty contracts with 20–25% royalties and small advance

Production time: 10–12 weeks, bookstore distribution in 9–10 months

Number of books published per year: 180–200, 25–30 in the faith division

Tip: "Beginning our 22nd year in publishing. Over 6,000 titles and 25 million books in print. Top independent publisher—rated 10 times from *Publishers Weekly*—and distribution into 98% of the bookstores in North America, including over 180 online plus brick-and-mortar bookstores. Our books have been on the *New York Times* bestseller list over 28 times and over 200 times on the *Wall Street Journal* bestseller list.

"We offer free marketing and coaching training for authors and a private Facebook group with over 1,400 authors. Over the lifetime of the agreement, the author has access to an unlimited number of free ebooks to give away and is required to purchase 2,000 copies at the print cost plus $3. Our author support team builds a free BookFunnel page for each author to give away a free ebook to build their email list. These free downloads drive print sales and count against the book purchase requirement.

"Email your proposal with sample chapters or full manuscript. Only 30% of authors have literary agents."

REDEMPTION PRESS

70 S. Val Vista Dr., Ste. A3-442, Gilbert, AZ 85296 | 360-226-3488
acquisitions@redemption-press.com | *www.redemption-press.com*
Tracy Wren, director of acquisitions

Types: audiobooks, ebooks, gift books, hardcover, offset paperback, picture books, POD

Services: à la carte options, author websites, copyediting, design, distribution, indexing, manuscript evaluation, marketing, online bookstore, promotional materials, proofreading, substantive editing, theological review, foreign rights and translations

Production time: 6–12 months, depending on editing needed and word count

Number of books published per year: 75–100

Tip: "Don't rush the process—writing and launching a book is both a calling and a craft. Prayerfully invite a trusted circle to cover you in prayer, seek wise counsel from those who've walked the publishing road, and commit to excellence in every step. The impact of your message grows when it's prepared with both diligence and dependence on the Lord."

RENOWN PUBLISHING

424 W. Bakerview Rd., Ste. 105, Bellingham, WA 98248 | 360-836-0672
caleb@renownpublishing.com | renownpublishing.com
Caleb Breakey, founder

Types: audiobooks, ebooks, hardcover, offset paperback, POD
Service: legacy storytelling
Production time: 14–18 months
Number of books published per year: 10–20
Tip: "Let story do the work."

ROARING LAMBS PUBLISHING

18383 Preston Rd., Ste. 408, Dallas, TX 75252 | 972-380-0123
mlaine@RoaringLambs.org | www.roaringlambs.org/publishing
Marji Laine, director of publishing

Types: audiobooks, ebooks, hardcover, picture books, POD
Services: à la carte options, copyediting, design, distribution, manuscript evaluation, proofreading, substantive editing
Production time: six months
Number of books published per year: 20–30
Tip: "Your story is too important to leave on the computer. Share it with those who desperately need to hear it!"

SALVATION PUBLISHER AND MARKETING GROUP

PO Box 40860, Santa Barbara, CA 93140 | 805-252-9822
opalmaedailey@aol.com
Opal Mae Dailey, editor in chief

Types: ebooks, hardcover, offset paperback
Services: copyediting, design, manuscript evaluation, proofreading, substantive editing
Production time: six to nine months
Number of books published per year: five to seven
Tip: "Turning recorded messages into book form for pastors is a

specialty of ours. We do not accept any manuscript we would be ashamed to put our name on."

SERMON TO BOOK
424 W. Bakerview Rd., Ste. 105 #215, Bellingham, WA 98226 | 360-223-1877
info@sermontobook.com | *www.sermontobook.com*
Caleb Breakey, lead book director

   Types: audiobooks, ebooks, offset paperback, POD
   Services: author websites, copyediting, design, distribution, indexing, manuscript evaluation, marketing, online bookstore, packages of services, promotional materials, proofreading, substantive editing
   Production time: seven to nine months
   Number of books published per year: 60
   Tip: "Check out our materials at *SermonToBook.com*."

SPRINKLE PUBLISHING
1675 Lucia Ln., Mansfield, OH 44907-2778 | 419-709-1435
Dr.Sprinkle@wsministries.ws | *www.wsministries.ws/home/sprinkle-publishing*
Dr. Wanda J. Sprinkle, CEO and editor

   Types: audiobooks, hardcover, offset paperback
   Services: copyediting, design, manuscript evaluation, online bookstore, proofreading
   Production time: three to six months
   Number of books published per year: five
   Tip: "Write every day without corrections. Capture your thoughts and ideas immediately."

STONE OAK PUBLISHING
PO Box 2011, Friendswood, TX 77549 | 832-569-4282
stoneoakpublishing@gmail.com | *stoneoakpublishing.com*
Karen Porter, acquisitions

   Types: ebooks, hardcover, offset paperback, POD
   Services: à la carte options, coaching, copyediting, design, distribution, ghostwriting, indexing, manuscript evaluation, marketing, packages of services, promotional materials, proofreading, royalty contract, substantive editing
   Production time: six to eight months
   Number of books published per year: 10
   Tip: "Send us a well-thought-out email detailing the information about your book."

TEACH SERVICES, INC.

140 Industry Ln. SW, Calhoun, GA 30701 | 800-367-1844
publisher@TEACHServices.com | *teachservices.com/mss-review*
Michael W. Brazington, publisher

> **Types:** audiobooks, ebooks, hardcover, offset paperback, picture books, POD
> **Services:** à la carte options, author websites, copyediting, design, distribution, indexing, manuscript evaluation, marketing, online bookstore, packages of services, promotional materials, proofreading, royalty contract, substantive editing
> **Production time:** 12 months
> **Number of books published per year:** 80
> **Tip:** "'Now go write it in a book,' Isaiah 30:8."

THRILLING LIFE PUBLISHERS

PO Box 92522, Southlake, TX 76092 | 817-719-4333
victorya@victorya.com | *Thrillinglife.com*
Victorya Rogers, publisher

> **Types:** audiobooks, ebooks, hardcover, offset paperback, POD
> **Services:** à la carte options, author websites, copyediting, design, distribution, manuscript evaluation, marketing, packages of services, proofreading, substantive editing
> **Production time:** three to four months
> **Number of books published per year:** 6–12
> **Tip:** "We publish Christian nonfiction, primarily female authors."

TMP BOOKS

3 Central Plaza, Ste. 307, Rome, GA 30161 | 678-600-4617
info@tmpbooks.com | *www.TMPbooks.com*
Tracy Ruckman, publisher

> **Types:** audiobooks, ebooks, hardcover, picture books, POD
> **Services:** à la carte options, copyediting, design, distribution, manuscript evaluation, marketing, packages of services, promotional materials, proofreading, substantive editing
> **Production time:** two to three months
> **Number of books published per year:** six
> **Tip:** "We work one-on-one with authors, from the beginning stages of writing a book through the marketing phase, and customize our services to fit the author's needs. Affordable hybrid publishing. Authors receive 100% of royalties and pay cost for books."

TORCHBEARER PRESS

PO Box 306190, Nashville, TN 37230 | 877-474-2693
Torchbearer@rhboyd.com | rhboyd.com/pages/author-services
David Groves, director of publications

> **Types:** ebooks, hardcover, offset paperback
> **Services:** à la carte options, copyediting, design, proofreading
> **Tip:** "Torchbearer Press requires a minimum print run of 2,500 books."

TRILOGY CHRISTIAN PUBLISHING

PO Box A, Santa Ana, CA 92711 | 855-214-2665
www.trilogy.tv
Bryan Norris, director of publications

> **Types:** ebooks, hardcover, POD
> **Services:** copyediting, design, distribution, illustrations, marketing, online bookstore, proofreading
> **Tip:** "The Trinity Broadcasting Family of Networks is blazing a trail worldwide, with fresh, innovative programs that entertain, inspire, and change lives. In addition to the 8,000 cable and satellite affiliates that reach over 100 million homes across America and every inhabited continent, the TBN Family of Networks will continue to aggressively expand their reach as they deliver content across all social media and digital platforms. As part of your book release TBN will use its social media platforms with 1.8 million followers to promote it. From there, all of the social media strength of Trilogy Christian Publishing will be deployed."

THE WELL PUBLISHERS

PMB #533, 520 Butternut Dr., Ste. 8, Holland, MI 49424 | 616-212-0151
thewellpublishers@gmail.com | thewellpublishers.com
Kathy Bruins, owner

> **Types:** audiobooks, ebooks, gift books, hardcover, offset paperback, POD
> **Services:** à la carte options, copyediting, design, distribution, manuscript evaluation, marketing, packages of services, proofreading, substantive editing
> **Production time:** 3–12 months
> **Number of books published per year:** 10
> **Tip:** "Make your manuscript shine as much as possible (i.e., no spelling errors). Work as part of the team in getting your book published. Realize that this is a business."

WESTBOW PRESS

1663 Liberty Dr., Bloomington, IN 47403 | 844-714-3454

www.westbowpress.com

> **Types:** audiobooks, ebooks, gift books, hardcover, offset paperback, POD
>
> **Services:** book trailer, copyediting, design, distribution, illustrations, indexing, manuscript evaluation, marketing, packages of services, Spanish translation, substantive editing
>
> **Tip:** Independent publishing division of Thomas Nelson and Zondervan.

WILT AND WADE PUBLISHING

15418 Weir St. #105, Omaha, NE 68137 | 402-541-6997

tonya@wiltandwade.com | *wiltandwade.com*

Tonya Ludwig, founder

> **Types:** ebooks, hardcover, offset paperback, picture books, POD
>
> **Services:** author websites, copyediting, design, distribution, manuscript evaluation, marketing, online bookstore, packages of services, promotional materials, proofreading, royalty contract, substantive editing
>
> **Production time:** five months
>
> **Number of books published per year:** two
>
> **Tip:** "Submit a comprehensive proposal after you have completed 2–3 rounds of edits yourself. We appreciate seeing work that has been polished for best presentation."

WORD ALIVE PRESS

119 De Baets St., Winnipeg, MB R2J 3R9, Canada | 866-967-3782

jen@wordalivepress.ca | *www.wordalivepress.ca*

Jen Jandavs-Hedlin, publishing consultant

> **Types:** audiobooks, ebooks, gift books, hardcover, offset paperback, picture books, POD
>
> **Services:** à la carte options, copyediting, design, distribution, indexing, manuscript evaluation, marketing, online bookstore, packages of services, promotional materials, royalty contract
>
> **Production time:** three to six months
>
> **Number of books published per year:** 100
>
> **Tip:** "Start with a manuscript evaluation from a reputable editor or publisher. They will help you to identify and address any big-picture trouble spots prior to investing in copyediting or publishing."

XULON PRESS

555 Winderley Pl., Ste. 225, Maitland, FL 32751 | 407-339-4217

www.xulonpress.com

Donald Newman, executive director of publishing

Types: ebooks, hardcover, offset paperback, POD

Services: à la carte options, book trailer, copyediting, design, ghostwriting, illustrations, manuscript evaluation, marketing, online bookstore, packages of services, promotional materials, substantive editing

Production time: three to six months

Note: See "Editorial Services" and "Publicity and Marketing Services" for help with these needs.

4

DESIGN AND **PRODUCTION SERVICES**

1DOLLARSCAN
2470 Winchester Blvd., Ste. A, Campbell, CA 95008 | 669-212-0185
contact@1dollarscan.com | 1dollarscan.com

Contact: email
Services: document scanning, file conversion
Charges: custom, flat fee
Credentials/experience: "1DollarScan is the most affordable
scanning/digitizing service in the world. Through innovative
technology solutions and the best practices, we are able to create
the lowest priced and most affordable service with the best quality
in the business."

829 DESIGN | LINNÉ GARRETT
8749 Cortina Cir., Roseville, CA 95678-2940 | 408-410-8072
linne@829design.com | www.829design.com

Contact: email, phone, website form
Services: book-cover design, book-interior design, branding design,
ebook conversion, graphic design, illustrations, marketing design,
typesetting, website design
Charges: custom, flat fee, hourly rate
Credentials/experience: "For over two decades, our unwavering
commitment to delivering exceptional creative design services
has left a lasting impact on brands, ambitious startups, small
businesses, and private clients around the globe. While custom
book design remains one of our cherished specialties, our portfolio
encompasses a wide spectrum of offerings. From brand strategy
and identity design to publication design, user-centric digital
experiences with bespoke web development, and comprehensive
digital marketing services encompassing SEO and Google ads—we

deliver it all. Print design and brand collateral marketing are also part of our diverse expertise."

ABOVE THE SUN MEDIA | JESSE RIVAS

330 S. 3rd St., Cottage Grove, OR 97424 | 541-954-9479
team@abovethesun.org | *abovethesun.org*

Contact: email, website form

Services: audiobook, book-cover design, book-interior design, ebook conversion, printing, typesetting, website design

Charges: custom

Credentials/experience: "Jesse has over 20 years of experience as an author, mentor, editor, and publicist. He holds a bachelor's degree in education, graduated from the Rubart Writing Academy, and founded Above The Sun, where he and his team have guided hundreds of authors from inspiration to publication."

BACK·DOOR DESIGN

backdoordesign99@gmail.com | *backdoordesign99.wixsite.com/info*

Contact: email, website form

Services: book-cover design, book-interior design, ebook conversion, illustrations, typesetting

Charges: custom, flat fee

Credentials/experience: "At back•door DESIGN, our mission is to create high-quality book designs at DIY prices. We are all about book design, from front cover to back cover and everything in between. Adobe Certified Associate in Print & Digital Publication Using Adobe InDesign."

BBS PUBLISHING AND COMMUNICATIONS LLC | PAMELA GOSSIAUX

734-846-0112
pam@pamelagossiaux.com | *BestsellingBookShepherd.com*

Contact: email

Services: book-cover design, book-interior design, ebook conversion, newsletter design, printing, social-media posts, website design

Charges: custom, flat fee, hourly rate

Credentials/experience: "Let me turn your fiction or nonfiction manuscript into a bestseller! Experienced book shepherd can help you with design, publication, distribution, and more. I've coached and promoted authors to Amazon, *USA Today* and *Wall Street Journal* bestsellers. Degrees in Creative Writing &

English Language and Literature from University of Michigan. International bestselling author."

BELIEVERS BOOK SERVICES | DAVE SHEETS

2329 Farragut Ave., Colorado Springs, CO 80907 | 719-641-7862
dave@believersbookservices.com | *www.believersbookservices.com*

> **Contact:** website form
> **Services:** book-cover design, book-interior design, ebook conversion, illustrations, printing, typesetting
> **Charges:** custom
> **Credentials/experience:** "Our team has decades of experience in traditional publishing (Tyndale, Multnomah, Harvest House, NavPress), book wholesaling (STL Distribution), book distribution (Advocate Distribution Solutions), book printing (Bethany Press, Snowfall Press), book retailing (Glen Eyrie Bookstore), and independent publishing (Believers Press, BelieversBookServices). We know how to help our clients achieve their goals while maintaining control over their own book project. We have helped hundreds of authors successfully publish, both in the United States and around the world."

BLUE LEAF BOOK SCANNING | DON O'DANIEL

618 Crowsnest Dr., Ballwin, MN 63021 | 314-606-9322
blue.leaf.it@gmail.com | *www.blueleaf-book-scanning.com*

> **Contact:** email, website form
> **Services:** audiobook, document scanning, ebook conversion
> **Charges:** flat fee
> **Credentials/experience:** "We have been providing low-cost scanning services since 2008."

BREE ROSE CREATIVE LLC | BREE BYLE

Grand Rapids, MI
brc@breerosecreative.com | *www.BreeRoseCreative.com*

> **Contact:** email, website form
> **Services:** book photography for marketing, illustrations, typesetting, website design
> **Charges:** flat fee
> **Credentials/experience:** "I've worked with many publishers, agencies, and independent authors to provide design and photography services."

BRIAN WHITE DESIGN | BRIAN WHITE

Lawrence, KS | 785-841-5500
brianwhite.design

> **Contact:** phone, website form
> **Services:** app design, book-cover design, graphic design, illustrations, logo design, website design
> **Charges:** flat fee, hourly rate
> **Credentials/experience:** Twenty years in the design/web design/ branding industry.

BUTTERFIELD EDITORIAL SERVICES | DEBRA L. BUTTERFIELD

4810 Gene Field Rd. #2, Saint Joseph, MO 64506 | 816-752-2171
deb@debralbutterfield.com | themotivationaleditor.com

> **Contact:** email
> **Services:** book-cover design, book-interior design, ebook conversion, typesetting
> **Charges:** custom
> **Credentials/experience:** "I began my interior design work with my own books and moved into typesetting and design for CrossRiver Media Group. For over six years I have been helping my freelance clients with book-cover and interior design for print and ebooks."

CELEBRATION WEB DESIGN | JONATHAN SHANK

844 Runner Oak St., Celebration, FL 34747 | 877-313-7593
info@celebrationwebdesign.com | celebrationwebdesign.com

> **Contact:** email, phone, website form
> **Services:** marketing, SEO, website design
> **Charges:** flat fee, hourly rate
> **Credentials/experience:** "Celebration Web Design's team is enthusiastic with focused analysts, developers, and designers who have a passion for technology and online marketing solutions. Since 2002, our expert staff has been helping individuals and organizations enhance their online presence. Celebration Web Design develops handcrafted websites, branding packages, and marketing solutions. We consider it a privilege to help individuals and organizations with their website and online marketing needs."

COLLIN SMITH CREATIVE | COLLIN SMITH

607 County Hwy. 241, Benton, MO 63736 | 573-225-7992
collinsmithcreative@gmail.com | collinsmithcreative.com

Contact: email

Services: book-cover design, book-interior design, ebook conversion, graphic design, typesetting, website design

Charges: custom, flat fee, hourly rate

Credentials/experience: "Over the last five years, I've been helping indie authors and publishers with book-cover design, typesetting, and web design. I have experience submitting books for print at large presses and on-demand printers, such as IngramSpark and Amazon KDP. I can also help with promotional graphics for social media, Amazon A+ Ads, trade-show displays, and any other graphic design needs you may have!"

CREATIVE CORNERSTONES | CAYLAH COFFEEN and GALADRIEL COFFEEN

Huntsville, AL | 318-553-1625

creativecornerstones@gmail.com | *creativecornerstones.com/pre-release-materials*

Contact: email, website form

Services: audiobook, book trailer, book-cover design, book-interior design, ebook conversion, illustrations, typesetting, website design

Charges: custom

Credentials/experience: "Creative Cornerstones is a team of creatives who can make your book stand out from the crowd. We can create all your designs in one place: book exterior, interior, and visual marketing. Galadriel is an artist with over 10 years of experience. She can bring your vision to life, creating a sharp, hyperrealistic digital cover, character illustrations, maps, and even audiobooks. She specializes in fantasy and sci-fi art and can make the inside of a book pop as much as the outside. Caylah is a designer with experience creating WordPress websites, book trailers, and illustrations for social media and has worked as a content creator for Monster Ivy Publishing and Eschler Editing. We'll create a plan for each design step with our knowledge of the industry, so you can focus on what you love: writing."

DAVID & SALLIE | DAVID BORRINK

341 Glen Arbor Dr. NE, Rockford, MI 49341 | 616-326-5594

david@davidandsallie.com | *davidandsallie.com*

Contact: email, phone, website form

Services: book-cover design, book-interior design, illustrations, information graphics, typesetting

Charges: flat fee, hourly rate

Credentials/experience: "Many years' experience in book cover and interior book design, fiction and nonfiction genres in both print and ebook versions (PDF, EPUB, KPF). Very flexible and easy to work with."

DESERT RAIN EDITING | GLENIECE LYTLE

PO Box 8163, Hualapai, AZ 86412 | 928-715-7125
desert.rain.editing@gmail.com | *desertrainediting.com*

Contact: email, website form
Services: book-interior design, ebook conversion, typesetting
Charges: flat fee, page rate
Credentials/experience: "I began the typesetting journey several years ago when one of my editing clients was dissatisfied with her final printed book from a vanity publisher. I learned quickly and discovered how much I enjoy interior-book design! I create clean, elegant, and readable print-ready PDFs and compile EPUB ebook files using HTML and CSS styles. Typesetting takes patience and a flair for the standout, yet simple flourishes. At Desert Rain Editing, I take great joy in making my clients' books look as polished and professional as they read."

DESIGN CORPS | JOHN WOLLINKA

1370 Carlson Dr., Colorado Springs, CO 80910 | 719-260-0500
john@designcorps.us | *designcorps.us*

Contact: email
Services: book-cover design, book-interior design, ebook conversion, illustrations, typesetting
Charges: custom
Credentials/experience: "For over 25 years Design Corps has helped Christian publishers and self-publishing authors. Our experience includes fiction, nonfiction, children's books, curriculum, and Bibles. We have done work for the following publishers: Moody Publishers, Zondervan, Intervarsity Press, Wesleyan Publishing House, The American Bible Society, and Life Publishers International."

DIGGYPOD | KEVIN OSWORTH

301 Industrial Dr., Tecumseh, MI 49286 | 877-944-7844
www.diggypod.com

Contact: phone, website form
Services: book-cover design, printing
Charges: custom
Credentials/experience: "DiggyPOD has been printing books since 2001. All facets of the book printing take place in our facility."

EAH CREATIVE | EMILIE HANEY

PO Box 69, Taylorsville, IN 47280

eahendryx@gmail.com | *www.eahcreative.com*

Contact: website form
Services: book-cover design, book-interior design
Charges: custom, flat fee
Credentials/experience: "Emilie works with small and large traditional publishers, as well as independent authors to create vibrant and marketable covers and graphics. Over the last six years her covers have finaled for awards and allowed her opportunities to speak about cover design and other aspects of graphic design specifically for authors. She approaches each new project with the desire to make the best and most marketable cover that will be at home on the digital or physical shelf."

EDENBROOKE PRODUCTIONS | MARTY KEITH

615-415-1942

johnmartinkeith@hotmail.com | *www.edenbrookemusic.com/booktrailers*

Contact: email, phone, website form
Service: book trailer
Charges: flat fee
Credentials/experience: "Edenbrooke Productions believes your story deserves a unique soundtrack. We've produced music for everyone from CBS Television to Discovery Channel, and now we want to give your story the star treatment."

ERIN ULRICH CREATIVE | ERIN ULRICH

PO Box 80282, Simpsonville, SC 29680

hello@erinulrichcreative.com | *erinulrichcreative.com*

Contact: website form
Service: website design
Charges: flat fee
Credentials/experience: "After 15 years of designing and building WordPress sites, I've mapped out a strategic plan that allows us to work faster and smarter, completing website projects in just one day, because no one has time for long, drawn-out projects."

FINDLEY FAMILY VIDEO PUBLICATIONS | MARY C. FINDLEY

mjmcfindley@gmail.com | *findleyfamilyvideopublications.com/the-design-in-your-mind*

Contact: email
Services: book-cover design, book-interior design
Charges: flat fee
Credentials/experience: "Twenty plus years in publishing, including work for a university press and design and formatting for multiple indie authors. Many testimonials, affordable pricing, and multigenre examples are on the website."

FISTBUMP MEDIA LLC | DAN KING
115 E. 4th Ave., Ste. 212, Mount Dora, FL 32757 | 941-681-8015
sales@fistbumpmedia.com | fistbumpmedia.com

Contact: email
Services: SEO, website design
Charges: flat fee, hourly rate
Credentials/experience: "With our roots in building an online presence as a blogger-author and growing authentic social-media community, we are a digital marketing (and managed WordPress hosting) agency which knows how to grow a brand online from the ground up. We're WordPress specialists, and our goal is to help you manage the technical side of being online."

HANNAH LINDER DESIGNS | HANNAH LINDER
hannah@hannahlinderdesigns.com | www.hannahlinderdesigns.com

Contact: email, website form
Services: book-cover design, book-interior design
Charges: custom, flat fee
Credentials/experience: "Hannah Linder Designs specializes in professional book-cover design with affordable prices. Having designed for both traditional publishing houses and individual authors, including *New York Times*, *USA Today*, national, and international bestsellers, Hannah understands the importance of an attractive book cover and the trends of today's industry. Also, Hannah is a *magna cum laude* Graphic Design Associates Degree graduate and an award-winning book-cover designer."

HISWAY GRAPHIC DESIGN | KIMBERLY MORRISON
133 Hudspeth Rd., Statesville, NC 28677
kim@onlyhisway.com | onlyhisway.com

Contact: email, website form
Services: book trailer, book-cover design, book-interior design, ebook conversion, website design

Charges: custom, flat fee

Credentials/experience: "Kimberly is a graphic designer and self-published author who feels called to use her creative gifts to serve the Kingdom. With over seven books independently published, she understands both the beauty and the challenges of the self-publishing journey. In addition to her own writing, she has helped numerous authors successfully bring their books to life—offering thoughtful design, guidance, and encouragement every step of the way. She also partners with churches to create impactful graphic design and websites that support ministry and outreach, all with the heart to glorify God through her work."

INKSNATCHER | SALLY HANAN

429 S. Avenue C, Elgin, TX 78621 | 512-265-6403
inkmeister@inksnatcher.com | *inksnatcher.com*

Contact: email, phone, website form

Services: book-cover design, book-interior design, ebook conversion, typesetting, website design

Charges: flat fee

Credentials/experience: "Sally Hanan, an author herself, started Inksnatcher in 2008 with just editing services. Today, Inksnatcher provides self-publishing authors with every service they need to produce and publish with excellence. Inksnatcher is an approved service provider with the Alliance of Independent Authors, the Christian Editor Connection, and Reedsy."

JAMIE FOLEY

Giddings, TX
jamie@jamiefoley.com | *jamiefoley.com/typesetting*

Contact: email

Services: book-interior design, typesetting

Charges: flat fee, hourly rate

Credentials/experience: "Specializing in efficient digital typesetting and custom interior-book design, Jamie has been working in the Christian publishing industry since 2008. Starting at Thomas Nelson, she is currently the typesetter at Enclave Publishing, Sky Turtle Press, and The Christian Writers Institute, and has served many independent authors, including the estate for the *New York Times* bestselling Christy novels. She also has creative director experience, including press checks and printer relations, and a BA in arts and technology from the University of Texas at Dallas."

JDLAKE STUDIOS | JOHN "JD" LAKE

11077 W. Forest Home Ave. #213, Hales Corners, Wi 53130-2552 | 608-792-3419

john@jdlake.com | jdlake.com

> **Contact:** email
> **Service:** audiobook
> **Charges:** flat fee, hourly rate, royalty share
> **Credentials/experience:** "A theatre and English major in college, JD used his skills in the corporate and small-business world, primarily as a live-delivery trainer and consultant—first in the classroom, then added video/virtual training to his experience. He went on to include producing (writing, performing, editing) training videos for manufacturing, computer software, and employee process applications. JD has returned to the microphone to relaunch an original skillset."

JENNIFER EDWARDS COMMUNICATIONS | JENNIFER EDWARDS

2839 Sleeping Bear Rd., Montrose, CO 81401 | 916-768-4207

mail.jennifer.edwards@gmail.com | jedwardsediting.net

> **Contact:** email
> **Services:** author coaching for self-publishers, book-cover design, book-interior design, ebook conversion, production management for self-publishing
> **Charges:** flat fee
> **Credentials/experience:** "Jennifer Edwards is a professional book editor and self-publishing consultant of Christian nonfiction works. She helps self-publishing authors through the editing process and produces their works for publication on the KDP Amazon and IngramSpark platforms. Her services include coordinating the cover and interior designs, setting up self-publishing accounts, developing and managing metadata, and teaching the author to manage their titles. She has produced over 75 self-publishing titles, including hardcovers, paperbacks, ebooks, and audiobooks."

JENNIFER WESTBROOK

14030 Connecticut Ave. #6813, Silver Spring, MD 20916

support@jenwestwriting.com | www.jenwestwriting.com/web-design

> **Contact:** phone
> **Service:** website design
> **Charges:** flat fee

Credentials/experience: "I build Wix websites that pack a punch, complete with all the must-haves you need to keep thriving online. As a copywriter and web designer with over eight years of experience, I create the right mix of words, design, and behind-the-scenes systems to make everything work together seamlessly so you can get next-level results."

KELLIE BOOK DESIGN | KELLIE PARSONS

Unit 1, 23 Apara Way, Nollamara, WA 6061, Australia | 0412 591 687
kellie@kelliemaree.com | *kelliemaree.com*

Contact: email
Services: book-cover design, book-interior design, ebook conversion, typesetting, website design
Charges: flat fee
Credentials/experience: "Ten years' experience in graphic design, communications, and marketing. Book-design specialist for the last nine years. BA Creative Industries (Graphic Design, Interactive Media and Photography)."

LAUNCH MISSION CREATIVE | TRAVIS D. PETERSON

travis@launchmissions.com | *www.launchmissioncreative.com*

Contact: website form
Services: book-cover design, book-interior design
Charges: custom
Credentials/experience: "Not only am I an award-winning Christian children's author myself, but also an award-winning print designer with over a decade of experience both in-house for a couple of internationally recognized ministries and as a freelancer. I hold a degree in Computer Graphics Technology from Purdue University."

LEMUEL STUDIO | LEMUEL MASSUIA

Brazil
lemuel@lemuelmassuia.com | *www.lemuelmassuia.com*

Contact: email, website form
Services: book-cover design, book-interior design, illustrations
Charges: flat fee, hourly rate, page rate
Credentials/experience: "I'm an illustrator and graphic designer with a degree in visual arts, a bachelor's in advertising, and additional training through various fine arts courses. I have over 10 years of experience working in editorial design and illustration,

with a specialization in children's books. My academic background and hands-on expertise allow me to create visually engaging, concept-driven work that supports clear storytelling and strong communication."

LISAVDESIGNS LLC | LISA VON DE LINDE

Dayton, OH

hello@lisavdesigns.com | *www.lisavdesigns.com*

Contact: website form

Services: book-cover design, book-interior design, ebook conversion, graphic design, typesetting, website design

Charges: custom, flat fee, page rate

Credentials/experience: "My book-design career started at an agency with large Christian publishing houses as our main clients. I worked with them for six and a half years. Since then, I've partnered with self-publishing authors to bring their books to life with publishing-house-quality design services. In total I have over 20 years' experience designing books."

MARTIN PUBLISHING SERVICES | MELINDA MARTIN

Palestine, TX 903-948-4893

martinpublishingservices@gmail.com | *melindamartin.me*

Contact: phone

Services: book-cover design, book-interior design, typesetting

Charges: flat fee

Credentials/experience: "Over the last 10+ years, I've helped close to 1,000 authors with their publishing projects. Although my primary focus is on children's books these days, my business was founded on serving the adult nonfiction community. I still love to work with nonfiction authors."

MISSION AND MEDIA | MICHELLE RAYBURN

11510 County Highway M, New Auburn, WI 54757

info@missionandmedia.com | *missionandmedia.com*

Contact: email

Services: book-cover design, book-interior design, ebook conversion, typesetting

Charges: flat fee, free consultation, hourly rate

Credentials/experience: "Michelle works with indie and self-published authors to design a quality book cover and interior. She also coaches those who want to create their own imprint with full control of their own publishing process. Her area of specialty is with Amazon KDP. Michelle has more than 20 years of experience on the writing and editing side of publishing. Portfolio and additional information are available on the website."

MOUNTAIN CREEK BOOKS LLC | KARA STARCHER

PO Box 21, Chloe, WV 25235
kara@mountaincreekbooks.com | *mountaincreekbooks.com*

Contact: website form
Services: book-cover design, book-interior design, ebook conversion, typesetting
Charges: custom, flat fee
Credentials/experience: "BA in publishing; over 20 years of experience."

PAGE & PIXEL PUBLICATIONS | SUSAN MOORE

La Crosse, WI
pageandpixelpublications@gmail.com | *pageandpixelpublications.com*

Contact: email
Services: book trailer, book-cover design, book-interior design, ebook conversion, typesetting
Charges: hourly rate
Credentials/experience: "Are you preparing to self-publish? I can format your manuscript to give it that professional look within the parameters of your publishing house. The design would include the entire interior of your book. A digital, print-ready PDF of your book's completed interior layout is provided. I can convert your manuscript into the digital format that is readable on devices like Kindle, Nook, tablets, phones, computers, and notebooks, as well as generic brand e-readers. Working from your original document in Microsoft Word, InDesign, PDF, or other format, I will provide you with a digital file that you can upload to Amazon, Barnes and Noble, or other suppliers. Your finished product will feature a navigable table of contents and hyperlinked footnotes, as well as any graphic images that you choose to include."

PROFESSIONAL PUBLISHING SERVICES | CHRISTY CALLAHAN

PO Box 1164, Frankston, TX 75763 | 912-388-1898
professionalpublishingservices@gmail.com | *professionalpublishingservicesus.weebly.com*

Contact: email

Services: book-cover design, book-interior design, ebook conversion, typesetting

Charges: custom

Credentials/experience: "Christy graduated Phi Beta Kappa from Carnegie Mellon University, where she first learned how to use Adobe software. While she earned her MA in Intercultural Studies from Fuller Seminary, she edited sound files for distance-learning classes for the Media Center and designed ads as Women's Concerns Committee chairperson. Christy is an Adobe Certified Associate in Print & Digital Publication Using Adobe InDesign, leveraging her expertise as an editor and proofreader and extensive knowledge of *Chicago* style to create professional-looking book covers and interior layouts."

RICK STEELE EDITORIAL SERVICES | RICK STEELE

26 Dean Rd., Ringgold, GA 30736 | 706-937-8121
rsteelecam@gmail.com | *steeleeditorialservices.myportfolio.com*

Contact: website form

Services: typesetting

Charges: page rate

Credentials/experience: "With decades of experience using page-layout software, Rick Steele Editorial Services has the skills to take your edited manuscript to printed-page format with a professional, attractive page layout. If you wish to publish your manuscript with Amazon's KDP or similar platform, I can help prepare your manuscript file for print and ebook submission."

ROSEANNA WHITE DESIGNS | ROSEANNA WHITE

roseannamwhite@gmail.com | *www.RoseannaWhiteDesigns.com*

Contact: website form

Services: book-cover design, book-interior design, promotional graphics (digital and print), typesetting

Charges: flat fee

Credentials/experience: "Roseanna has been designing and typesetting books for more than ten years, combining her keen eye and artistic skills with her insider knowledge of the industry. As an author herself, she knows how important it is for the appearance of a book to match the words and strives to bring your story to life at a single glance. She has worked for publishing houses and independently for some of Christian fiction's top authors."

SCOTT LA COUNTE

Anaheim, CA | 714-404-7182

Roboscott@gmail.com | *scottdouglas.org/coaching*

Contact: website form

Services: book-cover design, book-interior design, self-publishing coach

Charges: flat fee

Credentials/experience: "I've worked in publishing for over 20 years (both in traditional publishing and self-publishing). Over those years, I have helped indie publishers sell over 2,000,000 books."

SFP DESIGNS

Oregon

author@suzannefyhrieparrott.com | *www.SuzanneFyhrieParrott.com*

Contact: website form

Services: book-cover design, book-interior design, ebook conversion, illustrations, promotional materials

Charges: custom

Credentials/experience: "Designer, illustrator, and publishing professional since 1981. I offer freelance services for self-publishing authors and small businesses."

STORMHILL MEDIA | JIM CAMOMILE

15226 County Rd. 434, Lindale, TX 75771 | 512-914-8458

jim@stormhillmedia.com | *www.stormhillmedia.com*

Contact: email, phone, website form

Services: ebook conversion, SEO, website design

Charges: hourly rate

Credentials/experience: "Award-winning author-website designers and developers of MyBookTable for WordPress. Stormhill Media has over 10 years of experience invested in designing and building attractive and highly effective author websites that sell books and get noticed. You need a website that looks great and competes in search engines. We specialize in both. Let's work together to make a website that achieves your goals."

STORYWRAP.CA | LYSA AND KAYLEY ROWAN

Saskatchewan, Canada

designer@storywrap.ca | *storywrap.ca*

Contact: email, website form

Services: book-cover design, book-interior design, marketing design

Charges: custom, flat fee, hourly rate

Credentials/experience: "Storywrap.ca is owned and operated by two graphic designers from Canada. We've been in business for three years, are self taught, and strive to provide great service affordably. If we don't have the expertise to do a great job, we'll let the customer know before accepting the project. Always learning new skills and ready to put them to work for our customers. We love graphic design!"

TINNSY WINNSY EDITORIAL AND DESIGN STUDIO | BRENDA WILBEE

7595 Birch Bay Dr. #2, Blaine, WA 98230 | 360-389-6895
Brenda@BrendaWilbee.com | www.BrendaWilbee.com

Contact: email

Services: book-cover design, promotional materials, typesetting

Charges: custom, flat fee, hourly rate

Credentials/experience: "I hold an MA in professional writing and a degree in graphic design. I taught college composition for seven years, commercial writing for twenty, and in the past have worked as a designer for an international company. Some of my clients include Habitat for Humanity, PageMill Press, DDA Publishing, Forever Books, Lauren Myers, Carol Lawrence, Lisa Weitkamp, Deanna Nowadnick, Scott Wyatt, and so many other writers just like you."

TLC BOOK DESIGN | TAMARA DEVER

Austin, TX
tamara@tlcbookdesign.com | www.TLCBookDesign.com

Contact: website form

Services: book-cover design, book-interior design, ebook conversion, printing, typesetting

Charges: custom

Credentials/experience: "We are a small, Christ-loving group of professionals honored to share this ministry with authors worldwide. Whether you need complete production or just design, we're here to build your book—editorial, design, printing—and coach you through the process. Serving the publishing industry for over 30 years, our books have garnered more than 375 awards. We'd love to add you to the TLC family of authors and publishers!"

TWO WORDS PUBLISHING | CLATON BUTCHER

3213 W. Main St. #166, Rapid City, SD 57702 | 605-939-5913
cbutcher@twowordspublishing.com | www.twowordspublishing.com

Contact: email
Service: audiobook
Charges: hourly rate
Credentials/experience: "Two Words Publishing has published and/ or produced audiobooks from most major Christian publishers, as well as authors and their agents. With an Audie (considered the Oscars of audiobooks), Earphones Award, Voice Arts Awards, and more, you can expect top-notch audiobook quality."

TYPEWRITER CREATIVE CO. | TARYN NERGAARD
support@typewritercreative.co | www.typewritercreative.co

Contact: website form
Services: book-cover design, book-interior design, ebook conversion, illustrations, typesetting
Charges: flat fee
Credentials/experience: "Backed by 100+ books for over 60 authors, Typewriter Creative Co. expertly handles cover design, interior formatting, and publishing setup, so authors can publish professionally while keeping full rights and royalties."

VIVID GRAPHICS | LARRY VANHOOSE
2273 Snow Hill Rd., Galax, VA 24333 | 276-235-7044
me@larryvh.com | www.vivid-graphics.com

Contact: email
Services: book-cover design, book-interior design, ebook conversion
Charges: flat fee, hourly rate
Credentials/experience: "Vivid Graphics is a full-service graphic design, web design, commercial photography, and video design agency. Our client list includes John Deere-Hitachi, Volvo HT, Tico, Amano, UPS, Nissan, and Yadtel Telecom. Larry Van Hoose is the Creative Director for Vivid Graphics and has over 25 years of experience in design, writing, photography, and marketing."

YO PRODUCTIONS LLC | YOLONDA SANDERS
7185 E. Main St., Unit 1543, Reynoldsburg, OH 43068 | 614-452-4920
info_4u@yoproductions.net | www.yoproductions.net

Contact: email, phone, website form
Services: book-cover design, book-interior design, typesetting
Charges: custom
Credentials/experience: "We work side by side with our clients to understand their needs and create high-quality designs using the

latest software. Don't have a clear idea yet? Don't worry—we're happy to help you brainstorm! We treat every project like it's our own, giving it the time and attention it deserves to turn it into a masterpiece."

ZAQ DESIGNS + D.E. WEST ART & PHOTOGRAPHY | DOUG WEST

13518 Heritage Dr., Bonner Springs, KS 66012 | 913-827-2225
doug@zaqdesigns.com | *www.zaqdesigns.com*

Contact: website form

Services: audiobook, book trailer, book-cover design, book-interior design, ebook conversion, illustrations, printing, typesetting, website design

Charges: custom, flat fee, page rate

Credentials/experience: "We specialize in offering book design and production services. With more than 29 years of experience in graphic design, printing, and illustration, we ventured into the book design and publishing business in 2010. ZAQ Designs is dedicated to providing high quality, stunning cover designs and production services. Don't hesitate to contact us and see what we can do for you!"

Note: See "Editorial Services" and "Publicity and Marketing Services" for help with these needs.

5

DISTRIBUTION SERVICES

AMAZON SELLER CENTRAL
sell.amazon.com

Amazon has two selling plans: individual for 99¢ per book and professional for $39.99 per month. Both plans have other selling fees as well. You can manage inventory, update pricing, communicate with buyers, contact support, and add new products all from the Seller Central website.

BCH FULFILLMENT & DISTRIBUTION
33 Oakland Ave., Harrison, NY 10528 | 914-835-0015

bookch@aol.com | www.bookch.com/home.taf

Provides exclusive fulfillment and distribution services, including relationships with wholesalers and bookstores, warehousing your books, taking orders from wholesalers and bookstores, fulfilling those orders, billing and collecting monies, processing returns, and getting your books into Ingram if you qualify. Fees vary, depending on the services.

MIDPOINT TRADE BOOKS
814 N. Franklin St., Ste. 100, Chicago, IL 60610 | 312-337-0747

frontdesk@ipgbook.com | www.midpointtrade.com/christian_marketplace

A full-service book distribution division of Independent Publishers Group. Provides warehousing, fulfillment, and catalog inclusion under Covenant Media Resources, an extension of sales and distribution services specifically tailored to meet the needs of the Christian marketplace. In addition to reaching the traditional CBA market, it has access to a wide range of general bookstores and wholesalers that successfully sell Christian and other likeminded titles.

PATHWAY BOOK SERVICE
34 Production Ave., Keene, NH 03431 | 800-345-6665

pbs@pathwaybook.com | www.pathwaybook.com

Provides warehousing, order fulfillment, and trade distribution. It is a longtime distributor to Ingram and Baker & Taylor, the vendors of choice for most bookstores. Pathway uploads new-title spreadsheets to Ingram and Baker & Taylor, as well as to *Amazon.com*, Barnes & Noble, and Books-A-Million on a weekly basis. Distribution outside of North America is available through Gazelle Book Services in the United Kingdom. Also provides the option of having Pathway add titles to its Amazon Advantage account, which is at a lower discount and often a lower shipping cost per book than individual accounts.

PUBLISHERS STORING AND SHIPPING
660 S. Mansfield, Ypsilanti, MI 48197 | 734-487-9720
pssc.com

Provides warehousing, call center, order fulfillment, and returns for single-title self-publishers to large publishing houses. Has a second facility at 46 Development Rd., Fitchburg, MA 01420; 978-345-2121.

PART 3

PERIODICAL PUBLISHERS

6

TOPICS AND TYPES

This chapter is not an exhaustive list of types of manuscripts and topics periodical editors are looking for, but it is a starting place for some of the more popular ones. For instance, almost all periodicals take manuscripts in categories like Christian living, so they are not listed here. Plus writers guidelines tend to outline general areas, not every specific type and topic an editor will buy.

COLUMNS

Almost an Author
Blue Ridge Christian News
Christian Courier
Christian Herald
Christian Leader
Forward
Fusion Next
Holiness Today
HomeLife
InSite
Light
The Mother's Heart
Power for Living
Teachers of Vision
Velocity
Words for the Way

DEVOTIONS

Blue Ridge Christian News
Brio

DevoKids
Faith on Every Corner
Focus on the Family Clubhouse
Forward
Mature Living
ParentLife
Power for Living
StarLight Magazine
Teachers of Vision

ESSAYS

America
The Canadian Lutheran
The Christian Century
Commonweal
Faith Today
Faithfully Magazine
The Lutheran Witness
Poets & Writers Magazine
U.S. Catholic
Writer's Digest

EVANGELISM

Baptist Standard
Blue Ridge Christian News
Christian Herald
Christian Leader
Evangelical Missions Quarterly
Fusion Family
Mature Living
Outreach
The War Cry

FAMILY

Angels on Earth
The Baptist Bulletin
Baptist Standard
Columbia
Creative Inspirations
Faith & Friends
Focus on the Family
Gems of Truth
Guideposts
HomeLife
Influence
Inspire a Fire
Joyful Living Magazine
Light
Mature Living
Ministry
The Mother's Heart
ParentLife
St. Anthony Messenger

FICTION

See Short Story.

FILLERS

Angels on Earth
Bible Advocate

Blue Ridge Christian News
Focus on the Family Clubhouse
Focus on the Family Clubhouse Jr.
Ignited by the Word
LIVE
The Mother's Heart
StarLight Magazine
Words for the Way

HOW-TO

Almost an Author
Baptist Standard
Blue Ridge Christian News
Cadet Quest
Canada Lutheran
Celebrate Life Magazine
Christian Herald
Christian Standard
DevoKids
Evangelical Missions Quarterly
Faith Today
Focus on the Family
Focus on the Family Clubhouse
Forward
HomeLife
Influence
InSite
The Journal of Adventist Education
Joyful Living Magazine
Just Between Us
Leading Hearts
Light
LIVE
The Lutheran Witness
Mature Living
Ministry
The Mother's Heart
Mutuality
Outreach

ParentLife
Poets & Writers Magazine
Sharing: A Journal of Christian
   Healing
Teachers of Vision
Words for the Way
Writer's Digest
WritersWeekly.com
Writing Corner

INTERVIEWS

The Arlington Catholic Herald
The Baptist Bulletin
Baptist Standard
The Brink
Brio
byFaith
Cadet Quest
Canada Lutheran
Celebrate Life Magazine
Charisma
The Christian Century
Christian Herald
Christianity Today
Columbia
DevoKids
DTS Magazine
Evangelical Missions Quarterly
Faith & Friends
Faith Today
Faithfully Magazine
Focus on the Family
Focus on the Family Clubhouse
Forward
Friends Journal
Fusion Family
Guide
Influence
InSite

Joyful Living Magazine
Leading Hearts
The Lutheran Witness
The Marketplace
The Messianic Times
Nature Friend
Outreach
Peer
Poets & Writers Magazine
Power for Living
Relevant
Sports Spectrum
St. Anthony Messenger
testimony/Enrich
Today's Christian Living
U.S. Catholic
The War Cry
Writer's Digest

ISSUES

Anglican Journal
Celebrate Life Magazine
The Christian Century
Christianity Today
Columbia
Faith Today
Ministry
Now What?
St. Anthony Messenger
The War Cry

LEADERSHIP/MINISTRY

The Baptist Bulletin
Baptist Standard
Christian Leader
Evangelical Missions Quarterly
Holiness Today
Influence

InSite
Ministry
Outreach
testimony/Enrich

MARRIAGE

Angels on Earth
The Baptist Bulletin
Boundless
Faith & Friends
Focus on the Family
Fusion Next
Gems of Truth
Guideposts
HomeLife
Joyful Living Magazine
Mature Living
St. Anthony Messenger

NATURE

Angels on Earth
Cadet Quest
Creation Illustrated
Creative Inspirations
DevoKids
Focus on the Family Clubhouse Jr.
Guide
Nature Friend
Our Little Friend
Primary Treasure
StarLight Magazine

NEWSPAPERS

Anglican Journal
The Arlington Catholic Herald
Blue Ridge Christian News
Christian Courier

Christian Herald
Good News
The Messianic Times

OPINION

Canadian Mennonite
The Christian Century
Christian Courier
Christianity Today
Commonweal
Faithfully Magazine
The Messianic Times
Relevant
U.S. Catholic

PARENTING

The Baptist Bulletin
Columbia
Focus on the Family
Fusion Family
Fusion Next
HomeLife
Light
Mature Living
The Mother's Heart
ParentLife

PERSONAL EXPERIENCE

Almost an Author
Angels on Earth
Anglican Journal
The Baptist Bulletin
Bible Advocate
Blue Ridge Christian News
The Breakthrough Intercessor
The Brink
Café

Canada Lutheran
Canadian Mennonite
Celebrate Life Magazine
Christian Leader
Creation Illustrated
DTS Magazine
Faith & Friends
Faith on Every Corner
Forward
Friends Journal
Fusion Family
Gather
Gems of Truth
Guide
Guideposts
Highway News
Holiness Today
Ignited by the Word
Inspire a Fire
The Journal of Adventist Education
Joyful Living Magazine
Just Between Us
Leading Hearts
LEAVES
LIVE
The Lutheran Witness
Mature Living
The Mother's Heart
Mutuality
Now What?
Power for Living
Standard
Teachers of Vision
testimony/Enrich
Today's Christian Living
The War Cry
Words for the Way

POETRY

America
Bible Advocate
The Breakthrough Intercessor
The Christian Century
Christian Courier
Commonweal
Creative Inspirations
DevoKids
Faith on Every Corner
Focus on the Family Clubhouse Jr.
Forward
Friends Journal
Fusion Next
Gems of Truth
Ignited by the Word
Ink & Quill Quarterly
Inspire a Fire
LEAVES
LIVE
The Lutheran Witness
Power for Living
Sharing: A Journal of Christian
    Healing
Sojourners
StarLight Magazine
Teachers of Vision
Time Of Singing: A Journal of
    Christian Poetry
U.S. Catholic
Velocity
Words for the Way

PROFILES
See Interviews.

REVIEWS

Anglican Journal
byFaith
Canadian Mennonite
Caring Magazine
Celebrate Life Magazine
Charisma
The Christian Century
Christian Courier
Christian Herald
Christianity Today
Evangelical Missions Quarterly
Faith & Friends
Faith Today
HeartBeat
Ignited by the Word
The Journal of Adventist Education
Leading Hearts
LEAVES
Light
The Messianic Times
Ministry
The Mother's Heart
Mutuality
Sojourners
Time Of Singing: A Journal of
    Christian Poetry
Words for the Way

SHORT STORIES

Beginner's Friend
Blue Ridge Christian News
Brio
Cadet Quest
Creation Illustrated
DevoKids
Explorers
Faith on Every Corner

Focus on the Family Clubhouse
Focus on the Family Clubhouse Jr.
Forward
Fusion Next
Gems of Truth
Ignited by the Word
LIVE
Mature Living
Nature Friend
Sharing: A Journal of Christian
    Healing
St. Anthony Messenger
StarLight Magazine
Teachers of Vision
Velocity
Youth Compass

SUNDAY SCHOOL
TAKEHOME PAPERS

Beginner's Friend
Explorers
Gems of Truth
Guide
LIVE
Our Little Friend
Power for Living
Primary Treasure
Standard
Youth Compass

TEACHING

The Baptist Bulletin
Bible Advocate
The Breakthrough Intercessor
byFaith
The Canadian Lutheran
Celebrate Life Magazine
DTS Magazine

Focus on the Family
Friends Journal
Influence
The Lutheran Witness
Mature Living
The Messianic Times
Ministry
ParentLife
Relevant
St. Anthony Messenger

TESTIMONIES

Bible Advocate
Christian Leader
Faith & Friends
Friends Journal
Just Between Us
LEAVES
Peer
Today's Christian Living

7

ADULT MARKETS

AMERICA

106 W. 56th St., New York, NY 10019-3803 | 212-581-4640
www.americamagazine.org
Sam Sawyer, S.J., editor in chief
   Denomination: Catholic
   Parent company: America Media/Jesuit Conference of the United
      States and Canada
   Type: monthly digital and print magazine; circulation: 46,000
   Audience: primarily Catholic, two-thirds laypeople, college educated
   Purpose: to provide a smart Catholic take on faith and culture
   Submissions: Only accepts complete manuscript or query letter through
      the website. Unsolicited freelance: 100%. Responds in two weeks.
   Types of manuscripts: articles, essays, poetry
   Length: articles and essays, 800–2,000 words; poetry, 40 lines maximum
   Topics: Christian living/spirituality, culture, trends
   Rights: electronic, first
   Payment: competitive rates, on acceptance
   Guidelines: *americamedia.submittable.com/submit*
   Sample: *www.americamagazine.org/magazine*
   Tip: "We are known across the Catholic world for our unique brand
      of excellent, relevant, and accessible coverage. From theology and
      spirituality to politics, international relations, arts and letters, and the
      economy and social justice, our coverage spans the globe."

ANGELS ON EARTH

100 Reserve Rd., Ste. E200, Danbury, CT 06810 | 800-431-2344
submissions@angelsonearth.org | *guideposts.org/shop/product/*
   angels-on-earth-magazine
Colleen Hughes, editor-in-chief
   Parent company: Guideposts

Type: bimonthly digital and print magazine; circulation: 89,000

Audience: general

Purpose: to tell true stories of heavenly angels and earthly ones who find themselves on a mission of comfort, kindness, or reassurance

Submissions: Email complete manuscript with cover letter. Unsolicited freelance: 90%. Responds in two months or not interested.

Types of manuscripts: fillers, personal experience, recipes

Length: articles, 1,200–1,500 words; shorter features, 300–600 words; departments, 175–400 words

Topics: Christmas, Easter, family, friendship, loneliness, marriage, nature, pets, prayer, travel, worry

Rights: all

Payment: $25–400, on publication

Kill fee: sometimes

Manuscripts accepted per year: 40–60

Seasonal submissions: six months in advance

Guidelines: *www.guideposts.org/writers-guidelines*

Sample: *order.emags.com/angels_on_earth*

Tip: "*Angels on Earth* magazine is filled with true, first-person stories of heavenly angels and earthly ones who find themselves on a mission of comfort, kindness, or reassurance. Contributors have received angelic messages in dreams and daydreams, during mysterious encounters or random run-ins, from a strain of music heard by chance or a gust of wind on a still day. Angels take surprising forms as they deliver God's messages. We've seen inspiration come from stray animals, unexpected blooms, cloud formations, hidden treasures, and shells washed ashore. We depend on unique situations to add variety to our pages."

ANGLICAN JOURNAL

80 Hayden St., Toronto, ON M4Y 3G2, Canada | 416-924-9199
editor@national.anglican.ca | *www.anglicanjournal.com*
Tali Folkins, editor

Denomination: Anglican

Parent company: Anglican Church of Canada

Type: 10 times a year; digital and print newspaper; circulation: 78,000; accepts ads

Audience: denomination

Purpose: to share compelling news and features about the Anglican Church of Canada and the Anglican communion and religion in general

Submissions: Query first by email or mail. Responds in two weeks.

Types of manuscripts: news, personal experience, reviews
Length: 500–1,000 words
Topics: Christian living/spirituality, denomination, events, issues
Rights: first
Payment: $75–100, on acceptance
Seasonal submissions: two months in advance
Preferred Bible version: NRSV
Guidelines: *anglicanjournal.com/about/posting-policy*
Sample: on the website
Tip: "Stories should be of interest to a national audience. They are usually about a national event or a local issue that reflects the larger picture."

THE ARLINGTON CATHOLIC HERALD

200 N. Glebe Rd., Ste. 600, Arlington, VA 22203 | 703-841-2590
editorial@catholicherald.com | *www.catholicherald.com*
Ann M. Augherton, managing editor
Kevin Schweers, executive editor
Denomination: Catholic
Parent company: Arlington, Virginia, Diocese
Type: weekly digital and print newspaper; circulation: 100,000; accepts ads
Audience: denomination
Purpose: to support the church's mission to evangelize by providing news from a Catholic perspective
Submissions: Query first by email.
Types of manuscripts: feature articles, news, profiles
Sample: on the website

THE BAPTIST BULLETIN

244 S. Randall Rd. #1188, Elgin, IL 60123 | 888-588-1600
submissions@BaptistBulletin.org | *baptistbulletin.org*
Matt Olmstead, managing editor
Denomination: General Association of Regular Baptist Churches
Parent company: Regular Baptist Ministries
Type: quarterly digital and print magazine; circulation: 5,300
Audience: denomination
Purpose: to provide a "kitchen table" where church members gather to discuss important topics
Submissions: Only accepts complete manuscript through the website.
Types of manuscripts: personal experience, profiles, teaching

Length: 800–2,000 words

Topics: Christian living, denomination, discipleship, family, marriage, ministry, parenting

Rights: all

Preferred Bible version: ESV

Guidelines: *baptistbulletin.org/write-for-us*

Tip: "The magazine is your gateway to articles addressing current issues from a Baptist perspective, inspiring stories about people who serve in unique ways, and exciting coverage of what's happening in Regular Baptist Ministries."

BAPTIST STANDARD

PO Box 941309, Plano, TX 75094 | 214-630-4571
kencamp@baptiststandard.com | *www.baptiststandard.com*
Ken Camp, managing editor, news, features, book reviews
Eric Black, executive director and editor, opinion articles,
  eric.black@baptiststandard.com

Denomination: Baptist

Parent company: Baptist Standard Publishing

Type: quarterly website

Audience: denomination

Purpose: to connect God's story and God's people through information, inspiration, and challenge

Submissions: Email complete manuscript as attachment.

Types of manuscripts: how-to, profiles

Length: articles, 750–1,000 words; book reviews, 250–500 words

Topics: evangelism, family, leadership, ministry, missions, Texas Baptist history

Rights: all

Guidelines: *www.baptiststandard.com/submissions*

Tip: "When we consider something for publication, we ask: Does a news story or opinion piece inform, inspire or challenge people to live like Jesus? If so, it passes the most general test for consideration. Does a news story involve Baptists, in general? If so, we consider it. Does a story involve or have importance to Baptists in Texas? If so, we consider it. Does it involve the Baptist General Convention of Texas and Texas Baptists? An almost automatic yes."

BIBLE ADVOCATE

PO Box 33677, Denver, CO 80233
bibleadvocate@cog7.org | *baonline.org*

Sherri Langton, associate editor

Denomination: Church of God (Seventh Day)

Parent company: General Conference of the Church of God (Seventh Day)

Type: bimonthly digital and print magazine; circulation: 10,500

Audience: denomination, general

Purpose: to advocate the Bible and represent the Church of God (Seventh Day)

Submissions: Email complete manuscript. Unsolicited freelance: 50–75%. Responds in 4–10 weeks.

Types of manuscripts: fillers, personal experience, poetry, teaching, testimonies

Length: 600–1,300 words

Topics: Christian living/spirituality, theme-related

Rights: electronic, first, onetime, reprint (with info on where/when previously published)

Payment: articles, $25–65; poems and fillers, $20; on publication

Manuscripts accepted per year: 20–25

Preferred Bible version: NKJV

Theme lists: available on website

Guidelines: *baonline.org/write-for-us-2*

Sample: 9"x12" envelope with three stamps

Tip: "Please read past issues of the magazine before you submit and become familiar with our style. No snail mail submissions or PDFs. No Christmas or Easter manuscripts. We do not pay writers who live outside the US or Canada."

BLUE RIDGE CHRISTIAN NEWS

152 Summit Ave., Spruce Pine, NC 28777 | 828-765-6800
cathyp@brcnews.com | *blueridgechristiannews.com*
Cathy Pritchard, managing editor

Parent company: The Ninevah Productions, Inc.

Type: monthly digital and print newspaper; circulation: 12,000; accepts ads

Audience: people seeking to know more about God

Purpose: to proclaim biblical truth, strengthen believers, and share the love of Christ with the world

Submissions: Only accepts email. Unsolicited freelance: 10%. Responds in one week.

Types of manuscripts: columns, devotions, fillers, how-to, news, personal experience, short stories

Length: 1,000 words

Topics: Christian living/spirituality, evangelism

Rights: all, electronic, first, reprint (with info on where/when previously published)

Payment: none

Manuscripts accepted per year: 100

Seasonal submissions: one month in advance

Preferred Bible versions: KJV, NKJV, NASB

Guidelines: not available

Sample: *blueridgechristiannews.com/past-issues*

Tip: "We welcome new voices who want to share biblical truth and personal stories that uplift and inspire."

BOUNDLESS

See entry in "Teen/Young Adult Markets."

THE BREAKTHROUGH INTERCESSOR

PO Box 121, Lincoln, VA 20160-0121 | 540-338-4131
breakthrough@intercessors.org | *www.intercessors.org/our-publications*
Sarah Merly, editor

Parent company: Breakthrough

Type: quarterly digital and print magazine; circulation: 4,000

Audience: adults interested in growing their prayer lives

Purpose: to encourage people to pray and equip them to do so more effectively

Submissions: Email or mail complete manuscript.

Types of manuscripts: personal experience, poetry, teaching

Length: 600–1,000 words

Topic: prayer

Rights: electronic, first, onetime

Payment: none

Sample: on the website

byFAITH

1700 N. Brown Rd., Ste. 105, Lawrenceville, GA 30043 | 678-825-1005
info@byfaithonline.com | *byfaithonline.com*
Richard Doster, editor

Denomination: Presbyterian

Parent company: Presbyterian Church in America

Type: website; accepts ads

Audience: denomination

Purpose: to inform, encourage, and edify PCA churches and members as they seek to be faithful to the Scriptures, true to the Reformed faith, and obedient to the Great Commission

Submissions: Email complete manuscript.

Types of manuscripts: news, profiles, reviews, teaching

Length: 500–3,000 words

Topics: Christian living/spirituality, culture, denomination, theology

Guidelines: *byfaithonline.com/about*

Sample: on the website

Tip: "Theologically, the writers are Reformed and believe the faith is practical and applicable to every part of life. Most of our writers (though not all) come from the PCA."

CAFÉ

See entry in "Teen/Young Adult Markets."

CANADA LUTHERAN

400-185 Carlton St., Winnipeg, MB R3C 3J1, Canada | 888-786-6707
editor@elcic.ca | canadalutheran.ca
Sarah Malina, editor
Rachel Genge, British Columbia Synod, csynodeditor@gmail.com
Terrie Coombs, Synod of Alberta and the Territories, terrie4645@gmail.com
Anno Bell, Saskatchewan Synod, clsaskeditor@gmail.com
Michelle Collins, Manitoba/Northwestern Ontario Synod, mcollins@elcic.ca
Liz Zehr, Eastern Synod, ezehr@elcic.ca

Denomination: Evangelical Lutheran Church in Canada

Parent company: Evangelical Lutheran Church in Canada

Type: monthly print magazine; circulation: 6,000+

Audience: denomination

Purpose: to engage the Evangelical Lutheran Church in Canada in a dynamic dialogue in which information, inspiration, and ideas are shared in a thoughtful and stimulating way

Submissions: Only accepts email.

Types of manuscripts: documentary, how-to, personal experience, profiles

Length: 700–1,200 words

Topics: Christian living/spirituality, denomination, seasonal

Rights: onetime

Sample: *canadalutheran.ca/look-inside*

Tip: "As much as is possible, the content of the magazine is chosen from the work of Canadian writers. The content strives to reflect the Evangelical Lutheran Church in Canada in the context of our Canadian society."

THE CANADIAN LUTHERAN

3074 Portage Ave., Winnipeg, MB R3K 0Y2, Canada | 800-588-4226
editor@lutheranchurch.ca | www.canadianlutheran.ca
Matthew Block, editor
Michelle Heumann, regional news
> **Denomination:** Lutheran
> **Parent company:** Lutheran Church–Canada
> **Type:** bimonthly digital and print magazine; circulation: 12,000, hits: 10,000
> **Audience:** denomination
> **Purpose:** to inspire, motivate, and inform
> **Submissions:** Only accepts complete manuscript by email.
> **Types of manuscripts:** essays, news, teaching
> **Topics:** culture, denomination, theology
> **Rights:** first
> **Payment:** none
> **Preferred Bible version:** ESV
> **Guidelines:** *www.canadianlutheran.ca/editors-and-submissions*
> **Sample:** *issuu.com/thecanadianlutheran*
> **Tip:** "All feature articles with doctrinal content must go through doctrinal review to ensure fidelity to the Scriptures. As a result, authors may occasionally be asked to rewrite some sections of their article before publication."

CANADIAN MENNONITE

490 Dutton Dr., Unit C5, Waterloo, ON N2L 6H7, Canada | 519-884-3810
submit@canadianmennonite.org | canadianmennonite.org
Will Braun, editor
Susan Fish, associate editor
> **Denomination:** Mennonite
> **Parent company:** Canadian Mennonite Publishing Service
> **Type:** monthly digital and print magazine; circulation: 9,000; accepts ads
> **Audience:** denomination
> **Purpose:** to educate, inform, inspire, and foster dialogue on issues facing Mennonites in Canada
> **Submissions:** Query first by email as attachment or in body of message. Gives assignments to known writers. Accepts simultaneous submissions. Unsolicited freelance: 10%. Responds in three weeks. Accepts submissions from children and teens.

Types of manuscripts: opinion, personal experience, reviews, sermons
Length: 750 words
Topics: theme-related
Rights: first
Payment: 12¢/word, on publication
Manuscripts accepted per year: few; primarily publishes the writing of correspondents and related organizations
Seasonal submissions: three months in advance
Preferred Bible version: none
Theme lists: available on website
Guidelines: *canadianmennonite.org/submissions*
Sample: on the website
Tip: "Our content is focused on the Mennonite experience in Canada. We do not usually take submissions from USA. If the writer is in Canada and has a suggestion for a topic of known interest to Mennonites, we'd like to hear about it."

CARING MAGAZINE

30840 Hawthorne Blvd., Rancho Palos Verde, CA 90275 | 562-491-8343
caring@usw.salvationarmy.org | *caringmagazine.org*
Karen Gleason, senior editor
Hillary Jackson, managing editor, hillary.jackson@usw.salvationarmy.org
Denomination: The Salvation Army
Parent company: The Salvation Army USA Western Territory
Type: monthly digital and print magazine; circulation: 18,000
Audience: denomination in the territory
Purpose: to help people who care to make an impact for good
Submissions: Email query letter first.
Types of manuscripts: articles, reviews
Topics: denomination
Sample: *issuu.com/caringmagazine*
Tip: "Shares information from across The Salvation Army world, reports that analyze effective programs to identify the unique features and trends for what works, tips to help local congregations better engage in the issues of today, and influential voices on relevant (and sometimes controversial) matters."

CELEBRATE LIFE MAGAZINE

PO Box 6170, Falmouth, VA 22403 | 540-659-4171
clmag@all.org | *www.clmagazine.org*
Susan Ciancio, editor
Denomination: Catholic

Parent company: American Life League
Type: quarterly digital and print magazine; circulation: 7,500; accepts ads
Audience: pro-life
Purpose: to inspire, encourage, and educate pro-life activists
Submissions: Only accepts complete manuscript as email attachment. Unsolicited freelance: 25%. Responds in one to two months.
Types of manuscripts: how-to, interviews, personal experience, reviews, teaching
Length: 1,500 words maximum, including sidebars
Topics: ethics, issues; see list of possible topics in the guidelines
Rights: first
Payment: 10–25¢/word, on publication
Kill fee: sometimes
Manuscripts accepted per year: six
Seasonal submissions: six months in advance
Preferred Bible version: Jerusalem Bible
Guidelines: *www.clmagazine.org/submission-guidelines*
Sample: *shop.all.org/collections/celebrate-life-magazine/download*
Tip: "Current-events articles, holiday articles, and articles with appropriate photos or artwork get top priority in our processing procedure."

CHARISMA

PO Box 954027, Lake Mary, FL 32795 | 407-333-0600
robert.caggiano@charismamedia.com | *www.charismamag.com*
Robert Caggiano, content manager

Denomination: Charismatic/Pentecostal
Parent company: Charisma Media
Type: monthly digital and print magazine; circulation: 207,000; accepts ads
Audience: passionate, Spirit-filled Christians
Purpose: to empower believers for life in the Spirit
Submissions: Only accepts emailed query letter. Unsolicited freelance: 20%. Responds in two to three months.
Types of manuscripts: feature articles, interviews, profiles, reviews
Length: 700–2,600 words
Topics: Christian living/spirituality, Christmas, Easter, prayer, prophecy, seasonal, spiritual warfare
Rights: all
Payment: on publication
Seasonal submissions: five months in advance
Preferred Bible version: MEV
Guidelines: *charismamag.com/about/write-for-us*

Sample: *mycharisma.com/current-issue*
Tip: "Please take time to read—even study—at least one or two of our recent issues before submitting a query. Sometimes people submit their writing without ever having read or understood our magazine or its readers; and sometimes people will have read our magazine years ago and think it's the same as it has always been, but magazines undergo many changes through the years."

THE CHRISTIAN CENTURY

900 W. Jackson Blvd., Ste. 7W, Chicago, IL 60607 | 312-263-7510
submissions@christiancentury.org | *www.christiancentury.org*
Steve Thorngate, managing editor
Jill Peláez Baumgaertner, poetry, poetry@christiancentury.org
Dawn Araujo-Hawkins, news

Type: monthly digital and print magazine; accepts ads
Audience: ecumenical, mainline ministers, educators, and church leaders
Purpose: to explore what it means to believe and live out the Christian faith in our time
Submissions: Only accepts emailed query letter. Unsolicited freelance: 90%. Responds in one month. If you are interested in becoming a reviewer, mail your résumé and a list of subjects of interest to Attn: Book reviews.
Types of manuscripts: essays, humor, interviews, opinion, poetry, reviews
Length: articles, 1,500–3,000 words; poetry, to 20 lines
Topics: culture, issues, justice
Rights: all, reprint (with info on where/when previously published)
Payment: articles, $100–300; poems, $50; reviews, to $75; on publication
Manuscripts accepted per year: 150
Seasonal submissions: four months in advance
Preferred Bible version: NRSV
Guidelines: *www.christiancentury.org/submission-guidelines*
Sample: *www.christiancentury.org/magazine*
Tip: "Keep in mind our audience of sophisticated readers, eager for analysis and critical perspective that goes beyond the obvious. We are open to all topics if written with appropriate style for our readers."

CHRISTIAN COURIER

PO Box 124, Wainfleet, ON L0S 1V0, Canada | 800-275-9185
editor@christiancourier.ca | *www.christiancourier.ca*
Angela Reitsma Bick, editor-in-chief

Marlene Bergsma, features, features@christiancourier.ca
Adele Gallogly, reviews, reviews@christiancourier.ca
Maaike Vandermeer, poetry, maaike@christiancourier.ca

Denomination: Christian Reformed
Parent company: Reformed Faith Witness
Type: biweekly digital and print newspaper; circulation: 2,500; accepts ads
Purpose: to connect Christians with a network of culturally savvy partners in faith for the purpose of inspiring all to participate in God's renewing work with His creation
Submissions: Email complete manuscript or query letter. Accepts simultaneous submissions. Responds in one to two weeks, only if accepted.
Types of manuscripts: columns, feature articles, news, opinion, poetry, reviews
Length: articles, 700–1,200 words; reviews, 750 words
Rights: onetime, reprint (with info on where/when previously published)
Payment: articles, $50–70; reviews, $30–70; poetry, $45; reprints, none; all CAD; on publication
Seasonal submissions: three months in advance
Preferred Bible version: NIV
Guidelines: *www.christiancourier.ca/write-for-us*
Sample: *www.christiancourier.ca/past-issues*
Tip: "Suggest an aspect of the theme which you believe you could cover well, have insight into, could treat humorously, etc. Show that you think clearly, write clearly, and have something to say that we should want to read. Have a strong biblical worldview and avoid moralism and sentimentality."

CHRISTIAN HERALD

PO Box 68526, Brampton, ON L6R 0J8, Canada | 905-874-1731
info@christianherald.ca | christianherald.ca
Fazal Karim Jr., publisher, editor

Type: monthly digital and print newspaper; circulation: 25,000; accepts ads
Audience: Christians living in the Greater Toronto Area
Purpose: to serve the Christian community in the greater Toronto area
Submissions: Email complete manuscript or query by attachment. Gives assignments; to get one, contact editor by email indicating topics of interest. Unsolicited freelance: 5%. Responds in two weeks.
Types of manuscripts: columns, feature articles, how-to, interviews, reviews, sidebars
Length: 500–950 words
Topics: Christian history, Christian living/spirituality, evangelism, events, finances

Rights: electronic, first, onetime, reprint (with info on where/when previously published)
Payment: 10¢/word, on publication
Kill fee: sometimes
Manuscripts accepted per year: eight
Seasonal submissions: 40 days in advance
Theme lists: available via email
Guidelines: *www.christianherald.ca/writing-guidelines.html*
Sample: on the website
Tip: "Looking for event coverage, reviews, and ministry profiles."

CHRISTIAN LEADER
PO Box 155, Hillsboro, KS 67063 | 620-947-5543
editor@usmb.org | christianleadermag.com
Lacey Scully, editor
    Denomination: Mennonite
    Parent company: U.S. Conference of Mennonite Brethren Churches
    Type: bimonthly digital and print magazine; circulation: 7,800
    Audience: denomination
    Purpose: to inspire, inform, educate, and challenge church members and attendees, as well as to provide a "kitchen table" around which our diverse denomination can gather
    Submissions: Only accepts complete manuscript by email.
    Types of manuscripts: columns, feature articles, personal experience, testimonies
    Length: feature articles, 800–1,200 words; columns, 550 words
    Topics: church planting, discipleship, evangelism, leadership
    Rights: first
    Payment: on publication
    Guidelines: *christianleadermag.com/about-cl/cl-history*
    Sample: *issuu.com/christianleader*
    Tip: "We give preference to writers who are from North American Mennonite Brethren congregations, ministries and educational institutions. We welcome articles by writers from within the Anabaptist and Mennonite family of denominations. Articles by Mennonite Brethren and those from other Mennonite writers that focus on personal experiences are encouraged. Please do not submit personal testimonies or stories unless you are a Mennonite Brethren or Mennonite writer."

CHRISTIAN STANDARD
16965 Pine Ln., Ste. 202, Parker, CO 80134 | 800-543-1353
cs@christianstandardmedia.com | www.christianstandard.com

Shawn McMullen, editor

Denomination: Christian Churches, Churches of Christ
Parent company: Christian Standard Media
Type: bimonthly digital and print magazine
Audience: paid and volunteer leaders
Purpose: to leverage the power of our unity and to resource Christian churches to fulfill Christ's commission
Submissions: Only accepts query letter. Unsolicited freelance: 5%; 95% assigned. Responds in one to three months.
Types of manuscripts: Communion meditations for website, how-to
Length: maximum 1,800 words, prefers 500–1,200 words
Topics: theme-related
Rights: first, reprint (with info on where/when previously published)
Payment: $50–250, on acceptance
Kill fee: sometimes
Manuscripts accepted per year: 15
Seasonal submissions: six to eight months in advance
Preferred Bible version: NIV
Theme lists: available on website
Guidelines: *christianstandard.com/writersguidelines*
Sample: on the website
Tip: "Writers with journalism backgrounds who are interested in covering stories, conducting interviews, and writing news articles are invited to contact us about becoming a freelance general assignment reporter. These reporters may develop their own leads or they may write on assignment by editors; they should be available to write news stories on relatively short notice. If you are interested in being considered, please email us and include your journalism education and experience as well as several published clips."

CHRISTIANITY TODAY
465 Gundersen Dr., Carol Stream, IL 60188-2498 | 630-260-6200
editor@christianitytoday.com | *www.christianitytoday.com*
Ashley Hales, editorial director, print
Matt Reynolds, books editor, mreynolds@christianitytoday.com
Daniel Silliman, news editor, dsilliman@christianitytoday.com
Parent company: Christianity Today International
Type: bimonthly digital and print magazine; circulation: 100,000; hits: 3.5 million page views/month; accepts ads
Audience: Christian leaders throughout North America
Purpose: to equip Christians to renew their minds, serve the church,

and create culture to the glory of God

Submissions: Only accepts query letter through the website. Unsolicited freelance: few. Responds in three weeks or not interested.

Types of manuscripts: feature articles, interviews, opinion, profiles, reviews

Length: 300–1,800 words

Topics: Christian living/spirituality, culture, issues

Rights: electronic, first

Payment: varies, on acceptance

Preferred Bible version: NIV

Guidelines: *help.christianitytoday.com/hc/en-us/ articles/360047411253-How-do-I-write-for-CT*

Sample: articles are on the website

Tip: "We are most interested in stories of Christians living out their faith in unique ways that impact the world for the better and communicate truth in a way that is deep, nuanced, and challenging."

COLUMBIA

1 Columbus Plaza, New Haven, CT 06510-3326 | 203-752-4398
columbia@kofc.org | *www.kofc.org/en/news-room/columbia/index.html*
Alton J. Pelowski, editor

Denomination: Catholic

Parent company: Knights of Columbus

Type: monthly digital and print magazine; circulation: 1.7 million

Audience: general Catholic family

Submissions: Query first by email or mail. No simultaneous submissions.

Types of manuscripts: feature articles, profiles

Length: 700-1,500 words

Topics: current events, family, finances, health, issues, parenting, trends

Rights: first

Payment: varies, on acceptance

Seasonal submissions: six months in advance

Guidelines: *www.kofc.org/en/news-room/columbia/guidelines.html*

Sample: *issuu.com/columbia-magazine*

COMMONWEAL

475 Riverside Dr., Rm. 405, New York, NY 10115 | 212-662-4200
editors@commonwealmagazine.org | *www.commonwealmagazine.org*
Matthew Boudway, senior editor
Alexander Stern, editor, features

Denomination: Catholic

Type: monthly print magazine; circulation: 20,000; accepts ads

Audience: liberal Catholics

Purpose: to provide a forum about faith, public affairs, and the arts, centered on belief in the common good

Submissions: Only accepts complete manuscript or query through the website. Responds in six to eight weeks.

Types of manuscripts: essays, news, opinion, poetry

Length: articles, 1,000–2,000 and 2,500–5,000 words; "Last Word" column, 750–1,500

Topics: literature and the arts, public affairs

Rights: all

Payment: varies, on publication

Guidelines: *commonweal.submittable.com/submit*

Sample: most of the articles are on the website

Tip: "Articles should be written for a general but well-educated audience. While religious articles are always topical, we are less interested in devotional and 'churchy' pieces than in articles which examine the links between 'worldly' concerns and religious beliefs. Articles fall into three categories:

• 'Short Takes,' running from 1,000–2,000 words, are brief, 'newsy' and reportorial, giving facts, information, and some interpretation behind the 'headlines of the day.'

• Feature articles, running from 2,500–5,000 words, are more reflective and detailed, bringing new information or a different point of view to a subject, raising questions, and/or proposing solutions to the dilemmas facing the world, nation, church, or individual.

• 'Last Word' columns, running from 750–1,500 words, are more personal reflections on some aspect of the human condition: spiritual, individual, political, or social."

CREATION ILLUSTRATED

PO Box 141103, Spokane Valley, WA 99214 | 530-269-1424
ci@creationillustrated.com | *creationillustrated.com*
Jennifer Ish, associate editor

Parent company: Creation Illustrated Ministries, Inc.

Type: quarterly digital and print magazine; circulation: 15,000; accepts ads

Audience: families, homeschoolers

Purpose: to help one get away to nature and reconnect to the knowledge, power, and beauty found in God's creation

Submissions: Email query with clips. Unsolicited freelance: 75%+. Responds in four weeks.

Types of manuscripts: articles, personal experience, short stories, travel
Length: 700–1,500 words
Topic: nature
Rights: first, reprint (with info on where/when previously published)
Payment: $75–100, 30 days past publication
Kill fee: sometimes
Manuscripts accepted per year: 32
Seasonal submissions: two to three months in advance
Preferred Bible versions: KJV, NKJV, NASB, ESV
Guidelines: *www.creationillustrated.com/writer-and-photo-guidelines*
Sample: *www.creationillustrated.com/free-digital-copy*
Tip: "Send a good query (helps us avoid repeating a subject recently covered) that is focused on one of the key features. Make sure it can be illustrated with stunning photographs, as each story is beautifully illustrated with many full-colored photos. Looking especially for articles about creatures, nature up close, children's stories that have nature and character-building lessons, and gardening."

CREATIVE INSPIRATIONS

PO Box 19051, Kalamazoo, MI 49009 | 269-348-5712
creativeinspirations01@gmail.com | *www.cipoetrypublication.com*
MJ Reynolds, publisher and editor
   Type: bimonthly digital magazine
   Audience: poets and people who appreciate poetry
   Purpose: to publish inspirational poetry
   Submissions: Email or mail manuscript. Unsolicited freelance: 100%. Responds in one to two weeks. Accepts submissions from teens.
   Type of manuscripts: poetry
   Topics: Christian living/spirituality, family, nature
   Rights: onetime
   Payment: none
   Manuscripts accepted per year: varies
   Preferred Bible version: NIV
   Guidelines: *www.cipoetrypublication.com/ci-news–info.html*
   Sample: request by email
   Tip: "Follow the submission guidelines."

DTS MAGAZINE

3909 Swiss Ave., Dallas, TX 75204 | 800-387-9673
magazine@dts.edu | *voice.dts.edu/article*
Neil Coulter, editor

Parent company: Dallas Theological Seminary (DTS)
Type: quarterly digital and print magazine; circulation: 35,000
Audience: evangelical laypeople, students, alumni, donors, and friends
Purpose: to apply biblical truth to life as a ministry to friends of Dallas Theological Seminary
Submissions: Only accepts complete manuscript through the website. Responds in three weeks.
Types of manuscripts: personal experience, profiles, teaching
Length: 600–1,500 words
Topic: Christian living/spirituality
Rights: first, reprint
Payment: $300, $100 for reprints, $50-100 for web articles, on publication
Seasonal submissions: six months in advance
Preferred Bible version: NET
Guidelines: *voice.dts.edu/magazine/editorial-policies*
Sample: *voice.dts.edu/magazine*
Tip: "*DTS Magazine* is a ministry of Dallas Theological Seminary. We prioritize articles written by our alumni, faculty, students, staff, board members, donors and their families."

EVANGELICAL MISSIONS QUARTERLY

PO Box 398, Wheaton, IL 60187 | 678-392-4577
Editor@MissioNexus.org | missionexus.org/emq
Evelyn Hibbert, editor
David Dunaetz, book review editor
Parent company: Missio Nexus
Type: quarterly digital journal
Audience: missionaries, mission agency executives, mission professors, missionary candidates, students, mission pastors, mission-minded church leaders, mission supporters, and agency board members
Purpose: to increase the effectiveness of the evangelical missionary enterprise
Submissions: Email query as attachment. Submit complete manuscript through the website.
Types of manuscripts: how-to, profiles, reviews
Length: 2,000–3,000 words
Topics: church planting, culture, discipleship, evangelism, leadership, missions, trends
Rights: all
Theme lists: available on website

Guidelines: *missionexus.org/emq/submit-an-article-to-emq*

Tip: "We are not a scholarly journal written for academics, but desire material that is academically respectable, reflecting careful thought and practical application to missions professionals, and especially working missionaries. We like to see problems not only diagnosed, but solved either by way of illustration or suggestion."

FAITH & FRIENDS

The Salvation Army, 2 Overlea Blvd., Toronto, ON M4H 1P4, Canada | 416-422-6226

faithandfriends@salvationarmy.ca | *salvationist.ca/editorial/faith-and-friends*
Ken Ramstead, editor

Denomination: The Salvation Army

Parent company: The Salvation Army Canada and Bermuda

Type: bimonthly digital and print magazine; circulation: 14,600

Audience: general

Purpose: to show Jesus Christ at work in the lives of real people and to provide spiritual resources for those who are new to the Christian faith

Submissions: Only accepts complete manuscript emailed as attachment.

Types of manuscripts: personal experience, profiles, reviews, testimonies

Length: 600–900 words

Topics: Christian living/spirituality, family, marriage, theology

Rights: first, reprint

Payment: none

Preferred Bible version: NIV

Guidelines: *salvationist.ca/editorial/writer-s-guidelines*

Sample: on the website

Tip: "Looking for stories about people whose lives have been changed through an encounter with Jesus: conversion, miracles, healing, faith in the midst of crisis, forgiveness, reconciliation, answered prayers, and more. Profiles of people who have found hope and healing through their ministries, including prisoners, hospital patients, nursing-home residents, single parents in distress, addicts, the unemployed, or homeless."

FAITH ON EVERY CORNER

159 Hudson Cajah Mountain Rd., Hudson, NC 28638 | 828-305-8570
team@faithoneverycorner.com | *www.faithoneverycorner.com/magazine*

Karen Ruhl, publisher and editor in chief
   Parent company: Faith On Every Corner, LLC
   Type: monthly digital magazine; circulation: 35,000
   Audience: families, seekers
   Purpose: to reach as many people as we can with the Good News
   Submissions: Email manuscript as attachment. Unsolicited freelance:
      20%. Responds in one week. Accepts submissions from teens.
   Types of manuscripts: devotions, personal experience, poetry, short
      stories
   Length: 500–1,000 words
   Topic: Christian living/spirituality
   Rights: onetime
   Payment: none
   Manuscripts accepted per year: 400
   Seasonal submissions: two months
   Preferred Bible version: NIV
   Theme lists: available via email
   Guidelines: *www.faithoneverycorner.com/submission-guidelines.html*
   Sample: on the website
   Tip: "Looking for true Christian stories, devotions, poetry, life events
      that brought you to Christ."

FAITH TODAY

275 Slater St., Ste. 810, Ottawa, ON K1P 5H9, Canada | 866-302-3362
editor@faithtoday.ca | www.faithtoday.ca
Bill Fledderus, senior editor
   Parent company: The Evangelical Fellowship of Canada
   Type: bimonthly digital and print magazine; circulation: print, 18,000;
      online, 9,500; accepts ads
   Audience: Canadian evangelicals
   Purpose: to connect, equip, and inform Canada's four million
      evangelical Christians from Anglican and Baptist to Pentecostal
      and The Salvation Army
   Submissions: Only accepts emailed query letter with clips.
      Unsolicited freelance: 10%. Responds in one week.
   Types of manuscripts: essays, feature articles, how-to, news, profiles,
      reviews
   Length: 350–1,800 words
   Topics: church, issues, trends
   Rights: electronic, first, onetime, reprint (with info on where/when
      previously published)

Payment: 30–40¢ CAD/word, on acceptance
Kill fee: sometimes
Manuscripts accepted per year: 100
Seasonal submissions: four months in advance
Guidelines: *www.faithtoday.ca/writers*
Sample: *www.faithtoday.ca/digital*
Tip: "What is the Canadian angle? How does your approach include diverse Canadian voices from different churches, regions, generations, etc.?"

FAITHFULLY MAGAZINE

397 Hillside Ave. #5154, Hillside, NJ 07205
contact@faithfullymagazine.com | *faithfullymagazine.com*
Nicola A. Menzie, managing editor
　　Parent company: Faithfully Media, LLC
　　Type: daily website; accepts ads
　　Audience: ethnically diverse millennials and post-millennials
　　Purpose: to report on issues, conversations, and events impacting Christian communities of color for an ethnically inclusive audience
　　Submissions: Query first by email. Responds in three days or not interested.
　　Types of manuscripts: biography, essays, feature articles, news, opinion, profiles
　　Length: feature and essay, varies; opinion and analysis, 1,000–1,200 words; news and trends, 400–500 words; profile and historical biography, 500–800 words
　　Topics: wide variety
　　Rights: all, first
　　Payment: $20–200
　　Guidelines: *faithfullymagazine.com/submissions*
　　Sample: see website
　　Tip: "Although we work with new writers, our time limits us to working with writers whose clips show they are well-practiced in their craft."

FOCUS ON THE FAMILY

8605 Explorer Dr., Colorado Springs, CO 80920 | 800-232-6459
FocusMagSubmissions@family.com | *www.focusonthefamily.com/magazine*
Andrea Gutierrez, managing editor
　　Parent company: Focus on the Family
　　Type: bimonthly print magazine; circulation: 240,000
　　Audience: married parents with children in the home
　　Purpose: to support couples in their marriage and parents when

training their children

Submissions: Email complete manuscript. Unsolicited freelance: 20%. Responds in eight weeks. Also buys articles on parenting and marriage for online. Length: 800–1,500 words. Email to *Rhonda. Robinson@fotf.org*.

Types of manuscripts: how-to, profiles, teaching

Length: 400 words maximum

Topics: grandparenting, marriage, parenting

Rights: first

Payment: $125, on acceptance

Kill fee: always

Manuscripts accepted per year: 100

Seasonal submissions: nine months in advance

Preferred Bible version: ESV

Guidelines: *www.focusonthefamily.com/magazine/call-for-submissions*

Sample: articles are on the website; free subscription, email *HELP@focusonthefamily.com*

Tip: "Start with 'Hacks & Facts' for parenting, extended family, grandparenting, and adult kids. Find any calls for submissions on our site, and follow the directions for that specific article."

FRIENDS JOURNAL

1501 Cherry St., Philadelphia, PA 19102 | 215-563-8629
martin@friendsjournal.org | *www.friendsjournal.org*
Martin Kelly, senior editor

Denomination: Quaker

Parent company: Religious Society of Friends

Type: monthly digital and print magazine

Audience: denomination

Purpose: to communicate Quaker experience in order to connect and deepen spiritual lives

Submissions: Only accepts email through the website.

Types of manuscripts: personal experience, poetry, profiles, teaching, testimonies

Length: 1,200–2,500 words; departments, around 1,500 words or fewer

Topics: theme-related

Rights: first

Payment: none

Manuscripts accepted per year: varies; poems, 22–33

Theme lists: available on website

Guidelines: *www.friendsjournal.org/submissions*

Sample: articles are on the website

Tip: "*Friends Journal* prefers articles with a constructive approach to spiritual seeking. We seek an open, curious and respectful tone even when discussing controversial subjects. We prefer articles rooted in the author's own experiences of the divine. Submissions should show an awareness of Friends' ways and concerns, as well as sensitivity to them."

FUSION FAMILY

114 Bush Rd., Nashville, TN 37217 | 800-877-7030
david.jones@d6family.com | *store.randallhouse.com/product/fusion-family-devotional-study-guide-so*
David Jones, senior editor

Denomination: Free Will Baptist
Parent company: D6 Family Ministry
Type: bimonthly print magazine
Audience: parents with children at home
Purpose: to integrate truth, faith, and life
Submissions: Only email as attachment. Unsolicited freelance: 10%. Responds in one week.
Types of manuscripts: interviews, narrative, personal experience
Length: 500–1,500
Topics: Christian life, evangelism, parenting, theology
Rights: all
Payment: $50–150, on acceptance
Manuscripts accepted per year: 24
Seasonal submissions: six months in advance
Preferred Bible version: ESV
Guidelines: by email
Sample: buy from website
Tip: "It helps to zero-in on a very specific topic. Since our magazine already contains devotionals, we're not looking for another devotional-type piece."

FUSION NEXT

114 Bush Rd., Nashville, TN 37217 | 800-877-7030
kathy.murphy@d6family.com | *store.randallhouse.com/product/fusion-next-devotional-study-guide-so*
Kathy Murphy, editor

Denomination: Free Will Baptist
Parent company: D6 Family Ministry

Type: bimonthly print magazine

Audience: empty nesters, grandparents

Purpose: to strengthen the faith of seniors and guide them as they disciple their adult children and grandchildren

Submissions: Only accepts email as Word document attachment. Unsolicited freelance: 10%. Responds in one week. Email editor for assignments. Devotions are by assignment only.

Types of manuscripts: articles, columns, poetry, short stories

Length: 900–1,500 words

Topics: Christian service, grandparenting, marriage, parenting adult children, spiritual disciplines

Rights: all, electronic, first, onetime, reprint (with info on where/when previously published)

Payment: 900 words, $90; 1,200 words, $120; etc.

Manuscripts accepted per year: 72

Seasonal submissions: four to six months

Preferred Bible version: ESV

Guidelines: by email

Sample: email *david.womack@d6family.com*

Tip: "Topics needed most: grandparenting, spiritual growth in the empty-nester years."

GATHER

8765 W. Higgins Rd., Chicago, IL 60631 | 844-409-0576
gather@elca.org | *www.gathermagazine.org*
Elizabeth Hunter, editor

Denomination: Evangelical Lutheran Church in America

Parent company: Women of the Evangelical Lutheran Church in America

Type: quarterly digital and print magazine

Audience: Lutheran women

Purpose: to help readers grow in faith and engage in ministry and action

Submissions: Email query letter with clips. Accepts simultaneous submissions. Responds only if interested.

Type of manuscripts: personal experience

Topics: theme-related

Rights: first, onetime, reprint (with info on where/when previously published)

Payment: on publication

Seasonal submissions: seven months in advance

Guidelines: *www.gathermagazine.org/write-for-gather*

Sample: article samples are on the website

Tip: "Please know that most of what we publish is assigned—we ask particular established authors to write on specific themes far in advance of publication. We publish very few articles that originated as unsolicited manuscripts or queries."

GEMS OF TRUTH

PO Box 4060, Overland Park, KS 66204 | 913-432-0331
sseditor@heraldandbanner.com | *heraldandbanner.com/product/gems-of-truth*
Arlene McGehee, Sunday school editor

Denomination: Church of God
Parent company: Herald and Banner Press
Type: weekly Sunday school take-home paper; circulation: 4,750
Audience: denomination
Purpose: to build character values without being preachy
Submissions: Email or mail manuscript. Unsolicited freelance: 50%. Responds in nine months.
Types of manuscripts: biography, personal experience, poetry, short stories
Length: 1,000–2,000 words
Topics: Christian living/spirituality, family, marriage, prayer
Rights: first, reprint
Payment: prose, .0005¢/word; poetry, 25¢/line; reprints, 50%; on publication
Manuscripts accepted per year: varies
Seasonal submissions: six months in advance
Preferred Bible version: KJV
Guidelines: by email
Sample: 9"x12" SASE with $3.50 postage
Tip: Looking for seasonal stories.

GOOD NEWS

PO Box 670368, Coral Springs, FL 33067 | 954-564-5378
ShellyP@goodnewsfl.org | *www.goodnewsfl.org*
Shelly Pond, editor

Parent company: Good News Media Group LLC
Type: monthly digital and print newspaper; circulation: 80,000 print, 30,000 digital; accepts ads
Audience: Florida residents
Submissions: Only accepts emailed query letter with clips.
Types of manuscripts: articles

Length: 500–800 words
Payment: 10¢/word
Sample: on the website

GUIDEPOSTS

100 Reserve Rd., Ste. E200, Danbury, CT 06810 | 800-431-2344
submissions@guideposts.org | *guideposts.org/shop/product/guideposts-magazine*
Evan Miller, senior editor
Nikki Notare, editor

Parent company: Guideposts
Type: bimonthly digital and print magazine; circulation: 700,000
Audience: general
Purpose: to provide inspirational content so that people can grow and thrive by practicing hope and positivity in their daily lives; to encourage, inform, entertain, and tell true stories of personal change; to unite rather than divide, nurture spiritual wellness, and serve believers and seekers
Submissions: Email complete manuscript or query as attachment. Unsolicited freelance: 70%. Responds in two months or not interested. Specific departments also welcome submissions: Mysterious Ways, "more than coincidence" stories that show God's hand at work, *mw@guideposts.org;* Someone Cares, short stories of kindness and caring, *sc@guideposts.org.*
Types of manuscripts: personal experience
Length: articles, 1,200–1,500 words; shorter features, 350–600 words; departments, 175–400 words
Topics: close calls (action-adventure), everyday life, family, friendship, marriage, miracles, new beginnings, personal change, pets and animals
Rights: all
Payment: varies, minimum of $100 per printed page, on acceptance
Kill fee: sometimes
Manuscripts accepted per year: 40–60
Seasonal submissions: six months in advance
Guidelines: *guideposts.org/writers-guidelines*
Sample: *order.emags.com/guideposts* to order a digital edition of our current issue
Tip: "*Guideposts* magazine features true, first-person stories about everyday people who have been changed, in ways large or small, by an experience they've had. Narrators face challenges in their lives that they resolve through leaning on their faith and on God. The challenge can involve everything from day-to-day relationship issues,

to life transitions, such as caregiving, divorce, retirement or job loss, to close calls. Our stories deliver hope and inspiration with a clear spiritual point that readers can apply to everyday difficulties in their own lives. Study the magazine and how our stories are told. Stories can be your own or ghostwritten for someone else. We don't publish essays, sermons, testimonials, fiction, or poetry."

HEARTBEAT

PO Box 9, Hatfield, AR 71945 | 870-389-6196
heartbeat@cmausa.org | cmausa.org/Resources/Heartbeat
Misty Bradley, editor

Parent company: Christian Motorcyclists Association
Type: monthly digital and print magazine; circulation: 18,000
Audience: motorcyclists
Purpose: to inspire leaders and members to be the most organized, advanced, equipped, financially stable organization, full of integrity in the motorcycling industry and the Kingdom of God
Submissions: Only accepts complete manuscript by email.
Types of manuscripts: articles, reviews
Topic: motorcycling
Rights: all
Payment: none

HIGHWAY NEWS

1525 River Rd., Marietta, PA 17547 | 717-426-9977
editor@tfcglobal.org | tfcglobal.org/highway-news-current-issue
Lynn Bolster, editor

Parent company: TFC Global
Type: monthly digital and print magazine; circulation: 18,000–20,000
Audience: truck drivers and their families
Purpose: to lead truck drivers, as well as the trucking community, to Jesus Christ and help them grow in their faith
Submissions: Only accepts complete manuscript by email. Unsolicited freelance: 10–20%.
Types of manuscripts: news, personal experience
Length: 800–1,000 words
Topic: trucking life
Rights: first, reprint
Payment: none
Seasonal submissions: six months in advance
Preferred Bible version: ESV

Guidelines: by email

Sample: on the website

Tip: "Articles submitted for publication do not have to be religious in nature; however, they should not conflict with or oppose guidelines and principles presented in the Bible."

HOLINESS TODAY

17001 Prairie Star Pkwy., Lenexa, KS 66220 | 913-577-0500
holinesstoday@nazarene.org | *www.holinesstoday.org*
Nathanael T. Gilmore, content editor

Denomination: Nazarene

Parent company: General Board of the Church of the Nazarene

Type: bimonthly digital and print magazine; circulation: 8,000; accepts ads

Audience: denomination

Purpose: to keep readers connected with the Nazarene experience and provide tools for everyday faith

Submissions: Only accepts complete manuscript as email attachment. Unsolicited freelance: 30%. Accepts submissions from children and teens.

Types of manuscripts: columns, personal experience

Length: 700–1,100 words

Topics: denomination, ministry, teaching

Rights: first, reprint (with info on where/when previously published)

Payment: $135, on publication

Kill fee: yes

Manuscripts accepted per year: six to eight

Preferred Bible version: NIV

Theme lists: available via email

Guidelines: by email

Tip: "We are always interested in hearing from Nazarene pastors, lay leaders, and experts in their fields. We are a Nazarene publication that wants our articles to be relevant and applicable to real-life scenarios and the world we live in."

HOMELIFE

200 Powell Pl., Ste. 100, Brentwood, TN 37027 | 615-251-2196
homelife@lifeway.com | *www.lifeway.com/en/product-family/home life-magazine*
David Bennett, managing editor

Denomination: Southern Baptist

Parent company: Lifeway Christian Resources

Type: monthly print magazine; circulation: 140,000

Audience: parents

Purpose: to offer biblical and practical encouragement that champions life-changing discipleship, dynamic marriages, and effective parenting

Submissions: Only accepts complete manuscript as attachment. Gives assignments. Unsolicited freelance: 20%. Responds only if interested.

Types of manuscripts: columns, how-to, narrative, sidebars

Length: 500, 750, 1,500 words

Topics: family, living on mission, marriage, parenting

Rights: first

Payment: $100–500, on acceptance

Kill fee: sometimes

Manuscripts accepted per year: 18

Seasonal submissions: six months in advance

Preferred Bible version: CSB

Guidelines: by email

Sample: on the website

Tip: "Be familiar with the magazine and the Faith-Family-Life format."

INFLUENCE

1445 N. Boonville Ave., Springfield, MO 65802 | 417-862-2781
editor@influencemagazine.com | *influencemagazine.com*
Christina Quick, lead editor

Denomination: Assemblies of God

Parent company: The General Council of the Assemblies of God

Type: quarterly digital and print magazine; circulation: 33,000; accepts ads

Audience: pastors and other leaders

Purpose: to provide a Christ-centered, Spirit-empowered perspective that propels people to engage their faith—as individuals, in community, and with the global Church

Submissions: Only accepts emailed query letter.

Types of manuscripts: how-to, profiles, teaching

Length: 700–1,000 words

Topics: ethics, family, leadership, ministry, worship

Rights: first

Preferred Bible version: NIV

Guidelines: *influencemagazine.com/submission-guidelines*

Sample: *influencemagazine.com/en/issues*

Tip: "We'd love to hear more about your background in leadership and how that might connect to your pitch. Links to sites, social-media profiles, or other writing samples are encouraged. Reprints or excerpts are considered on a case-by-case basis, but original content is preferred."

INSITE

PO Box 62189, Colorado Springs, CO 80962-2189 | 888-922-2287
editor@ccca.org | www.ccca.org/ccca/Publications.asp
Jen Howver, editor

> **Parent company:** Christian Camp and Conference Association
> **Type:** five times/year; digital and print magazine; circulation: 5,200; accepts ads
> **Audience:** Christian camping staff and professionals
> **Purpose:** to maximize ministry for member camps and conference centers
> **Submissions:** Email manuscript as attachment. Gives assignments. Unsolicited freelance: 0%. Responds in one to two weeks.
> **Types of manuscripts:** columns, how-to, interviews
> **Length:** features, 1,500 words
> **Topics:** camping ministry, facilities, finances, hospitality, HR, marketing
> **Rights:** all
> **Payment:** features, $300; on publication
> **Kill fee:** sometimes
> **Preferred Bible version:** NIV
> **Guidelines:** by email
> **Sample:** email editor
> **Tip:** "We're open to finding new writers for taking feature article assignments. An email with sample writing and experience may open a door for a freelancer to get onto our list. If you have experience with interview- or research-based writing, samples will be helpful."

INSPIRE A FIRE

dianaflegal@gmail.com | inspireafire.com
Diana Flegal, senior editor
Eddie Jones, executive editor, WritersCoach.us@gmail.com

> **Parent company:** Christian Devotions Ministry
> **Type:** daily website; circulation: 38,000
> **Audience:** Christians looking for encouragement and inspiration
> **Purpose:** to deliver life-giving articles that inspire hope, convey God's truth, and accompany believers on their spiritual journeys
> **Submissions:** Unsolicited freelance: 40%. Responds in one week.

Types of manuscripts: personal experience, poetry
Length: 1,500 words
Topics: Christian living, culture, family, relationships
Rights: first, reprint if retitled and reworded 25%
Payment: none
Theme lists: available on website
Guidelines: *inspireafire.com/submissions-guidelines*
Sample: on the website
Tip: *"Inspire a Fire* is looking for committed writers familiar with WordPress, or willing to learn, to post a monthly article in accordance with submission guidelines. If you would like to become a monthly contributor, email Diana or Eddie to schedule a phone call or Zoom interview."

THE JOURNAL OF ADVENTIST EDUCATION

12501 Old Columbia Pike, Silver Spring, MD 20904-6600 | 301-680-5069
mcgarrellf@gc.adventist.org | *www.journalofadventisteducation.org*
Faith-Ann A. McGarrell, editor
Denomination: Seventh-day Adventist
Parent company: General Conference of Seventh-day Adventists
Type: quarterly digital journal; circulation: 10,000–16,000; accepts ads
Audience: educators and administrators
Purpose: to aid professional teachers and educational administrators worldwide, kindergarten to higher education
Submissions: Only accepts complete manuscript through the website. Unsolicited freelance: 10%. Responds in four to six weeks.
Types of manuscripts: how-to, personal experience, reviews, sidebars
Length: 1,500–4,000 words; book reviews, 900–1,100 words
Topic: Christian education
Rights: first, reprint (with info on where/when previously published)
Payment: varies, on publication
Manuscripts accepted per year: 32
Seasonal submissions: six months in advance
Preferred Bible version: NIV
Guidelines: *www.journalofadventisteducation.org/author-guidelines*
Sample: download from the website
Tip: *"JAE* accepts invited and freelance submissions from educators, educational administrators, and individuals working in education. Authors must be familiar with Adventist Christian education—its philosophy, structure, and historical foundations."

JOYFUL LIVING MAGAZINE

PO Box 311, Palo Cedro, CA 97073 | 530-227-9330
joyfullivingmagazineredding@gmail.com | *joyfullivingmagazine.com*
Cathy Jansen, editor in chief

> **Type:** quarterly digital magazine; accepts ads
> **Audience:** general
> **Purpose:** to share encouragement and hope, to help readers grow spiritually and emotionally, and to help them in their everyday lives with practical issues
> **Submissions:** Only accepts complete manuscript emailed as attachment.
> **Types of manuscripts:** how-to, personal experience, profiles, recipes
> **Length:** 200–700 words
> **Topics:** aging, Christian living/spirituality, depression, family, finances, health, marriage, singleness, work
> **Payment:** none
> **Guidelines:** *www.joyfullivingmagazine.com/writers-info*
> **Sample:** on the website
> **Tip:** "Articles need to be uplifting and encouraging for singles, seniors, young people, and families. Each article needs to inspire the reader to grow spiritually, emotionally, and help them in their everyday lives with very practical issues."

JUST BETWEEN US

777 S. Barker Rd., Brookfield, WI 53045 | 262-786-6478
cherie@justbetweenus.org | *www.justbetweenus.org*
Cherie Burbach, digital editor

> **Type:** weekly digital magazine and quarterly print magazine; circulation: 10,000
> **Audience:** women
> **Purpose:** to encourage and equip women for a life of faith and service
> **Submissions:** Only accepts complete manuscript emailed as attachment. Responds in six to eight weeks or not interested.
> **Types of manuscripts:** how-to, personal experience, testimonies
> **Length:** 800–1,100 words
> **Topics:** theme-related
> **Rights:** first
> **Payment:** none
> **Preferred Bible version:** NIV
> **Theme lists:** available on website
> **Guidelines:** *justbetweenus.org/magazine/writers-guidelines*
> **Sample:** *justbetweenus.org/magazine-sample-issue*

Tip: "We especially appreciate articles that reflect authentic spiritual growth—stories of lessons learned through personal struggles and the wisdom gained along the way. Your journey could be exactly the encouragement someone else needs."

LEADING HEARTS

PO Box 6421, Longmont, CO 80501 | 303-835-8473
amber@leadinghearts.com | leadinghearts.com
Amber Weigland-Buckley, editor

Parent company: Right to the Heart Ministries
Type: bimonthly digital magazine; circulation: 10,000; accepts ads
Audience: women leaders
Purpose: to encourage Christian women who lead hearts at home, work, community and church
Submissions: Assignment only; 50–60% assigned. To audition for an assignment, email an article of 1,200 words maximum and a short résumé.
Types of manuscripts: how-to, personal experience, profiles, reviews
Length: articles, 800 words maximum; columns, 250–500 words
Topics: theme-related
Rights: first, reprint
Payment: none
Preferred Bible version: NIV
Guidelines: *leadinghearts.com/writers-guidelines*
Sample: on the website
Tip: Gives preferred consideration to members of AWSA.

LEAVES

PO Box 87, Dearborn, MI 48121-0087 | 313-561-2330
editor.leaves@mariannhill.us | www.mariannhill.us/leaves.html

Denomination: Catholic
Parent company: Marianhill Mission Society
Type: bimonthly print magazine; circulation: 10,000
Audience: Catholics, primarily in the Detroit, Michigan, area
Purpose: to promote devotion to God and testimony of His blessings
Submissions: Email or mail complete manuscript.
Types of manuscripts: personal experience, poetry, reviews, testimonies
Length: 250 words
Topics: Christian living/spirituality, prayer
Rights: first, reprint
Payment: none

Manuscripts accepted per year: 40
Preferred Bible version: RSV Catholic edition
Sample: articles are on the website
Tip: Greatest need is for personal testimonies.

LIGHT

901 Commerce St., Ste. 550, Nashville, TN 37203 | 615-244-2495
nicolet@erlc.com | erlc.com/resources
Lindsay Nicolet, editor

Denomination: Southern Baptist
Parent company: The Ethics and Religious Liberty Commission
Type: biannual digital and print journal; circulation: 8,000; accepts ads
Audience: church and ministry leaders
Purpose: to bear witness to the gospel by speaking to congregations and consciences with a thoroughly Christian moral witness
Submissions: Email complete manuscript as attachment. Unsolicited freelance: 10%. Responds in one week.
Types of manuscripts: columns, how-to, news, reviews
Length: 1,500 words
Topics: culture, ethics, family, justice, parenting, politics
Rights: all
Payment: depends on article and writer
Manuscripts accepted per year: 10
Preferred Bible version: CSB
Guidelines: not available
Sample: on the website
Tip: "Looking for articles tied to current events and focus on local church ministry."

LIVE

1445 N. Boonville Ave., Springfield, MO 65802-1894 | 417-862-2781
rl-live@gph.org | myhealthychurch.com
Wade Quick, editor

Denomination: Assemblies of God
Parent company: Gospel Publishing House
Type: weekly Sunday school take-home paper; circulation: 40,000
Audience: denomination
Purpose: to encourage Christians in living for God through stories that apply biblical principles to everyday problems
Submissions: Email as attachment or mail manuscript. Unsolicited freelance: 100%. Responds in six weeks.

Types of manuscripts: fillers, how-to, personal experience, poetry, short stories

Length: articles, 200–1,200 words; poetry, 12–25 lines

Topic: Christian living/spirituality

Rights: first, reprint

Payment: 10¢/word for first rights, 7¢/word for reprint, $35–60 for poetry, on acceptance

Seasonal submissions: 18 months in advance

Preferred Bible version: NLT

Guidelines: *myhealthychurch.com/store/startcat.cfm?cat=tWRITGUID*

Tip: "Stories should be encouraging, challenging, and/or humorous. Even problem-centered stories should be upbeat. Stories should not be preachy, critical, or moralizing. They should not present pat, trite, or simplistic answers to problems. No Bible fiction or sci-fi. Make sure the stories have a strong Christian element, are written well, have strong takeaways, but do not preach."

THE LUTHERAN WITNESS

1333 S. Kirkwood Rd., St. Louis, MO 63122-7226 | 800-248-1930
lutheran.witness@lcms.org | *witness.lcms.org*
Roy S. Askins, managing editor

Denomination: Lutheran Church Missouri Synod

Parent company: The Lutheran Church Missouri Synod

Type: monthly print magazine; circulation: 100,000

Audience: denomination

Purpose: to interpret the contemporary world from a Lutheran perspective

Submissions: Query via email, or submit complete manuscript through the website. Responds in at least three months only if interested.

Types of manuscripts: Bible studies, essays, how-to, humor, personal experience, poetry, profiles, teaching

Length: 500, 1,000, or 1,500 words

Topics: theme-related

Rights: electronic, first

Payment: based on both article length and complexity and author's credentials, on acceptance

Preferred Bible version: ESV

Theme lists: available on website

Guidelines: *witness.lcms.org/contribute*

Sample: articles are on the website

Tip: "Because of the magazine's long lead time, and because many features are planned at least six months in advance of the publication date, your story should have a long-term perspective that keeps it relevant several months from the time you submit it."

THE MARKETPLACE

PO Box 1771, Lancaster, PA 17608 | 800-665-7026
mstrathdee@meda.org | www.meda.org/the-marketplace
Mike Strathdee, content editor

Denomination: Mennonite

Parent company: Mennonite Economic Development Associates (MEDA)

Type: bimonthly digital and print magazine; circulation: 12,000; accepts ads

Audience: Christian entrepreneurs and farmers, people who are interested in economic development as a way to lessen poverty in the global South

Purpose: to explore the intersection of faith and business and show the impact of MEDA's efforts to create business solutions to poverty in the global South

Submissions: Query first by email attachment. Unsolicited freelance: 16%. Responds in a few days. To get an assignment, send a note explaining your relevant experience.

Types of manuscripts: inspirational, profiles

Length: 500–1,500 words

Topics: business

Rights: electronic, first, reprint (with info on where/when previously published)

Payment: 15–30¢/word, on publication

Seasonal submissions: six months

Preferred Bible versions: NRSV, NIV

Guidelines: *www.meda.org/the-marketplace/style-guide*

Sample: *www.meda.org/the-marketplace/issues*

Tip: "Read the guidelines and a few issues of the magazine before writing."

MATURE LIVING

200 Powell Pl., Ste. 100, Brentwood, TN 37027-7707 | 615-251-2000
matureliving@lifeway.com | www.lifeway.com/en/product-family/mature-living-magazine
Debbie Dickerson, managing editor

Denomination: Southern Baptist

Parent company: LifeWay Christian Resources

Type: monthly print magazine

Audience: ages 55 and older

Purpose: to equip mature adults as they live a legacy of leadership, stewardship, and discipleship

Submissions: Assignment only; not accepting unsolicited manuscripts or queries. Email for possible assignment.

Types of manuscripts: devotions, how-to, personal experience, puzzles, recipes, short stories, teaching

Topics: caregiving, evangelism, family, marriage, parenting, relationships, theology

Preferred Bible version: CSB

Guidelines: by email

Sample: on the website

Tip: Open for "Kicks and Grins," fun stories of your grandkids, 25–125 words; challenging, biblical, word-search puzzles; and crossword puzzles.

THE MESSENGER

440 Main St., Steinbach, MB R5G 1Z5, Canada | 204-326-6401
messenger@emconference.ca | *emcmessenger.ca*
Rebecca Roman, editor

Denomination: Mennonite

Parent company: Evangelical Mennonite Conference

Type: bimonthly digital and print magazine; circulation: 2,600

Audience: members and adherents of Evangelical Mennonite Conference churches

Purpose: to inform concerning events and activities in the denomination, instruct in godliness and victorious living, inspire to earnestly contend for the faith

Submissions: Assignment only; contact the editor for assignment requirements. Responds in one month.

Type of manuscripts: feature articles

Length: 2,000 words

Topics: wide variety

Rights: first

Payment: 15¢/word, on publication

Kill fee: sometimes

Manuscripts accepted per year: 18

Preferred Bible version: NIV

Guidelines: *emcmessenger.ca/submission-guidelines*

Sample: *www.emcmessenger.ca/current-issue*

Tip: "We don't accept unsolicited material."

THE MESSIANIC TIMES

50 Alberta Dr., Amhurst, NY 14226 | 866-612-7770
editor@messianictimes.com | *www.messianictimes.com*
Kayla Levy, editorial coordinator

Denomination: Messianic
Parent company: The Messianic Times, Inc.
Type: monthly digital and print newspaper; accepts ads
Audience: Messianic community and Christians interested in Jewish roots of their faith
Purpose: to provide accurate, authoritative, and current information to unite the international Messianic Jewish community, teach Christians the Jewish roots of their faith, and proclaim that Yeshua is the Jewish Messiah
Submissions: Only accepts emailed query letter.
Types of manuscripts: news, opinion, profiles, reviews, teaching
Sample: on the website
Tip: Looking for writers with some acquaintance with the Messianic movement.

MINISTRY

12501 Old Columbia Pike, Silver Spring, MD 20904 | 301-680-6518
ministrymagazine@gc.adventist.org | *www.ministrymagazine.org*
Jeffrey Brown, associate editor

Denomination: Seventh-day Adventist
Parent company: General Conference of Seventh-day Adventists
Type: monthly digital and print magazine; circulation: 18,000+
Audience: pastors, church leaders, church elders
Purpose: to deepen spiritual life, develop intellectual strength, and increase pastoral and evangelistic effectiveness of all ministers in the context of the three angels' messages of Revelation 14:6–12
Submissions: Only accepts complete manuscript emailed as attachment. Accepts simultaneous submissions.
Types of manuscripts: Bible studies, how-to, reviews, teaching
Length: articles, 1,500–2,000 words; reviews, 600 words maximum
Topics: family, issues, ministry, pastoral/preaching, relationships, theology
Rights: all
Payment: determined on amount of research done and other work needed to prepare manuscript, on acceptance
Preferred Bible version: any but easily understood by English-as-a-second-language readers
Guidelines: *www.ministrymagazine.org/about/article-submission*

Sample: articles are on the website

Tip: "Because *Ministry*'s readership includes individuals from all over the world, you will want to use words, illustrations, and concepts that will be understood by readers in various parts of the world. Avoid illustrations that are understood in one country but may be confusing in others."

THE MOTHER'S HEART

PO Box 275, Tobaccoville, NC 27050 | 336-775-8519
KymAWright@gmail.com | *www.the-mothers-heart.com*
Kym A. Wright, publisher and editor

Parent company: alWright! Publishing

Type: bimonthly digital magazine; circulation: 100,000; accepts ads

Audience: moms at home, homeschoolers, large families, homesteaders, DIYers

Purpose: to serve and encourage mothers in the many facets of staying at home and raising a family

Submissions: Submit only via email, either as attachment or in body of message. Accepts simultaneous submissions. Unsolicited freelance: 20%. Responds in two months.

Types of manuscripts: columns, fillers, how-to, personal experience, reviews

Length: 750–1,000 and 1,250–1,750 words

Topics: adoption story, Christian living/spirituality, DYI, family, fostering, gardening, homeschooling, hospitality, organization, parenting, special needs, time management

Rights: first

Payment: $10–75, on publication, or 1/8-page ad

Manuscripts accepted per year: 30

Seasonal submissions: six months in advance

Preferred Bible version: any

Guidelines: *tmhmag.com/Writers%20Guidelines%202023-2026.pdf*

Sample: *tmhmag.com/subscribe.htm*

Tip: "Break in with an adoption story, homeschool, gardening, parenting, DIY."

MUTUALITY

122 W. Franklin Ave., Ste. 610, Minneapolis, MN 55404 | 612-872-6898
mutuality@cbeinternational.org | *www.cbeinternational.org/primary_page/
mutuality-blogmagazine*
Carrie Silveira, editor

Parent company: Christians for Biblical Equality

Type: quarterly digital and print magazine +weekly blog; circulation: 400; hits: 40,000

Audience: laypeople, church leaders, and academics who are passionate about advancing women's equality in the home, church, and world

Purpose: to provide inspiration, encouragement, and information on topics related to a biblical view of mutuality between men and women in the home, church, and world

Submissions: Email complete manuscript or query letter as attachment. Responds in four weeks or longer.

Types of manuscripts: how-to, personal experience, reviews

Length: articles, 800–1,800 words; reviews, 500–800 words

Topics: theme-related

Rights: first

Payment: subscription

Preferred Bible version: NIV

Theme lists: available on website

Guidelines: *www.cbeinternational.org/primary_page/mutuality-writer-guidelines*

NOW WHAT?

PO Box 33677, Denver, CO 80233
nowwhat@cog7.org | nowwhat.cog7.org
Sherri Langton, associate editor

Denomination: Church of God (Seventh Day)

Type: monthly digital magazine

Audience: seekers

Purpose: to address the felt needs of the unchurched

Submissions: Email complete manuscript. Unsolicited freelance: 100%. Responds in four to ten weeks.

Type of manuscripts: personal experience

Length: 1,000–1,500 words

Topics: issues, salvation

Rights: electronic, first, reprint (with info on where/when previously published)

Payment: $25–65, on publication

Manuscripts accepted per year: 15–20

Preferred Bible version: NIV

Guidelines: *nowwhat.cog7.org/send-us-your-story*

Sample: on the website

Tip: "Avoid unnecessary jargon or technical terms. No Christmas or
Easter pieces or fiction. Think how you can explain your faith, or
how you overcame a problem, to a non-Christian. Use storytelling
techniques, like dialogue, scenes, etc., with the conflict clearly stated."

OUTREACH

5550 Tech Center, Colorado Springs, CO 80919 | 800-991-6011, x3208
tellus@outreachmagazine.com | *www.outreachmagazine.com*
James P. Long, editor

Type: bimonthly print magazine; circulation: 31,000

Audience: pastors and church leadership, as well as laypeople who are
passionate about outreach

Purpose: to further the Kingdom of God by empowering Christian
churches to reach their communities for Jesus Christ

Submissions: Email complete manuscript with clips and cover letter or
query letter with clips. Responds in eight weeks.

Types of manuscripts: how-to, profiles

Length: feature articles, 1,500–2,500 words; ideas, 300 words

Topics: church outreach, evangelism, ministry, small groups

Rights: first, reprint (with info on where/when previously published)

Payment: $700–1,000 for feature articles

Seasonal submissions: six months in advance

Guidelines: *www.outreachmagazine.com/magazine/3160-writers-
guidelines.html*

Sample: some articles are on the website

Tip: "While most articles are assigned, we do accept queries and
manuscripts on speculation. Please don't query us until you've
studied at least one issue of *Outreach*. If you're interested in writing
on assignment, submit a cover letter, published writing samples,
résumé, and a list of topics you specialize in or are interested in
covering. We keep these on file and do not respond to all writing
queries or return writing samples."

PARENTLIFE

200 Powell Pl., Ste. 100, Brentwood, TN 37027-7707 | 615-251-2196
parentlife@lifeway.com | *www.lifeway.com/en/product-family/parentlife-
magazine*
Nancy Cornwell, content editor

Denomination: Southern Baptist

Parent company: LifeWay Christian Resources

Type: monthly print magazine

Audience: parents of children from birth to preteen

Purpose: to encourage and equip parents with biblical solutions that will transform families

Submissions: Email complete manuscript or query letter. Responds in six to twelve months.

Types of manuscripts: devotions, how-to, sidebars, teaching

Length: 500–1,500 words

Topics: discipline, education, family, parenting, spiritual growth

Preferred Bible version: CSB

Guidelines: by email

Sample: order from the website

Tip: "Serves as a springboard for parents who may feel exasperated or overwhelmed with information by offering a biblical approach to raising healthy, productive children. Offers practical ideas and information for individual parents and couples."

POWER FOR LIVING

4050 Lee Vance Dr., Colorado Springs, CO 80918 | 719-536-0100
Powerforliving@davidccook.com | *davidccook.org*
Karen Scalf Bouchard, managing editor

Parent company: David C Cook

Type: weekly Sunday school take-home paper

Audience: general, ages 50 and older

Purpose: to connect God's truth to real life

Submissions: Email complete manuscript.

Types of manuscripts: columns, devotions, interviews, personal experience, poetry

Length: features, 1,200–1,500 words; poems, 20 lines or fewer; columns, 750 words; devotions, 400 words

Topics: Christian living, holidays

Rights: first, onetime, reprint

Payment: $375 for articles, $50 for poems, $150 for columns, $100 for devotions, on acceptance

Manuscripts accepted per year: feature articles, 20; poems, 6–12; columns, 5–8; devotions, rare

Seasonal submissions: 12–18 months in advance

Preferred Bible versions: NIV, KJV

Guidelines: *davidccook.org/wp-content/uploads/Power-for-Living-Writers-Guidelines.pdf*

Sample: buy from website

Tip: "Looking for inspiring stories and articles about famous and ordinary people whose experiences and insights show the power of Christ at work in their lives. We are often on the lookout for well-written seasonal pieces related to holidays and special days, including Christmas, Thanksgiving, Veteran's Day, Memorial Day, and Independence Day."

RELEVANT
See entry in "Teen/Young Adult Markets."

SHARING: A Journal of Christian Healing
1081 Woodward Ave., South Bend, IN 46616 | 877-992-5222
sharing@OSLToday.org | osltoday.org/sharing-magazine
Jamie Richard, editor
> **Parent company:** The International Order of St. Luke the Physician
> **Type:** bimonthly digital and print magazine; circulation: 3,500
> **Audience:** membership
> **Purpose:** to promote the healing of body, soul, and spirit
> **Submissions:** Email manuscript as attachment. Unsolicited freelance: 10%. Responds in two days.
> **Types of manuscripts:** how-to, poetry, short stories
> **Length:** 1,200–2,000 words
> **Topic:** healing
> **Rights:** first, reprint (with info on where/when previously published)
> **Payment:** none
> **Manuscripts accepted per year:** six
> **Theme lists:** by email
> **Guidelines:** by email
> **Sample:** email for a copy
> **Tip:** "Write on Christian healing or closely related topics. Being a current OSL member is desired but not required."

SOJOURNERS
400 C St. NE, Washington, DC 20002 | 202-328-8842
queries@sojo.net | sojo.net/magazine/current
Julie Polter, editor
news, news@sojo.net
reviews, reviews@sojo.net
poetry, poetry@sojo.net
> **Type:** bimonthly digital and print magazine; circulation: 19,000; accepts ads
> **Audience:** community influencers

Purpose: to inspire hope and action by articulating the biblical call to racial and social justice, life and peace, and environmental stewardship

Submissions: Email query letter in body of message. Responds in six weeks.

Types of manuscripts: feature articles, poetry, reviews

Length: articles, 1,800–2,000 words; poetry, 25 lines maximum

Topics: Christian living/spirituality, culture, faith, justice, politics

Rights: all

Payment: varies; poetry, $50, on publication

Guidelines: *sojo.net/magazine/write*

Sample: buy from website

SPORTS SPECTRUM

333 Inverness Dr. S, Ste. 110, Englewood, CO 80112 | 866-821-2971
jon@sportsspectrum.com | *sportsspectrum.com/magazine*
Jon Ackerman, managing editor

Parent company: Pro Athletes Outreach

Type: quarterly digital and print magazine; circulation: 4,000; accepts ads

Audience: sports fans

Purpose: to share stories of sports persons displaying an athletic lifestyle pleasing to God

Submissions: Email query letter with clips as attachment. Gives assignments. Accepts simultaneous submissions. Unsolicited freelance: 10%. Responds in one week.

Types of manuscripts: feature articles, interviews, profiles

Length: 1,500–2,000 words

Topic: sports

Rights: all

Payment: 15¢/word, on acceptance

Manuscripts accepted per year: two or three

Seasonal submissions: two to three months in advance

Preferred Bible version: NIV

Guidelines: not available

Sample: call the office

Tip: "Come with a story idea and plan for executing it."

ST. ANTHONY MESSENGER

28 W. Liberty St., Cincinnati, OH 45202-6498 | 513-241-5615
MagazineEditors@Franciscanmedia.org | *www.FranciscanMedia.org/ st-anthony-messenger*

Christopher Heffron, editorial director
Denomination: Catholic
Parent company: Franciscan Media
Type: monthly print magazine
Audience: family-oriented, majority are women ages 40–70
Purpose: to promote deeper faith, stronger family life, good citizenship, and greater economic justice—all in the spirit of St. Francis
Submissions: Email query letter, complete manuscript for fiction. Responds in eight weeks.
Types of manuscripts: profiles, short stories, teaching
Length: 2,000–2,500 words
Topics: church, education, family, issues, marriage, sacraments, spiritual growth
Rights: first
Payment: 25¢/published word, on acceptance
Manuscripts accepted per year: short stories, 12
Seasonal submissions: one year in advance
Preferred Bible version: NAB
Guidelines: *www.franciscanmedia.org/writers-guidelines*
Sample: articles are on website
Tip: "Our articles are popular and accessible in tone."

STANDARD

PO Box 843336, Kansas City, MO 4184-3336 | 816-931-1900
standard.foundry@gmail.com | *www.thefoundrypublishing.com/
  curriculum/adult.html*
Jeanette Gardner Littleton, editor
Denomination: Nazarene
Parent company: The Foundry Publishing
Type: weekly Sunday school take-home paper; circulation: 40,000
Audience: denomination
Purpose: to encourage and inspire our audience and to reinforce curriculum
Submissions: Only accepts email. Primarily assignment only; to get an assignment, send clips of personal-experience articles. Response time varies.
Type of manuscripts: personal experience
Length: 400 and 800–900 words
Topics: theme-related
Rights: all, first, reprint
Payment: $35 and $50. on acceptance

Manuscripts accepted per year: 104
Seasonal submissions: one year in advance
Preferred Bible version: NIV
Theme lists: available via email
Guidelines: by email
Sample: email request
Tip: "Writers should know basics of Wesleyan-Arminian theological perspective. Write to the theme list; please indicate which theme you're proposing it for. Nonfiction cannot be preachy. Put full contact information in the body of the manuscript, not only in the email. It helps to know if you're Nazarene or another Wesleyan/holiness denomination."

TEACHERS OF VISION

PO Box 981, Yorba Linda, CA 92885 | 888-798-1124
dmolnar@christianeducators.org | *christianeducators.org/tov*
Dawn Molnar, managing editor

Parent company: Christian Educators Association International
Type: triannual digital and print magazine; circulation: 20,000; accepts ads
Audience: Christian public-school educators
Purpose: to provide biblically principled resources that encourage, equip, and empower Christian educators
Submissions: Only accepts email as attachment. Unsolicited freelance: less than 10%. Responds in two weeks. Accepts submissions from children and teens. For writers we have a history with, we send out assignments via email.
Types of manuscripts: columns, devotions, how-to, personal experience, poetry, short stories, sidebars
Length: 500–2,000 words
Topics: discipleship, teaching
Rights: first, reprint
Payment: $150, on publication
Manuscripts accepted per year: 20
Seasonal submissions: five months in advance
Theme lists: available on website
Guidelines: *christianeducators.org/tov-write-for-us*
Sample: request by phone
Tip: "Most of our writers are current or retired teachers/educators. Many are high school English language arts teachers specifically, who have something to share about their experience of carrying Christ into their public school classrooms."

TESTIMONY/ENRICH

2450 Milltower Ct., Mississauga, ON L5N 5Z6, Canada | 905-542-7400
testimony@paoc.org | *testimony.paoc.org*
Stacey McKenzie, editor

Denomination: Pentecostal

Parent company: Pentecostal Assemblies of Canada

Type: quarterly digital and print magazine; circulation: 2,200

Audience: general and leaders

Purpose: to celebrate what God is doing in and through the Fellowship, while offering encouragement to believers by providing a window into the struggles that everyday Christians often encounter

Submissions: Only accepts emailed query letter. Responds in six to eight weeks.

Types of manuscripts: interviews, personal experience, sidebars

Length: 800–1,000 words

Topics: Christian living/spirituality, denomination, discipleship, leadership

Rights: first

Seasonal submissions: four months in advance

Preferred Bible version: NIV

Guidelines: *testimony.paoc.org/submit*

Tip: "Our readership is 98% Canadian. We prefer Canadian writers or at least writers who understand that Canadians are not Americans in long underwear. We also give preference to members of this denomination, since this is related to issues concerning our fellowship."

TIME OF SINGING: A Journal of Christian Poetry

PO Box 5276, Conneaut Lake, PA 16316 | 814-439-0914
timesing@zoominternet.net | *thebluecollarartist.com/time-of-singing*
Lora Zill, editor

Parent company: Wind & Water Press

Type: quarterly print journal; circulation: 200

Audience: those who love language and its expression through the art and craft of poetry

Purpose: to provide poets and readers a platform for thought-provoking and reflective work

Submissions: Only accepts emailed or mailed complete manuscript. Gives assignments for book reviews of *Time Of Singing* poets; inquire for an assignment. Unsolicited freelance: 95%. Responds in three months. Accepts submissions from teens.

Types of manuscripts: poetry, reviews

Length: 40 lines maximum

Rights: first, onetime, reprint (with info on where/when previously published)

Payment: none

Manuscripts accepted per year: 150

Seasonal submissions: six months in advance

Preferred Bible version: any

Guidelines: *www.thebluecollarartist.com/time-of-singing*

Sample: $5 each, including postage (checks, money orders payable to Wind & Water Press)

Tip: "I want poems that aren't afraid to take chances or think outside the theological box. Challenge my assumptions about faith, living the Christian life, and loving God. I prefer poems that don't try to provide answers but fearlessly wrestle with the questions. Trust your reader to 'get it.' It's really best to pick up a back issue to analyze to see what I like. I don't publish greeting-card style poetry or sermons that rhyme. I love fresh rhyme, free verse, and beg for forms."

TODAY'S CHRISTIAN LIVING

PO Box 5000, Iola, WI 54945 | 715-445-5000
michellea@jpmediallc.com | *www.todayschristianliving.org*
Michelle Adserias, editor

Parent company: JP Media LLC

Type: bimonthly digital and print magazine; circulation: 12,000; accepts ads

Audience: general, ages 45 and older

Purpose: to engage, equip, and encourage readers through inspirational true stories

Submissions: Email complete manuscript attached as a Word document. Accepts simultaneous submissions. Unsolicited freelance: 25%. Responds in two months. No teaching articles, essays, poetry, or devotions.

Types of manuscripts: humor, ministry spotlights, personal experience, profiles, testimonies

Length: 700–1,500 words

Topics: Christian living/spirituality, humor

Rights: all

Payment: $75–150, $25 for short humorous anecdotes, 45 days after publication

Kill fee: yes

Manuscripts accepted per year: 24

Seasonal submissions: six months in advance

Preferred Bible version: none
Guidelines: *todayschristianliving.org/writers-guidelines*
Sample: *todayschristianliving.org/free-digital-issue-with-newsletter-signup*
Tip: "Turning Point and Grace Notes columns are good starting points. No particular topics."

U.S. CATHOLIC
205 W. Monroe St., 9th floor, Chicago, IL 60606 | 312-544-8169
submissions@uscatholic.org | *www.uscatholic.org*
Emily Sanna, managing editor
    Denomination: Catholic
    Parent company: Claretian Missionaries
    Type: monthly digital and print magazine
    Audience: denomination
    Purpose: to explore the wisdom of the Catholic faith tradition and apply that faith to the challenges of 21st-century life
    Submissions: Email complete manuscript or query letter. Responds in six to eight weeks.
    Types of manuscripts: essays, feature articles, opinion, poetry, profiles
    Length: feature articles, 2,500–3,500 words; essays, 800–1,600 words; opinion, 1,400 words; reviews, 315 words; poetry, 10–30 lines
    Topics: denomination
    Rights: first
    Payment: $75–500
    Seasonal submissions: six months in advance
    Guidelines: *uscatholic.org/writers-guide*
    Tip: "*U.S. Catholic* does not consider submissions that have simultaneously been sent to any other publication or that have appeared elsewhere in any form, either in print or online. This includes articles published on personal blogs or excerpts from books, published or unpublished."

THE WAR CRY
615 Slaters Ln., Alexandria, VA 22314 | 703-684-5500
www.thewarcry.org
Lt. Colonel Lesa Davis, editor-in-chief
    Denomination: The Salvation Army
    Parent company: The Salvation Army in the United States
    Type: monthly digital and print magazine; circulation: 185,000; accepts ads
    Audience: denomination and general public

Purpose: to communicate the Christian gospel, to bring people to experience Jesus Christ as Savior, and inspire them by His example

Submissions: Only accepts submissions through the website. Accepts simultaneous submissions. Unsolicited freelance: 50%. Responds in three to four weeks.

Types of manuscripts: personal experience, profiles

Length: articles, 800–1,250 words; news items and sidebars, 100–400 words

Topics: Christian living/spirituality, culture, discipleship, evangelism, issues, The Salvation Army, trends

Rights: first, reprint

Payment: 35¢/word, 15¢/word for reprints; on acceptance

Kill fee: sometimes

Manuscripts accepted per year: 40

Seasonal submissions: six months in advance

Preferred Bible version: NLT

Theme lists: available on website

Guidelines: *www.thewarcry.org/submission-guidelines*

Sample: on the website

Tip: "Some association/connection/explication of The Salvation Army is helpful when possible."

8

TEEN/YOUNG ADULT MARKETS

BOUNDLESS

8605 Explorer Dr., Colorado Springs, CO 80920 | 719-531-3400

editor@boundless.org | www.boundless.org

Lisa Anderson, director

Bry Shirin, digital content specialist

Parent company: Focus on the Family

Type: website; monthly hits: 300,000

Audience: single young adults in 20s and 30s

Purpose: to help Christian young adults grow up, own their faith, date with purpose, and prepare for marriage and family

Submissions: Only accepts query letter with clips. Responds only if interested.

Types of manuscripts: articles, blog posts

Length: articles, about 1,200 words, occasionally up to 2,000 words; blog posts, 500–800 words

Topics: adulthood, Christian living/spirituality, dating, marriage, relationships

Rights: all

Preferred Bible version: ESV

Guidelines: *www.boundless.org/write-for-us*

Sample: website

Tip: "We don't typically publish unsolicited articles, but we are always open to considering new writers. If you think you've got what it takes to have your work published on *Boundless,* please feel free to send us a sample or two of your writing, a link to your blog, and a proposal of what you're interested in writing about."

THE BRINK

114 Bush Rd., Nashville, TN 37217 | 800-877-7030

david.jones@d6family.com | *store.randallhouse.com/product/brink-devotional-study-guide-so*

David Jones, senior editor

Denomination: Free Will Baptist
Parent company: D6 Family Ministry
Type: bimonthly print magazine
Audience: young adults
Purpose: to help young adults in the church to belong, grow, and serve
Submissions: Only accepts email as attachment. Unsolicited freelance: 10%. Responds in one week.
Types of manuscripts: interviews, narrative, personal experience, devotions
Length: 500–1,500
Topics: Christian life, church, politics, relationships, theology, young-adult life
Rights: all
Payment: $50-150, on acceptance
Manuscripts accepted per year: 24
Seasonal submissions: six months in advance
Preferred Bible version: ESV
Guidelines: by email
Sample: buy from website
Tip: "The more specific the topic the better." Devotions are written on assignment only; email editor to get an assignment.

BRIO

8605 Explorer Dr., Colorado Springs, CO 80920 | 719-531-3400

FocusMagSubmissions@family.org | *www.focusonthefamily.com/parenting/brio-magazine-2*

Laura Pottkotter, managing editor

Parent company: Focus on the Family
Type: bimonthly print magazine; circulation: 47,000
Audience: teen girls
Purpose: to provide inspiring stories, fashion insights, fun profiles, and practical tips, all from a biblical worldview
Submissions: Email as attachment or mail complete manuscript.
Types of manuscripts: articles, devotions, profiles, short stories
Length: profiles, 1,200–1,400 words; character traits, 650–750 words; entertainment/social media, 800–900 words; prayer, 200–300 words;

relationships, 800–900 words; fiction, 1,200–1,300 words
Topics: beauty, culture, entertainment, fashion, health, prayer, relationships, seasonal, social media
Rights: first
Payment: minimum 30¢ per word, on acceptance
Guidelines: *www.focusonthefamily.com/magazine/call-for-submissions*
Sample: on the website

CADET QUEST

See entry in "Children's Markets."

CAFÉ

8765 W. Higgins Rd., Chicago, IL 60631 | 800-638-3522
cafe@elca.org | *www.boldcafe.org*
Elizabeth McBride, editor

Denomination: Evangelical Lutheran Church in America
Parent company: Women of the Evangelical Lutheran Church in America
Type: monthly website
Audience: women ages 18–35+
Purpose: to share stories written by bold, young women who write about faith, relationships, advocacy, and more
Submissions: Email query letter with clips. Accepts simultaneous submissions. Responds only if interested.
Type of manuscripts: personal experience
Length: 700–1,000 words
Topics: theme-related
Rights: first, onetime, reprint (with info on where/when previously published)
Payment: $20 per 100 published words, excluding biblical text
Seasonal submissions: seven months in advance
Preferred Bible version: NRSV
Guidelines: *www.boldcafe.org/add-voice-boldcafe*
Sample: see the website
Tip: "We ask particular established authors to write on specific themes far in advance of publication. We publish very few articles that originated as unsolicited manuscripts or queries. Those we do accept are most likely to be accepted from Christian women (though we accept queries from men) that include stories about women or reflections that especially speak to young adult women."

CREATION ILLUSTRATED

See entry in "Adult Markets."

FORWARD

114 Bush Rd., Nashville, TN 37217 | 800-877-7030

katie.greenwood@d6family.com | *store.randallhouse.com/product/forward-devotional-study-guide-so*

Katie Greenwood, curriculum director

Denomination: Free Will Baptist
Parent company: D6 Family Ministry
Type: bimonthly print magazine; circulation: 2,000
Audience: teens
Purpose: to help teens study Scripture on their own and provide them with biblical resources
Submissions: Only accepts email as attachment. Unsolicited freelance: 15%. Responds in one or two days.
Types of manuscripts: columns, devotions, how-to, interviews, personal experience, poetry, reviews, short stories
Length: 500–1,200
Topics: Christian life, college prep, dating, decision-making, emotions, peer pressure
Rights: all
Payment: $50–120, on acceptance
Manuscripts accepted per year: 30+
Seasonal submissions: four to six months in advance
Preferred Bible version: ESV, KJV
Guidelines: by email
Sample: email *david.womack@d6family.com*
Tip: Devotions are by assignment only; email editor for assignments. Especially looking for fiction and interviews.

GUIDE

See entry in "Children's Markets."

IGNITED BY THE WORD

See entry in "Children's Markets."

INSPIRE A FIRE

See entry in "Adult Markets."

NATURE FRIEND
See entry in "Children's Markets."

PEER
615 Sisters Ln., Alexandria, VA 22314 | 703-684-5500
peer@usn.salvationarmy.org | *peermag.org*
Lt. Colonel Lesa Davis, editor-in-chief
   Denomination: The Salvation Army
   Parent company: The Salvation Army in the United States
   Type: monthly print and digital magazine; circulation: print 30,000, digital 34,000; accepts advertising
   Audience: ages 16–22
   Purpose: to ignite a faith conversation that will deepen biblical perspective, faith, and holy living by addressing topics related to faith, community, and culture
   Submissions: Submit complete manuscript or query through the website. Responds in one week. Accepts submissions from teens.
   Types of manuscripts: articles, profiles, testimonies
   Length: 300–800 words
   Topics: Christian living/spirituality, culture, current events
   Rights: first, onetime
   Payment: 35¢/word, 15¢/word for reprints
   Preferred Bible version: NLT
   Guidelines: *peermag.org/contribute*
   Tip: "We are *always* welcoming new submissions from young writers. Do you love to write? Do you consider yourself an expert on a topic that would interest 16- to 22-year-olds? *Peer* is a national publication, and you can most certainly add the experience of writing for us on your résumé!"

REJOICE!
See entry in "Devotional Booklets and Websites."

RELEVANT
55 W. Church St., Ste. 211, Orlando, FL 32801 | 407-660-1411
submissions@relevantmediagroup.com | *relevantmagazine.com*
Emily Brown, managing editor
   Type: bimonthly digital magazine plus annual print
   Audience: ages 20s and 30s
   Purpose: to challenge people to go further in their spiritual journeys;

live selflessly and intentionally; care about positively impacting the world around them; and find the unexpected places God is speaking in life, music, and culture

Submissions: Email complete manuscript or query letter as attachment. Responds in one to two weeks or not interested.

Types of manuscripts: interviews, opinion, teaching

Length: 750–1,000 words

Topics: Christian living/spirituality, culture, faith, justice

Payment: none

Guidelines: *relevantmagazine.com/write*

Sample: on the website

TAKE 5 PLUS

See entry in "Devotional Booklets and Websites."

UNLOCKED

See entry in "Devotional Booklets and Websites."

VELOCITY

114 Bush Rd., Nashville, TN 37217 | 800-877-7030

kathy.murphy@d6family.com | *store.randallhouse.com/product/velocity-devotional-study-guide-so*

Kathy Murphy, editor

Denomination: Free Will Baptist

Parent company: D6 Family Ministry

Type: bimonthly print magazine

Audience: middle schoolers

Purpose: to strengthen the faith of middle schoolers with devotions, relatable articles, practical columns, and fun pages

Submissions: Email as Word document attachment only. Unsolicited freelance: 10%. Responds in one week.

Types of manuscripts: articles, columns, poetry, short stories, devotions

Length: 500–1,200

Topics: bullying, middle-school life, social issues, spiritual disciplines

Rights: all, electronic, first, onetime, reprint (with info on where/when previously published)

Payment: 500 words, $50; 1,200 words, $120

Manuscripts accepted per year: 54

Seasonal submissions: four to six months in advance

Preferred Bible version: ESV

Guidelines: by email
Sample: email *david.womack@d6family.com*
Tip: Devotions are by assignment only; email editor for assignments.

YOUTH COMPASS

PO Box 4060, Overland Park, KS 66204 | 913-432-0331
sseditor@heraldandbanner.com | *heraldandbanner.com/product/*
  youth-compass
Arlene McGehee, Sunday school editor

Denomination: Church of God
Parent company: Herald and Banner Press
Type: weekly Sunday school take-home paper
Audience: grades 7–12
Purpose: to apply Christian principles on junior high and high school level
Submissions: Email or mail manuscript. Responds in nine months.
Types of manuscripts: biography, short stories
Length: 800–1,500 words
Topic: Christian living
Rights: first, reprint (with info on where/when previously published)
Payment: .005¢/word, .0025¢/word for reprints, on publication
Manuscripts accepted per year: varies
Seasonal submissions: six months in advance
Preferred Bible version: KJV
Guidelines: by email
Sample: 9"x12" SASE with $3.50 postage
Tip: Looking for seasonal stories.

9

CHILDREN'S MARKETS

BEGINNER'S FRIEND

PO Box 4060, Overland Park, KS 66204 | 913-432-0331
sseditor@heraldandbanner.com | *heraldandbanner.com/product/
beginners-friend*
Arlene McGehee, Sunday school editor

Denomination: Church of God
Parent company: Herald and Banner Press
Type: weekly Sunday school take-home paper; circulation: 575
Audience: ages 2–5
Purpose: to apply biblical truths to daily life in an understandable way
Submissions: Email or mail manuscript. Unsolicited freelance:
33%. Responds in one year.
Type of manuscripts: short stories
Length: 500–800 words
Topic: Christian life
Rights: first, reprint (with info on where/when previously published)
Payment: .005¢/word, .0025¢/word for reprints, on publication
Manuscripts accepted per year: 10
Seasonal submissions: six months in advance
Preferred Bible version: KJV
Guidelines: by email
Sample: 9"x12" SASE with $3.50 postage
Tip: Needs seasonal manuscripts most.

CADET QUEST

4695 44th St. SE, Ste. B-130, Kentwood, MI 49512 | 616-241-5616
submissions@CalvinistCadets.org | *www.calvinistcadets.org/cadet-quest-magazine*
Steve Bootsma, executive editor

Parent company: Dynamic Youth Ministries
Type: monthly October–April print magazine; circulation: 5,800

Audience: boys ages 9–14

Purpose: to help boys grow more Christlike in all areas of life

Submissions: Email or mail complete manuscript. Unsolicited freelance: 25%. Responds when an issue is ready. Accepts submissions from children and teens.

Types of manuscripts: how-to, profiles, short stories

Length: 700–1,500 words

Topics: Christian athletes, Christian character, nature, sports, theme-related

Rights: first, reprint (with info on where/when previously published)

Payment: 10¢/word for first rights, less for reprints, on publication

Manuscripts accepted per year: 15–20

Seasonal submissions: four months in advance

Preferred Bible version: NIV

Theme lists: available on website

Guidelines: download from *www.calvinistcadets.org/cadet-quest-magazine*

Sample: email the submissions address

Tip: "Looking for short-story fiction, nonfiction that is theme related, and nothing that sounds too preachy or cliché."

CREATION ILLUSTRATED

See entry in "Adult Markets."

DEVOKIDS

377 Woodcrest Dr., Kingsport, TN 37663 | 423-384-4821

WritersCoach.us@gmail.com | *devokids.com*

Eddie Jones, acquisitions editor

Parent company: Christian Devotions Ministries

Type: weekly website; circulation: 2,230

Audience: ages 4–8

Purpose: to help guide young hearts in discovering God's goodness and love through exciting, age-appropriate content

Submissions: Only accepts email as attachment. Unsolicited freelance: 75%. Responds in one week.

Types of manuscripts: activities, coloring pages, crafts, devotions, games, how-to, poetry, profiles, puzzles, recipes, short stories

Length: 75–250 words

Topics: adventure, animals, creation, finances, nature

Rights: exclusive distribution for three months

Payment: none

Manuscripts accepted per year: 60
Seasonal submissions: two months in advance
Guidelines: *devokids.com/write-for-us*
Tip: "Think like a child. Act like a child. Write to appeal to a child. Jesus connected with kids. We can too."

EXPLORERS

PO Box 4060, Overland Park, KS 66204 | 913-432-0331
sseditor@heraldandbanner.com | *heraldandbanner.com/product/explorers*
Arlene McGehee, Sunday school editor

Denomination: Church of God
Parent company: Herald and Banner Press
Type: weekly Sunday school take-home paper
Audience: grades 1–6
Purpose: to apply Christian principles to elementary students
Submissions: Email or mail manuscript. Responds in nine months.
Types of manuscripts: biography, puzzles, short stories
Length: 500–1,500 words
Rights: first, reprint (with info on where/when previously published)
Payment: .005¢/word, .0025¢/word for reprints, on publication
Manuscripts accepted per year: varies
Seasonal submissions: six months in advance
Preferred Bible version: KJV
Guidelines: by email
Sample: 9"x12" SASE with $3.50 postage
Tip: Looking for seasonal stories. Accepts serial stories.

FOCUS ON THE FAMILY CLUBHOUSE

8605 Explorer Dr., Colorado Springs, CO 80920 | 719-531-3400
focusonthefamily.com/clubhouse-magazine
Rachel Peiffer, editor

Parent company: Focus on the Family
Type: monthly print magazine; circulation: 90,000
Audience: ages 8–12
Purpose: to inspire, entertain, and teach Christian values to children
Submissions: Only accepts complete manuscript by mail. Unsolicited freelance: 15%. Responds in three months. Accepts submissions from children and teens.
Types of manuscripts: activities, articles, crafts, devotions, how-to, interviews, personality features of kids, quizzes, recipes, short stories

Length: fiction, 1,800–2,000 words; nonfiction, 400–500 or 800–1,000 words

Topics: apologetics, archaeology, Christian life

Rights: first

Payment: 15–25¢ per word, on acceptance

Kill fee for assigned manuscripts: sometimes

Manuscripts accepted per year: 80

Seasonal submissions: eight months in advance

Preferred Bible version: CSB

Guidelines: *focusonthefamily.com/clubhouse-magazine/about/submission-guidelines*

Sample: $4.99 at *store.focusonthefamily.com/clubhouse-magazine-single-issue*

Tip: "We are always looking for unique and interesting nonfiction stories and articles, especially stories about real-life kids. Every article should have a Christian angle, though it shouldn't be overbearing. The concepts and vocabulary should be appropriate for our audience's ages."

FOCUS ON THE FAMILY CLUBHOUSE JR.

8605 Explorer Dr., Colorado Springs, CO 80920 | 719-531-3400

focusonthefamily.com/clubhouse-jr-magazine

Grace Kelley, associate editor

Parent company: Focus on the Family

Type: monthly print magazine; circulation: 50,000

Audience: ages 3–7

Purpose: to inspire, entertain, and teach Christian values to children

Submissions: Only accepts complete manuscript by mail. Unsolicited freelance: 15%. Responds in three months. Accepts submissions from children and teens.

Types of manuscripts: activities, Bible stories retold, crafts, poetry, rebus stories, recipes, short stories

Length: fiction, 800–1,000 words; rebus stories, 200 words; nonfiction, 250–400 words

Topics: animals, Bible stories, Christian life, nature, science

Rights: first

Payment: 15–25¢ per word, on acceptance

Manuscripts accepted per year: 50

Seasonal submissions: eight months in advance

Preferred Bible version: NIrV

Guidelines: *www.focusonthefamily.com/clubhouse-jr-magazine/about/*

submission-guidelines

Sample: $4.99 at *store.focusonthefamily.com/clubhouse-jr-magazine-single-issue*

Tip: "Read the magazine to learn our style and reading level. Aim at early and beginning readers. Rebus and Bible stories are a great way to break in."

GUIDE

PO Box 5353, Nampa, ID 83653-5353

guide.magazine@pacificpress.com | *www.guidemagazine.org*

Randy Fishell, editor

Denomination: Seventh-day Adventist

Parent company: Pacific Press Publishing Association

Type: weekly Sunday school take-home paper; circulation: 26,000

Audience: ages 10–14

Purpose: to show readers, through stories that illustrate Bible truth, how to walk with God now and forever

Submissions: Mail complete manuscript, or query via email or through the website. Unsolicited freelance: 75%; 20% assigned. Responds in four to six weeks. Accepts submissions from teens.

Types of manuscripts: biography, humor, personal experience, profiles, quizzes

Length: 450–850 words

Topics: adventure, Christian living/spirituality, missions, nature

Rights: first, reprint (with info on where/when previously published)

Payment: 7–10¢ per word, $25–40 for games and puzzles, on acceptance

Seasonal submissions: eight months in advance

Preferred Bible version: NKJV

Guidelines: *www.guidemagazine.org/writers-guidelines*

Tip: "Use your best short-story techniques (dialogue, scenes, a sense of plot) to tell a true story starring a kid ages 10–14. Bring out a clear spiritual/biblical message. We publish multipart true stories regularly, two to twelve parts. All topics indicated need to be addressed within the context of a true story."

IGNITED BY THE WORD

1894 Georgetown Center Dr., Jenison, MI 49428 | 616-457-5970

ignitedbytheword.org

David Harbach, editor-in-chief

Denomination: Reformed
Parent company: Reformed Free Publishing Association
Type: four to six times/year print magazine; circulation: 800
Audience: ages 4–14
Purpose: to ignite the spark within every young believer and to glorify God by publishing stories, activities, and artwork for and by young saints
Submissions: Only accepts manuscripts through the website. Unsolicited freelance: 10%. Responds in one month. Accepts submissions from children and teens.
Types of manuscripts: activities, biography, crafts, fillers, personal experience, poetry, reviews, short stories
Length: 500 words
Topics: Bible stories, Christian life, church history, devotional
Rights: all
Payment: none
Seasonal submissions: three months in advance
Preferred Bible version: AKJV
Guidelines: by email
Tip: "We welcome article submissions and artwork from all ages. Regarding in-depth doctrine, our staff subscribes to the Three Forms of Unity (Heidelberg Catechism, Canons of Dort, Belgic Confession)."

KEYS FOR KIDS DEVOTIONAL

See entry in "Devotional Booklets and Websites."

LIVING FAITH KIDS

See entry in "Devotional Booklets and Websites."

NATURE FRIEND

4253 Woodcock Ln., Dayton, VA 22821 | 540-867-0764
editor@naturefriendmagazine.com | *www.naturefriendmagazine.com*
Kevin Shank, editor

Parent company: Dogwood Ridge Outdoors
Type: monthly print magazine; circulation: 10,000
Audience: ages 6–14, 80% are ages 8–12
Purpose: to increase awareness of God and appreciation for God's works and gifts, to teach accountability toward God's works, and to teach natural truths and facts

Submissions: Only accepts complete manuscript by email attachment. Accepts simultaneous submissions. Unsolicited freelance: 55%. Accepts submissions from children and teens.

Types of manuscripts: articles, crafts, experiments, photo features, profiles, projects, short stories

Length: 500–1,000 words

Topics: animals, astronomy, first aid, flowers, gardening, marine life, nature, photography, science, weather

Rights: all, first, reprint

Payment: all rights, 10¢/edited word; first rights, 8¢/edited word; reprints, 5¢/edited word; on publication

Manuscripts accepted per year: 40–50

Seasonal submissions: four months in advance

Preferred Bible version: KJV only

Guidelines: *naturefriendmagazine.com/contributors/writers-guide-for-freelance-writers*

Sample: *naturefriendmagazine.com/sample-issues*

Tip: "While talking animals can be interesting and teach worthwhile lessons, we have chosen to not use them in *Nature Friend*. Excluded are puzzle-type submissions, such as 'Who Am I?'"

OUR LITTLE FRIEND

PO Box 5353, Nampa, ID 83653

janelle.sundin@pacificpress.com | *primarytreasure.com*

Janelle Sundin, managing editor

Denomination: Seventh-day Adventist

Parent company: Pacific Press Publishing Association

Type: weekly Sunday school take-home paper; circulation: 16,000

Audience: ages 1–5

Purpose: to teach about Jesus and the Christian life

Submissions: Only accepts complete manuscript by email attachment. Responds in one month.

Type of manuscripts: true stories

Length: one to two double-spaced pages

Topics: Christian living, God's love, holidays, nature

Rights: electronic, onetime

Payment: $25–50, on acceptance

Manuscripts accepted per year: 52

Seasonal submissions: eight to nine months in advance

Preferred Bible versions: ICB, NIrV

Theme lists: available via mail with SASE

Guidelines: *www.primarytreasure.com/for-writers*

Tip: "Stories that are humorous, yet teach a spiritual lesson, rate high in this office because they rate high with kids."

PRIMARY TREASURE

PO Box 5353, Nampa, ID 83653

janelle.sundin@pacificpress.com | *www.primarytreasure.com*

Janelle Sundin, managing editor

Denomination: Seventh-day Adventist

Parent company: Pacific Press Publishing Association

Type: weekly Sunday school take-home paper; circulation: 14,000

Audience: ages 6–9

Purpose: to teach children about the love of God and the Christian life through true stories

Submissions: Only accepts complete manuscript emailed as attachment. Unsolicited freelance: 80%. Responds in one month.

Type of manuscripts: true stories

Length: four to five double-spaced pages

Topics: Christian living, holidays, nature

Rights: electronic, onetime

Payment: $25–50, on acceptance

Manuscripts accepted per year: 104

Seasonal submissions: eight months in advance

Theme lists: available via mail with SASE

Guidelines: *www.primarytreasure.com/for-writers*

Tip: "We look for stories that avoid stereotypical roles for men and women. More than half of today's mothers work outside the home. Stories should reflect that some of the time. A more traditional lifestyle setting is OK too. We also want more stories with Dad as the adult character. We get plenty with Mom."

STARLIGHT MAGAZINE

704 W. Madison St., La Grange, KY 40031 | 704-578-0858

editor@starlightmagazine.com | *www.starlightmagazine.com*

Jean Hall, editor

Type: eight times/year digital magazine; circulation: 450

Audience: ages 5–10

Purpose: to shine God's truth through children's literature

Submissions: Only accepts complete manuscript emailed as attachment. Unsolicited freelance: 90%. Responds in two weeks.

Types of manuscripts: Bible stories retold, biography, devotions, fillers, poetry, puzzles, quizzes, short stories, sidebars, trivia

Length: ages 5–7, 500 words; ages 8–10, 1,000 words

Topics: animals, Bible stories, Christian living, Christmas, creation, Easter, heavenly bodies, love of reading, nature, school, science

Rights: electronic, reprint (with info on where/when previously published)

Payment: none

Manuscripts accepted per year: 100

Seasonal submissions: three months in advance

Preferred Bible versions: NIV, NLT

Theme lists: available on website

Guidelines: *starlightmagazine.com/starlight-magazine-writers-guidelines*

Sample: on the website

Tip: "We especially need contemporary fiction related to daily life for children." To get an assignment, email the editor.

10

WRITERS MARKETS

ALMOST AN AUTHOR

editor@almostanauthor.com | www.almostanauthor.com
Norma Poore, editor

> **Parent company:** Serious Writer
> **Type:** daily website; circulation: 1,000·
> **Audience:** aspiring writers
> **Purpose:** to help writers learn craft, launch career, and build platform
> **Submissions:** Email query with clips first; no attachments. Unsolicited freelance: 20%. Responds in one to two days.
> **Types of manuscripts:** columns, how-to, inspirational, personal experience
> **Length:** 400–900 words
> **Topics:** business, encouragement, marketing, writing
> **Rights:** onetime
> **Payment:** none
> **Manuscripts accepted per year:** 120 guest articles and 240 columns
> **Seasonal submissions:** 30 days in advance
> **Preferred Bible version:** any
> **Guidelines:** *www.almostanauthor.com/submissions-3*
> **Sample:** website
> **Tip:** "We accept guest posts on a wide variety of writing topics. Please review our site and our submission guidelines before sending your proposed article. We will consider guest-post queries based on how well it fits our mission and on our current editorial needs."

INK & QUILL QUARTERLY

1053 E. 1400 N, Milford, IN 46542 | 574-658-3960
wishesandjoy@gmail.com
Amy Schlabach, prose editor
Arielle C. Walters, poetry

> **Type:** quarterly print magazine; circulation: 400; advertising accepted

Audience: primarily Anabaptist poets and writers
Purpose: to give inspiration to beginning and experienced writers alike
Submissions: Email complete manuscript as attachment, or mail it. Cover letter required. Unsolicited freelance: 10%. Responds in one month.
Types of manuscripts: articles, poetry, writing exercises
Length: 600–800 words
Topics: literature appreciation, writing
Rights: first, reprint (with info on where/when previously published)
Payment: articles, $30; poetry, 50¢/line; on acceptance
Manuscripts accepted per year: 80
Seasonal submissions: three months in advance
Preferred Bible version: KJV
Guidelines: by email or mail with SASE
Sample: write or email *mjhofstetter@hotmail.com* and request a sample copy; back issues are $5 each
Tip: "We put a special emphasis on poetry, especially traditional verse forms with rhyme and meter. We currently need high-quality poetry of all kinds (nature, Christian living, devotional, personal, narrative, and the kinds of poems poets write for fun.)"

POETS & WRITERS MAGAZINE

90 Broad St., Ste. 2100, New York, NY 10004-2272 | 212-226-3586
editor@pw.org | *www.pw.org*
Emma Komlos-Hrobsky, senior editor

Parent company: Poets & Writers, Inc.
Type: bimonthly print magazine; circulation: 65,000; advertising accepted
Audience: writers of poetry, fiction, and creative nonfiction
Purpose: to provide practical guidance for getting published and pursuing writing careers
Submissions: Only accepts query letter with clips by email or mail. Responds in four to six weeks.
Types of manuscripts: essays, how-to, interviews, news, profiles
Length: 500–3,000 words
Topic: writing
Rights: all
Payment: $150–500, when scheduled for production
Seasonal submissions: four months in advance
Guidelines: *www.pw.org/about-us/submission_guidelines*
Sample: sold at large bookstores and online
Tip: Most open to "News & Trends," "The Literary Life," and "The Practical Writer."

WORDS FOR THE WAY

5042 E. Cherry Hills Blvd., Springfield, MO 65809 | 417-832-8409

ozarksACW@yahoo.com | www.ozarksacw.org

Jeanetta Chrystie, managing editor

Parent company: Ozarks Chapter of American Christian Writers

Type: monthly/digital newsletter; circulation: 95; advertising accepted

Audience: writers at all levels

Purpose: to encourage and educate Christians to follow their call to write and learn to write well

Submissions: Submit complete manuscript or query letter by email only. Unsolicited freelance: 95%. Responds in three weeks. Accepts submissions from teens.

Types of manuscripts: columns, fillers, how-to, personal experience, poetry, reviews, sidebars

Length: features, 600–900 words; general writing how-to, 400–600 words; sidebars, 200–400 words; reviews, 200–400 words; devotions, 250–500 words; poetry, 12–40 lines

Topic: writing

Rights: electronic, first, onetime, reprint (with info on where/when previously published)

Payment: none

Manuscripts accepted per year: 45

Seasonal submissions: two months in advance

Preferred Bible version: any

Guidelines: *www.OzarksACW.org/guidelines.php*

Sample: request by email

Tip: "We want content that speaks to our Christian writers by teaching and encouraging them. Specific current needs: how to write in a specific genre (your choice), how to grow spiritually through writing, how to organize a book, how to handle taxes as a freelancer. Also, we need devotions for the website that encourage, inspire, and teach (not preach) Christians to follow their calling to write." Advertising is usually free.

WRITER'S DIGEST

PO Box 42534, Cincinnati, OH 45242

rbrower@aimmedia.com | www.writersdigest.com

Robert Lee Brower, senior editor

Parent company: Active Interest Media

Type: bimonthly print and digital magazine; circulation: 40,000;

advertising accepted

Audience: aspiring and professional writers

Purpose: to celebrate the writing life and what it means to be a writer in today's publishing environment

Submissions: Email complete manuscript as attachment, or query through the website. Responds in two to four months.

Types of manuscripts: essays, how-to, humor, profiles, sidebars

Length: feature articles, 1,600–2,500 words; columns, 1,200–1,500 words

Topic: writing

Rights: electronic, first

Payment: 50¢ per word, on acceptance

Kill fee for assigned manuscripts: 25%

Seasonal submissions: eight months in advance

Theme lists: available on website

Guidelines: *www.writersdigest.com/resources/submission-guidelines*

Sample: available at newsstands and through *www.writersdigestshop.com*

Tip: "Although we welcome the work of new writers, we believe the established writer can better instruct our readers. Please include your publishing credentials related to your topic with your submission."

WRITERSWEEKLY.COM

12441 N. Main St. #38, Trenton, GA 30752 | 305-768-0261

brian@writersweekly.com | *writersweekly.com*

Brian Whiddon, managing editor

Parent company: BookLocker.com

Type: weekly digital newsletter; circulation: 23,000

Audience: professional freelance writers

Purpose: to help professional writers find new markets and ways to increase their freelance income

Submissions: Only accepts query letter through the website. Unsolicited freelance: 20%. Responds in one week.

Types of manuscripts: feature articles, how-to

Length: 600 words

Topics: marketing, writing

Rights: first, reprint

Payment: first rights, $60; reprints, $30; on acceptance

Manuscripts accepted per year: 100

Guidelines: *writersweekly.com/writersweekly-com-writers-guidelines*

Sample: on the website

Tip: "Understand that we are not a publication about writing but earning income through writing. Proofread your query letter; spelling, capitalization, and punctuation errors leap out at us and tell us what we can expect from you as a writer. *Sell* us your idea; don't just say, 'I want to write about . . . .'"

WRITING CORNER

contests@writingcorner.com | writingcorner.com

Type: website

Audience: writers at all levels

Purpose: to provide concrete, useful advice from those who have been in the trenches and made a successful journey with their writing

Submissions: Email complete manuscript or query letter. Responds in two days.

Types of manuscripts: how-to

Length: 600–900 words

Topic: writing

Rights: onetime, reprint

Payment: none

Guidelines: *writingcorner.com/submission-guidelines*

Sample: website

Tip: "Our site visitors are from all areas of writing, so keep that audience in mind when writing for us."

PART 4

SPECIALTY MARKETS

11

DEVOTIONAL BOOKLETS AND **WEBSITES**

Many of these markets assign all manuscripts. If there is no information listed on getting an assignment, request a sample copy and writers guidelines if they are not on the website. Then write two or three sample devotions to fit that particular format, and send them to the editor with a request for an assignment.

CHRIST IN OUR HOME

PO Box 1209, Minneapolis, MN 55440-1209 | 800-328-4648
afsubmissions@augsburgfortress.org | *www.augsburgfortress.org/store/ category/286996/Devotionals*
Heidi Hyland Mann, editor

Denomination: Lutheran—ELCA
Parent company: Augsburg Fortress/1517 Media
Audience: adults
Type: print
Frequency: quarterly
Submissions: Assignments only. Submit sample devotions as explained in the guidelines.
Length: maximum of 1190 characters, including spaces
Rights: all
Bible: NRSV
Guidelines: download from *ms.augsburgfortress.org/downloads/ Submission%20Guidelines.pdf?redirected=true*
Tip: "*Christ in Our Home* is read by people in many nations, so avoid thinking only in terms of those who live in the U.S."

CHRISTIAN DEVOTIONS

377 Woodcrest Dr., Kingsport, TN 37663 | 423-384-4821

martin@christiandevotions.us | ChristianDevotions.us

Martin Wiles, managing editor; Cindy Sproles, executive editor

Parent company: Christian Devotions Ministries
Audience: adults
Type: website
Frequency: daily
Submissions: Accepts freelance submissions of single devotions. Email as attached Word document.
Length: 300–400 words
Rights: onetime
Bible: any
Guidelines: *www.christiandevotions.us/writeforus*
Payment: none
Tip: "We use the Hook, Book, Look, and Took method for our devotions. Work to achieve a good hook, a nice anecdotal story, a strong application, and takeaway."

DEVOTIONS

See *The Quiet Hour*.

FORWARD DAY BY DAY

412 Sycamore St., Cincinnati, OH 45202-4110 | 800-543-1813

editorial@forwardmovement.org | www.forwardmovement.org

Richelle Thompson, managing editor

Denomination: Episcopal
Parent company: Forward Movement
Audience: adults
Type: print
Frequency: quarterly
Submissions: Devotions are written on assignment. To get an assignment, send three sample meditations based on three of the following Bible verses: Psalm 139:21; Mark 8:31; Acts 4:12; Revelation 1:10. Responds in six weeks. Authors complete an entire month's worth of devotions.
Length: maximum of 220 words, including Scripture
Guidelines: *forwardmovement.org/wp-content/uploads/2025/04/ SubmissionGuidelines_ForwardDaybyDay.pdf*
Payment: $300 for a month

Tip: "*Forward Day by Day* is not the place to score points on controversial topics. Occasionally, when the Scripture passage pertains to it, an author chooses to say something about such a topic. If you write about a hot-button issue, do so with humility and make certain your comment shows respect for persons who hold a different view."

FRUIT OF THE VINE

211 N. Meridian St., Ste. 101, Newberg, OR 97132 | 503-538-9775

fv@barclaypress.com | *www.barclaypress.com*

Eric Muhr, executive editor, emuhr@barclaypress.com

Denomination: Quaker
Parent company: Barclay Press
Audience: adults
Type: print
Frequency: quarterly
Submissions: Accepts freelance submissions, one week at a time with a theme for the week.
Length: about 250 words, maximum 290 words
Rights: onetime
Bible: primarily NIV
Guidelines: *www.barclaypress.com/s/Writer-Guidelines-for-Fruit-of-the-Vine.pdf*
Payment: one-year subscription
Tip: "Effective devotionals usually contain examples or personal experiences to illustrate their themes. Such illustrations engage the reader and allow the work to be more persuasive. Devotionals often provide new insights on familiar ideas or passages or acquaint the reader with the unfamiliar. They are Bible-centered, challenging, and encouraging. We aim for content comprehensible and applicable to the diverse group of subscribers."

INKSPIRATIONS ONLINE

6175 Hickory Flat Hwy., Ste. 110-215, Canton, GA 30115 | 813-505-7676

tina@inkspirationsonline.com | *inkspirationsonline.com*

Tina Yeager, publisher

Audience: writers
Type: website
Frequency: weekly
Submissions: Accepts freelance submissions. Email as an attached Word document.

Length: 400 words
Rights: first, reprint, onetime
Bible: any
Guidelines: *inkspirationsonline.com/submission-guidelines*
Payment: none
Tip: "*Inkspirations Online* exists to encourage writers. Please ensure your devotion relates to writers and conveys inspiration."

KEYS FOR KIDS DEVOTIONAL

2060 43rd St. SE, Grand Rapids, MI 49508 | 888-224-2324
editorial@keysforkids.org | *www.keysforkids.org*
Courtney Lasater, editor

Parent company: Keys for Kids Ministries
Audience: children
Type: print
Frequency: quarterly
Submissions: Takes only freelance submissions. Buys 30–40 per year. Seasonal four to five months ahead.
Length: 375 words, including short fiction story
Rights: all
Bible: NKJV
Guidelines: *keysforkids.org/writersguidelines*
Payment: $30 each, on acceptance
Tip: "Include illustration in devotional story that uses a real-world object/situation to help kids understand a spiritual truth. Download free PDFs of past issues for sample stories at *www.keysforkids.org/pdf*." Also does a phone app.

LIGHT FROM THE WORD

13300 Olio Rd., Fishers, IN 46037 | 317-774-3868
submissions@wesleyan.org | *www.wesleyan.org/communication/dailydevo*
Susan LeBaron, publishing services director

Denomination: Wesleyan
Parent company: Wesleyan Publishing House
Audience: adults
Type: print
Frequency: quarterly
Submissions: Must be affiliated with The Wesleyan Church. Email three sample devotions to fit the format and request an assignment. Write "Devotion Samples" in the subject line.

Length: 200–240 words
Rights: all
Bible: NIV
Guidelines: *finelink.com/wphstoreretail/writers-guidelines.html*
Payment: $200 for seven
Tip: "Writing must lead readers to discover a biblical truth and *apply* that truth to their lives."

LIVING FAITH

PO Box 292824, Kettering, OH 45429 | 800-246-7390
info@livingfaith.com | *livingfaith.com*
Pat Gohn, editorial director

Denomination: Catholic
Parent company: Bayard, Inc.
Audience: adults
Type: print
Frequency: quarterly
Submissions: Assignments only; email one or two samples and credentials to request an assignment.
Bible: NAB
Tip: "*Living Faith* provides daily reflections based on a Scripture passage from the daily Mass. With readings for daily Mass listed at the bottom of each devotion, this booklet helps Catholics pray and meditate in spirit with the seasons of the Church Year."

LIVING FAITH KIDS

PO Box 292824, Kettering, OH 45429 | 800-246-7390
editor@livingfaithkids.com | *www.livingfaith.com/kids*
Connie Clark, editor

Denomination: Catholic
Parent company: Bayard, Inc.
Audience: children
Type: print
Frequency: quarterly
Submissions: Assignments only; email samples and credentials to request an assignment.
Tip: "*Living Faith Kids* features daily devotions based on the daily Scripture readings from the Catholic Mass. Each quarterly issue helps children 8–12 develop the habit of daily prayer and build their relationship with Jesus and the Church."

LOVE LINES FROM GOD

128 Leyland Ct., Greenwood, SC 29649 | 864-554-3204

mandmwiles@gmail.com | *lovelinesfromgod.blogspot.com*

Martin Wiles, managing editor

> **Audience:** adults
> **Type:** website
> **Frequency:** daily
> **Submissions:** Accepts freelance submissions. Email as an attachment.
> **Length:** 300–400 words
> **Rights:** first
> **Bible:** NIV
> **Guidelines:** *lovelinesfromgod.blogspot.com/p/write-for-us_3.html*
> **Payment:** none
> **Tip:** "We are looking for devotions that encourage, not preach. Following the submission guidelines will result in a better chance of having the submission accepted."

OPEN WINDOWS

200 Powell Pl., Ste. 100, Brentwood, TN 37027-7707 | 615-251-2000

openwindows@lifeway.com | *lifeway.com/en/product-family/open-windows-magazine*

David Bennett, managing editor

> **Denomination:** Southern Baptist
> **Parent company:** Lifeway Christian Resources
> **Audience:** adults
> **Type:** print
> **Frequency:** quarterly
> **Submissions:** Assignment only.
> **Length:** 300 words
> **Rights:** first
> **Bible:** KJV, CSB
> **Guidelines:** by email
> **Payment:** $30–40 each
> **Tip:** "Writers must be conservative evangelicals."

PORTALS OF PRAYER

3558 S. Jefferson Ave., St. Louis, MO 63118-3968 | 800-325-3040

portals@cph.org | *www1.cph.org/portals*

Scot Kinnaman, senior editor

Denomination: Lutheran—Missouri Synod
Parent company: Concordia Publishing House
Audience: adults
Type: print
Frequency: quarterly
Submissions: Assignment only. To get an assignment, email a completed author profile and two sample devotions based on 1 Kings 19:14–21 and Matthew 6:24–34 and two on texts of your own choosing. Writers are chosen two years in advance.
Length: 245–250 words, including verse and prayer
Payment: $1,000 for a month
Guidelines: *www1.cph.org/portals/write.aspx*

THE QUIET HOUR

4050 Lee Vance Dr., Colorado Springs, CO 80919

thequiethour@davidccook.com | *davidccook.org/submissions-and-writer-guidelines*

Karen Cain, editor

Parent company: David C Cook
Audience: adults
Type: print
Frequency: quarterly
Submissions: *Devotions* and *The Quiet Hour* jointly publish new devotionals. By assignment only. To get an assignment for a week of devotions, submit a sample on a key verse you select in a Scripture passage of your choice. Begin with an anecdotal opening, then transition to relevant biblical insight and encouragement for a life of faith rooted in the key verse. Must have North American postal address for contract and payment.
Length: about 200 words
Rights: all
Bible: NIV, KJV
Guidelines: *davidccook.org/wp-content/uploads/Devotions-and-Quiet-Hour-Writers-Guidelines.pdf*
Payment: $170 for seven
Tip: "Write conversationally as a companion on the journey of faith. Aim for balance in the amount of copy dedicated to each of the three body elements. Concluding prayers may be shorter. Note that the devotional is not meant to be a Bible teaching, a retelling of the Scripture text, or a review of background information."

REFLECTING GOD

PO Box 419427, Kansas City, MO 64141 | 800-877-0700

dbrush@thefoundrypublishing.com | *reflectinggod.com;*
  www.thefoundrypublishing.com/reflecting-god-rg-son25.html
Duane Brush, editor

>**Denomination:** Nazarene
>**Parent company:** The Foundry Publishing
>**Audience:** adults
>**Type:** print
>**Frequency:** quarterly
>**Submissions:** Only Wesleyan writers. Send a couple of sample devotions to fit the format and request an assignment. Also available as a podcast and by email.
>**Length:** 180–200 words.
>**Payment:** $115 for seven
>**Tip:** "Our purpose is the pursuit to embrace holy living. We want to foster discussion about what it means to live a holy life in the 21st century."

REJOICE!

718 N. Main St., Newton, KS 67114 | 800-245-7894

RejoiceEditor@MennoMedia.org | *www.mennomedia.org/rejoice*
April Yamasaki, editor

>**Denomination:** Mennonite
>**Parent company:** MennoMedia
>**Audience:** adults, teens
>**Type:** print
>**Frequency:** quarterly
>**Submissions:** Devotions, limited poetry, and additional devotional material on assignment only. To be considered for an assignment, submit a sample devotion and bio demonstrating familiarity with the Mennonite and Mennonite Brethren Church and reflecting Anabaptist content.
>**Length:** 265 words
>**Rights:** first, electronic
>**Bible:** CEB
>**Guidelines:** via email
>**Payment:** devotions, $125 for a week; articles, $50; poems, $25; on publication
>**Tip:** "Most readers affiliate with Mennonite or Mennonite Brethren

churches and are from a variety of ages, backgrounds, cultures, and life settings in Canada and the United States. Content reflects Anabaptist emphases on commitment, community, reconciliation, and renewal."

THE SECRET PLACE

1075 First Ave., King of Prussia, PA 19406 | 610-768-2084

thesecretplace@judsonpress.com | *www.judsonpress.com/Products/ CategoryCenter/JPSEC/The-Secret-Place.aspx*

Katelyn Morgan, administrator

Denomination: American Baptist
Parent company: Judson Press
Audience: adults
Type: print
Frequency: quarterly
Submissions: Accepts freelance submissions; does not give assignments. Prefers email. Submit seasonal devotions 9–12 months in advance. Do not submit more than six devotions at a time, one per email. May take up to two years to respond; rejections generally sent in one to two months.
Length: 250 words
Rights: first plus unlimited electronic
Bible: NRSVue
Guidelines: *www.judsonpress.com/Content/Site189/ BasicBlocks/102582024GUIDEL_00000167979.pdf*
Payment: $20 each
Tip: "Write for comfort, inspiration, and hope in people's everyday lives."

STRENGTH & GRACE

100 Reserve Rd., Ste. E200, Danbury, CT 06810 | 800-431-2344

Kelkins@guideposts.org | *guideposts.org/shop/product/strength-and-grace-magazine*

Kimberly Elkins, lead editor

Parent company: Guideposts
Audience: adults, caregivers
Type: print
Frequency: bimonthly
Submissions: Accepts freelance submissions written in first person. Buys 365 devotions/year. Email query letter. Responds in two

months. Topics: caregiving for those who are aging and/or dealing with a long-term illness or disability, including parents, children, siblings, or even friends.

Length: 230–270 words inclusive of everything (title, devotion, Bible verse, short prayer)

Rights: all

Guidelines: by email

Payment: $75 each, on acceptance

Tip: "Each devotion should work as a stand-alone story with a clear beginning, middle, and end and a clear takeaway for the reader."

TAKE 5 PLUS

1445 N. Boonville Ave., Springfield, MO 65802 | 417-862-2781

wquick@ag.org | myhealthychurch.com

Wade Quick, team leader

Denomination: Assemblies of God

Parent company: Gospel Publishing House

Audience: teens

Type: print

Frequency: quarterly

Submissions: Assignment only. Request writers guidelines and sample assignment (unpaid) via email. After samples are approved, writers will be added to the list for assignments.

Length: 210–235 words

Rights: all

Bible: NIV

Payment: $25 each, on acceptance

Tip: "Study the publication before attempting the sample assignment."

UNLOCKED

2060 43rd St. SE, Grand Rapids, MI 49508 | 616-647-4500

editorial@unlocked.org | unlocked.org

Hannah Howe, editor

Parent company: Keys for Kids Ministries

Audience: teens

Type: print

Frequency: quarterly

Submissions: Accepts only freelance submissions. Submit through the website. Publishes devotional essays, 200–315 words (personal stories, book-of-the-Bible summaries, church history pieces, tough topics, etc.); fiction, 200–350 words (primarily looking for allegorical fiction, especially sci-fi and fantasy; sometimes accepts contemporary fiction stories with characters, situation, and dialogue that are not too young; when in doubt, write for an older audience, not a younger one); and poetry, 16–23 lines. Takes teen writers. Also available on the website and as a podcast. Sample: *unlocked.org/about.*

Rights: all

Bible: CSB, NIV, NLT, WEB.

Guidelines: *unlocked.org/contribute*

Payment: $30 each, on acceptance

Tip: "We recommend all interested writers sign up for our writer's newsletter for monthly updates and more details about the kinds of submissions we are looking for (topics, genres, etc.): *unlocked.org/writers-newsletter.*"

THE UPPER ROOM

1908 Grand Ave., Nashville, TN 37212 | 615-340-6000

ureditorial@upperroom.org | upperroom.org

Lindsay Gray, editorial director

Parent company: The Upper Room

Audience: adults

Type: print

Frequency: bimonthly

Submissions: Accepts freelance submissions. Submit through the website form (preferred), by mail, or by email.

Length: 350–400 words, which include everything on the printed page

Rights: first, electronic

Bible: NIV, NRSV, CEB, KJV

Guidelines: *submissions.upperroom.org/en/guidelines/meditations*

Payment: $30 each, on publication

Tip: "*The Upper Room* is meant for an international, interdenominational audience. We want to encourage Christians in their personal life of prayer and discipleship. We seek to build on what unites us and to connect Christians together in prayer around the world. We are usually short on meditations that focus on church holidays (Easter, Lent, Christmas, etc.)."

THE WORD IN SEASON

Augsburg Fortress, PO Box 1209, Minneapolis, MN 55440-1209

rochelle@writenowcoach.com | *www.augsburgfortress.org/store/*
   category/286106/The-Word-in-Season

Rochelle Melander, managing editor

>**Denomination:** Lutheran—ELCA
>**Parent company:** Augsburg Fortress/1517 Media
>**Audience:** adults
>**Type:** print
>**Frequency:** quarterly
>**Submissions:** Assignment only. To be considered for an assignment, email for guidelines, then submit three trial devotions by email.
>**Length:** 250 words
>**Rights:** all
>**Bible:** NRSVue
>**Payment:** $40 each
>**Tip:** "We are seeking writers with an ELCA or mainline denomination perspective (Episcopal, United Church of Christ, United Methodist, Presbyterian). We focus on a grace-filled God who accepts and loves us."

12

DRAMA

CHRISTIAN PUBLISHERS

PO Box 248, Cedar Rapids, IA 52406 | 844-841-6387

editor@christianpub.com | *www.christianpub.com*

Audiences: adult, children, teens

Types: children's Christmas and Easter pageants, full-length musicals, full-length plays, one-act musicals, one-act plays

Submissions: Publishes plays for the Christian market, including but not limited to elementary through high school, adults, and youth groups. Submit complete script through the website form. Response time varies according to the time of the year.

Payment: 10% royalty, often to a fixed amount; no advance

Guidelines: *www.christianpub.com/default.aspx?pg=ag*

Tip: "Be sure your play builds. People have short attention spans, and if the story is too bogged down in excessive dialogue, or if the play wanders aimlessly, they will simply tune out. If the comedy or suspense doesn't build from scene to scene, if we're not involved with the main character(s) or the dramatic question, then the play isn't going anywhere."

CSS PUBLISHING COMPANY, INC.

5450 N. Dixie Hwy., Lima, OH 45807 | 419-227-1818

editor@csspub.com | *www.csspub.com*

David Runk, president

Audiences: adult, teens

Types: monologues, one-act plays, reader's theatre, short skits, skit compilations

Submissions: Publishes three to five skits per year. Receives 10 submissions per year. Length: 20–30 minutes. Primarily interested in Advent/Christmas/Epiphany and Lent/Easter. Doesn't publish lengthy dramatic works. Email or mail complete script. Responds in six months. Simultaneous submissions OK.

Payment: negotiated, no advance

Guidelines: *store.csspub.com/page.php?Custom%20Pages=10*

Tip: "Must be unique to the Christmas and Easter seasons."

DRAMA MINISTRY

2814 Azalea Pl., Nashville, TN 37204 | 866-859-7622

service@dramaministry.com | *www.dramaministry.com*

Vince Wilcox, general manager

Audiences: adult, children, teens

Types: monologues, reader's theatre, short skits

Submissions: Open to all topics, including seasonal/holidays. Email or mail script. Buys all rights.

Guidelines: *www.dramaministry.com/faq*

ELDRIDGE CHRISTIAN PLAYS AND MUSICALS

PO Box 4904, Lancaster, PA 17604 | 850-385-2463

newworks@histage.com | *www.95church.com*

Susan Shore, senior editor

Audiences: adult, children, teens

Types: full-length musicals, full-length plays, monologues, musicals, one-act plays, reader's theatre, short skits, skit compilations

Submissions: Publishes 10–15 scripts per year; receives 150–200 submissions annually. Length: plays and musicals, minimum 30 minutes, maximum two hours. Submit complete script via email attachment with cover letter in the body of the message. Simultaneous OK. Responds in two months.

Payment: 50% royalty plus 10% copy sales, no advance

Guidelines: *95church.com/submission-guidelines*

Tip: "Please submit plays and musicals suitable for performance by all kinds and sizes of churches. We are an independent publisher not supported by any specific religious denomination. We welcome shows on all subjects; however, Christmas plays are very popular."

WORDCRAFTS THEATRICAL PRESS

912 E. Lincoln, Tullahoma, TN 37388 | 615-397-8376

wordcrafts@wordcrafts.net | *wordcrafts.net*

Mike Parker, publisher

Audiences: adult, children, teens

Types: full-length plays, one-act plays

Submissions: Publishes two to four plays per year. Receives 8–10 submissions. Email query letter. Accepts simultaneous submissions. Responds in four to six weeks.

Payment: royalties on script and performance license fees per performance, advance

Guidelines: *www.wordcrafts.net/how-to-submit*

Tip: "Write a great script we can't resist."

13

GIFTS AND GREETING CARDS

BLUE MOUNTAIN ARTS

Editorial Dept., PO Box 1007, Boulder, CO 80306 | 303-449-0536

editorial@sps.com | www.sps.com

Audience: adult

Product: greeting cards

Submissions: General card publisher with some inspirational cards. Not looking for rhymed poetry, religious verse, or one-liners. Length: 50–300 words. Buys all rights. Accepts freelance submissions by email (no attachments), website form, or mail. Responds in two months or not interested. Holiday deadlines: Christmas and general holidays, May 15; Valentine's Day, July 12; Easter, September 8; Mother's Day and graduation, October 13; Father's Day, December 7.

Payment: $300 for cards, $50 per poem to use in a book

Guidelines: *www.sps.com/greeting-card-guidelines-submissions*

Tip: "Because our cards capture genuine emotions on topics such as love, friendship, family, missing you, and other real-life subjects, we suggest that you have a friend, relative, or someone else in your life in mind as you write. We are looking for new, original, and creative writings that do not sound like anything we have already published."

CHRISTIAN ART GIFTS

359 Longview Dr., Bloomingdale, IL 60108 | 800-521-7807

info@christianartpublishing.com | www.christianartgifts.com

Rob Teigen, vice president of publishing

Audiences: adult, children

Products: box of blessings, coloring books, devotionals, gift books, gifts, journals, mugs, activity books

Submissions: Interested in devotionals, prayer books, seasonal books, and kids resources. Submit query through the website form. Buys all rights.

Payment: 10–14% royalty, sometimes offers advance

Guidelines: *christianartpublishing.com/get-started*

Tip: "Looking for devotionals, kids devotionals, prayer books, and thoughtful gift books."

DICKSONS, INC.

709 B Ave. E, Seymour, IN 47274 | 812-522-1308

submissions@dicksonsgifts.com | *www.dicksonsgifts.com*

Thom Hunter, director of product development

Audience: adult

Products: gifts

Submissions: Two to eight lines, maximum 16, suitable for plaques, bookmarks, etc. Email submission. Responds in three months. Subjects can cover any gift-giving occasion and Christian, inspirational, and everyday social-expression topics. Phrases or acrostics of one or two lines for bumper stickers are also considered. Buys reprint rights.

Payment: royalty, negotiable

Tip: Looking for religious verses.

ELLIE CLAIRE

830 Crescent Center Dr., Franklin, TN 37067 | 615-932-7600

www.hachettebookgroup.com/imprint/hachette-nashville/worthy-books/ ellie-claire-gifts

Audience: adult

Products: devotionals, gift books, journals

Submissions: Submit through agents only. Buys all rights.

Payment: flat fee, royalty

Tip: "We operate in the gift market, and the writing will need to reflect that. We are not interested in Bible studies but in inspirational and encouraging devotions, funny stories with a spiritual component, and compilations from a Christian worldview."

INK & WILLOW

10807 New Allegiance Dr., Ste. 500, Colorado Springs, CO 80921 | 719-590-4999

info@waterbrookmultnomah.com | *waterbrookmultnomah.com/ink-and-willow*

Jamie Lapeyrolerie, acquisitions editor

Leslie Calhoun, acquisitions editor

Audience: adult

Products: coloring books, inspirational cards, journals, planners

Submissions: Takes submissions only from agents.

Tip: "Ink & Willow encompasses a line of interactive products that infuse contemplation and inspiration into the regular spiritual practice of creative-minded Christians, wherever they are in their faith journey. Each thoughtfully curated gift product is based in biblical truth and sparks a reminder of how God reveals beauty in the midst of our ordinary."

WARNER PRESS

2902 Enterprise Dr., Anderson, IN 46013 | 800-741-7721

editors@warnerpress.org | *www.warnerpress.org*

Robin Loisch, kids and family ministry editor

Audiences: adult, children

Products: greeting cards

Submissions: Themes include birthday, anniversary, baby congratulations, sympathy, get well, kid's birthday and get well, thinking of you, friendship, Christmas, praying for you, encouragement. Use a conversational tone with no lofty poetic language, such as *thee, thou, art*. Don't preach or use a negative tone. Strive to share God's love and provide a Christian witness. Length: average of four lines. Responds in six to eight weeks. Email as attachment. Buys all rights. Deadlines: everyday, July 31; Christmas, October 1.

Payment: $25–50

Guidelines: *www.warnerpress.org/submission-guidelines*

Tip: "Include your name, address, and email address with each page of submissions. We prefer email submissions with verses sent as an attachment. We seldom buy rhyming verse. Greeting cards are sold as boxed sets. No individual counter-line cards. Verses should be general enough that they would be appropriate to send to multiple people. Including a Scripture for your verse is also appreciated (KJV and NIV preferred)."

14

TRACTS

The following companies publish gospel tracts but do not have writers guidelines. If you are interested in writing for them, email or phone to find out if they currently are looking for submissions. Also check your denominational publishing house to see if it publishes tracts.

FELLOWSHIP TRACT LEAGUE
3733 Snook Rd., Morrow, OH 45152 | 513-494-1075
mail@fellowshiptractleague.org | *fellowshiptractleague.org*

GOSPEL TRACT SOCIETY, INC.
PO Box 1118, Independence, MO 64051 | 816-461-6086
gospeltractsociety@gmail.com | *www.gospeltractsociety.org*

   Submissions: Considers "any work that has Christian value, is based on the truth of God's Word, is relevant to today's lifestyle, furthers the Kingdom of God and promotes the Gospel of Jesus Christ. The writing must be copyright-free." A team of proofreaders and leaders makes the final decision but doesn't notify writers. "To know if your writing became an official GTS tract, periodically check the website to see if it was published and available for distribution. Unfortunately, with the number of submissions we receive, we don't have the capacity to reach back out when/if approved or denied. On a lighter note, we *love* seeing people's work and encourage you to send us whatever messages you have. You just never know what God will do."

PILGRIM TRACT SOCIETY
PO Box 126, Randleman, NC 27317 | 336-495-1241
pilgrim@northstate.net | *www.pilgrimtract.org*
   Submissions: Submit full manuscript.

TRACT ASSOCIATION OF FRIENDS

1501 Cherry St., Philadelphia, PA 19102
info@tractassociation.org | tractassociation.org

Audience: Quakers
Submissions: Writers must be Quakers.

15

BIBLE CURRICULUM

This list includes only the major, nondenominational curriculum publishers. If you are in a denominational church, also check its publishing house for curriculum products. Plus some organizations, like Awana and Pioneer Clubs, produce curriculum for their programs.

Since Bible curriculum is written on assignment only, you'll need to get samples for age groups you want to write for (from the company's website, large Christian bookstores, or your church) and study the formats and pieces. Look for editors' names on the copyright or contents pages of teachers manuals, or call the publishing house for this information.

Then write query letters to specific editors. Tell why you're qualified to write curriculum for them, include a sample of curriculum you've written or other sample of your writing, and ask for a trial assignment. Since the need for writers varies widely, you may not get an assignment for a year or more.

Some of these companies also publish undated, elective curriculum books that are used in a variety of ministries. Plus some book publishers publish lines of Bible-study guides. (See "Traditional Book Publishers.") These are contracted like other books with a proposal and sample chapters.

DAVID C COOK
4050 Lee Vance Dr., Colorado Springs, CO 80918 | 719-536-0100
davidccook.org/curriculum
> **Type:** Sunday school, children's ministry
> **Imprints:** Bible-in-Life, Echoes, Gospel Light, HeartShaper, Scripture Press, SEEN, Standard Lesson, Tru, Wonder Ink

GROUP PUBLISHING (a ministry of David C Cook)
1515 Cascade Ave., Loveland, CO 80538 | 800-447-1070
info@group.com | *www.group.com*
> **Types:** Sunday school, vacation Bible school, children's worship

Imprints: BE BOLD, DIG IN, FaithWeaver NOW, Following Jesus, Hands-On Bible Curriculum, LIVE, Simply Loved, KidsOwn Worship, Play-n-Worship

LIFESTONE MINISTRIES (formerly Union Gospel Press)

19695 Commerce Pkwy., Middleburg Hts., OH 44130 | 216-749-2100
info@lifestoneministries.org | *lifestoneministries.org*

Type: Sunday school, homeschool, Christian school
Imprints: Christian Life Series, Illuminate Bible Series

PENSACOLA CHRISTIAN COLLEGE

PO Box 17900, Pensacola, FL 32522-7900 | 877-356-9385
www.joyfullifesundayschool.com

Type: Sunday school
Imprint: Joyful Life

UMI (Urban Ministries, Inc.)

1551 Regency Ct., Calumet City, IL 60409-5448 | 800-860-8642
support@urbanministries.com | *urbanministries.com*

Types: Sunday school, vacation Bible school

16

MISCELLANEOUS

These companies publish a variety of books and other products that fall into the specialty-markets category, such as puzzle books, game books, children's activity books, craft books, charts, church bulletins, and coloring books.

BARBOUR PUBLISHING, INC.
See entry in "Traditional Book Publishers."

BEAMING BOOKS
See entry in "Traditional Book Publishers."

BROADSTREET PUBLISHING GROUP
See entry in "Traditional Book Publishers."

CF4K
See entry in "Traditional Book Publishers."

CREATIVE COMMUNICATIONS FOR THE PARISH
See entry in "Traditional Book Publishers."

DAVID C COOK
See entry in "Traditional Book Publishers."

THE GOOD BOOK COMPANY
See entry in "Traditional Book Publishers."

GOOD BOOKS
See entry in "Traditional Book Publishers."

JUST FOR KIDS

2 Overlea Blvd., Toronto, ON M4H 1P4, Canada | 416-425-2111
justforkids@salvationarmy.ca | *salvationist.ca/editorial/just-for-kids/
2025-back-issues*
Abbigail Oliver, editor

Parent company: The Salvation Army in Canada and Bermuda
Audience: ages 5–12
Type: weekly activity page
Submissions: Puzzles that relate to a biblical story or concept, common themes (seasons, holidays, sports, animals, etc.), and Salvation Army distinctives (junior soldiers, Salvation Army flag, etc.); jokes and tongue twisters; general knowledge and Salvation Army trivia questions; news photos (junior soldier enrollment, achievement or recognition of a young person or group of young people, a corps activity for or by young people, etc.) with caption of 75 words maximum.
Payment: none
Bible: NIrV
Guidelines: *salvationist.ca/files/salvationarmy/Magazines/Just-for-Kids-Guidelines.pdf*

ROSE PUBLISHING

See entry in "Traditional Book Publishers."

ROSEKIDZ

See entry in "Traditional Book Publishers."

TWENTY-THIRD PUBLICATIONS

See entry in "Traditional Book Publishers."

TYNDALE KIDS

See entry in "Traditional Book Publishers."

WARNER PRESS

2902 Enterprise Dr., Anderson, IN 46013 | 800-741-7721
editors@warnerpress.org | *www.warnerpress.org*
Robin Loisch, kids and family ministry editor

Children's coloring and activity books: Most activity books focus on a Bible story or biblical theme, such as love and forgiveness. Ages range from preschool (ages 2–5) to upper elementary (ages 8–10).

Include activities and puzzles in every upper-elementary book. Coloring-book manuscripts should present a picture idea and a portion of the story for each page. Deadlines: May 1 and October 1. Payment varies.

Children's teaching resources: Books with skits, science experiments, and crafts. Length: 48–144 pages. Activities must be interesting for kids, teach important biblical lessons, and be easy to use in a class. Payment varies.

Guidelines: *www.warnerpress.org/submission-guidelines*

PART 5

SUPPORT
FOR
WRITERS

17

LITERARY AGENTS

Asking editors and other writers is a great way to find a reliable agent. You may also want to visit *www.sfwa.org/other-resources/for-authors/writer-beware/agents* for tips on avoiding questionable agents and choosing reputable ones.

The general market has the Association of American Literary Agents (*aalitagents.org*), also known as AALA. To be a member, the agent must agree to a code of ethics. The website has a searchable list of agents. Some listings below indicate at least one agent belongs to the AALA. Lack of such a designation, however, does not indicate the agent is unethical; most Christian agents are not members.

AKA LITERARY MANAGEMENT
11445 Dallas Rd., Peyton, CO 80831 | 646-846-2478
submissions@akaliterary.com | *akalm.net*
   Agent: Terrie Wolf
   Agency: Established in 2009. Represents more than 50 clients. Member of Association of American Literary Agents. Responds in 8–12 weeks. Specializes in rights management, including transmedia, film, TV, and foreign.
   Types of books: adult fiction, adult nonfiction, children's fiction, cookbook, general-market children's, general-market fiction, general-market nonfiction, home arts, teen/YA nonfiction, wellness, young adult
   New clients: Open to all writers. First contact: emailed proposal, website form, or referral from current client. Query via the instructions on the website through Submittable or Query Manager. Simultaneous OK.
   Commission: 15%
   Tip: "(1) Make sure we're open to submissions. Those received when our window is not open will be discarded. (2) Get to know us

on social media. (3) Please provide well-formatted submissions that include your query, your quick synopsis, the first three chapters (or full manuscript for children's works or full proposal for nonfiction works), and take the time to help us understand why you would like to work with us."

ALIVE LITERARY AGENCY

5001 Centennial Blvd. #50742, Colorado Springs, CO 80908

admin@aliveliterary.com | *www.aliveliterary.com*

Agents: Bryan Norman, Lisa Jackson, Rachel Jacobson, Kathleen Kerr, Carly Kellerman, Rory Green

Agency: Established in 1989. Represents 250 clients.

Types of books: adult nonfiction

New clients: Open only to well-established book writers. Initial contact: referral from current client. Responds in three weeks.

Commission: 15%

Tip: "We only accept manuscripts by referral or request. Writers considering representation can follow Alive on Instagram @aliveliteraryagency."

AMBASSADOR LITERARY

PO Box 50358, Nashville, TN 37205 | 615-370-4700

wes@AmbassadorAgency.com | *www.AmbassadorAgency.com*

Agent: Wes Yoder

Agency: Established in 1997. Represents 20 clients. Also offers national media representation for select clients.

Types of books: adult nonfiction

New clients: Open only to well-established book writers. Contact by email with a full proposal. Responds in two weeks.

Commission: 15%

Tip: "Looking for great storytellers!"

AUTHORIZEME LITERARY AGENCY

PO Box 1816, South Gate, CA 90280 | 310-508-9860

AuthorizeMeNow@gmail.com | *lifethatmatters.net/authorizeme#literary_agency*

Agent: Dr. Sharon Norris Elliott

Agency: Established in 2020. Represents 60+ clients. Other services: See entry in "Editorial Services."

Types of books: Bible study, Christian living, devotionals, early readers, family, leadership, parenting, picture books, spiritual growth

New clients: Open to writers from established to those seeking their first contract. Contact: email with one-sheet. Responds in one to three months.

Commission: 15%

Tip: "Love Jesus; be teachable, patient, and humble; possess a strong desire to reach for excellence; smile a lot."

BANNER LITERARY

PO Box 1828, Winter Park, CO 80482

mike@mikeloomis.co | www.mikeloomis.co

Agent: Mike Loomis

Agency: Established in 2004. Represents 48 clients. Other services: See entries in "Editorial Services" and "Publicity and Marketing Services."

Types of books: adult nonfiction, business, inspiration, politics, self-help

New clients: Open to writers who have not published a book and self-published writers. Contact through email or website form. Responds in two weeks.

Commission: 15%

Tip: "Send your web address with query."

BBH LITERARY

david@bbhliterary.com | www.bbhliterary.com

Agents: David Bratt; Laura Bardolph, *laura@bbhliterary.com*

Agency: Established in 2021. Represents 30 clients. Other services: See entries in "Editorial Services" and "Publicity and Marketing Services."

Types of books: adult nonfiction

New clients: Open to all book writers. Contact: query letter via website form or referral from current client. Accepts simultaneous submissions. Responds in one week.

Commission: 15%

Tip: "Please tell us why your book has some urgency to its message. We are most interested in books that speak to real life in a complicated world with nuance and wisdom."

THE BINDERY

3250 Birnamwood Dr., Colorado Springs, CO 80920 | 719-351-4897

info@thebinderyagency.com | www.thebinderyagency.com

Agents: Alex Field, Trinity McFadden, Ingrid Beck, John Blase,

Morgan Strehlow

Agency: Established in 2017. Represents 200+ clients. Member of Association of American Literary Agents.

Types of books: adult fiction, adult nonfiction, biography, children's fiction, children's nonfiction, Christian living, cultural issues, health/wellness, history, memoir, parenting, relationships, self-help, social issues, sports

New clients: Open to potential clients from all backgrounds. Initial contact: emailed full proposal or query or a referral from current client. Accepts simultaneous submissions. Responds in 8–10 weeks.

Commission: 15%

Tip: "Please include the following in the body of your email: a clear summary of your book concept, an author biography, the table of contents (for nonfiction), at least two sample chapters, plus a one-page synopsis for fiction, relevant contact information, and any publishing history. Include the word *QUERY* in the email subject line; and if you've completed a book proposal, please attach that document to your email. You may address your query to one agent or to The Bindery as a whole. Before sending, you can find out what each agent is seeking on the ABOUT page on our website."

THE BLYTHE DANIEL AGENCY, INC.

PO Box 64197, Colorado Springs, CO 80962-4197

submissions@theblythedanielagency.com | *www.theblythedanielagency.com*

Agents: Blythe Daniel, *blythe@theblythedanielagency.com*; Stephanie Alton, *stephanie@theblythedanielagency.com*

Agency: Established in 2005. Represents 115 clients. Sells to general-market too. Other services: See entry in "Publicity and Marketing Services."

Types of books: adult fiction, apologetics, business, Christian living, current events, devotionals, family, gift books, leadership, marriage, parenting, social issues, spiritual growth, women's issues, youth

New clients: Open to all writers from those who have never been published through well-published ones. Contact: Email proposal and three sample chapters. Responds in 8–12 weeks if interested.

Commission: 15%

Tip: "We want to work with authors who are open to feedback and suggestions and are willing to work hard. We are looking for writers who are saying something no one else is saying, are committed to becoming authors who are building their audience, and whom we can build a relationship with over time."

BOOKS & SUCH LITERARY MANAGEMENT

representation@booksandsuch.com | www.booksandsuch.com

Agents: Janet Kobobel Grant, *janet@booksandsuch.com;* Wendy Lawton, *wendy@booksandsuch.com;* Rachel Kent, *rachel@booksandsuch.com;* Cynthia Ruchti, *cynthia@booksandsuch.com;* Barb Roose, *barb@ booksandsuch.com*

Agency: Established in 1996. Represents 275 clients.

Types of books: adult fiction, adult nonfiction, Christian living, devotionals, discipleship, family, health/wellness, leadership, marriage, middle grade, ministry, teen/YA fiction, teen/YA nonfiction

New clients: Open to writers who have not published a book. Contact by email with query first. Responds in one month.

Commission: 15%

Tip: "We're especially interested in writers who have developed a social-media presence and have a website."

CHRISTIAN LITERARY AGENT

PO Box 428, Newburg, PA 17257 | 717-423-6621

keith@christianliteraryagent.com | www.christianliteraryagent.com

Agent: Keith Carroll

Agency: Established in 2010. Represents 10–15 new clients annually. Other service: writer coach.

Types of books: adult nonfiction

New clients: Open to first-time book authors and self-published writers. Initial contact: phone, mail application form. Responds in two to four weeks.

Commission: 10%

Fee: $90 administrative fee

Tip: "I try to help you make your material more of an effective read."

THE CHRISTOPHER FEREBEE AGENCY

submission@christopherferebee.com | christopherferebee.com

Agents: Christopher Ferebee, Angela Scheff, Jonathan Merritt, Kyle Negrete

Agency: Established in 2011.

Types of books: adult fiction, adult nonfiction

New clients: Submit query letter and proposal as email attachment. Responds in four weeks.

Tip: "As a small agency, we focus our efforts on a very select group of authors. Our primary focus and attention is always on existing client relationships. But we are looking for the right authors with important ideas."

C.Y.L.E. AGENCY (CYLE YOUNG LITERARY ELITE)

PO Box 1, Clarklake, MI 49230 | 330-651-1604

submissions@cyleyoung.com | *cyleyoung.com*

> **Agents:** Cyle Young, Tessa Emily Hall, Del Duduit, Megan Burkhart, Antwan Houser, Andy Clapp
>
> **Agency:** Established in 2018. Represents 80 clients. Member of Association of American Literary Agents. Specialty: children's and nonfiction. Acquires general-market books too.
>
> **Types of books:** adult fiction, adult nonfiction, children's fiction, children's nonfiction, middle grade, teen/YA fiction, teen/YA nonfiction
>
> **New clients:** Some of the agents are currently closed to queries and proposals except when meeting writers at a conference or an online writing event. Check the website to see who is open to submissions. Simultaneous submissions OK. Responds in three months or not interested.
>
> **Commission:** 15%
>
> **Tip:** "We look for projects with great writing, big ideas, and great platform."

DUNAMIS WORDS

www.cherylricker.com/dunamis-words

> **Agent:** Cheryl Ricker
>
> **Agency:** Established in 2015. Represents more than 20 clients.
>
> **Types of books:** adult fiction, business, charismatic, Christian living, current events, devotionals, gift books, leadership, marriage, memoir, ministry, parenting, social issues, women's issues
>
> **New clients:** Accepts queries—maximum of six pages—only through the website. If interested, will ask for more information and sample chapters.
>
> **Tip:** "One's heart matters as much as one's calling and ability to write. These authors work diligently at growing their craft and tuning their antennae to the Creator and wellspring of life. From a deep abiding relationship with Christ flows the richest substance and wisdom."

EMBOLDEN MEDIA GROUP

PO Box 953607, Lake Mary, FL 32795

submissions@emboldenmediagroup.com | *emboldenmediagroup.com*

> **Agents:** Jevon Bolden, Deidra Riggs, Rebekah Von Lintel, Kathy Green, Joylanda Jamison, Mytecia Myles
>
> **Agency:** Established in 2017. Represents more than 100 clients. Also offers content development, editorial, writing coaching.

Types of books: adult fiction, adult nonfiction, African American, charismatic, children's fiction, children's nonfiction, Christian living, devotionals, health/wellness, leadership, memoir

New clients: Open to writers at every level, including self-published. Contact: email query, website form, or current client referral. Accepts simultaneous submissions. Responds in eight weeks.

Commission: 15%

Tip: "Follow us and our agents on social media; keep up with the kind of authors we represent and themes that catch our hearts and eyes."

GARDNER LITERARY

248 Misty Creek Dr., Monument, Colorado 80132 | 719-440-0069

gardnerliterary@gmail.com | *gardner-literary.com*

Agents: Rachelle Gardner, *rachelle@gardner-literary.com;* Sherri Johnson, *Sherri@gardner-literary.com;* Candice Benbow, *Candice@gardner-literary.com*

Agency: Established in 2021. Represents 100 clients.

Types of books: adult fiction, adult nonfiction

New clients: Open to any writer. Novels must be complete. Nonfiction authors should have a platform. First contact: query through Query Tracker. Responds in 30 days. Welcomes subject matter experts on any topic, behind-the-scenes in any profession or walk of life, thoughtful nonfiction on just about any topic.

Commission: 15%

Tip: "Please understand the importance of platform, especially for nonfiction writers."

THE GATES GROUP

don@the-gates-group.com | *www.the-gates-group.com*

Agent: Don Gates

Agency: Established in 2013. Represents more than 50 authors. Member of Association of American Literary Agents.

Types of books: nonfiction

New clients: Open only to well-established book writers and writers who currently have an agent. Initial contact: website form. Responds in two days.

Commission: 15%

GOLDEN WHEAT LITERARY

jessica@goldenwheatliterary.com | *goldenwheatliterary.com*

Agent: Jessica Schmeidler

Agency: Established in 2015. Also sells to the general market.

Types of books: adult fiction, devotionals, general-market fiction, memoir

New clients: Email query letter and first three chapters, all in body of message; no attachments. If no response in six months, assume not interested.

Tip: "If our lack of response has been due merely to a time availability issue, then we have been known to respond to queries that have gone unanswered for six months or longer. So, if you do not wish to receive a response after a certain time, for your own sanity and/ or record-keeping reasons, please note that in your initial query. Likewise, if your manuscript is no longer available for consideration, please do remember to withdraw the submission."

ILLUMINATE LITERARY AGENCY

7265 Falcon Crest Dr., Redmond, OR 97756

submissions@illuminateliterary.com | illuminateliterary.com

Agent: Jenni Burke

Agency: Established in 2006. Represents 40 clients. Specialty: adult nonfiction.

Types of books: adult nonfiction, Bible studies, business, children's fiction, children's nonfiction, Christian living, culture, devotionals, gift books, leadership, memoir, personal development, spiritual growth

New clients: Open to writers with a strong platform, clear writing, and a powerful message. Welcomes submissions that include a proposal via the Submissions page on the website or a referral from a current client. Responds in four weeks if proposal catches her interest.

Commission: 15%

Tip: "Please thoroughly review the Submissions page on our website prior to submitting."

LINDA S. GLAZ LITERARY AGENCY

51670 Washington St., New Baltimore, MI 48047 | 586-822-1061

linda@lindasglaz.com | lindasglaz.com

Agent: Linda S. Glaz

Agency: Established in 2022. Represents 35 clients.

Types of books: adult fiction, adult nonfiction, general-market fiction, general-market nonfiction

New clients: Open to new book and self-published authors but prefers those met at conferences or referred by other agents or authors. First contact: email with full proposal, referral through current client. Accepts simultaneous submissions. Responds in two months but generally much sooner. Not looking for children's, speculative fiction, and memoirs.

Commission: 15%

Tip: "Be sure to research everything I do and do not handle, please."

LITERARY MANAGEMENT GROUP

531 Montgomery St., Miamisburg, OH 45342 | 615-812-4445

brucebarbour@literarymanagementgroup.com |
www.literarymanagementgroup.com

Agent: Bruce R. Barbour

Agency: Established in 1995. Represents 100+ clients.

Types of books: adult nonfiction, business, Christian living, inspiration, motivational, prayer, women's issues

New clients: Open only to well-established writers with traditional publishers. Contact: Email proposal according to the website template and sample chapters. Accepts simultaneous submissions. Responds in two weeks.

Commission: 15%

Tip: "We represent a wide range of categories and published authors but are not able to review unpublished proposals or manuscripts."

MacGREGOR AND LUEDEKE COLLABORATIVE LLC

PO Box 1316, Manzanita, OR 97130

www.macgregorandluedeke.com

Agents: Amanda Luedeke, *amanda@macgregorliterary.com;* Alina Mitchell; Bethany Jett

Agency: Established in 2006; rebranded in 2025. Member of Association of American Literary Agents. Represents 50–75 clients. Specialty: Christian nonfiction.

Types of books: adult fiction, business, children's, Christian living, devotionals, finance, leadership, memoir, sports

New clients: Open to writers with great ideas and platforms. Initial contact: Query your agent of choice using their preferred query method. Responds in six weeks.

Commission: 15%

Tip: "Have a great book proposal (nonfiction) or manuscript (fiction)."

MARY DEMUTH LITERARY

2150 Heather Glen Dr., Rockwall, TX 75087 | 214-475-9083

query@marydemuthliterary.com | *marydemuthliterary.com*

Agent: Mary DeMuth

Agency: Established in 2022; former agent with Books & Such Literary Management. Represents 42 clients. Other service: mentoring writers in platform and proposal writing.

Types of books: Christian living

New clients: Open to all writers. First contact: emailed query. Responds in one week.

Commission: 15%

Tip: "Read the website for all the instructions you need."

PAPE COMMONS

11327 Rill Pt., Colorado Springs, CO 80921 | 719-648-4019

don@papecommons.com | *papecommons.com*

Agent: Don Pape

Agency: Established in 2021. Represents 50 clients.

Types of books: adult fiction, adult nonfiction, children's fiction, children's nonfiction

New clients: No self-published writers. Looking for writers pursuing their craft and community. Contact: website form. Responds in two to three days.

Commission: 15%

Tip: "Pape Commons is a community of writers interested in the craft of writing and the art of doing this together with monthly Zoom calls to offer that sense of camaraderie and an opportunity to become aware of the greater world of book publishing."

THE SEYMOUR AGENCY

4100 Corporate Sq., Ste. 140, Naples, FL 34104 | 239-398-8209

www.theseymouragency.com

Agent: Julie Gwinn, *querymanager.com/JulieGwinn*

Agency: Established in 1992. Primarily a general-market agency; Julie handles the Christian books.

Types of books: adult fiction, adult nonfiction

New clients: Open to writers who have not published a book and self-published writers. First contact: email query through Query Manager. Responds in three weeks to queries or not interested.

Commission: 15%

Tip: "Hone your craft. Take advantage of writers groups, critique partners, etc., to polish your manuscript into the best shape it can be."

THE STEVE LAUBE AGENCY

24 W. Camelback Rd. A-635, Phoenix, AZ 85013

info@stevelaube.com | www.stevelaube.com

Agents: Steve Laube, *krichards@stevelaube.com;* Tamela Hancock Murray, *ewilson@stevelaube.com;* Bob Hostetler, *rgwright@ stevelaube.com;* Dan Balow, *vseem@stevelaube.com;* Lynette Eason, *ehumphries@stevelaube.com*

Agency: Established in 2004. Represents more than 300 clients. See website blog post by each agent for what he or she is looking for.

Types of books: adult fiction, adult nonfiction

New clients: Open to unpublished authors. Email proposal as attachment according to the guidelines on the website. Steve Laube also will take proposals by mail. Accepts simultaneous submissions. Responds in 8–12 weeks.

Commission: 15%; foreign, 20%

Tip: "Please follow the guidelines! Since your book proposal is like a job application, you want to present yourself in the most professional manner possible. Your proposal will be a simple vehicle to convey your idea to us and, ultimately, to a publisher. Don't call the office to pitch your book idea. We'd rather read the proposal."

TRACIE MILES LITERARY

3618 Walter Nelson Rd., Mint Hill, NC 28227 | 704-975-1958

traciemiles.com/tracie-miles-literary

Agent: Tracie Miles

Agency: Established in 2024. Number of clients: 20+. Member of Association of American Literary Agents.

Types of books: adult fiction, adult nonfiction, Bible studies, children's fiction, children's nonfiction, Christian living, curriculum, middle grade, self-help, teen/YA fiction. Looking for Christian nonfiction on trending topics and key issues that have a unique angle; no dystopian or fantasy; clean Christian adult romance, historical, and suspense fiction; Christian living focused on spiritual growth, personal growth, self-help, lifestyle, relationships, mental health, anxiety, loneliness, friendship, neurodiverse topics, practical material, family, and parenting.

New clients: Open to aspiring writers, especially professional experts in their topic or leaders in women's ministries, who have solid writing, strong platforms, a unique angle on their topic, an email subscriber base, and working on building an online presence. Contact: website form. Responds in four weeks.

Commission: 15%

Tip: "Must submit a complete book proposal with three sample chapters."

WESTWOOD CREATIVE ARTISTS

386 Huron St., Toronto, Ontario, Canada M1S 2G6

submissions@wcaltd.com | www.wcaltd.com

Agent: Bridgette Kam, *bridgette@wcaltd.com*

Agency: Established in 1995. Has 16 clients. Responds in 12 weeks. Initial contact: email.

Types of books: adult fiction, memoir, middle-grade fiction, narrative nonfiction, picture books, teen/YA fiction

New clients: Open to self-published and new book writers.

Commission: 15%

Fees: none

Tip: "Westwood Creative Artists is a longstanding North American agency based in Canada, helping writers place successful book deals across the US, Canada, and the English-speaking world and beyond."

WILLIAM K. JENSEN LITERARY AGENCY

119 Bampton Ct., Eugene, OR 97404 | 541-688-1612

queries@wkjagency.com | www.wkjagency.com

Agent: William K. Jensen

Agency: Established in 2005. Represents more than 50 clients.

Types of books: adult nonfiction

New clients: Open to unpublished authors. Contact by email only; no attachments. See the website for complete query details. Accepts simultaneous submissions. Responds in one month or not interested.

Commission: 15%

Tip: "Due to the changes in book retailing over the last ten years, publishers will only accept authors with a robust social-media and/or speaking platform. That being the case, we can only consider queries by writers with at least 20,000 online followers and/or a dynamic speaking ministry."

WINTERS & KING

2448 E. 81st St., Ste. 5900, Tulsa, OK 74137-4259 | 918-494-6868

twinters@wintersking.com | wintersking.com/practice-areas/ publishing-agent-services

Agent: Thomas J. Winters

Agency: Established in 1983. Part of a law firm. Other services: legal review of publishing contracts, drafting of work-for-hire agreements to contract writer/editor services, copyright/trademark filing.

Types of books: adult nonfiction, government

New clients: Open only to well-established book writers and well-known business and government figures. Contact by email. Response time varies.

Commission: varies

Tip: "Please note we rarely accept unsolicited offers but anyone is welcome to reach out via email."

WOLGEMUTH & WILSON

info@wolgemuthandwilson.com | wolgemuthandwilson.com

Agents: Austin Wilson, Erik Wolgemuth, Andrew Wolgemuth

Agency: Established in 1992. Represents 150+ clients. Responds in two weeks if interested.

Types of books: adult nonfiction, Bible notes, Bible studies, children's fiction, children's nonfiction

New clients: Open only to well-established authors or who are referred by a client. First contact: email query or referral. Simultaneous submissions OK.

Commission: 15%

Tip: "Real-life relational networks and online presence are important factors."

WORDSERVE LITERARY GROUP

700 Colorado Blvd. #318, Denver, CO 80206

admin@wordserveliterary.com | www.wordserveliterary.com

Agents: Greg Johnson; Keely Boeving, *Keely@wordserveliterary.com;* Emma Fulenwider, *Emma@wordserveliterary.com*

Agency: Established in 2003. Represents 200 clients. General-market nonfiction is limited to military, history, business, health, wellness, YA/children, some memoir. Other service: movie options.

Types of books: all faith-based adult and children's, general-market nonfiction

New clients: Open to writers who have not published a book. Contact: email query or referral from a current client. Accepts simultaneous submissions. Responds in four to six weeks.

Commission: 15%

Tip: "Keep your pitch letter sharp."

WORDWISE MEDIA SERVICES

4083 Avenue L, Ste. 255, Lancaster, CA 93536

submit@wordwisemedia.com | www.wordwisemedia.com/agency

Agents: Steven Hutson, David Fessenden, Michelle S. Lazurek

Agency: Established in 2011. Member of Association of American Literary Agents. Represents 60 clients.

Types of books: almost everything

New clients: Open to unpublished book authors. Contact: downloadable query form submitted as email attachment. Accepts simultaneous submissions. Responds in one month; OK to nudge after then.

Commission: 15%, more for movie deals

Tip: "Follow directions carefully. Meet us at a conference. Specify the agent's name in the email subject line if you have a preference."

YATES & YATES

1551 N. Tustin Ave., Ste. 710, Santa Ana, CA 92705 | 714-480-4000

email@yates2.com | *www.yates2.com*

Agents: Sealy Yates, Matt Yates, Curtis Yates, Mike Salisbury, Karen Yates

Agency: Established in 1988. Represents fewer than 50 clients.

Types of books: adult nonfiction

New clients: No unpublished book authors. Contact: Query through the website. Responds in one to two months. Other service: author coaching.

Commission: negotiable

Tip: "We serve passionate, articulate, gifted Christian communicators, using our strengths to guide, counsel and protect them, fiercely advocate for them, and help them advance life- and culture-transforming messages for the sake of the Kingdom."

18

WRITERS CONFERENCES AND SEMINARS

Note: This chapter is divided by states, international countries, and online, each section in alphabetical order. Many directors had not set dates and details for 2026 when this book went to print, so check the websites for up-to-date information.

ALABAMA

BLUE LAKE CHRISTIAN WRITERS CONFERENCE
Andalusia, AL | March 18–21 | *BLCWC.com*
> **Director:** Susan Neal, 850-393-3681, *SusanNeal@Bellsouth.net*
> **Description:** "At Blue Lake Christian Writers Conference, you'll enjoy the depth and diversity of a large writers conference but with a personal touch that makes all the difference. For example, you'll receive 30-minutes of mentoring with faculty, not a short, 15-minute appointment. Whether you're just beginning your writing journey or are an established author, our conference caters to both fiction and nonfiction enthusiasts along with a poetry flare."
> **Faculty:** agents, editors, publishers
> **Plenary speakers:** Michelle Medlock Adams, Linda Evans Shepherd, Babbie Mason
> **Scholarships:** partial
> **Attendance:** 100
> **Contests:** Living Water Awards for unpublished works

SOUTHERN CHRISTIAN WRITERS CONFERENCE
Leeds, AL (Birmingham area) | June | *www.facebook.com/groups/81752677629*
> **Director:** Cheryl Wray, 205-534-0595, *scwritersconference@gmail.com*
> **Description:** "The SCWC is a two-day conference for beginners or experienced writers that focuses on several genres: nonfiction books, magazines, fiction, grammar, business aspects, legal aspects, etc."
> **Faculty:** agents, editors
> **Attendance:** 160–200

ARIZONA

FAITH, HOPE, & LOVE CHRISTIAN WRITERS IN-PERSON CONFERENCE
Phoenix, AZ | September 25–27 | *fhlchristianwriters.com/in-person-conference*
> **Director:** Pamela Tracy, *Pamela@fhlchristianwriters.com*
> **Description:** "This conference brings together publishing industry leaders including top-selling authors, agents, and editors to offer in-depth teaching to writers at all stages of their careers. Focusing on the smaller conference setting allows participants to form groups and connections that will further their careers."
> **Faculty:** agents, editors, publishers
> **Scholarships:** full, partial
> **Attendance:** 100

CALIFORNIA

VISION CHRISTIAN WRITERS CONFERENCE
Mt. Hermon, CA (near Santa Cruz) | March 27–31 | *vcwconf.com*
> **Director:** Robynne Elizabeth Miller, *director@vcwconf.com*
> **Description:** "All-inclusive conference for beginners through advanced writers with over 50 teaching options and an industry-leading faculty to attendee ratio. Free pitch/advice appointments, contest entry, and writing critiques, set in the stunning coastal redwoods."
> **Special track:** advanced writers
> **Faculty:** agents, editors, publishers
> **Plenary speakers:** Jim Rubart, Bill Myers, Robin Jones Gunn, Cynthia Ruchti
> **Scholarships:** full, partial

Attendance: 150–200

Contest: Vision Writing Contest: themed, for nonfiction and fiction, no fee for attendees, cash prize

WEST COAST CHRISTIAN WRITERS CONFERENCE

Roseville, CA | October/November | *www.westcoastchristianwriters.com*

Directors: Sarah Sundin and Sarah Barnum, 800-660-0747, *info@westcoastchristianwriters.com*

Description: "The annual West Coast Christian Writers conference is a hybrid in-person/online event with a reputation for high-value teaching, expert speakers and mentors, hands-on help, a welcoming atmosphere, and innovation. Our faculty members are industry professionals—agents, editors, authors, and marketing and business experts—chosen to represent a variety of publishing methods, genres, interests, and ethnicities."

Faculty: agents, editors, publishers

Scholarships: partial

Attendance: 300

Contest: The Goldie Awards is a writing contest for original, unpublished submissions by conference attendees. Categories include fiction, nonfiction, memoir, poetry, children/YA, and "bad writing."

COLORADO

ILLUMIFY WRITERS CONFERENCE

Littleton, CO (Denver area) | October 3 | *www.IllumifyMedia.com*

Director: Michael J. Klassen, 303-523-4813, *mklassen@illumifymedia.com*

Description: "Every year Illumify Media hosts a one-day conference based on their proprietary 360-Degree Author philosophy, a comprehensive model for authorship that spans from the creative spark to the bookstore shelf—and beyond."

Special track: advanced writers

Faculty: editors, publishers

Attendance: 70

ROCKY MOUNTAIN CHRISTIAN WRITERS CONFERENCE

Lakewood, CO | May | *rmcw.us*

Director: Michael Klassen, *mklassen@illumifymedia.com*

Description: "The Rocky Mountain Christian Writers Conference is a day filled with inspiration, learning, and networking with fellow writers. Whether you're a seasoned writer or just starting out, this event at Colorado Christian University is the perfect place to grow your skills and connect with like-minded individuals. Don't miss this opportunity to take your writing to the next level."

Faculty: agents, editors, publishers

Plenary speakers: Catherine DeVries, Linda Evans Shepherd

WRITE IN THE SPRINGS

Colorado Springs, CO | March 27–28 | *www.acfwcosprings.com/wits-2026*

Director: Felicia Ferguson, 270-779-9685, *conference@acfwcosprings.com*

Description: "Pepper Basham, Jaime Jo Wright, and Lisa Phillips join forces for a genre-track conference with a half-day indie publishing intensive. Appointment times with each speaker will be available for brainstorming, critique, or specific Q/A time. Pitch opportunities with an agent/editor."

Special tracks: advanced writers, teens

Faculty: agents, editors, publishers

Scholarships: full, partial

Attendance: 60

CONNECTICUT

reNEW—SPIRITUAL RETREAT FOR WRITERS AND SPEAKERS

Litchfield, CT | October 15–18 | *reNEWwriting.com*

Director: Rachel Britton, 978-758-9574, *info@renewwriting.com*

Description: "reNEW is a community of Christ-following writers and speakers, both beginners and seasoned, growing inwardly so we can be effective outwardly."

Special track: speaking

Plenary speaker: Edie Melson

Scholarships: partial

Attendance: 70

FLORIDA

FLORIDA CHRISTIAN WRITERS CONFERENCE

Leesburg, FL | October 21–25 | *Word-Weavers.com/FloridaEvents*

Directors: Eva Marie Everson and Taryn Souders, 407-209-4141, *FCWCManager@aol.com*

Description: "Florida in autumn—what could be better? Add to the glorious weather 10 continuing classes, all-day intensives, and four days of 1- and 3-hour workshops, VIP Breakfasts (with speakers), Just-Write Getaways, inspiring praise and worship, Brainstorming with the Experts, and the best in keynote speakers. Writers of all levels are welcome!"

Special tracks: advanced writers, speaking

Faculty: agents, editors, publishers

Scholarships: full, partial

Attendance: 250

Contests: SonShine Awards, see website for details

REALM MAKERS WINTER RETREAT

Panama City Beach, FL | February 15–19 | *www.realmmakers.com/winter-retreat*

Director: Rebecca Minor, *becky@realmmakers.com*

Description: "The Realm Makers Winter Retreat seeks to gather writers of all experience levels in an encouraging, intimate setting where they can learn from a master writer and experience fellowship along the way. Writers will enjoy time gaining new skills, as well as opportunities to focus on the manuscript of their choosing."

Plenary speaker: Lindsay A. Franklin

Attendance: 40

GEORGIA

WRITING FOR YOUR LIFE

Atlanta, GA | April or May | *writingforyourlife.com/conferences*

Director: Kate Rademacher, 919-357-0099, *wfylinfo@gmail.com*

Description: "Writing for Your Life is committed to offering a wide variety of useful resources and services to support spiritual writers. We offer in-person writing conferences and online events and videos featuring leading spiritual writers and publishing-industry experts. Authors discuss and teach about various aspects of spiritual writing. Industry experts offer advice on how to get published and how to market."

Faculty: agents, editors, publishers

Scholarships: partial

Attendance: 100

ILLINOIS

WRITE TO PUBLISH CONFERENCE

Wheaton, IL (Chicago area) | June 9-12 | *writetopublish.com*

> **Director:** Becky Antkowiak, *becky@christianwritersinstitute.com*
> **Description:** "No matter where you are in your writing career—beginning the journey to becoming a published writer, exploring the process of becoming a working writer, or an experienced professional desiring to stay connected and growing—the Write to Publish Conference is your key to reaching those goals."
> **Faculty:** agents, editors, publishers
> **Scholarships:** full, partial
> **Attendance:** 300

INDIANA

TAYLOR UNIVERSITY PROFESSIONAL WRITERS CONFERENCE

Upland, IN | July 24-25 with intensive track July 23-24 | *taylorprofessional writersconference.weebly.com*

> **Director:** Linda K. Taylor, Taylor University, 1846 Main St., Upland, IN 46989; 765-998-5591; *taylorpwrconference@gmail.com*
> **Description:** "This conference is for all types of writers—beginners who have never been to a conference, teens (16+) who want to explore their desire to write, older folks who finally want to put pen to paper, and even seasoned writers who just want to soak in some training and be around other writers. This is a perfect conference to begin or continue your writing journey."
> **Plenary speaker:** Steven James
> **Special track:** advanced writers
> **Faculty:** agents, editors
> **Attendance:** 120

WINONA CHRISTIAN WRITERS CONFERENCE

Winona Lake, IN | July 16-18 | *www.grace.edu/about/the-winona-christian-writers-conference*

> **Director:** Lauren Rich, Grace College, 1 Lancer Way, Winona Lake, IN 46590; 574-904-3101; *richlg@grace.edu*
> **Description:** "Located on Grace College campus near beautiful Winona

Lake, Indiana, the Winona Christian Writers Conference welcomes emerging writers of all walks: from college students and graduate students to teachers and other adults seeking to improve and publish their writing. Drawn together by our unique perspective as believers, WCWC focuses on excellence, beauty, and craft."
Plenary speaker: Jessica Hooten Wilson
Scholarships: full, partial
Attendance: 65

IOWA

CEDAR FALLS CHRISTIAN WRITERS CONFERENCE

Cedar Falls, IA | June 4–6 | *cfcwc.org*

Directors: Nick and Mary Portzen, 563-235-9408, *cfcwconference@gmail.com*
Description: "We welcome new writers, established writers, and everyone interested in the writer's craft. Our purpose is to glorify God and His Son Jesus Christ through all we do as we encourage others in the craft of writing."
Faculty: editors, publishers
Plenary speaker: James C. Magruder
Scholarships: partial
Attendance: 30

KENTUCKY

KENTUCKY CHRISTIAN WRITERS CONFERENCE

Elizabethtown, KY | October | *www.kychristianwriters.com*

Director: Sara R. Turnquist, *info@kychristianwriters.com*
Description: "Our purpose is to provide an annual, interdenominational event to equip and encourage writers in their quest for publication. The conference provides a safe environment where writers can discover their gifts and share their work."
Faculty: agents, editors, publishers
Attendance: 75

MICHIGAN

FESTIVAL OF FAITH & WRITING

Grand Rapids, MI | April 16–18 | *ccfw.calvin.edu/festival-of-faith-and-writing*

>**Director:** Jennifer Holberg, Director, Calvin Center for Faith & Writing, *ccfw@calvin.edu*
>
>**Description:** "The Festival of Faith & Writing is a unique celebration. For three days every other April, we gather on the campus of Calvin University in Grand Rapids, Michigan, to explore the power of belief and the written word. Through lectures, readings, and engaging conversations, we bring together a vibrant community of readers and writers for a genuinely inspiring experience."
>
>**Special track:** speaking
>
>**Highlighted speakers:** Robin Wall Kimmerer, Laurie Halse Anderson, Ross Gay, Barbara Brown Taylor, Ariel Lawhon
>
>**Scholarships:** partial
>
>**Attendance:** 1,200

SPEAK UP CONFERENCE

Grand Rapids, MI | July 10–12 | *speakupconference.com*

>**Director:** Bonnie Emmorey, 316-882-9400, *bonnie@speakupconference.com*
>
>**Description:** "The Speak Up Conference is a three-day event where Christian communicators gather to learn how to spread the gospel and build up the body of Christ through speaking and writing."
>
>**Special track:** speaking
>
>**Faculty:** agents, editors, publishers
>
>**Scholarships:** partial
>
>**Attendance:** 250

THE WELL CONFERENCE

Zeeland, MI (Grand Rapids area) | April 30–May 2 | *seeyouatthewell.net*

>**Director:** Victoria Chapin, 616-886-8636, *victoriaatthewell@gmail.com*
>
>**Description:** "Come and be equipped and refreshed as you network with our creative community."
>
>**Special tracks:** advanced writers, speaking
>
>**Faculty:** agents, editors, publishers
>
>**Scholarships:** full, partial
>
>**Attendance:** 150
>
>**Contest:** Oasis Awards for unpublished Christian fiction and nonfiction

manuscripts, devotionals, play scripts, and screenplays. Winners will receive The Well OASIS Award and a publishing prize for their submitted work. For more info: *seeyouatthewell.net/contests/oasis-awards*.

MISSOURI

REALM MAKERS WRITERS CONFERENCE

St. Louis, MO | July 24–27 | *www.realmmakers.com/annual-conference*

Director: Becky Minor, *becky@realmmakers.com*

Description: "Realm Makers is a writers conference for Christian authors writing in the genres of fantasy, science fiction, or horror. Agents and editors from both Christian publishing and the general market can be found at Realm Makers." Note: This conference changes location every year.

Special tracks: advanced writers, teens

Faculty: agents, editors, publishers

Scholarships: full, partial

Attendance: 525

NORTH CAROLINA

ASHEVILLE CHRISTIAN WRITERS CONFERENCE

Asheville, NC | February 27–March 1 | *www.ashevillechristianwriters conference.com*

Director: Cindy Sproles, *cindyksproles@gmail.com*

Description: "ACWC equips new writers, refines seasoned writers, and then celebrates their successes."

Special track: advanced writers

Faculty: agents, editors

Plenary speakers: Bob Hostetler, Eva Marie Everson

Scholarships: partial

Attendance: 120

Contest: Sparrow Award Book Contest for unpublished manuscripts

BLUE RIDGE MOUNTAINS CHRISTIAN WRITERS CONFERENCE

Black Mountain, NC | May 25–29 | *www.BlueRidgeConference.com*

Director: Edie Melson, 864-373-4232, *ediegmelson@gmail.com*

Description: "This is a multidiscipline conference that caters to writers of all levels. In addition to outstanding craft/industry instruction, there is a strong focus on preparing spiritually to follow God as He directs our words for His glory."

Special tracks: advanced writers, speaking, teens
Faculty: agents, editors, publishers
Scholarships: partial
Attendance: 550
Contests: Selah Awards (industry-wide published books), Directors' Choice Awards (for former attendees and those in attendance at the 2026 event), Foundation Awards (restricted to unpublished writers who are attending the 2026 event)

MOUNTAINSIDE NOVELIST RETREAT

Black Mountain, NC | November | *www.BlueRidgeConference.com/ mountainside-retreats*

Director: Edie Melson, 864-373-4232, *ediegmelson@gmail.com*
Description: "Through small-group instruction and hands-on exercises from bestselling writers, the craftsman is able to focus on building strengths from challenges. Writers developing all levels of their careers will benefit from one-on-one consultations, brainstorming, and instruction. This event is a guided intensive where all participants have the opportunity to practice what they're learning under experienced team leaders."
Attendance: 40

SHE SPEAKS CONFERENCE

Charlotte, NC | July 17–18 | *shespeaksconference.com*

Director: Lisa Allen, Proverbs 31 Ministries, PO Box 3189, Matthews, NC 28106; 704-849-2270; *shespeaks@Proverbs31.org*
Description: Speaking and writing tracks. For women only.
Special track: speaking
Faculty: agents, editors
Attendance: 700

OKLAHOMA

OKLAHOMA CHRISTIAN FICTION WRITERS MINICON

Edmond, OK | April | *okchristianfictionwriters.com*

Director: Kristy Werner, 405-714-2935, *authors@okchristianfictionwriters.com*

Description: "One-day writer's conference. VIP luncheon with speakers is available."
Attendance: 25

OREGON

CASCADE CHRISTIAN WRITERS CONFERENCE
Canby, OR (Portland area) | June 14–17 | *cascadechristianwriters.org*
Director: Christina Suzann Nelson, CCW, PO Box 22, Gladstone, OR 97027; *business@cascadechristianwriters.org*
Description: "A multi-day conference with a focus on improving craft, fellowship with other writers, and increasing publishing opportunities. We write for both Christian and secular publishers/publications."
Special tracks: advanced writers, teens
Faculty: agents, editors, publishers
Scholarships: partial
Attendance: 200
Contest: Cascade Awards with multiple opportunities to enter and gain invaluable feedback from three experienced writing/publishing judges; opens in January

CASCADE CHRISTIAN WRITERS FALL ONE-DAY CONFERENCE
Tualatin, OR (Portland area) | October | *www.cascadechristianwriters.org*
Director: Christina Suzann Nelson, CCW, PO Box 22, Gladstone, OR 97027; *business@cascadechristianwriters.org*
Description: "A one-day conference with a focus on improving craft, fellowship with other writers, and increasing publishing opportunities. We write for both Christian and secular publishers/publications."
Faculty: agents
Attendance: 100+

PENNSYLVANIA

LANCASTER CHRISTIAN WRITERS CONFERENCE
New Holland, PA | November | *lancasterchristianwriters.org*
Director: Cheryl Weber, email through the website

MONTROSE CHRISTIAN WRITERS CONFERENCE

Montrose, PA | July 13–17 | *www.montrosebible.org*

Director: Amy Radford, *directormcwc@gmail.com*

Description: "In a family atmosphere at the restored home and conference center of evangelist R.A. Torrey, the conference always offers a faculty of best-selling authors, agents, editors, and publishers who present classes for beginners as well as published authors, teaching fiction, nonfiction, children's fiction and nonfiction, marketing, poetry, music, drama, and numerous subgenres. Private critiques are always offered, as well as works-in-progress sessions."

Special tracks: advanced writers, teens

Faculty: agents, editors, publishers

Scholarships: partial

Attendance: 70

Contest: The Shirley Brinkerhoff Scholarship Fund offers $200 to the best entry of a 300-piece submission based on the year's theme.

ST. DAVIDS CHRISTIAN WRITERS' CONFERENCE

Meadville, PA | June 24–28 | *stdavidswriters.com*

Director: Sue A. Fairchild, *sueafairchild74@gmail.com*

Description: "St. Davids Christian Writers' Conference has been equipping writers since 1957 with our intimate gathering each June that provides an opportunity to build a network of friends, mentors, and encouragers, all seeking to share God's message with the world. Each conference strives to provide teaching for a wide range of genres and writing levels."

Special track: speaking

Faculty: agents, editors, publishers

Scholarships: full, partial

Attendance: 70

Contest: A wide variety of contest categories and winners receive a discount off next year's conference registration. First-place winners have their entries read at the Saturday night banquet.

SOUTH CAROLINA

CAROLINA CHRISTIAN WRITERS CONFERENCE

Greer, SC | March | *www.carolinacwc.com*

Director: Linda Gilden, 864-309-8644,
info@carolinachristinwritersconference.com

Description: "Focus is on learning to write to reach others with the love of Jesus. Special features include panel discussions for all levels of writers, one-on-one appointments with publishers, editors, and agents. Pastors Day is Thursday for pastors and ministry leaders. This is separate to help pastors to learn how to reuse their research to create books and articles from the research they have done for their sermons and Sunday School lessons. Publishers and editors will be there to assist them."

Special tracks: advanced writers, pastors, speaking

Faculty: agents, editors, publishers

Scholarships: full

Attendance: 125

Contest: Kudos contest for book and article writers, published and unpublished

TENNESSEE

ACFW CONFERENCE

Memphis, TN | October 29–November 1 | *www.acfw.com/conference*

Director: Robin Miller, *director@acfw.com*

Description: "Each year, hundreds of veteran authors and those just learning the craft of Christian fiction gather ... to hear skilled instructors, inspiring keynoters ... to gain from the insights of industry professionals ... to interact with other writers ... and to present their ideas to agents and editors looking for stories like theirs, or to mentors who can help them move forward in their writing career. If you write Christian fiction—or want to learn how— the ACFW conference is an investment worth making." Note: This conference changes location every year.

Special track: advanced writers

Faculty: agents, editors, publishers

Scholarships: full

Attendance: 500

Contests: The Genesis Contest is for unpublished writers whose Christian fiction manuscript is completed. The Carol Awards honor the best of Christian fiction from the previous calendar year.

THE CHRISTY AWARD® ART OF WRITING CONFERENCE

Nashville, TN | November | *thechristyaward.com*

> **Director:** Cindy Carter, ECPA, 5801 S. McClintock Dr., Ste. 104, Mesa, AZ 85283; 480-966-3998; *TheChristyAward@ecpa.org*
>
> **Description:** "A focused conference for writers, storytellers, and publishing curators that features four top-of-the-moment topics with excellent speakers and panelists in the know. The conference immediately precedes the evening Gala of The Christy Award® program."
>
> **Faculty:** agents, editors, publishers
>
> **Attendance:** 125

EVANGELICAL PRESS ASSOCIATION ANNUAL CONVENTION

Franklin, TN | May 11–13 | *epaconvention.com*

> **Director:** Lamar Keener, EPA, PO Box 1787, Queen Creek, AZ 85142; 888-311-1731; *director@evangelicalpress.com*
>
> **Description:** "The annual EPA Christian media convention is your chance to step away from daily activities to engage and interact with the EPA community. Join together to explore new ideas and learn from one another through powerful seminars, workshops, discussions and presentations—all focused on creating content for writers, editors and designers." Note: This conference changes location every year.
>
> **Faculty:** editors
>
> **Attendance:** 200
>
> **Contests:** Freelance writers with EPA membership may submit articles and/or blog entries into Awards of Excellence and Higher Goals in Journalism.

MID-SOUTH CHRISTIAN WRITERS CONFERENCE

Collierville, TN (Memphis area) | March 21 | *midsouthchristianwriters.com*

> **Director:** Beth Gooch, 901-277-5525, *beth@bethgooch.com*
>
> **Description:** "Mid-South Christian Writers Conference is an affordable, one-day conference, with a balance of fiction and nonfiction. We also have optional add-on workshops the day before the conference."
>
> **Faculty:** agents, editors
>
> **Plenary speaker:** DiAnn Mills
>
> **Scholarships:** partial
>
> **Attendance:** 100

TEXAS

DECLARE CONFERENCE

New Hope, TX (Dallas area) | September | *declareconference.com/declare-conference*

> **Director:** Eryn Hall, *eryn@wearedeclare.com*
>
> **Description:** "The Declare Conference empowers and equips Christian women who influence, lead, speak, write, communicate, and create content. Prepare for a restorative time with networking opportunities, productive work, and interactive sessions. Whether you're attending to learn, collaborate, work, or rest, the Declare Conference will be a game-changer. If you come with a hungry heart, you will encounter God and experience holy restoration."

WASHINGTON

NORTHWEST CHRISTIAN WRITERS RENEWAL

Bellevue, WA | April 25–26 | *nwchristianwriters.org/Conference*

> **Director:** *admin@nwchristianwriters.org*
>
> **Description:** "This conference is where writers, editors, and publishers can connect, network, and collaborate. Conferees will sharpen their skills, learn strategies, and form connections to boost their success on the writing journey."
>
> **Faculty:** agents, editors, publishers
>
> **Scholarships:** full
>
> **Attendance:** 130

AUSTRALIA

OMEGA WRITERS CONFERENCE

Adelaide, South Australia | October | *www.omegawriters.com.au*

> **Director:** Karen Roper, *secretary@omegawriters.com.au*
>
> **Description:** "For Christian writers or aspiring Christian writers in Australia and New Zealand, Omega Writers Conference rotates between retreats in odd years and in-person conferences in even years. They offer focused craft workshops, genre groups, networking opportunities, as well as sessions on essential skills for writers. In-person conferences also offer the opportunity for

271

one-on-one appointments with editors, agents, and publishers and walking away with friendships and Christian encouragement."
Attendance: 100

CANADA

InSCRIBE CHRISTIAN WRITERS' FELLOWSHIP CONFERENCE

Saskatoon, SK, Canada | September | *inscribe.org/fall-conference*

Director: *president@inscribe.org*

Description: "InScribe's fall conference features a seasoned author, publisher, or other expert as the keynote speaker; plus we offer a variety of workshop topics and presenters. It's a weekend where writers—whether they are seasoned or beginning—can connect for fellowship, encouragement, and support."

Scholarships: partial

Contests: See *www.inscribe.org/contests*.

ONLINE

ACFW DFW READY WRITERS MINI-CONFERENCE

April 11 | *www.facebook.com/DFWReadyWriters*

Director: Paula Peckham, 817-454-5218, *acfwdfw@gmail.com*

Description: "Four speakers will each present a class and a keynote speaker. The classes are targeted toward Christian fiction writers on various levels of experience."

Faculty: agents

Attendance: 30–35

ACFW VIRGINIA ROYAL WRITERS VIRTUAL CONFERENCE

November 6–7 | *acfwvirginia.com/writers-conference*

Director: Kelly Goshorn, 540-454-4144, *acfwvirginia@gmail.com*

Description: "The Royal Writers Conference is geared to Christian fiction writers and seeks to extend your knowledge of the business and craft of writing, fill you with inspiration, and provide the tools you need to write for His glory. Over two days, you'll enjoy two keynote addresses, 24 workshops, connection opportunities with writers, and appointments with agents, editors, and authors, all for

an unbelievably affordable price."
Faculty: agents, editors, publishers
Scholarships: full, partial
Attendance: 200–250

CASCADE CHRISTIAN WRITERS SPRING ONE-DAY CONFERENCE

March 14 | *cascadechristianwriters.org*

Director: Christina Suzann Nelson, CCW, PO Box 22, Gladstone, OR 97027; *business@cascadechristianwriters.org*

Description: "A one-day conference with a focus on improving craft, fellowship with other writers, and increasing publishing opportunities. We write for both Christian and secular publishers/publications."

Faculty: agents
Attendance: 100+

FAITH, HOPE, & LOVE CHRISTIAN WRITERS VIRTUAL CONFERENCE

March 21 | *fhlchristianwriters.com/virtual-conference*

Director: Edwina Kiernan, *vp@fhlchristianwriters.com*

Description: "A one day conference offering teachings on both the craft and business side of writing." For writers of Christian romance and women's fiction with romantic elements.

Attendance: 75

MT ZION RIDGE PRESS ONLINE WRITING CONFERENCE

April 30–May 2 | *mzrpchristianwritingconference.com*

Director: Penny McGinnis, 937-402-0782, *penny.frost.mcginnis@gmail.com*

Description: "The online conference with an in-person experience."

Faculty: agents, editors, publishers
Attendance: 60

PENCON

May 6–8 | *PENCONeditors.com*

Director: Liz Tolsma, *director@PENCONeditors.com*

Description: "Our three-day conference offers sessions for both fiction and nonfiction editors to improve their skills, to connect with one another, and to learn from some of the industry's top professionals."

Faculty: editors
Scholarships: partial
Attendance: 65

PUBLISHING IN COLOR
spring and fall | *publishingincolor.com*

> **Director:** Joyce Dinkins, PO Box 150, Grand Junction, MI 49056; *JoyceDinkinsPublishing@gmail.com*
> **Description:** "Publishing in Color is a bridge for Black and Indigenous People of Color (BIPOC) striving to publish content that shares biblical truths with everyone. Through its conferences and network, PIC helps connect creatives with publishers addressing historic underrepresentation."
> **Faculty:** agents, editors, publishers
> **Plenary speaker:** Joyce Dinkins
> **Scholarships:** full
> **Attendance:** 100

STORY EMBERS SUMMIT
May | *storyembers.org/summit*

> **Director:** Brianna Storm Hilvety, *brianna@storyembers.org*
> **Description:** "The Story Embers Summit is a 3-day virtual event where Christian authors and editors give actionable advice on how to exceed readers' expectations, develop authentic characters, convey resonant themes, and other topics focused on either craft or mindset, all with a strong faith component."
> **Faculty:** agents, editors
> **Scholarships:** full, partial
> **Attendance:** 150

WEST COAST CHRISTIAN WRITERS CONFERENCE
October/November | *www.westcoastchristianwriters.com*
See entry in California.

WRITE HIS ANSWER CONFERENCE
end of June or mid-August | *conference.writehisanswer.com*

> **Director:** Marlene Bagnull, 267-436-2503, *mbagnull@aol.com*
> **Description:** "The former Colorado and Greater Philly Christian Writers Conferences combine into one huge online conference with faculty of more than 60 editors, agents, and authors. All the features of an in-person conference, including 7 keynotes, 9 learning labs, 9 continuing sessions, and 63 workshops. Everything is live—no prerecords. For a nominal fee conferees can purchase access to over 100 hours of video replays through the end of the year. In addition

to small-group breakouts, round tables, critique groups, 6 panels, and preconference events, conferees get 3 free appointments with editors or agents."

Faculty: agents, editors, publishers

Scholarships: partial

Attendance: 250

Contest: Poetry (12–30 lines) or prose (500–800 words) on our conference theme, "Write His Answer"—not only how He is calling you to "write His answer" but also what you have found to be His answer in the struggles you have faced as you have sought to "live His answer." Published and not-yet published writers are judged in separate categories. This is a win-win contest since everyone who enters receives their choice of a free ebook, either *Sleeping Near the Ark* or *Write His Answer: A Bible Study for Christian Writers*.

WRITE2IGNITE MASTER CLASSES

April and September | *write2ignite.com*

Director: Jean Matthew Hall, 704-578-0858, *jeanmatthewhall@outlook.com*

Description: "Master Classes are designed to educate, inspire, and encourage Christian writers of literature for children and young adults."

Faculty: agents, editors

Attendance: 30

19

WRITERS ORGANIZATIONS AND GROUPS

Note: In addition to the groups listed here, check the writers organizations for new groups in your area and information about starting a group.

WRITERS ORGANIZATIONS

540 WRITERS COMMUNITY

540writerscommunity.com

> **Contact:** Becky Antkowiak, PO Box 133, Sutherland, VA 23885; *becky@540writerscommunity.com*
>
> **Services:** Free, stellar education accessible to every writer. We offer educational sessions, writing accountability, peer-to-peer feedback, 24/7 Write-in Zoom, and more—all online, free, and accessible.
>
> **Members:** 1,700+
>
> **Membership fee:** none

ADVANCED WRITERS & SPEAKERS ASSOCIATION (AWSA)

awsa.com

> **Contact:** Linda Evans Shepherd, 303-709-9043, *LindaReply@gmail.com*
>
> **Services:** "Advanced Writers and Speakers Association is a professional group made up of the top 10 percent of Christian women in the publishing and speaking world. Our main event is the annual AWSA conference prior to the opening of the Christian Product Expo. We host online mastermind groups for community, as well as the Golden Scroll Awards Banquet where we honor authors, editors and publishers for their excellence. Our communication

centers around an online loop where we find connection and prayer support with those who are traveling similar journeys. We are also the publishers of *Leading Hearts,* the award-winning magazine to empower Christian women for leadership and a daily devotional, *Arise Daily."* Also offers online training and coaching and different levels of membership.

Members: 800+

Membership fee: $50/year

AMERICAN CHRISTIAN FICTION WRITERS

acfw.com

Contact: Robin Miller, PO Box 101066, Palm Bay, FL 32910-1066; *director@acfw.com*

Services: Email loop, genre Facebook pages, online courses, critique groups, and local and regional chapters. Sponsors contests for published and unpublished writers and conducts the largest Christian fiction writers conference annually.

Members: 2,600+

Membership fee: $75 to join, $49/year to renew

CASCADE CHRISTIAN WRITERS

cascadechristianwriters.org

Contact: President, PO Box 22, Gladstone, OR 97027; *business@cascadechristianwriters.org*

Services: Monthly Zoom gatherings, critique groups, online writing groups, group Facebook page, discounts for conferences and contest entries, newsletter.

Membership fee: $55/year; 30 and younger, $40/year; seniors, $44/year

CHRISTIAN AUTHORS NETWORK

ChristianAuthorsNetwork.com

Contact: Susan U. Neal, 850-393-3681, *contact@christianauthorsnetwork.com*

Services: "CAN is a group of traditionally published Christian authors who have joined together in a supportive association to spread the news about books to book lovers everywhere. We operate as a cooperative, Christ-centered marketing organization, to encourage and teach one another, and get the word out about CAN authors' books to readers, retailers, and librarians. Membership is open to authors with two or more published books. One must be a Christian book published by a traditional royalty-paying publisher

(with no financial input by the author), whose books are currently available in publication (in any and all formats) at the date of the membership application."
Members: 140
Membership fee: $90/year

CHRISTIAN INDIE AUTHOR NETWORK
www.christianindieauthors.com

Contact: Mary C. Findley, 918-805-0669, *mjmcfindley@gmail.com*
Services: Provides a readers site to connect independently published books to readers, several Facebook groups for both authors and readers, and book promotion opportunities.
Members: 400+
Membership fee: none

THE CHRISTIAN PEN: Proofreaders and Editors Network
www.TheChristianPEN.com

Contact: Jayna Baas, *director@TheChristianPEN.com*
Services: "The Christian PEN: Proofreaders and Editors Network provides aspiring, beginning, established, and professional editors and proofreaders with networking, community, and industry discounts. If you are an editor or proofreader, or are thinking about becoming one, join this community of like-minded professionals who share our knowledge and experience with one another."
Members: 200
Membership fee: $30–90/year

FAITH, HOPE, & LOVE CHRISTIAN WRITERS
fhlchristianwriters.com

Contact: Lori Altebaumer, *president@fhlchristianwriters.com*
Services: "To promote excellence in Christian fiction and/or fiction written from a Christian worldview. To help Christian writers establish their careers and to provide continuing support for writers within the fiction-publishing industry. We accomplish this stated purpose through our email groups, our online programs, our contests and awards, etc."
Membership fee: $35/year

INSPIRE CHRISTIAN WRITERS

www.inspirewriters.com

Contact: Dina Preuss, *communications@inspirewriters.com*

Services: "Through Inspire you'll find a community of writers working together to achieve writing and publication goals. By taking advantage of our online and in-person critique groups, you'll give and receive feedback and grow in your craft. We offer web-based and local training through workshops and conferences to help you navigate publishing decisions, create your online presence, and polish your writing until it shines. You'll have opportunities to network with other writers—multipublished as well as those just starting out." Sponsors the Vision Christian Writers Conference at Mt. Hermon.

Members: 150

Membership fee: $50/year

REALM MAKERS

www.realmmakers.com

Contact: Ralene Burke, membership director, *membership@ realmmakers.com*

Services: "Realm Makers supports writers and artists who create science fiction and fantasy in their journeys from idea to marketplace. Whether participating artists wish to gear their content for inspirational or mainstream audiences, Realm Makers seeks to encourage them from a faith-friendly perspective. Offers a membership program, where authors can connect throughout the year, critique one another's work, and participate in periodic webinars to keep their writing and marketing toolkits sharp." Sponsors the Realm Makers conference and Realm Makers Winter Retreat.

Members: 100

Membership fee: ranges from $7.99/month or $79.99/year to $14.99/month or $149.99/year

WORD WEAVERS INTERNATIONAL

www.Word-Weavers.com

Contact: Eva Marie Everson, CEO, PO Box 520224, Longwood, FL 32752; *WordWeaversInternational@aol.com*

Services: "Local traditional chapters and Zoom online pages for manuscript critiquing using our unique form of critique. Sponsors Florida Christian Writers Conference."

Members: 1,200

Membership fee: $55/year, traditional or online; $75/year, traditional plus online; teens: $45/year, traditional or online; $65/year, traditional plus online

WORDGIRLS

www.kathycarltonwillis.com/wordgirls

Contact: Kathy Carlton Willis, 956-642-6319, *kathy@kathycarltonwillis.com*

Services: "WordGirls is a special sisterhood of writing support for women writing from a biblical worldview (whether for the faith market or general market). Services include one-on-one coaching, topical monthly video sessions, writing accountability, prayer support, and more. In-person and virtual getaways are hosted several times a year. Sessions offer how-tos for the nonwriting side of the writing business, as well as honing writing skills. From want-to-be a writer to the multipublished, experienced professional, WordGirls helps each writer get to the next step of her writing journey. Membership is limited in order to customize services to the needs of the group. WordGirls is a group of fun, female believers from across America who are serious about writing."

Members: 30–40

Membership fee: $300/year; $250/year to renew; women only

NATIONAL AND INTERNATIONAL ONLINE GROUPS

ACFW BEYOND THE BORDERS

www.facebook.com/groups/ACFWBeyondtheBorders

Contact: Iola Goulton, *BeyondBorders@acfwchapter.com*

Members: 100, in all countries outside the US

Membership fee: national fee

Affiliation: American Christian Fiction Writers

ACFW KIDLIT

www.acfwkidlit.com, *www.facebook.com/groups/acfwkidlit*

Contact: Bettie Boswell, *acfwkidlit@acfwchapter.com*

Members: 165

Membership fee: national fee plus $10/year

Affiliation: American Christian Fiction Writers

WORD WEAVERS ONLINE GROUPS

Contact: Susan Simpson, *SimpsonCircle@gmail.com*
Members: 375
Membership fee: national fee
Affiliation: Word Weavers

ALABAMA

ACFW ALABAMA

www.facebook.com/groups/acfwalabama

Meetings: online, second Tuesdays; Huntsville, twice a year
Contact: Jenny Erlingsson, *Alabama@acfwchapter.com*
Members: 28
Membership fee: national fee
Affiliation: American Christian Fiction Writers

WORD WEAVERS NORTH ALABAMA

Facebook.com/Word Weavers North Alabama

Meetings: East Highland Baptist Church, 1030 Main St. E, Hartsell;
third Thursdays, 10:00 a.m.–noon
Contact: Bonita McCoy, *byvette.mccoy@gmail.com*
Members: 14
Membership fee: national fee
Affiliation: Word Weavers

ARIZONA

ACFW ARIZONA/CHRISTIAN WRITERS OF THE WEST

www.christianwritersofthewest.com

Meetings: Denny's Restaurant, 3315 N. Scottsdale Rd., Scottsdale;
second Saturdays, noon–2:00 p.m.
Contact: Jennifer Cary, *arizona@acfwchapter.com*
Members: 30
Membership fee: national fee plus $15/year
Affiliation: American Christian Fiction Writers

READY WRITERS PSALM 45:1
Meetings: Move City Church, 200 North Ave., Sierra Vista; second Saturdays, 10:00 a.m.–noon
Contact: Charity Plumb, 520-255-3020, *cplumbwrites@gmail.com*
Members: 7
Membership fee: none

WORD WEAVERS NORTHERN ARIZONA
Meetings: Verde Community Church, 102 S. Willard, Cottonwood; second Saturdays, 9:30–11:30 a.m.
Contact: Merrilyn Jones, *merrilynsgarden@protonmail.com*
Membership fee: national fee
Affiliation: Word Weavers

WORD WEAVERS SOUTHEAST ARIZONA
Meetings: Valley Christian Church, 5968 E. Fairmount St., Tuscan; third Saturdays, 10:00 a.m.–noon
Contact: Charity Plumb, *cplumbwrites@gmail.com*
Members: 5
Membership fee: national fee
Affiliation: Word Weavers

ARKANSAS

ACFW NW ARKANSAS
www.facebook.com/groups/127662834752320
Meetings: Springdale; first Mondays, 5:30 p.m.
Contact: Robyn Hook, *NWArkansas@acfwchapter.com*
Members: 20
Membership fee: national fee
Affiliation: American Christian Fiction Writers

CALIFORNIA

ACFW CALIFORNIA
Meetings: online, first Thursdays
Contact: Jennifer Hendricks, *california@acfwchapter.com*
Membership fee: national fee
Affiliation: American Christian Fiction Writers

WORD WARRIORS

www.facebook.com/wordwarriorswriters

> **Meetings:** online, first Tuesdays September–June, 7:00 p.m.
> **Contact:** Debbie Jones Warren, *debbiencj812@gmail.com*
> **Members:** 10
> **Membership fee:** none

COLORADO

ACFW COLORADO SPRINGS

acfwcosprings.net

> **Meetings:** Penrose Library, 20 N. Cascade, Colorado Springs; first
> Saturdays, 10:00–11:30 a.m.
> **Contact:** Felicia Ferguson, *info@acfwcosprings.com*
> **Services:** Sponsors the Write in the Springs Conference.
> **Members:** 60
> **Membership fee:** national fee plus $25/year
> **Affiliation:** American Christian Fiction Writers

WOLF CREEK CHRISTIAN WRITERS NETWORK

wolfcreekwriters.com

> **Meetings:** Grace in Pagosa and Zoom, 1044 Park Ave., Community
> Room, Pagosa Springs; Mondays except holidays, 9:00–11:00 a.m.
> **Contact:** Cathy McIver, 970-946-3554, *cmciver@pagosaheat.com*
> **Members:** 20
> **Membership fee:** $40/year

WORD WEAVERS PIKES PEAK

www.facebook.com/groups/415291469231448

> **Meetings:** Springs Church, 1515 Auto Mall Loop, Colorado Springs;
> third Saturdays, 9:15–11:45 a.m.
> **Contact:** Dan Daetz, *dan@scifipilot.com*
> **Members:** 20
> **Membership fee:** national fee plus $25
> **Affiliation:** Word Weavers

WORD WEAVERS WESTERN SLOPE

www.facebook.com/groups/568085077249557

> **Meetings:** Church on the Rock, 2170 Broadway, Grand Junction; fourth Saturdays, 10:00 a.m.–noon
> **Contact:** Templa Melnick, 970-261-7230, *templa.melnick@gmail.com*
> **Members:** 8
> **Membership fee:** national fee
> **Affiliation:** Word Weavers

WRITERS ON THE ROCK ARVADA

www.facebook.com/groups/281086379291783

> **Meetings:** email or call for location, Arvada; last Thursdays, 6:30–8:30 p.m.
> **Contact:** Sue Roberts, 303-467-0286, *srobertswithjoy@yahoo.com*
> **Membership fee:** none
> **Affiliation:** Writers on the Rock

WRITERS ON THE ROCK CASTLE ROCK

www.facebook.com/groups/193369214634778

> **Meetings:** Phillip Miller Library, 100 S. Wilcox St., Castle Rock; third Mondays, 6:30 p.m.
> **Contact:** Amber Baughman, *amberjbaughman@gmail.com*
> **Membership fee:** none
> **Affiliation:** Writers on the Rock

WRITERS ON THE ROCK COLORADO SPRINGS

www.facebook.com/groups/1916955675297782

> **Meetings:** Penrose Library, 20 N. Cascade Ave., Colorado Springs; second Thursdays, 6:30 p.m.
> **Contact:** April Musekamp, 719-650-1480
> **Membership fee:** none
> **Affiliation:** Writers on the Rock

WRITERS ON THE ROCK HIGHLANDS RANCH

www.facebook.com/groups/1509730649342640

> **Meetings:** 6653 S. Grant St., Centennial; first Thursdays, 6:30 p.m.
> **Contact:** Michael J. Klassen, 303-523-4813, *mklassen@illumifymedia.com*
> **Members:** 12
> **Membership fee:** none
> **Affiliation:** Writers on the Rock

WRITERS ON THE ROCK LAKEWOOD
www.writersontherock.com/groups

> **Meetings:** Green Mountain Recreation Center, 13198 W. Green Mountain Dr., Lakewood; fourth Tuesdays, 7:00–8:30 p.m.
> **Contact:** Amy Young, *amy.young@swissmail.org*
> **Membership fee:** none
> **Affiliation:** Writers on the Rock

WRITERS ON THE ROCK NORTH METRO DENVER
www.facebook.com/groups/1110986532338485

> **Meetings:** Crossroads Church, 10451 Huron St., Northglenn; first Mondays, 6:30–8:30 p.m.
> **Contact:** Marla Lindstrom Bentroth, *tellyourstorytoo@msn.com*
> **Membership fee:** none
> **Affiliation:** Writers on the Rock

WRITERS ON THE ROCK NORTHERN COLORADO
www.facebook.com/groups/445776855860806

> **Meetings:** Panera Bread, 1550 Fall River Dr., Loveland; third Thursdays, 7:00–8:30 p.m.
> **Contact:** Jen Grams, *jennygrams@gmail.com*
> **Membership fee:** none
> **Affiliation:** Writers on the Rock

DELAWARE

DELMARVA CHRISTIAN WRITERS' ASSOCIATION
www.facebook.com/groups/219751814716191

> **Meetings:** Georgetown; third Saturdays, 9:00 a.m.–noon
> **Contact:** *delmarvachristianwriters@yahoo.com*
> **Members:** 20
> **Membership fee:** none

FLORIDA

ACFW CENTRAL FLORIDA
www.facebook.com/CFACFW

> **Meetings:** online, third Saturdays

Contact: Kelly Underwood, *centralflorida@acfwchapter.com*
Membership fee: national fee
Affiliation: American Christian Fiction Writers

SUNCOAST CHRISTIAN WRITERS GROUP

Meetings: The Haus Coffee Shop, 12199 Indian Roacks Rd., Largo; third Wednesdays, 10:00 a.m.
Contact: Elaine Creasman, 727-251-3756, *emcreasman@aol.com;* contact her before attending first meeting
Members: 10–20
Membership fee: none

WORD WEAVERS BREVARD COUNTY

Meetings: Freedom Christian Center, 7250 Lake Andrew Dr., Melbourne; second Saturdays, 10:00 a.m.–noon
Contact: Irene Wintermeyer, *iwintermeyer@yahoo.com*
Members: 11
Membership fee: national fee
Affiliation: Word Weavers

WORD WEAVERS CLAY COUNTY

www.facebook.com/groups/WordWeaversClayCounty

Meetings: Panera Bread, 1510 County Rd. 220, Fleming Island; second Saturdays, 9:00–11:30 a.m.
Contact: Evelyn Collins, *wawacollins5@gmail.com*
Members: 9
Membership fee: national fee
Affiliation: Word Weavers

WORD WEAVERS DESTIN

Meetings: Crosspoint Bluewater, 4400 Highway 20 E, Ste. 600, Niceville; second Saturdays, 9:30 a.m.
Contact: Alice Murray, *pstyre@aol.com*
Members: 20
Membership fee: national fee
Affiliation: Word Weavers

WORD WEAVERS GAINESVILLE

Meetings: online, second Sundays, 2:00–4:30 p.m.
Contact: Lori Roberts, *authorLorilynRoberts@gmail.com*
Members: 6

Membership fee: national fee
Affiliation: Word Weavers

WORD WEAVERS JENSEN BEACH
www.facebook.com/groups/851396695481639

Meetings: Coastal Style Kitchens, conference room, 11274 Business Park Pl., Jensen Beach; third Saturdays, 9:30 a.m.–noon
Contact: Penny Cooke, *LifeCoachPenny@yahoo.com*
Membership fee: national fee
Affiliation: Word Weavers

WORD WEAVERS LAKE COUNTY
www.facebook.com/groups/1790245144535020

Meetings: Leesburg Public Library, 100 E. Main, Leesburg; third Saturdays, 9:30 a.m.–noon
Contact: Michael Anderson, *andersonwriter@gmail.com*
Members: 25
Membership fee: national fee
Affiliation: Word Weavers

WORD WEAVERS OCALA CHAPTER

Meetings: Belleview Public Library, 13145 S.E. County Hwy. 484, Belleview; second Fridays, 10:00 a.m.–12:30 p.m.
Contact: Yeny "Jenny" Rowley, *yenyrowley@yahoo.com*
Members: 18
Membership fee: national fee
Affiliation: Word Weavers

WORD WEAVERS ORLANDO
www.facebook.com/groups/216603998394619

Meetings: Calvary Chapel, 5015 Goddard Ave., Orlando; second Saturdays, 10:00 a.m.–12:30 p.m.
Contact: Brenda Fink, *brenda.fink335@gmail.com*
Members: 60
Membership fee: national fee
Affiliation: Word Weavers

WORD WEAVERS PACE

Meetings: Woodbine Baptist Church, 4912 CR 197A, Pace; first Thursdays, 6:30–8:30 p.m.
Contact: Ava Sturgeon, *avasturge@yahoo.com*

Membership fee: national fee
Affiliation: Word Weavers

WORD WEAVERS PENSACOLA

Meetings: Grace Lutheran Church, 6601 N. 9th Ave., Pensacola; second Tuesdays, 5:30–8:00 p.m.
Contact: Gretchen Huesmann, *gretchen.huesmann@gmail.com*
Members: 9
Membership fee: national fee
Affiliation: Word Weavers

WORD WEAVERS SANFORD

Meetings: 8224 Emerald Forest Ct., Sanford; second Tuesdays, 10:00 a.m.–noon
Contact: Suzanne Bennett, *SuzyB3699@hotmail.com*
Membership fee: national fee
Affiliation: Word Weavers

WORD WEAVERS SARASOTA

Meetings: 6807 48th Ter. E, Bradenton; third Sundays, 2:00–4:30 p.m.
Contact: Deb Entsminger, *Navgirladventures@gmail.com*
Members: 7
Membership fee: national fee
Affiliation: Word Weavers

WORD WEAVERS TAMPA

Meetings: 1901 S. Village Ave., Tampa; first Saturdays, 9:30 a.m.–noon
Contact: Sharron Cosby, *sharroncosby@gmail.com*
Members: 25
Membership fee: national fee
Affiliation: Word Weavers

WORD WEAVERS TREASURE COAST

www.facebook.com/groups/480150568723000
Meetings: First Church of God Vero Beach, 1105 58th Ave., Vero Beach; first Saturdays, 9:30 a.m.–noon
Contact: Del Bates, *Del@DelBates.com*
Members: 10
Membership fee: national fee
Affiliation: Word Weavers

WORD WEAVERS VOLUSIA COUNTY

www.facebook.com/groups/227447203952675

> **Meetings:** Faith Church, 4700 S. Clyde Morris Blvd., Port Orange; first Mondays, 7:00 p.m.
> **Contact:** Donna Collins Tinsley, *ThornRose7@aol.com*
> **Members:** 25
> **Membership fee:** national fee
> **Affiliation:** Word Weavers

GEORGIA

ACFW GEORGIA

acfwnga.wordpress.com, www.facebook.com/groups/acfwga

> **Meetings:** Zoom, second Tuesdays, 6:30–8:30 p.m.
> **Contact:** Janette Melson, *georgia@acfwchapter.com*
> **Members:** 56
> **Membership fee:** national fee plus $15/year
> **Affiliation:** American Christian Fiction Writers

CHRISTIAN AUTHORS GUILD

www.christianauthorsguild.org

> **Meetings:** Sojourn Woodstock, 8816 Main St., Woodstock; first Mondays, 7:00 p.m.
> **Contact:** Deborah Crawford, *deborahrdcrawford@gmail.com*
> **Members:** 30
> **Membership fee:** $30/year

WORD WEAVERS BROOKHAVEN

www.facebook.com/groups/200656040663612

> **Meetings:** Westminster Presbyterian Church, 1438 Sheridan Rd. NE, Atlanta; second Saturdays, 10:00 a.m.–12:30 p.m.
> **Contact:** Maria Gosa, *MariposaArt@Live.com*
> **Members:** 13
> **Membership fee:** national fee
> **Affiliation:** Word Weavers

WORD WEAVERS COLUMBUS

www.facebook.com/groups/541016626433688

> **Meetings:** Columbus Public Library, 3000 Macon Rd., Columbus;

third Mondays, 6:00–8:30 p.m.
Contact: Terri Miller, *wordweaverscolumbus@gmail.com*
Members: 8
Membership fee: national fee
Affiliation: Word Weavers

WORD WEAVERS CONYERS
www.facebook.com/groups/638509006538934
Meetings: Bethel Christian Church, 1930 Bethel Rd. NE, Conyers;
third Saturdays, 10:00 a.m.–noon
Contact: Terri Webster, *TerriJWebster@gmail.com*
Members: 8
Membership fee: national fee
Affiliation: Word Weavers

WORD WEAVERS GREATER ATLANTA
Meetings: 4541 Vendome Pl. NE, Roswell; first Saturdays,
9:30 a.m.–noon
Contact: Kathleen Metzger, *mkmetzger45@hotmail.com*
Members: 15
Membership fee: national fee
Affiliation: Word Weavers

WORD WEAVERS MACON–BIBB
www.facebook.com/groups/173188826644758
Meetings: Central City Church, 621 Foster Rd., Macon; second
Sundays, 3:00–5:30 p.m.
Contact: Robin Dance, *RobinDance.me@gmail.com*
Members: 45
Membership fee: national fee
Affiliation: Word Weavers

WORD WEAVERS VALDOSTA
Meetings: Corinth Baptist Church, 4089 Corinth Church Rd., Lake
Park; third Saturdays, 2:00–4:00 p.m.
Contact: Christy Adams, *ChristyAdams008@gmail.com*
Membership fee: national fee
Affiliation: Word Weavers

ILLINOIS

ACFW CHICAGO
www.facebook.com/acfwchicago, chicagoacfw.org
> **Meetings:** Panera Bread, 100 W. Higgins Rd., South Barrington; second Fridays, 6:30–8:30 p.m.
> **Contact:** Lori Davis, *chicago@acfwchapter.com*
> **Members:** 20
> **Membership fee:** national fee plus $35/year
> **Affiliation:** American Christian Fiction Writers

WORD WEAVERS LAND OF LINCOLN
> **Meetings:** Liberty Baptist Church, 2105 Sheridan Rd., Pekin; second Saturdays, 10:00 a.m.–noon
> **Contact:** Rita Klundt, *RitaKlundt@ymail.com*
> **Members:** 4
> **Membership fee:** national fee
> **Affiliation:** Word Weavers

WORD WEAVERS ON THE BORDER
> **Meetings:** Panera Bread, 254 E. Rollins Rd., Round Lake; fourth Thursdays, 7:00–8:30 p.m.
> **Contact:** Harold Tomesch, *hgt@cuw.edu*
> **Members:** 10
> **Membership fee:** national fee
> **Affiliation:** Word Weavers

INDIANA

ACFW INDIANA
www.acfwindiana.com
> **Meetings:** Zoom monthly; various locations, usually Kokomo, 1–2 times/year
> **Contact:** Rebecca Reed, *acfwindianachapter@gmail.com*
> **Members:** 20
> **Membership fee:** national fee plus $15/year
> **Affiliation:** American Christian Fiction Writers

HEARTLAND CHRISTIAN WRITERS
www.facebook.com/HeartlandChristianWriters
> **Meetings:** Mount Pleasant Christian Church, 381 N. Bluff Rd.,
> Greenwood; third Mondays except December, 12:30–3:00 p.m.
> **Contact:** Joyce Long, 317-306-0284, *joyce.e.long@gmail.com*
> **Members:** 12
> **Membership fee:** none

WORD WEAVERS INDY
> **Meetings:** Carmel-Clay Public Library, 425 E. Main St., Carmel; third
> Tuesdays, 6:30–8:30 p.m.
> **Contact:** Mandy Young, *wwindychap@gmail.com*
> **Membership fee:** national fee
> **Affiliation:** Word Weavers

IOWA

WORD WEAVERS DES MOINES
www.facebook.com/groups/495808943830132
> **Meetings:** Union Park Baptist Church, 821 Arthur Ave., Des Moines;
> last Mondays, 6:30–8:30 p.m.
> **Contact:** Gayl Siegel, *dragonsmom13@earthlink.net*
> **Members:** 12
> **Membership fee:** national fee
> **Affiliation:** Word Weavers

KANSAS

HEART OF AMERICA CHRISTIAN WRITERS NETWORK
www.hacwn.org
> **Meetings:** Colonial Presbyterian Church, 12501 W. 137th St.,
> Overland Park; second Thursdays, 7:00 p.m.
> **Contact:** Karen Morerod, *HACWN@earthlink.net*
> **Members:** 150
> **Membership fee:** active member, $35/year; professional member,
> $45/year

WORD WEAVERS HEARTLAND

www.facebook.com/groups/1368154937494713

Meetings: Central Christian College of Kansas, 1200 S. Main St., McPherson; second Saturdays, 9:00 a.m.–noon
Contact: Elaine McAllister, *bffgramma@gmail.com*
Members: 12
Membership fee: national fee
Affiliation: Word Weavers

KENTUCKY

ACFW KENTUCKY

www.facebook.com/groups/1876813595891979

Meetings: Southeast Christian Church, 950 Blankenbaker Rd., Louisville; second Saturdays, 10:30 a.m.–noon
Contact: Janet Morris Grimes, 615-400-1198, *acfwlouisville@gmail.com*
Members: 42
Membership fee: national fee plus $10
Affiliation: American Christian Fiction Writers

WORD WEAVERS BOONE COUNTY

www.facebook.com/groups/349709925923088

Meetings: Grace Fellowship Church, 9379 Gunpowder Rd., Florence; first Saturdays, 10:30 a.m.–12:30 p.m.
Contact: Pamela Walker, *pswalker1010@yahoo.com*
Members: 15
Membership fee: national fee
Affiliation: Word Weavers

WORD WEAVERS EAST CENTRAL KENTUCKY

www.facebook.com/groups/2153776371685141

Meetings: Montgomery County Public Library, 328 N. Maysville St., Mt. Sterling; second Saturdays, 10:30 a.m.–12:30 p.m.
Contact: Sarah Chafins, *sarah.chafins@gmail.com*
Membership fee: national fee
Affiliation: Word Weavers

LOUISIANA

ACFW LOUISIANA
www.facebook.com/ACFWLouisiana
> **Meetings:** Barksdale Baptist Church, 1714 Jimmie Davis Hwy.,
> Bossier City; last Saturdays, 11:00 a.m.
> **Contact:** Charles Sutherland, *louisiana@acfwchapter.com*
> **Membership fee:** national fee
> **Affiliation:** American Christian Fiction Writers

SOUTHERN CHRISTIAN WRITERS
scwguild.com
> **Meetings:** Gospel Bookstore and Zoom, 91 Westbank Expressway,
> Gretna; third Saturdays except November and December, 10:30 a.m.
> **Contact:** Teena Myers, *scwg@cox.net*
> **Members:** 40
> **Membership fee:** none; premium members with extra benefits, $50/year

SOUTHERN CHRISTIAN WRITERS RIVER PARISHES
scwguild.com
> **Meetings:** St. Charles United Methodist Church, front meeting room,
> 1905 Ormond Blvd., Destrehan; third Saturdays, 10:15 a.m.
> **Contact:** Teena Myers, *scwgnola@gmail.com*
> **Membership fee:** none; premium members with extra benefits, $50/year

MICHIGAN

ACFW GREAT LAKES
acfwgreatlakes.wordpress.com, www.facebook.com/groups/
527572863929168
> **Meetings:** various locations, first Saturdays, 10:00 a.m.
> **Contact:** Beth Foreman, *acfwgreatlakes@gmail.com*
> **Members:** 43
> **Membership fee:** national fee plus $10/year
> **Affiliation:** American Christian Fiction Writers

WORD WEAVERS WEST MICHIGAN GREENVILLE
> **Meetings:** Starbucks, 1720 W. Washington St., Greenville; first and
> third Tuesdays, 6:00–8:00 p.m.

Contact: Gene Koon, *koongene@gmail.com*
Members: 10
Membership fee: national fee
Affiliation: Word Weavers

WORD WEAVERS WEST MICHIGAN NORTH GRAND RAPIDS

Meetings: Russ's Restaurant, 3531 Alpine Ave. NW, Walker; first and
third Tuesdays, 6:00–8:00 p.m.
Contact: Gene Koon, *koongene@gmail.com*
Members: 10
Membership fee: national fee
Affiliation: Word Weavers

MINNESOTA

ACFW MINNESOTA N.I.C.E.

www.facebook.com/ACFW.MN.NICE

Meetings: Ridgewood Church, 4420 County Rd. 101, Minnetonka;
fourth Sundays, 6:00–8:00 p.m.
Contact: Linda Arrowood, *acfw.mn.nice@gmail.com*
Members: 25
Membership fee: national fee plus $25/year
Affiliation: American Christian Fiction Writers

MINNESOTA CHRISTIAN WRITERS GUILD

www.mnchristianwriters.com

Meetings: Oak Knoll Lutheran Church, 600 Hopkins Xrd.,
Minnetonka; second Mondays, September–May, 7:00–8:30 p.m.
Contact: Jason Sisam, *info@mnchristianwriters.com*
Members: 50
Membership fee: $90/year or $25/meeting

MISSISSIPPI

MID–SOUTH CHRISTIAN WRITERS ROUNDTABLE

www.facebook.com/groups/145426569547064

Meetings: various locations, Memphis metro area; third Saturdays
Contact: William G. Hill, 901-212-8020
Members: 10
Membership fee: none

MISSOURI

ACFW MOZARKS
www.acfwmozarks.com
> **Meetings:** The Library Center, 4653 S. Campbell Ave., Springfield; third Saturdays, 10:30 a.m.
> **Contact:** Erin Mifflin Shell, 417-251-1587, *mozarks@acfwchapter.com*
> **Members:** 10
> **Membership fee:** national fee plus $20/year
> **Affiliation:** American Christian Fiction Writers

ACFW ST. LOUIS
acfwstl.wordpress.com, www.facebook.com/groups/acfwstlouis
> **Meetings:** Festus Public Library, 400 W. Main St., Festus; second Saturdays, 11:30 a.m.
> **Contact:** Karen Sargent, 573-450-0514, *Karen@KarenSargent.com*
> **Members:** 20
> **Membership fee:** national fee plus $25/year
> **Affiliation:** American Christian Fiction Writers

OZARKS CHAPTER OF AMERICAN CHRISTIAN WRITERS
www.OzarksACW.org
> **Meetings:** University Heights Baptist Church and Zoom, 1010 S. National, Springfield; second Saturdays, September–May, 10:00 a.m.–noon
> **Contact:** Dr. Jeanetta Chrystie, 417-832-8409, *OzarksACW@yahoo.com*
> **Members:** 50
> **Membership fee:** $20/year; couple, $30; newsletter only, $10

NEBRASKA

MY THOUGHTS EXACTLY WRITERS
mythoughtsexactlywriters.wordpress.com
> **Meetings:** Keene Memorial Library, 1030 N. Broad St., Fremont; third Mondays, 6:30–8:00 p.m.
> **Contact:** Cheryl, *mythoughtse@gmail.com*
> **Membership fee:** none

NEW JERSEY

ACFW NY/NJ

www.facebook.com/groups/955365637934907

Meetings: Grace Bible Chapel, 100 Oakdale Rd., Chester; first Saturdays October–June, 10 a.m.–noon; critique groups at other times
Contact: Cherlyn Gatto, *nynj@acfwchapter.com*
Members: 65
Membership fee: national fee plus $20/year
Affiliation: American Christian Fiction Writers

NORTH JERSEY CHRISTIAN WRITERS GROUP

www.njcwg.blogspot.com

Meetings: High Mountain Church, conference room, 681 High Mountain Rd., North Haledon; first Saturdays, 10:00 a.m.–noon
Contact: Susan Panzica, 201-755-5730, *susan@susanpanzica.com*
Members: 15
Membership fee: none

NEW YORK

WORD WEAVERS WESTERN NEW YORK

Meetings: Marji Steven's art studio, 2458 Rush Mendon Rd., Honeoye Falls; third Mondays, 6:30–9:00 p.m.
Contact: Karen Rode, 585-571-7124, *karen.a.rode@gmail.com*
Members: 7
Membership fee: national fee
Affiliation: Word Weavers

NORTH CAROLINA

ACFW CHARLOTTE

Meetings: Charlotte; third Saturdays
Contact: Dianne Miley, *charlotte@acfwchapter.com*
Membership fee: national fee
Affiliation: American Christian Fiction Writers

WORD WEAVERS CHARLOTTE
www.facebook.com/share/g/16fRYf6btj/?mibextid=wwXIfr

Meetings: Charlotte Mecklenburg Library South County Regional,
5801 Rea Rd., Charlotte; first Saturdays, 10:00 a.m.–noon
Contact: Brandie Muncaster, *wordweaverscharlotte@gmail.com*
Members: 10
Membership fee: national fee
Affiliation: Word Weavers

WORD WEAVERS COASTAL CAROLINAS
www.facebook.com/groups/260975010218702

Meetings: Southwest Brunswick Branch Library, 9400 Ocean Hwy. W,
Carolina Shores; fourth Thursdays, 10:30 a.m.–1:00 p.m.
Contact: Jennifer E. Tirrell, *jenniferetirrell@gmail.com*
Members: 10
Membership fee: national fee

WORD WEAVERS HENDERSONVILLE
www.facebook.com/groups/746784416992918

Meetings: varies, Hendersonville; fourth Thursdays, 1:00–3:30 p.m.
Contact: Fred Von Kamecke, *FVonKamecke@comcast.net*
Members: 5
Membership fee: national fee
Affiliation: Word Weavers

WORD WEAVERS HICKORY–NEWTON

Meetings: Southwest Library, 2944 S. Hwy. 127, Hickory; first
Saturdays, 10:00 a.m.–noon
Contact: Norma Poore, *hickorynewtonwordweavers@gmail.com*
Members: 8
Membership fee: national fee
Affiliation: Word Weavers

WORD WEAVERS MAGGIE VALLEY
facebook.com/groups/2374738259340596

Meetings: Long's Chapel, room 229, 133 Old Clyde Rd., Waynesville;
third Thursdays, 12:30–2:30 p.m.
Contact: Linda Summerford, *Juleps2@yahoo.com*
Members: 10
Membership fee: national fee
Affiliation: Word Weavers

WORD WEAVERS PIEDMONT TRIAD

Meetings: The Mill: Coffee & Community, 615 Watson Cir., Thomasville; third Saturdays, 10:00 a.m.–noon
Contact: Genevieve Traversy, *genevieve.traversy@yahoo.com*
Members: 10
Membership fee: national fee plus $50/year
Affiliation: Word Weavers

WORD WEAVERS WILMINGTON

Meetings: Calvary Baptist Church, 423 23rd St., Wilmington; second Mondays, 6:30–8:30 p.m.
Contact: Laurel Senick, *LSenick6@gmail.com*
Members: 5
Membership fee: national fee
Affiliation: Word Weavers

WORD WEAVERS WINSTON–SALEM

www.facebook.com/groups/268156771940401

Meetings: 1038 Pine Place Dr., Germanton; second Saturdays, 9:30–11:30 a.m.
Contact: Diane Virginia Cunio, *Diane@dianevirginia.com*
Membership fee: national fee
Affiliation: Word Weavers

OHIO

ACFW OHIO

facebook.com/groups/220166801456380

Meetings: online, first Saturdays, 10:00 a.m.
Contact: Victor Hess, 504-258-2199, *ohio@acfwchapter.com*
Members: 45
Membership fee: national fee plus $12/year
Affiliation: American Christian Fiction Writers

COLUMBUS CHRISTIAN WRITERS ASSOCIATION

www.facebook.com/profile.php?id=100057586834554

Meetings: Zoom, second Sundays, 3:00–5:00 p.m.
Contact: Mina R. Raulston, 614–507–7893, *m_raulston@hotmail.com*
Members: 5
Membership fee: none

DAYTON CHRISTIAN SCRIBES

www.facebook.com/DaytonChristianScribes

Meetings: Kettering Seventh-day Adventist Church, 3939 Stonebridge Rd., Kettering; fourth Thursdays, 7:00–9:00 p.m.
Contact: Linore Rose Burkard, *Linore@LinoreBurkard.com*
Members: 20
Membership fee: $15/year

MIDDLETOWN AREA CHRISTIAN WRITERS/M.A.C. WRITERS

middletownwriters.blogspot.com

Meetings: Healing Word Assembly of God, 5303 S. Dixie Hwy., Franklin; second Tuesdays, 7:00–8:30 p.m.
Contact: Donna J. Shepherd, 513-373-5671, *donna.shepherd@gmail.com*
Members: 25
Membership fee: $30/year or $5/meeting

WORD WEAVERS KNOX COUNTY

www.facebook.com/groups/1440083346651013

Meetings: 303 S. Edgewood Rd., Mount Vernon; third Sundays, 3:00–5:00 p.m.
Contact: Steve Feazel, *SteveFeazel@gmail.com*
Membership fee: national fee
Affiliation: Word Weavers

WORD WEAVERS NORTHEAST OHIO

Meetings: Good Shepherd Villa, 726 Center St., Ashland; first Thursdays, 6:30–8:30 p.m.
Contact: Cherie Martin, *kitties395@yahoo.com*
Members: 10
Membership fee: national fee
Affiliation: Word Weavers

OKLAHOMA

ACFW OKLAHOMA CITY

www.okchristianfictionwriters.com

Meetings: New Hope Church of Christ, 700 W. 2nd St., Edmond; third Saturdays, 1:00–3:00 p.m.

Contact: Kristy Werner, *authors@okchristianfictionwriters.com*
Members: 35
Membership fee: national fee plus $20/year
Affiliation: American Christian Fiction Writers

FELLOWSHIP OF CHRISTIAN WRITERS

fellowshipofchristianwriters.org

Meetings: Kirk of the Hills Presbyterian Church, 4102 E. 61st St.,
Tulsa; second Tuesdays, 6:30–8:00 p.m.
Contact: Cheryl Barker, *cheryl@cherylbarker.net*
Members: 39
Membership fee: $30

WORDWRIGHTS

www.wordwrightsok.com

Meetings: The Last Drop Coffee Shop, 5425 N. Lincoln Blvd.,
Oklahoma City; second Saturdays, 10:00 a.m.
Contact: *info@wordwrightsok.com*
Members: 30
Membership fee: $20/year

PENNSYLVANIA

LANCASTER CHRISTIAN WRITERS

lancasterchristianwriters.org

Meetings: Petra Church and online, 565 Airport Rd., New Holland;
third Saturdays, 9:30 a.m.–noon
Contact: Cheryl Weber, email through the website
Membership fee: none

WORD WEAVERS HARRISBURG

Meetings: Living Water Community Church, 206 Oakleigh Ave.,
Harrisburg; second Saturdays, 1:30–3:30 p.m.
Contact: Mae Spradley, *Mae@2c1ministries.org*
Members: 7
Membership fee: national fee
Affiliation: Word Weavers

WORD WEAVERS PITTSBURGH

Meetings: Barnes & Noble at Waterworks Mall, 926 Freeport Rd., Pittsburgh; second Thursdays, 10:00 a.m.–12:30 p.m.
Contact: Darla Grieco, *dsgrieco@gmail.com*
Membership fee: national fee
Affiliation: Word Weavers

WRITE HIS ANSWER CRITIQUE GROUPS

writehisanswer.com/critiquegroups

Meetings: online; every other Thursday, 10:00 a.m. and alternating Thursdays, 8:00 p.m.
Contact: Marlene Bagnull, 267-436-2503, *mbagnull@aol.com*
Members: 15 each group
Membership fee: none

SOUTH CAROLINA

ACFW SOUTH CAROLINA LOWCOUNTRY

www.facebook.com/profile.php?id=100083299843252

Meetings: Wando Mt. Pleasant Library, 1400 Carolina Park Blvd., Mt. Pleasant; fourth Saturdays, 10:00 a.m.–noon
Contact: Laurie Larsen, 309-212-4157, *sclowcountry@acfwchapter.com*
Members: 16
Membership fee: national fee plus $20/year
Affiliation: American Christian Fiction Writers

ACFW UPSTATE SOUTH CAROLINA

www.acfwupstatesc.com

Meetings: Renovation Church Simpsonville, 611 Richardson St., Simpsonville; second Saturdays, 10:00 a.m.–1:00 p.m.
Contact: Isabella Skellenger, *upstatesc@acfwchapter.com*
Members: 30
Membership fee: national fee plus $20/year
Affiliation: American Christian Fiction Writers

WORD WEAVERS CHARLESTON

www.facebook.com/groups/2112701302307131

Meetings: St John's Parish Church, Resurrection Hall, 1811 Paulette Dr., Johns Island; third Saturdays, 10:00 a.m.–noon

Contact: Timothy Griggs, *timothygriggs@gmail.com*
Members: 25
Membership fee: national fee
Affiliation: Word Weavers

WORD WEAVERS LEXINGTON, SC
LexingtonWordWeavers.com

Meetings: Kittiwake Baptist Church, 420 Kitti Wake Dr., West Columbia; second Mondays, 6:45–9:00 p.m.
Contact: Jean Wilund, *Jwilund@icloud.com*
Members: 35
Membership fee: national fee
Affiliation: Word Weavers

WRITING 4 HIM

Meetings: Spartanburg First Baptist Church, The Hanger Room 215, 250 E. Main St., Spartanburg; second Thursdays, 9:45 a.m.
Contact: Linda Gilden, *linda@lindagilden.com*
Members: 20
Membership fee: none

TENNESSEE

ACFW KNOXVILLE
www.facebook.com/groups/341397182924371

Meetings: online, second Tuesdays; Parkway Baptist Church, 401 S. Peters Rd., Knoxville, twice/year
Contact: Mary Ostrander, *knoxville@acfwchapter.com*
Members: 20
Membership fee: national fee
Affiliation: American Christian Fiction Writers

ACFW MEMPHIS
facebook.com/groups/699561666820044

Meetings: M.R. Davis Library and online, 8554 Northwest Dr., Southaven
Contact: Shannon Leach, *memphis@acfwchapter.com*
Members: 32
Membership fee: national fee plus $20/year
Affiliation: American Christian Fiction Writers

ACFW MID–TENNESSEE

www.facebook.com/groups/250177678658399

> **Meetings:** Nashville; first Saturdays, 10:00 a.m.–noon
> **Contact:** Sheila Stovall, *midtennessee@acfwchapter.com*
> **Members:** 50
> **Membership fee:** national fee plus $24/year
> **Affiliation:** American Christian Fiction Writers

WORD WEAVERS KNOXVILLE

www.facebook.com/groups/336414403544597

> **Meetings:** Pleasant Grove Baptist Church, 3736 Tuckaleechee Pike,
> Maryville; third Saturdays, 9:30 a.m.–noon
> **Contact:** Les Burnette, 865-679-3370, *LesBurnette@gmail.com*
> **Members:** 12
> **Membership fee:** national fee
> **Affiliation:** Word Weavers

WORD WEAVERS NASHVILLE

www.facebook.com/groups/1321489534609537

> **Meetings:** Goodletsville Public Library, 205 Rivergate Pkwy.,
> Goodlettsville; second Saturdays, 10:00 a.m.–noon
> **Contact:** Kim Aulich, *KAAfterGodsOwnHeart@gmail.com*
> **Members:** 10
> **Membership fee:** national fee
> **Affiliation:** Word Weavers

WORD WEAVERS SOUTH MIDDLE TENNESSEE

www.facebook.com/share/g/1BKKvGg22G

> **Meetings:** Edgemont Baptist Church, 150 Fairfield Pike, Shelbyville;
> third Saturdays, 10:00 a.m.–noon
> **Contact:** Amanda E. West, *awestwrites@outlook.com*
> **Members:** 6
> **Membership fee:** national fee
> **Affiliation:** Word Weavers

TEXAS

67 WRITERS

roaringwriters.org/groups-locations

Meetings: A.H. Meadows Library, Bluebonnet Room, 922 S. 9th St., Midlothian; second Saturdays except December, 2:00–3:45 p.m.
Contact: Jan Johnson, email through website
Membership fee: none
Affiliation: Roaring Writers

ACFW DFW READY WRITERS

facebook.com/DFWReadyWriters

Meetings: George W. Hawkes Public Library and Zoom, 100 S. Center St. #327, Arlington; second Saturdays, 10:30 a.m.–noon; in-person once/quarter
Contact: Paula Peckham, 817-454-5218, *paula@paulapeckham.com*
Members: 42
Membership fee: national fee plus $25
Affiliation: American Christian Fiction Writers

ACFW THE WOODLANDS/WRITERS ON THE STORM

www.facebook.com/groups/122145464545775

Meetings: The Woodlands; third Saturdays
Contact: Linda Kozar, *wotsacfw@gmail.com*
Members: 40
Membership fee: national fee plus $20/year, $10/year for 70+
Affiliation: American Christian Fiction Writers

CHRISTIAN WRITERS WORKSHOP WACO

facebook.com/groups/374145049720167

Meetings: First Woodway Baptist Church, 101 Ritchie Rd., Woodway; Sundays September–November, January–April, 5:30–7:00 p.m.
Contact: Michelle Ruddell, 254-749-1740, *mruddell21@gmail.com*
Members: 50
Membership fee: none

CHRISTIAN WRITERS WORKSHOP DENTON

Meetings: Denton Bible Church, 131 University, Denton; Mondays, 1:00–3:00 p.m., September–May

Contact: Nancy McMinn, 254-339-3060, *reitahawthorne2@gmail.com*
Members: 22
Membership fee: donation
Affiliation: Roaring Writers

CHRISTIAN WRITERS WORKSHOP WOODWAY
roaringwriters.org/groups-locations

> **Meetings:** First Woodway Baptist Church, Room 210–211, 101 N.
> Ritchie Rd., Woodway; Sundays, 5:30–7:00 p.m., mid–January
> to the first week in April and mid–September through the end of
> October
> **Contact:** Michelle Ruddell, *mruddell21@gmail.com*
> **Affiliation:** Roaring Writers

HEART AND SOUL WRITERS
roaringwriters.org/groups-locations

> **Meetings:** Alsbury Baptist Church, 500 N.E. Alsbury Blvd., Burleson;
> third Tuesdays, 7:00–9:00 p.m.
> **Contact:** Lisa Bell, email through the website
> **Membership fee:** none
> **Affiliation:** Roaring Writers

INSPIRATIONAL WRITERS ALIVE! CENTRAL HOUSTON
www.centralhoustoniwa.com

> **Meetings:** First Baptist Church, Room 143, 7401 Katy Freeway,
> Houston; second Thursdays, 7:00–9:00 p.m.
> **Contact:** Connie Parks, 281-627-3011, *connie1.4@juno.com*
> **Members:** 15
> **Membership fee:** $20/year

INSPIRATIONAL WRITERS ALIVE! NORTHWEST HOUSTON
www.centralhoustoniwa.com

> **Meetings:** email for location, Houston; second Wednesdays, 2:00 p.m.
> **Contact:** Martha Roddy, 281-859-4208, *magnolia7787@gmail.com*
> **Members:** 15
> **Membership fee:** $20/year

LIVING WATERS
roaringwriters.org/groups-locations

> **Meetings:** Hood County Library, Pecan Room, 222 N. Travis,
> Granbury; second Fridays, 2:00–4:00 p.m.

Contact: Lisa Bell, email through the website
Membership fee: none
Affiliation: Roaring Writers

ROARING WRITERS MENTORING WITH FRANK BALL
www.roaringlambs.org/mentoring-sessions

Meetings: Frost Bank Conference Room, 8501 Davis Blvd., North Richland Hills; third Saturdays, 9:30 a.m.–12:30 p.m., March–November
Contact: Frank Ball, *fball@RoaringLambs.org*
Membership fee: $35 per session, $220 for eight sessions
Affiliation: Roaring Writers

ROCKWALL CHRISTIAN WRITERS GROUP
www.facebook.com/groups/rockwallchristianwritersgroup

Meetings: Redeemer Rockwall Annex, 303 E. Rusk St., Rockwall; first Mondays, 7:00–9:00 p.m.
Contact: Leslie Wilson, 214-505-5336, *leslieporterwilson@gmail.com*
Members: 15–20 in person, 380+ on Facebook page
Membership fee: none
Affiliation: Roaring Writers

WITNESS WRITERS
roaringwriters.org/groups-locations

Meetings: email for location and days, Plainview
Contact: Carole Bell, *caroleabell@gmail.com*
Membership fee: none
Affiliation: Roaring Writers

VIRGINIA

ACFW VIRGINIA
acfwvirginia.com

Meetings: Blue Ridge, Chesapeake, Leesburg; see website for days and times; plus monthly Zoom webinars
Contact: Deena Adams, *acfwvirginia@gmail.com*
Members: 75
Membership fee: national fee plus $15/year
Affiliation: American Christian Fiction Writers

WORD WEAVERS WOODBRIDGE
Meetings: Chinn Library Community Room, 13065 Chinn Park Dr., Woodbridge; last Saturdays, 10:00 a.m.–noon
Contact: Lauren Craft, *laurenchristianauthor@gmail.com*
Members: 4
Membership fee: national fee
Affiliation: Word Weavers

WASHINGTON

ACFW NORTHWEST
Meetings: online; includes Washington, Oregon, Idaho
Contact: Lisa Phillips, *northwest@acfwchapter.com*
Members: 110
Membership fee: national fee
Affiliation: American Christian Fiction Writers

VANCOUVER CHRISTIAN WRITERS
Meetings: email for address, Vancouver; first Mondays, 9:00 a.m.
Contact: Jon Drury, 510-909-0848, *jondrury2@yahoo.com*
Members: 8
Membership fee: none
Affiliation: Cascade Christian Writers

WISCONSIN

ACFW WI SOUTHEAST
www.facebook.com/wiseacfw
Meetings: Brookfield Library, 1900 N. Calhoun Rd., Brookfield; first Thursdays, 6:30–8:30 p.m.; three times/year; Zoom, eight months/year
Contact: Elizabeth Daghfal, *acfwwisconsin@gmail.com*
Members: 30
Membership fee: national fee plus $25/year
Affiliation: American Christian Fiction Writers

PENS OF PRAISE CHRISTIAN WRITERS
www.susanmarlene.com/writers–pens
Meetings: 4Given Coffee Shop, 1034 S. 18th St., Manitowoc; third Mondays, 1:30–3:00 p.m.

Contact: Susan Marlene Kinney, 920-242-3631, *susanmarlenewrites@gmail.com*
Members: 10
Membership fee: none

WORD AND PEN CHRISTIAN WRITERS

Meetings: St. Thomas Episcopal Church, 226 Washington St., Menasha; second Mondays, 7:30 p.m.; Zoom, January–March
Contact: Chris Stratton, 920-739-0752, *gcefsi@new.rr.com*
Members: 16
Membership fee: $10/year

WORD WEAVERS ST. CROIX

Meetings: First Congregational Church of Christ, 110 N. 3rd St., River Falls; second Saturdays, 10:00 a.m.–noon
Contact: Erin Maruska, *erin.maruska@gmail.com*
Members: 5
Membership fee: national fee
Affiliation: Word Weavers

AUSTRALIA AND NEW ZEALAND

NEW ZEALAND CHRISTIAN WRITERS

www.nzchristianwriters.org

Meetings: various places, see website
Contact: Kathryn Paul, *editor@nzchristianwriters.org*
Services: "NZ Christian Writers is a nationwide collective of around 300 authors, bloggers, editors, lyricists, poets, publishers, songwriters, storytellers, and writers throughout New Zealand. Along with our bimonthly magazines and competitions, we offer inspiring seminars and writers retreats to encourage, inspire, and upskill people in their writing. NZ Christian Writers' vision is to encourage and inspire Christian writers throughout New Zealand. We welcome both beginner and experienced writers to join us."
Members: 300
Membership fee: includes magazine; digital, $50, students $30; print, $75, students $55

OMEGA WRITERS

omegawriters.com.au

Meetings: online and various in-person locations, every other month

Contact: Karen Roper, *membership@omegawriters.org*

Services: Australian group with local and online chapters across the country and New Zealand. See the website for locations. Also sponsors an annual conference and the CALEB Award to recognize the best in Australasian Christian writing, published and unpublished.

Members: 160

Membership fee: $60/year

CANADA

InSCRIBE CHRISTIAN WRITERS' FELLOWSHIP

inscribe.org

Contact: Lorilee Guenter, *president@inscribe.org*

Services: "Inscribe Christian Writers' Fellowship has been encouraging and supporting Canadian Christian writers for over 25 years. You'll find our members in every province in Canada, ranging from beginner to experienced writers." See the website for locations. Also sponsors workshops, a fall conference, and contests and produces the quarterly magazine *FellowScript* that is included with membership.

Members: 160

Membership fee: varies, see website

MANITOBA CHRISTIAN WRITERS ASSOCIATION

Meetings: Bleak House, 1637 Main St., Winnipeg; first Saturdays September–June, 1:00–3:30 p.m.

Contact: Frieda Martens, 204-770-8023, *friedamartens1910@gmail.com*

Members: 18

Membership fee: $30

Affiliation: InScribe Christian Writers' Fellowship

THE WORD GUILD

www.thewordguild.com

Contact: 800-969-9010; *info@thewordguild.com;* Box 77001, Markham ON L3P 0C8, Canada

Services: "The Word Guild is a growing community of Canadian writers, editors, speakers, publishers, booksellers, librarians and other interested individuals who are Christian. From all parts of Canada and many denominational and cultural backgrounds, we affirm a common statement of faith and are united in our passion for the written word." Sponsors regional chapters across Canada and conferences, contests and awards for Canadian Christian writers.
Members: 325
Membership fee: $65/year

20

EDITORIAL SERVICES

Entries in this chapter are for information only, not an endorsement of editing skills. Before hiring a freelance editor, ask for references if they are not posted on the website; and contact two or three to help determine if this editor is a good fit for you. You may also want to pay for an edit of a few pages or one chapter before hiring someone to edit your complete manuscript.

A LITTLE RED INK | BETHANY KACZMAREK
115 1st St., Somerset, WI 54025 | 715-907-5144
contact@bethanykaczmarek.com | *www.bethanykaczmarek.com/little-red-ink2*
  Contact: website
  Services: copyediting, manuscript evaluation, substantive/
    developmental editing
  Types of manuscripts: adult, middle grade, novels, teen/YA
  Charges: hourly rate
  Credentials/experience: "An ACFW Editor of the Year finalist
    (2015), Bethany enjoys working with both traditional and indie
    authors. Several of her clients are award-winning and best-selling
    authors, though she does work with aspiring authors as well. She
    has edited speculative fiction for Enclave Fiction and Gilead, and
    general fiction for Sunrise Publishing."

AB WRITING SERVICES LLC | ANN BYLE
www.annbylewriter.com/ab-writing-services
  Contact: website
  Services: articles, back-cover copy, blog posts, book coaching, book
    proposals, coauthoring, consulting, ghostwriting, press releases,
    proofreading
  Types of manuscripts: adult, articles, blog posts, book proposals,
    devotionals, nonfiction books, novels

Charges: hourly rate

Credentials/experience: "Ann's experience includes years as a newspaper copy editor, freelance journalist for newspapers and magazines including *Publishers Weekly*, writing her own books including *Christian Publishing 101*, and co- and ghost-writing book projects."

ABOVE THE PAGES | PAM LAGORMARSINO

abovethepages@gmail.com | *www.abovethepages.com*

Contact: email, website

Services: back-cover copy, copyediting, discussion questions for books, manuscript evaluation, proofreading, substantive/developmental editing

Types of manuscripts: adult, articles, Bible studies, book proposals, children, cookbooks, curriculum, devotionals, easy readers, gift books, memoir, middle grade, ministry materials, nonfiction books, novels, picture books, query letters, short stories, teen/YA

Charges: custom, flat fee, word rate

Credentials/experience: "Pam Lagomarsino has owned and operated Above the Pages since early 2015, when she established it as a business. Pam has edited, proofread, or beta-read Christian nonfiction books, devotionals, sermons, Bible studies, homeschool curriculum, children's books, and Christian fiction. Additional experience includes working in a rural library, writing frequent articles for area newspapers, being a sales rep of children's books, and home teaching her children through high school. Her college coursework included English, literature, library science, and child development."

ABOVE THE SUN LLC | JESSE RIVAS

330 S. 3rd St., Cottage Grove, OR 97424 | 541-954-9479

team@abovethesun.org | *abovethesun.org/services/editing*

Contact: email, phone, website

Services: substantive/developmental editing, writing coach

Types of manuscripts: articles, devotionals, easy readers, middle grade, nonfiction books, novels, picture books, short stories, teen/YA

Charges: word rate

Credentials/experience: "Jesse has over 20 years of experience as an author, mentor, editor, and publicist. He holds a Bachelor's degree in Education, graduated from the Rubart Writing Academy, and founded Above The Sun, where he and his team have guided hundreds of authors from inspiration to publication."

ACEVEDO WORD SOLUTIONS LLC | JENNE ACEVEDO
editor@jenneacevedo.com | www.jenneacevedo.com

Contact: email

Services: back-cover copy, copyediting, discussion questions for books, project management, proofreading, substantive/developmental editing, writing coach

Types of manuscripts: adult, Bible studies, book proposals, curriculum, devotionals, gift books, middle grade, nonfiction books, query letters, teen/YA

Charges: hourly rate, word rate

Credentials/experience: "Consultant for private and corporate clients, proofreader for publishers. Cofounder of Christian Editors Association, former director of The Christian PEN, former director of PENCON, member of Christian Editor Connection, instructor for The PEN Institute, Editors' Choice Award judge. Founder and former director of Chandler Writers' Group."

AMBASSADOR COMMUNICATIONS | CLAIRE HUTCHINSON
13733 W. Gunsight Dr., Sun City West, AZ 85375 | 812-390-7907

clairescreenwriter@gmail.com | www.clairehutchinson.net

Contact: email

Services: coauthoring, copyediting, proofreading, screenwriting, substantive/developmental editing, writing coach

Types of manuscripts: scripts

Charges: flat fee

Credentials/experience: "M.A. English, Professional Program in Screenwriting UCLA, produced and award-winning screenwriter and producer and script analyst."

AMI EDITING | ANNETTE IRBY
editor@AMIediting.com | www.AMIediting.com

Contact: email

Services: copyediting, critiquing, manuscript evaluation (fiction only), proofreading, substantive/developmental editing

Types of manuscripts: novellas, novels, short stories

Charges: page rate

Credentials/experience: "Annette spent 5 years working as an acquisitions editor for a Christian book publisher. She has more than 20 years of experience editing freelance in the CBA marketplace. Her clients have included several well-known authors and publishers. She is a long-time member of ACFW and has served as a judge for their contests, including final-round evaluation. As a fiction author herself, she has published books of various lengths. Over the years, her writing has achieved top-three status in competitions, as well as placing first in BRMCWC's 2019 Selah Contest. In 2009, she founded Seriously Write, a co-hosted blog, which ran for 10 years with active participation from the Christian writing community. See her editing website for testimonials."

ANDREA MERRELL

60 McKinney Rd., Travelers Rest, SC 29690 | 864-616-5889
AndreaMerrell7@gmail.com | *www.AndreaMerrell.com*

Contact: email, website

Services: back-cover copy, copyediting, proofreading

Types of manuscripts: adult, articles, devotionals, nonfiction books, novels, short stories

Charges: hourly rate

Credentials/experience: "Professional freelance editor. Associate editor for Christian Devotions Ministries and former associate editor for LPC Books. Member of The Christian PEN: Proofreaders and Editors Network."

ANN KROEKER, WRITING COACH

ann@annkroeker.com | *annkroeker.com/writing-coach*

Contact: email, website

Services: writing coach

Types of manuscripts: adult, articles, blog posts, book proposals, nonfiction books, query letters, social-media content

Charges: flat fee, hourly rate, word rate

Credentials/experience: "A writing coach, author, speaker, and host of the *Ann Kroeker, Writing Coach* podcast, Ann works with clients one-to-one, through programs and courses like The Art & Craft of Writing, and through Your Platform Matters (YPM), her platform membership program. Her website has landed on *The Write Life*'s annual '100 Best Websites for Writers' list six years in a row thanks to years of valuable writing-related content.

"She leverages over three decades of experience in the writing and publishing world to support writers looking for input and confidence to advance their careers. Ann's clients have achieved personal goals, landed contracts, hit bestseller lists, and won awards. She's presented at conferences, retreats, and summits; coauthored *On Being a Writer: 12 Simple Habits for a Writing Life that Lasts*; and authored *Not So Fast: Slow-Down Solutions for Frenzied Families* and *The Contemplative Mom*."

ANOINTED EDITOR | TEMITOPE OYETOMI

244 Fifth Ave., Second Floor, New York, NY 10001 | 718-371-8190
director@anointededitor.com | *www.anointededitor.com*

Contact: email, website, WhatsApp
Services: back-cover copy, book-contract evaluation, coauthoring, copyediting, discussion questions for books, ghostwriting, indexing, manuscript evaluation, proofreading, self-publishing consulting, substantive/developmental editing, writing coach
Types of manuscripts: academic, articles, Bible studies, book proposals, devotionals, gift books, nonfiction books, novels, short stories
Charges: custom, flat fee, page rate, word rate
Credentials/experience: "Temitope founded Baal Hamon Publishers, a Christian publishing firm, in May 2006. He has been the Managing and Acquisitions Editor at Baal Hamon for 19 years. He launched a new publishing firm—the Grace Chapter—in 2023. The Anointed Editor is his latest outfit offering editorial and writing services to authors who desire to be more in control of their publishing process or who need to prepare their works for suitable publishers. He was the Scholarship Winner at Yale University's International Publishing Course (Leadership Strategies in Book Publishing) in the Summer of 2016. Temitope is also a distinguished and successful author. He employs his rich Christian experience, theological expertise and nearly two decades of publishing experience in delivering excellent editorial and writing services as 'the anointed editor.'"

AUTHORIZEME LITERARY FIRM LLC | DR. SHARON NORRIS ELLIOTT

PO Box 1816, South Gate, CA 90280 | 310-508-9860
AuthorizeMeNow@gmail.com | *lifethatmatters.net/authorizeme#services*

Contact: email, website
Services: back-cover copy, coauthoring, copyediting, discussion questions for books, ghostwriting, manuscript evaluation, proofreading, substantive/developmental editing, writing coach
Types of manuscripts: adult, articles, Bible studies, picture books, book proposals, curriculum, devotionals, easy readers, gift books, middle

grade, nonfiction books, novels, poetry, query letters, short stories

Charges: custom

Credentials/experience: "Over 35 years of experience in this business as an author, editor, writer, and speaker; AuthorizeMe business growing and in successful operation since 2008."

AUTHORS WHO SERVE | RACHEL HILLS

rachel@authorswhoserve.com | authorswhoserve.com

Contact: website

Services: back-cover copy, coauthoring, copyediting, discussion questions for books, ghostwriting, manuscript evaluation, substantive/developmental editing, writing coach

Types of manuscripts: adult, articles, devotionals, nonfiction books, novels, short stories

Charges: flat fee, word rate

Credentials/experience: "Rachel Hills has 25 years' experience editing. Besides a BA from Indiana University, she has certificates in copyediting, developmental editing, ghostwriting, and book coaching. With history as a freelance journalist, Rachel stays abreast of publishing trends to better serve you; she also enjoys interior formatting for a professional presentation."

AVODAH EDITORIAL SERVICES | CHRISTY DISTLER

www.avodaheditorialservices.com

Contact: website

Services: copyediting, manuscript evaluation, proofreading, substantive/developmental editing

Types of manuscripts: adult, devotionals, easy readers, nonfiction books, novels, picture books, poetry, short stories

Charges: word rate

Credentials/experience: "Educated at Temple University and University of California–Berkeley. Thirteen years of editorial experience, both as an employee and a freelancer. Currently works mostly for publishing houses but accepts freelance work as scheduling allows."

BANNER LITERARY | MIKE LOOMIS

mike@mikeloomis.co | www.MikeLoomis.co

Contact: email, website

Services: back-cover copy, book-contract evaluation, coauthoring, copyediting, discussion questions for books, ghostwriting, manuscript evaluation, substantive/developmental editing, writing coach

Types of manuscripts: articles, book proposals, devotionals, nonfiction books, query letters

Charges: custom, flat fee

Credentials/experience: "I have ghostwritten two *NYT* bestsellers, and advised internationally-known authors. But I truly enjoy helping aspiring authors develop their books, brands, and business."

BARBARA KOIS

7135 W. Amber Burst Ct., Tucson, AZ 85743 | 630-532-2941

barbara.kois@gmail.com

Contact: email

Services: back-cover copy, copyediting, proofreading, substantive/ developmental editing

Types of manuscripts: adult, Bible studies, children, devotionals, gift books, nonfiction books, novels, short stories, teen/YA

Charges: word rate

Credentials/experience: "Barbara has worked as a writer, ghostwriter, editor, teacher, coach, corporate communication consultant and journalist, and served as Writer in Residence at Tyndale House Publishers. She has written or co-written ten books, published more than 600 articles in the *Chicago Tribune*, and edited more than 250 books for various publishers and authors. Barbara has helped dozens of writers to prepare for the publication of their books, including both those who have published with traditional publishers and those who have chosen to self-publish. Her goals include making writing clear, memorable and even humorous where appropriate."

BBH LITERARY | DAVID BRATT

david@bbhliterary.com | www.bbhliterary.com/developmental-editing

Contact: email, website

Services: manuscript evaluation, substantive/developmental editing

Types of manuscripts: academic, articles, book proposals, nonfiction books, query letters

Charges: hourly rate

Credentials/experience: "Twenty-one years editing for Eerdmans Publishing; Ph.D. in American religion (Yale University, 1999)."

BECCA WIERWILLE EDITING AND COACHING SERVICES

becca@beccawierwille.com | beccawierwille.com/editing-services

 Contact: email, website

 Services: copyediting, manuscript evaluation, proofreading, substantive/developmental editing, writing coach

 Types of manuscripts: adult, book proposals, devotionals, easy readers, middle grade, novels, query letters, short stories, teen/YA

 Charges: word rate

 Credentials/experience: "Becca Wierwille is a freelance editor and writing coach who has worked with writers of various genres and experience levels. As a former newspaper reporter and avid critique group member, she has years of experience doing edits at every level. She loves partnering with authors to help make their stories shine and focuses on editing clean fiction, with a specialization in middle grade and YA. Her editing portfolio and testimonials are available upon request."

BESTSELLING BOOK SHEPHERD | PAMELA GOSSIAUX

pam@pamelagossiaux.com | BestsellingBookShepherd.com

 Contact: email

 Services: back-cover copy, coauthoring, copyediting, discussion questions for books, ghostwriting, manuscript evaluation, proofreading, substantive/developmental editing, writing coach

 Types of manuscripts: adult, articles, Bible studies, picture books, book proposals, devotionals, easy readers, gift books, middle grade, nonfiction books, novels, query letters, short stories, teen/YA

 Charges: custom, flat fee, hourly rate, packages

 Credentials/experience: "30 years experience writing, editing, journalism, book PR. Dual degree in Creative Writing & English Language and Literature from University of Michigan. International bestselling author. Have coached and promoted authors to Amazon, *USA Today* and *Wall Street Journal* bestsellers."

BOOK EDITS BY JESSI | JESSI RITA HOFFMAN

PO Box 433, Tenino, WA 98589 | 360-264-5480

jessihoffman8@gmail.com | www.JessiRitaHoffman.com

 Contact: email, website

 Services: copyediting, critiquing, manuscript evaluation, proofreading, substantive/developmental editing, writing coach

 Types of manuscripts: adult, book proposals, children, nonfiction books, novels, query letters

Charges: custom, flat fee

Credentials/experience: "A contributing editor to *Writer's Digest* with over twenty years in the publishing industry, Jessi Rita Hoffman specializes in helping aspiring authors and in editing Christian books of all varieties, both fiction and nonfiction. Her client list includes Donald Trump, U.S. Congressman Dennis Ross, and Pastor Monty Weatherall. Her website contains a blog with over a hundred articles on the craft and business of writing."

BOOKCAMP | CHAD R. ALLEN

chad@chadrallen.com | www.chadrallen.com

Contact: email

Services: substantive/developmental editing, writing coach

Types of manuscripts: adult, nonfiction books

Charges: custom

Credentials/experience: "25+ years in the traditional book publishing industry; independent writing coach for 7+ years."

BOOKHOUND EDITING | KATY SCHLOMACH

katy@bookhoundediting.com | www.bookhoundediting.com

Contact: email

Services: copyediting, manuscript evaluation, proofreading

Types of manuscripts: adult, novels, teen/YA

Charges: flat fee, packages, word rate

Credentials/experience: "Katy Schlomach is a freelance editor who helps authors captivate readers with their stories by removing any hindrance between the author's intent and the reader's perception. Her services are tailored to authors who know what story they want to tell and have worked out their plot but want to refine the writing to make sure they keep readers engaged. She exclusively works with fiction, specializing in the romance genre. She has a BA in communication (with a concentration in technical writing), completed training courses through Edit Republic and The PEN Institute, is a member of the Christian Editor Connection, and has served as a judge for the Editors' Choice Award and the Florida Tapestry Awards. See her website for more information about her services, testimonials of her work, and articles with self-editing tips."

BREAKOUT EDITING | DORI HARRELL

doriharrell@gmail.com | doriharrell.wixsite.com/breakoutediting

Contact: email

Services: copyediting, proofreading, substantive/developmental editing, website text

Types of manuscripts: adult, articles, book proposals, children, devotionals, memoir, middle grade, nonfiction books, novellas, novels, picture books, short stories, teen/YA

Charges: word rate

Credentials/experience: "Dori is a multiple-award-winning writer and a highly experienced editor who freelance edits full time and has edited more than 300 novels and nonfiction books. Breakout authors final in awards or win awards almost every year! She edits for publishers, including Gemma Halliday Publishing and Kregel Publications, and as an editor, she releases more than twenty books annually."

BUTTERFIELD EDITORIAL SERVICES | DEBRA L. BUTTERFIELD

4810 Gene Field Rd., Saint Joseph, MO 64506 | 816-752-2171

deb@debralbutterfield.com | *themotivationaleditor.com*

Contact: email

Services: copyediting, substantive/developmental editing, writing coach

Types of manuscripts: adult, devotionals, nonfiction books, novels, teen/YA

Charges: word rate

Credentials/experience: "For over fifteen years I've helped hundreds of writers polish their manuscripts for publication, many of which have won awards and Amazon bestselling status. I have ten years of experience as an editor for the publisher CrossRiver Media Group. I teach as I edit, so writers grow into better writers."

C. S. LAKIN | SUSANNE LAKIN

20406 Tiger Tail Rd., Grass Valley, CA 95949 | 530-200-5466

cslakin@gmail.com | *www.livewritethrive.com*

Contact: email, website

Services: back-cover copy, copyediting, critiquing, manuscript evaluation, proofreading, substantive/developmental editing, writing coach

Types of manuscripts: academic, adult, articles, Bible studies, book proposals, children, devotionals, easy readers, gift books, middle grade, nonfiction books, novels, picture books, poetry, query letters, short stories, teen/YA

Charges: flat fee, hourly rate, packages

Credentials/experience: "I've been a freelance professional copyeditor and writing coach for more than twenty years. I've worked with more than 1,000 writers in six continents, and I've taught more than 8,000 writers online via courses, master classes, and moderated critique groups. With more than 30 books published, fiction and nonfiction, in various genres, I bring a full range of expertise and experience to my work. I offer various packages and services, so be sure to check out my website, where I have more than 1 million words of instruction for writers!"

CATHY STREINER

Cathy@thecorporatepen.com | thecorporatepen.com

Contact: email

Services: back-cover copy, coauthoring, copyediting, discussion questions for books, proofreading, substantive/developmental editing, writing coach

Types of manuscripts: academic, adult, articles, Bible studies, devotionals, easy readers, gift books, middle grade, nonfiction books, novels, scripts, short stories, technical material, teen/YA

Charges: custom, flat fee, hourly rate, word rate

Credentials/experience: "Author of a Christian novel, I have experience with the start-to-finish self-publishing process. I also have extensive experience working with writers who need editing and proofreading services as well as limited coaching with constructive feedback."

CELTICFROG EDITING | ALEX McGILVERY

22-121 Ferry Rd., Clearwater, BC V0E 1N2, Canada | 250-819-4275

thecelticfrog@gmail.com | celticfrogediting.com

Contact: email, website

Services: manuscript evaluation, substantive/developmental editing, writing coach

Types of manuscripts: academic, adult, devotionals, easy readers, middle grade, nonfiction books, novels, short stories, teen/YA

Charges: flat fee

Credentials/experience: "I'm an author, content editor and publisher. After writing some four hundred reviews over a couple decades, I moved over to content editing and have worked with dozens of authors and hundreds of books. I also do manuscript assessments."

CHERI FIELDS EDITING

Cherifieldsediting@gmail.com | Cherifields.com

Contact: website

Services: copywriting, critiquing, substantive/developmental editing

Types of manuscripts: adult, articles, Bible studies, easy readers, middle grade, nonfiction books, picture books, teen/YA

Charges: flat fee, word rate

Credentials/experience: "I'm a graduate from the Institute of Children's Literature, have passed my gold level certification with The PEN Institute for nonfiction and children's editing. I am the managing editor for The Creation Club website (since 2019) and am currently earning my Master's degree in Biblical Counseling from Faith Bible Seminary. While many of my clients are early in their writing careers, you can see various finished books my clients have published by visiting my website. My specialty is to come alongside those who either need or want to go the self-publishing route, as I have done with my own books."

CHRISTIAN COMMUNICATOR MANUSCRIPT CRITIQUE SERVICE | SUSAN TITUS OSBORN

3133 Puente St., Fullerton, CA 92835 | 714-313-8651

susanosb@aol.com | www.christiancommunicator.com

Contact: email, phone, website

Services: back-cover copy, book-contract evaluation, coauthoring, copyediting, discussion questions for books, ghostwriting, manuscript evaluation, proofreading, writing coach

Types of manuscripts: academic, adult, articles, Bible studies, book proposals, curriculum, devotionals, easy readers, gift books, middle grade, nonfiction books, novels, picture books, poetry, query letters, scripts, short stories, technical material, teen/YA

Charges: hourly rate, page rate

Credentials/experience: "Our critique service, comprised of 14 professional editors, has been in business for almost 40 years. We are recommended by ECPA, the Billy Graham Association, and a number of publishing houses and agents."

CHRISTIAN EDITOR CONNECTION

director@ChristianEditor.com | www.ChristianEditor.com

Contact: email, website

Services: back-cover copy, coauthoring, copyediting, ghostwriting, indexing, manuscript evaluation, proofreading, substantive/

developmental editing, writing coach

Types of manuscripts: academic, adult, articles, Bible studies, book proposals, children, curriculum, devotionals, easy readers, German translation, gift books, middle grade, nonfiction books, novels, picture books, poetry, query letters, scripts, short stories, Spanish translation, technical material, teen/YA

Charges: custom, flat fee, hourly rate, page rate, word rate

Credentials/experience: "Christian Editor Connection is a 'matchmaking' service that personally connects authors and publishers with established, professional Christian editors."

CHRISTIANBOOKPROPOSALS.COM | SALLY CRAFT

2950 W. Ray Rd., Chandler, AZ 85224

scraft@ecpa.org | *ChristianBookProposals.com*

Contact: website

Services: copyediting, manuscript evaluation, online proposal-submission service, proofreading

Types of manuscripts: books of all kinds and all ages

Charges: $98 for six months

Credentials/experience: "The $98 basic proposal is created and edited by the author with prompts from an online form; the add-on services ($447 for book proposal evaluation and coaching; additional $50 for book proposal editing and proofreading (includes up to 3,000-word writing sample) are completed by professional editors with long experience in the Christian book publishing industry. Operated by the Evangelical Christian Publishers Association (ECPA), this book proposal submission service was created to help its member publishers manage and respond to unsolicited manuscripts from authors looking for a traditional, royalty-based relationship. It allows authors to submit their manuscript proposals in a secure, online format for review by editors from publishing houses that are members of ECPA."

COLLABORATIVE EDITORIAL SOLUTIONS | ANDREW BUSS

info@collaborativeeditorial.com | *collaborativeeditorial.com*

Contact: email

Services: copyediting, proofreading

Types of manuscripts: academic, adult, articles, Bible studies, devotionals, nonfiction books, technical material

Charges: hourly rate, page rate

Credentials/experience: "I'm a professional editor with more than five years of full-time experience working with authors and scholarly publishers such as InterVarsity Press, Reformation Heritage, P&R Publishing, Georgetown University Press, and Baylor University Press. Although I primarily work in the genre of scholarly nonfiction, I'm always keen to work with creative and thoughtful authors, whatever the topic or genre. I'm a member of the Editorial Freelancers Association and the Society of Biblical Literature."

COMMUNICATION ASSOCIATES | KEN WALKER

1566 Holderby Rd., Huntington, WV 25701 | 304-521-3943
kenwalker33@gmail.com | www.KenWalkerWriter.com

> **Contact:** email
> **Services:** back-cover copy, coauthoring, discussion questions for books, ghostwriting, substantive/developmental editing
> **Types of manuscripts:** adult, articles, Bible studies, devotionals, memoir, nonfiction books, teaching material
> **Charges:** flat fee, hourly rate
> **Credentials/experience:** "Have freelanced for 40-plus years; full-time since 1990. Have coauthored, ghosted or done substantive edits on more than 100 books. Experienced in both article writing and book writing & editing."

CREATIVE CORNERSTONES | CAYLAH COFFEEN

creativecornerstones@gmail.com | creativecornerstones.com/editing-2

> **Contact:** phone, website, WhatsApp
> **Services:** copyediting, manuscript evaluation, substantive/developmental editing
> **Types of manuscripts:** adult, articles, novels, scripts, teen/YA
> **Charges:** flat fee, word rate
> **Credentials/experience:** "Caylah Coffeen will give you the tools you need to make your fantasy or sci-fi novel shine! Don't be one in millions of 3 star books. Caylah will give your story a health checkup (manuscript evaluation), help you write characters that make readers laugh and cry (developmental edit), and make your turns of phrase clear and compelling (line edit). A member of the Editorial Freelancers Association, she has several years of freelance editing experience and also works with Monster Ivy Publishing and Eschler Editing. She is the founder of Creative Cornerstones, a book publishing services company which guides authors at each stage in the publishing journey: writing, design, and sales. Our team will take your story from 'great,' and elevate it to unforgettable."

CREATIVE EDITORIAL SOLUTIONS | CLAUDIA VOLKMAN
cvolkman@mac.com | claudiavolkman.com/home-1

Contact: phone

Services: copyediting, ghostwriting, proofreading, substantive/ developmental editing, writing coach

Types of manuscripts: adult, Bible studies, devotionals, gift books, nonfiction books, novels

Charges: flat fee, word rate

Credentials/experience: "I have more than 35 years of experience in the publishing world, most of it in Christian and Catholic trade publishing. Now as owner of Creative Editorial Solutions, I offer author coaching, developmental editing, and copyediting to entrepreneurs, coaches, speakers, and authors."

CREATIVE ENTERPRISES STUDIO | MARY HOLLINGSWORTH
1507 Shirley Way, Ste. A, Bedford, TX 76022-6737 | 817-312-7393
ACreativeShop@aol.com | www.creativeenterprisesltd.com

Contact: email

Services: coauthoring, copyediting, discussion questions for books, ghostwriting, manuscript evaluation, proofreading, substantive/ developmental editing

Types of manuscripts: adult, book proposals, curriculum, devotionals, easy readers, gift books, middle grade, nonfiction books, novels, picture books, short stories, teen/YA

Charges: custom

Credentials/experience: "CES is a publishing services company, hosting more than 150 top Christian publishing freelancers. We work with large, traditional Christian publishers on books by best-selling authors. We also produce custom, first-class books on a turnkey basis for independent authors, ministries, churches, and companies."

DENICA McCALL EDITING
denica@denicamccall.com | denicamccall.com/editing-services

Contact: website

Services: copyediting, manuscript evaluation, proofreading, substantive/developmental editing

Types of manuscripts: adult, Bible studies, children, devotionals, easy readers, middle grade, nonfiction books, novels, poetry, short stories, teen/YA

Charges: word rate

Credentials/experience: "I have been writing fiction for over sixteen years, completing a total of five manuscripts as well as a collection of short stories and hundreds of poems, some of which have been published in anthologies. I am a member of the Realm Makers writers community. I was also an intern and beta reader for Twenty Hills Publishing in 2023, an intern with Quill and Flame Publishers as a Junior Editor in 2024, and am currently a contracted editor with Scrivenings Press. I'm a graduate of the copyediting course, copyediting mentorship course, and the developmental editing course offered through Editorial Arts Academy."

DENISE HARMER

1695 Dorothea Ave., Fallbrook, CA 92028 | 760-505-0531
dharmeredits@gmail.com | *www.deniseharmer.weebly.com*

Contact: email

Services: copyediting, proofreading

Types of manuscripts: novels, short stories, teen/YA

Charges: word rate

Credentials/experience: "Denise Harmer specializes in copyediting and proofreading fiction and creative nonfiction. She started her editing experience in 1990 editing court transcripts, and over the last fifteen years she has had the privilege of working with several bestselling Christy and Carol Award-winning authors to help make their books the best that they can be."

DESERT RAIN EDITING | GLENIECE LYTLE

PO Box 8163, Hualapai, AZ 86412 | 928-715-7125
desert.rain.editing@gmail.com | *desertrainediting.com*

Contact: email, website

Services: back-cover copy, copyediting, proofreading

Types of manuscripts: adult, Bible studies, devotionals, memoir, nonfiction books

Charges: word rate

Credentials/experience: "At Desert Rain Editing, I line edit Bible studies, devotionals, and Christian living books, as well as memoirs, health and wellness, and business books from a Christian perspective for indie authors. Every editing project has taught me something new about the art of editing, the craft of writing, and life in general. I am a silver member of the Christian PEN: Proofreaders and Editors Network and use the current versions of the *Chicago Manual of Style, Merriam-Webster's Collegiate Dictionary,* and the *Christian Writer's Manual of Style* for my editing decisions. I look forward to partnering with each new client, nurturing their vision for their seedling manuscript, and turning it into a fully bloomed book."

ECHO CREATIVE MEDIA | BRENDA NOEL and DAWN SHERILL-PORTER

108 Springfield Dr., Smyrna, TN 37167 | 615-223-0754

echocreativemedia.com

Contact: email

Services: copyediting, discussion questions for books, ghostwriting, proofreading, substantive/developmental editing

Types of manuscripts: adult, articles, book proposals, curriculum, devotionals, easy readers, gift books, nonfiction books, picture books, short stories, teen/YA

Charges: flat fee, hourly rate

Credentials/experience: "More than 20 years of experience in the Christian publishing industry."

EDIT RESOURCE LLC | ERIC STANFORD

19265 Lincoln Green Ln., Monument, CO 80132 | 719-290-0757

info@editresource.com | www.editresource.com

Contact: email

Services: back-cover copy, book proposals, coauthoring, copyediting, discussion questions for books, ghostwriting, indexing, manuscript evaluation, proofreading, substantive/developmental editing, writing coach

Types of manuscripts: adult, Bible studies, book proposals, curriculum, devotionals, middle grade, nonfiction books, novels, query letters, teen/YA

Charges: depends on the service

Credentials/experience: "Owners Eric and Elisa have a combined 40 years of experience and have worked with numerous bestselling authors and books. They also represent a team of other top writing and editing professionals."

EDIT WITH CLAIRE | CLAIRE ERASMUS

editor@editwithclaire.com | editwithclaire.com

Contact: email

Services: copyediting, proofreading

Types of manuscripts: adult, Bible studies, devotionals, nonfiction books, novels, short stories, teen/YA

Charges: word rate

Credentials/experience: "I work with Christian authors to achieve excellence and help them prepare for publishing through line editing, copyediting, and proofreading across a variety of genres. I am trained in both UK and US styles, meaning I am able to assist authors with either set of conventions."

EDITING GALLERY LLC | CAROL CRAIG

2622 Willona Dr., Eugene, OR 97408 | 541-735-1834

editinggallery7@gmail.com | *www.editinggallery.com*

Contact: email, website

Services: coauthoring, manuscript evaluation, substantive/developmental editing, writing coach

Types of manuscripts: adult, book proposals, children, middle grade, novels, picture books, query letters, teen/YA

Charges: hourly rate

Credentials/experience: "For the past thirty years, I have had the privilege of working with an amazing group of writers, both those who are well-known and those who are new to the industry. I specialize in fiction novels: mystery, romance, mainstream, women's fiction, historical, and fantasy. I also like thrillers. As a developmental editor, I help you get your idea off the ground. I work closely with my clients and help them see it to the finished product, so if this is the type of editor you are looking for, please contact me."

EDITING INSIDERS | JANYRE TROMP

janyre@editinginsiders.com | *www.editinginsiders.com*

Contact: email

Services: back-cover copy, coauthoring, manuscript evaluation, substantive/developmental editing, writing coach

Types of manuscripts: adult, articles, Bible studies, book proposals, devotionals, nonfiction books, novels, query letters, short stories

Charges: hourly rate, word rate

Credentials/experience: "Award-winning nonfiction and fiction editor with more than 20 years of experience in acquiring, editing, and marketing books. I've edited more than 200 books written by new and seasoned authors. With an additional 10 years of experience in book marketing, I've written and edited marketing copy for a traditional publisher and had a hand in producing copy for several

Indie authors. I adore working with writers and equipping them to make their manuscripts the best they can be."

eDITMORE EDITORIAL SERVICES | TAMMY DITMORE
501-I S. Reino Rd. #194, Newbury Park, CA 91320 | 805-630-6809
tammy@editmore.com | *www.editmore.com*

Contact: email

Services: copyediting, discussion questions for books, manuscript evaluation, proofreading, substantive/developmental editing

Types of manuscripts: adult, articles, Bible studies, devotionals, nonfiction books, teen/YA

Charges: hourly rate

Credentials/experience: "Words are important. A poorly phrased paragraph or a badly organized book can confuse your readers. Typos and grammatical errors can undermine your credibility and overpower your ideas. I can help you shape and sharpen your words so that your finished work is polished, precise, and engaging. A writer and editor for more than 40 years, I have worked for newspapers, publishers, universities, and individual authors, and I specialize in Christian nonfiction publications."

EDITOR WORLD LLC | PATTI FISHER
info@editorworld.com | *www.editorworld.com*

Contact: website

Services: coauthoring, copyediting, discussion questions for books, ghostwriting, proofreading, substantive/developmental editing

Types of manuscripts: academic, adult, articles, Bible studies, book proposals, children, curriculum, devotionals, easy readers, gift books, middle grade, nonfiction books, novels, query letters, scripts, short stories, technical material, teen/YA

Charges: word rate

Credentials/experience: "Individual editor profiles provide detailed information on credentials and experience as well as previous client ratings. All writers and editors on our team are native English speakers from the US, UK, or Canada who have passed a stringent exam and review."

ELOQUENT EDITS | DENISE ROEPER
1025 Third St., Port Orange, FL 32129 | 386-290-4117
denise.eloquentedits@gmail.com | *www.eloquentedits.com*

Contact: email, website

Services: copyediting, proofreading, substantive/developmental editing

Types of manuscripts: academic, easy readers, memoir, middle grade, novels, short stories, teen/YA

Charges: word rate

Credentials/experience: "Fiction is my passion. I love to read it. I love to edit it. My clients will receive my full attention when I work on their creation."

EXEGETICA PUBLISHING | CATHY CONE

312 Greenwich #112, Lee's Summit, MO 64082

editor@exegeticapublishing.com | *exegeticapublishing.com/editing*

Contact: email, website

Services: copyediting, manuscript evaluation, proofreading, substantive/developmental editing

Types of manuscripts: academic, articles, Bible studies, curriculum, devotionals, nonfiction books

Charges: flat fee

Credentials/experience: "Exegetica editorial staff have more than 30 years editing experience with diverse media and publishers."

EXTRA INK EDITS | MEGAN EASLEY-WALSH

Ireland

Megan@ExtraInkEdits.com | *www.ExtraInkEdits.com*

Contact: email

Services: back-cover copy, copyediting, discussion questions for books, manuscript evaluation, proofreading, substantive/developmental editing, writing coach

Types of manuscripts: academic, adult, articles, Bible studies, devotionals, easy readers, gift books, middle grade, nonfiction books, novels, picture books, poetry, query letters, short stories, teen/YA

Charges: flat fee, word rate

Credentials/experience: "Megan Easley-Walsh, PhD History, is an author of historical fiction, a researcher, and a writing consultant and editor at Extra Ink Edits. She is an award-winning writer and has taught college writing in the UNESCO literature city of Dublin, Ireland. She is a dual American and Irish citizen and lives in Ireland with her Irish husband. Megan is a Professional Member of the Irish Writers' Centre, a Full Member of the Irish Writers' Union, a member of the Historical Novel Society, a Full Member of

ACES: The Society for Editing, a member of the Irish Association of Professional Historians, and a member of the American Historical Association. Additionally, she was shortlisted for the 2021 Hammond House International Literary Prize in Poetry."

FAITH EDITORIAL SERVICES | REBECCA FAITH

PO Box 184, Novelty, OH 44072 | 330-898-6365
rebecca@faitheditorial.com | *www.faitheditorial.com*

Contact: email, phone, website
Services: copyediting, manuscript evaluation, proofreading
Types of manuscripts: academic, adult, articles, Bible studies, book proposals, curriculum, devotionals, medical, nonfiction books, technical material
Charges: hourly rate
Credentials/experience: "My experience editing in the Christian market includes six years as managing editor for a Christian nonprofit, another eight years editing/transcribing content for a global Christian ministry, and copyediting nonfiction Christian books and devotionals. In addition I have eleven years experience editing technical, engineering, medical, and educational material for university presses, journal publishers, and independent clients. I hold membership in the EFA, the Christian PEN (Gold), and the Christian Editor Connection."

FAITHWORKS EDITORIAL & WRITING INC. | NANETTE THORSEN SNIPES

PO Box 1596, Buford, GA 30518 | 770-945-3093
nsnipes@bellsouth.net | *www.faithworkseditorial.com*

Contact: email, website
Services: copyediting, manuscript evaluation, proofreading, work-for-hire projects
Types of manuscripts: adult, articles, business materials, devotionals, easy readers, gift books, memoir, middle grade, nonfiction books, picture books, poetry, query letters, short stories
Charges: hourly rate, page rate
Credentials/experience: "Member: The Christian PEN (Proofreaders & Editors Network), Christian Editor Connection, Christian Editor Network. Proofreader for corporate newsletters, thirteen years. Published writer for more than twenty-five years. Published hundreds of articles in magazines and stories in more than sixty compilation books, including Guideposts, B&H, Regal,

and Integrity. Twelve years of editorial experience in both adult and children's short fiction and books, memoirs, short stories, devotions, articles, business. Rates are generally by page but, under specific circumstances, by the hour. Editorial clients have published with such houses as Zondervan, Tyndale, and Revell."

FINAL TOUCH PROOFREADING & EDITING LLC | HEIDI MANN
317 S. Central Ave., Ely, MN 55731 | 701-866-4299
mann.heidi@gmail.com

Contact: email
Services: copyediting, proofreading
Types of manuscripts: adult, Bible studies, devotionals, nonfiction books, novels, teen/YA
Charges: flat fee, hourly rate
Credentials/experience: "In addition to my editorial expertise, I bring experience and knowledge from my former work as a Lutheran (ELCA) pastor. I am passionate about editing that intersects with progressive Christian faith, theology, and biblical interpretation. I have many years' experience copyediting, proofreading, and providing developmental editing for Augsburg Fortress Publishers (the publishing house of the ELCA), including its several imprints. I have also assisted other ministry organizations, independent authors, and non-religious entities with their writing and editing needs."

THE FOREWORD COLLECTIVE | MOLLY HODGIN
1726 Charity Dr., Brentwood, TN 37027 | 615-497-4322
info@theforewordcollective.com | *www.theforewordcollective.com*

Contact: email
Services: back-cover copy, book-contract evaluation, coauthoring, ghostwriting, manuscript evaluation, substantive/developmental editing, writing coach
Types of manuscripts: adult, book proposals, children, devotionals, easy readers, gift books, middle grade, nonfiction books, novels, picture books, teen/YA
Charges: flat fee, hourly rate
Credentials/experience: "Molly Hodgin worked her way up the corporate publishing ladder in New York City as an editor for Penguin Young Readers Group and a Senior Editor for Scholastic, Inc., acquiring, editing, and managing products for brands such as Star Wars, Pokemon, Bakugan, and Barbie. Molly then served as the Editorial Director for the Specialty Division of Thomas Nelson

Publishing and then the Associate Publisher for the Specialty Division of HarperCollins Christian Publishing. There she acquired and created gift books, children's books, and new media products with authors and brands including Sarah Young, Max Lucado, Shauna Niequist, Candace Cameron Bure, Melanie Shankle, Ann Voskamp, Annie F. Downs, Lee Strobel, Karen Kingsbury, and Mark Batterson.

"In addition to Molly's editorial and consulting work, she's also written, co-written, and ghost-written over 50 children's books for films and TV shows and for brands including Strawberry Shortcake, Chuggington, Hot Wheels, Barbie, and American Girl. She has also ghost-written books for grown-ups with business professionals, speakers, and even with several country music legends, including a *New York Times* bestseller for Reba McEntire."

FRANK N. JOHNSON

PO Box 66525, Scotts Valley, CA 95067 | 831-345-7871
frank@franknjohnson.net | *www.franknjohnson.net*

- **Contact:** email, website
- **Services:** ghostwriting, manuscript evaluation
- **Types of manuscripts:** adult, articles, Bible studies, curriculum, devotionals, nonfiction books
- **Charges:** hourly rate, word rate
- **Credentials/experience:** "I am a seasoned writer with over thirty-five years of experience, specializing in writing content for missionaries, missions agencies and organizations, ministries, and churches. My experience includes nearly three years of experience serving in West Africa and France, over thirty years providing logistical support to missionaries, and over five years as the Chief Strategist and Primary Writer for a missions mobilization website (*hesed.com*)."

FRENCH AND ENGLISH COMMUNICATION SERVICES | DIANE GOULLARD

3104 E. Camelback Rd., PMB 124, Phoenix, AZ 85016-4502 | 602-870-1000
WorkingWithWords@cox.net | *frenchandenglish.com*

- **Contact:** email, mail, phone, website
- **Services:** copyediting, English to French translation, French to English translation, proofreading
- **Types of manuscripts:** academic, adult, articles, Bible studies, book proposals, children, curriculum, devotionals, easy readers, gift books, lyrics, middle grade, nonfiction books, novels, picture books,

query letters, scripts, short stories, technical material, teen/YA

Charges: custom, flat fee, hourly rate, page rate, word rate

Credentials/experience: "Diane has lifelong academic and occupational training, experience and skills, and loves the work. You reach a real person who thinks of you as a real person. Agreements are kept simple and to a minimum—no legalese unless absolutely necessary. She is communicative, supportive, thoughtful, honest, detail oriented, truthful, reasonable. Her preferred proofreading method is to give you a list of her observations, so you're free to review and incorporate them."

FULL CIRCLE EDITS | TANYA MINNICK

1150 S. Kansas Rd., Orrville, OH 44667 | 330-317-6603

Fullcircle.edits@gmail.com | *www.facebook.com/ profile.php?id=100069299295315*

Contact: email, phone

Services: back-cover copy, copyediting, proofreading, substantive/ developmental editing

Types of manuscripts: adult, articles, book proposals, curriculum, devotionals, easy readers, gift books, middle grade, nonfiction books, novels, picture books, short stories, technical material, teen/YA

Charges: custom, page rate

Credentials/experience: "Freelance experience in editing memoirs, devotionals, and children's story books—but willing to branch out to other areas as well. Participated in several book launch teams, with a focus on editing. Background in teaching English, applied linguistics, and language acquisition with extensive knowledge of grammar and syntax. Full Circle Edits provides 'noteworthy proofing that makes you stand out.'"

GINNY L. YTTRIP'S WORDS FOR WRITERS

3575 Arden Way #1093, Sacramento, CA 95864 | 916-276-7359

ginny@wordsforwriters.net | *wordsforwriters.net*

Contact: email

Services: manuscript evaluation, substantive/developmental editing, writing coach

Types of manuscripts: adult, book proposals, devotionals, memoir, nonfiction books, novels, query letters

Charges: word rate

Credentials/experience: "Ginny L. Yttrup is the author of seven novels, including *Words,* which won the Christy Award for Best First

Novel and was a Christy finalist for Best Contemporary Standalone. A developmental editor and coach, Ginny is the founder of Words for Writers, which offers inspiration and instruction for writers."

THE GRAMMAR QUEEN | RENEE GARRICK
1503 S. Park St., Red Wing, MN 55066 | 651-327-9686
renee@thegrammarqueen.net | TheGrammarQueen.net
   Contact: email, phone, website
   Services: copyediting, proofreading, substantive/developmental editing
   Types of manuscripts: Bible studies, devotionals, memoir, nonfiction books
   Charges: hourly rate
   Credentials/experience: "Since 2014 I've edited 7 books and proofed 3 more for TRISTAN Publishing in Minneapolis, MN; 3 of the editing projects have won a total of 4 awards. During the same time period, I've also edited for more than a dozen self-publishing authors and personal historians, along with providing services for 4 books for one 'boutique' publisher."

HANEMANN EDITORIAL | NATALIE HANEMANN
1865 Gunner Ln., Chapel Hill, TN 37034 |
nathanemann@gmail.com | www.nataliehanemann.com
   Contact: website
   Services: coauthoring, ghostwriting, substantive/developmental editing, writing coach
   Types of manuscripts: academic, nonfiction books, novels
   Charges: custom
   Credentials/experience: "After working in publishing for 20 years doing many forms of editing, I've honed my skillset to co-authoring, ghostwriting, and coaching. Will do developmental edits if it's a challenging manuscript that needs massive work (I'm a sucker for problem-solving!). Preferred categories include Catholic or Orthodox, academic (i.e. books with lots of footnotes and citations), social justice (poverty, disenfranchised people groups) and novels (adventure, general, historical, women's, biblical). Not accepting projects that are 'light reads' or strictly 'entertaining.' I like books that are well-thought out with deep messages that promote social change . . . or change of heart."

HEATHER KLEINSCHMIDT
heather@theseworthywords.com | www.theseworthywords.com
   Contact: email, phone

Services: consulting, copyediting, ghostwriting

Types of manuscripts: academic, adult, articles, curriculum, nonfiction books, technical material

Charges: flat fee, word rate

Credentials/experience: "For a 10% discount, use 'CWMG' in your email subject line (or mention that this is where you found me)! Nonfiction: I specialize in emotionally nuanced or complicated topics—or issues that are just generally difficult to articulate. Genres I work in include Health & Wellness, Psychology & Mental Health, Business & Finance. Academic: I've worked with universities and researchers to create high-impact curricula and research communications for both general and academic audiences."

HEATHER PUBOLS

heather.pubols@gmail.com | heatherpubols.com/editing-services

Contact: phone, website

Services: copyediting, proofreading, substantive/developmental editing

Types of manuscripts: academic, articles, Bible studies, nonfiction books, technical material

Charges: hourly rate

Credentials/experience: "More than 20 years of editorial experience working in corporate communications for Christian missions organizations. Freelance editor since 2018."

HENRY McLAUGHLIN

921 Silver Streak Dr., Saginaw, TX 76131 | 817-703-9875

henry@henrymclaughlin.org | www.henrymclaughlin.org

Contact: website

Services: ghostwriting, substantive editing & rewriting, writing coach

Types of manuscripts: adult, book proposals, novels, short stories

Charges: page rate

Credentials/experience: "Over 20 years as a novelist, coach/mentor, editor, teacher. Prize winning novelist. Successful ghostwriter. Teaching the craft at conferences, workshops, writers groups. Coaching and editing several clients to publication."

HISWAY GRAPHIC DESIGN | KIMBERLY MORRISON

kim@onlyhisway.com | www.onlyhisway.com

Contact: email, website

Services: back-cover copy, coauthoring, ghostwriting, manuscript evaluation, proofreading

Types of manuscripts: adult, Bible studies, children, devotionals, gift books, nonfiction books, novels, poetry, short stories, teen/YA

Charges: flat fee, word rate

Credentials/experience: "Kimberly is a graphic designer and self-published author who feels called to use her creative gifts to serve the Kingdom. With over seven books independently published, she understands both the beauty and the challenges of the self-publishing journey. In addition to her own writing, she has helped numerous authors successfully bring their books to life—offering thoughtful design, guidance, and encouragement every step of the way, all with the heart to glorify God through her work."

HONEST EDITING | WILLIAM CARMICHAEL

PO Box 2437, Sisters, OR 97759

www.honestediting.com

Contact: website

Services: copyediting, manuscript evaluation, proposal creation, substantive/developmental editing

Types of manuscripts: academic, adult, Bible studies, book proposals, devotionals, easy readers, gift books, middle grade, nonfiction books, novels, query letters, teen/YA

Charges: flat fee

Credentials/experience: "A professional editor with years of experience in Christian editing is assigned." A division of Writer's Edge Service.

INDEX BUSTERS LLC

2803 Philadelphia Pike, Claymont, DE 19703 | 610-364-6479

info@indexbusters.com | *www.indexbusters.com*

Contact: email

Services: indexing

Types of manuscripts: academic, adult, Bible studies, nonfiction books, technical material

Charges: page rate, word rate

Credentials/experience: "Index Busters is a professional book indexing company known for its expertise in producing high-quality indexes for academic and nonfiction publications. With decades of experience, their team of indexers brings diverse academic backgrounds, allowing them to cover a wide range of subjects across both the sciences and humanities. The company has worked with over 800 individual authors and contributed to more than

1,550 books. Their indexes have been prepared for titles published by leading university presses, including Cambridge University Press, Oxford University Press, and the University of Pittsburgh Press, among others. They also collaborate with several Christian publishers and are one of the few companies in the market offering specialized services in Scripture and Ancient Sources indexing."

THE INKY BOOKWYRM | GINA KAMMER

1054 Deer Ridge Ct. NW, Lonsdale, MN 55046 | 507-381-1887
ginakammer@inkybookwyrm.com | *www.inkybookwyrm.com*

Contact: website
Services: copyediting, manuscript evaluation, proofreading, query/submissions coaching, substantive/developmental editing, writing coach
Types of manuscripts: adult, easy readers, middle grade, novels, query letters, teen/YA
Charges: monthly fee, word rate
Credentials/experience: "Gina Kammer specializes in editing and book coaching for science fiction and fantasy. She is a former Capstone editor and Bethany Lutheran College writing/journalism instructor with 10+ years of experience in fiction and children's nonfiction. Using brain science hacks, hoarded craft knowledge, and solution-based direction, this book dragon helps science-fiction and fantasy authors get their stories—whether on the page or still in their heads—ready to enchant their readers."

INSPIRATION FOR WRITERS, INC. | SANDY TRITT

1527 18th St., Parkersburg, WV 26101 | 304-428-1218
IFWeditors@gmail.com | *Inspirationforwriters.com/editorial-services*

Contact: email
Services: copyediting, ghostwriting, manuscript evaluation, proofreading, substantive/developmental editing, writing coach
Types of manuscripts: academic, adult, articles, Bible studies, book proposals, children, devotionals, easy readers, gift books, memoir, middle grade, nonfiction books, novels, query letters, short stories, teen/YA
Charges: word rate
Credentials/experience: "Incorporated in 2009, Inspiration for Writers, Inc. has been on the web since 1999, making it one of the oldest continually operating online editing firms. Our clients hail from every state within the United States and from more than fifteen countries. More than 75 percent of our business is repeat business, which is perhaps the strongest indicator of client satisfaction. We believe

strongly in communication at every step of the editing process. Unlike other editing firms, we encourage clients to ask questions, and we offer free consulting to clients to steer them through the submissions and publishing processes."

JAMES PENCE EDITING

1551 County Road 4109, Greenville, TX 75401 | 214-460-0390
jamespence919@gmail.com | jamespence.com/writing-services

Contact: website
Services: copyediting, manuscript evaluation, proofreading, substantive/developmental editing
Types of manuscripts: nonfiction books, novels
Charges: flat fee, word rate
Credentials/experience: "Discover the writer within you with James Pence's expert guidance. As an experienced author, collaborator, and editor, James will help you bring your book-length project to fruition. Having authored ten books, many of which were published by major publishers such as Osborne/McGraw-Hill, Tyndale, Kregel, Baker, and Thomas Nelson (as a ghostwriter), James possesses a diverse range of writing skills across various genres, including fiction, nonfiction memoir, how-to, Christian living, and self-help."

JAMIE CHAVEZ

jamie.chavez@gmail.com

Contact: email
Services: copyediting, substantive/developmental editing
Types of manuscripts: nonfiction books, novels
Charges: flat fee
Credentials/experience: "Jamie Chavez worked for more than ten years in the Christian publishing industry (and more than twenty as a freelance copywriter) before she found her niche as an independent writer and editor in 2004. Specializing in content and line/copy editing, Chavez counts many national publishing houses as clients, many authors and agents as friends, and spends her days in the swanky second-floor office in the pink house with the green door making good books better."

JAMI'S WORDS | JAMI BENNINGTON

2615 5th St., Charleston, IL 61920 | 606-356-2867
jami@jamiswords.com | jamiswords.com

Contact: website

Services: copyediting, discussion questions for books, manuscript evaluation, proofreading

Types of manuscripts: adult, Bible studies, children, curriculum, devotionals, middle grade, nonfiction books, novels, short stories, teen/YA

Charges: hourly rate, word rate

Credentials/experience: "My almost ten years of editing experience includes a copyediting certificate earned through courses at the University of California at San Diego (UCSD), multiple editing courses through The Christian PEN, workshops through the EFA, and yearly conference attendance at PENCON. I am a member of The Christian PEN, the Editorial Freelancers Association (EFA), and American Christian Fiction Writers (ACFW)."

JANE RUBIETTA

418 W. Touhy Ave., Park Ridge, IL 60068 | 847-363-6364

janerubietta@gmail.com | *janerubietta.com*

Contact: email

Services: book-contract evaluation, coauthoring, copyediting, discussion questions for books, ghostwriting, manuscript evaluation, proofreading, writing coach

Types of manuscripts: adult, articles, book proposals, devotionals, gift books, nonfiction books

Charges: custom

Credentials/experience: "Jane has edited, shaped, formatted, rewritten, co-authored, and coached countless authors and want-to-be authors to the finished product of books and published articles. She has published hundreds of articles, 21 books, and multiple courses taught at Writers' Conferences. Jane founded Power Pen and Power Podium, and co-founded Life Launch Me, a service that helps people launch their dreams. She is an idea machine, helping direct a single idea into multiple articles."

JEANETTE GARDNER LITTLETON, PUBLICATION SERVICES

3706 N.E. Shady Lane Dr., Gladstone, MO 64119-1958 | 816-459-8016

jeanettedl@earthlink.net | *www.linkedin.com/in/ jeanette-littleton-b1b790101*

Contact: email

Services: back-cover copy, book-contract evaluation, copyediting, discussion questions for books, indexing, manuscript evaluation, proofreading, substantive/developmental editing

Types of manuscripts: adult, articles, Bible studies, book proposals, curriculum, devotionals, gift books, nonfiction books, novels, query letters, short stories, technical material, teen/YA

Charges: flat fee, hourly rate, page rate

Credentials/experience: "I've been a full-time editor and writer for more than thirty years for a variety of publishers. I've written five thousand articles and edited thousands of articles and dozens of books. Please see my profile at LinkedIn."

JEANETTE HANSCOME

jeanette@jeanettehanscome.com | *jeanettehanscome.com/ coaching-for-authors*

Contact: email, website

Services: manuscript evaluation, substantive/developmental editing, writing coach

Types of manuscripts: adult, devotionals, memoir, nonfiction books, novels, teen/YA

Charges: hourly rate, packages, word rate

Credentials/experience: "Jeanette is a multi-published author of both fiction and nonfiction and an established coach with thirty years of experience in the publishing industry. She has coached and edited in a variety of genres and thoroughly enjoys helping writers of all levels craft powerful stories."

JENNIFER EDWARDS COMMUNICATIONS

2839 Sleeping Bear Rd., Montrose, CO 81401 | 916-768-4207

mail.jennifer.edwards@gmail.com | *jedwardsediting.net*

Contact: email

Services: back-cover copy, coauthoring, copyediting, discussion questions for books, manuscript evaluation, proofreading, self-publishing consulting, substantive/developmental editing, writing coach

Types of manuscripts: academic, adult, Bible studies, book proposals, curriculum, devotionals, nonfiction books, query letters

Charges: hourly rate

Credentials/experience: "Jennifer Edwards is a professional editor, author coach, and self-publishing and production consultant specializing in Christian nonfiction books. With over 14 years of experience, she has worked with traditionally published and self-publishing authors, with over 150 titles. Her experience with Penguin Random House, Redemption Press, Lexham Press, PTLB Publishing, BMH Publishing, and 50+ self-publishing authors has made her an in-demand editor. Jennifer has a master's degree in Biblical Studies &

Theology from Western Seminary and is a standing Gold member of the Christian Editors & Proofreaders Network (PEN)."

JENNIFER GOTT

1769 Ridge Rd., Dickson, TN 37055 | 615-509-4644

jen@jennifergott.com | *jennifergott.com*

> **Contact:** email, website
>
> **Services:** back-cover copy, coauthoring, copyediting, discussion questions for books, ghostwriting, manuscript evaluation, proofreading, substantive/developmental editing, writing coach
>
> **Types of manuscripts:** Bible studies, book proposals, curriculum, devotionals, easy readers, gift books, middle grade, nonfiction books, picture books, query letters, teen/YA
>
> **Charges:** custom, flat fee, hourly rate, page rate, word rate
>
> **Credentials/experience:** "Jennifer Gott has worked in book publishing for 25 years. Most recently, Jennifer served as VP/Publisher for the gift division at HarperCollins Christian Publishing. She has spent her career in nonfiction, fiction, and childrens books, focusing for the last 13 years on high-design books in the gift, devotional, and lifestyle spaces (including cookbooks). She has worked with numerous bestselling authors over the years and was the lead editor for the Jesus Calling® brand, which has sold more than 45 million copies. Jennifer thrives on collaboration, concept ideation and development, marrying visuals and text, crafting messages based on trends and felt needs, and partnering with authors to clarify their message and enhance their unique voice on paper. She takes a 'first, do no harm' approach to editing—carefully and respectfully addressing each word and phrase with the author's message, audience, and voice at the forefront."

JESSICA SNELL BOOK SERVICES

jessicasnelledits@gmail.com | *jessicasnell.com/editing*

> **Contact:** email
>
> **Services:** copyediting, critiquing, ghostwriting, proofreading, substantive/developmental editing
>
> **Types of manuscripts:** adult, Bible studies, curriculum, devotionals, nonfiction books, novels, poetry, short stories, teen/YA
>
> **Charges:** flat fee, hourly rate
>
> **Credentials/experience:** "I am a member of the Christian Editor Connection (CEC) and a gold member of the Christian PEN (Proofreaders and Editors Network). I've also presented workshops at PENCON, the annual conference for Christian editors and

proofreaders. I have over a decade of professional experience, and I love helping authors polish their books so that their own voices shine through in a clear and compelling way."

JOANNE CREARY

joanne8340@gmail.com

    Contact: email
    Services: copyediting, substantive/developmental editing, writing coach
    Types of manuscripts: academic, articles, nonfiction books
    Charges: custom, hourly rate, page rate
    Credentials/experience: "I have extensive experience as a freelance editor, especially for academic book publishers, and as a newspaper feature writer. I'm also a trained Christian life coach passionate about helping you realize your dream! I'd love to bring this experience to help you polish your article or nonfiction book manuscript for publication. Contact me for a free 20-minute consultation."

JOHN HINDS FREELANCE | JOHN SLOAN

830 Grey Eagle Cir. N, Colorado Springs, CO 80919 | 719-888-0365
jsjohnsloan@gmail.com | *johnsloaneditorial.wordpress.com*

    Contact: website
    Services: coauthoring, substantive/developmental editing, writing coach
    Types of manuscripts: academic, adult, Bible studies, devotionals, easy readers, gift books, nonfiction books, short stories, teen/YA
    Charges: flat fee, hourly rate, word rate
    Credentials/experience: "I have worked in publishing and editorial roles for 40 years, with Multnomah Press and HarperCollins Christian Publishing, Zondervan. I am offering my services for freelance work in the areas of book development, collaboration, writer coaching, book doctoring, macro editing, content editing. I have worked with a broad spectrum of book and author types: I have edited the literary and general market works of authors like Philip Yancey and Frederick Buechner; the popular issues volumes of writers like Chuck Colson; the high visibility authors like Lee Strobel and Ben Carson; the broader market authors and pastors like John Ortberg and Mark Batterson; and I've worked in the area of the popular academic works."

JOT OR TITTLE EDITORIAL SERVICES | SAMUEL RYAN KELLY

sam@jotortittle.com | *jotortittle.com*

    Contact: email, phone
    Services: copyediting, manuscript evaluation, proofreading,

substantive/developmental editing, writing coach

Types of manuscripts: academic, adult, articles, Bible studies, devotionals, nonfiction books, novels, short stories

Charges: hourly rate

Credentials/experience: "Sam has a double BA in English and biblical and religious studies and an MA in theology. He specializes in academic writing and has a background in biblical languages, but he likes to bring his expertise to a variety of projects. In addition to his freelance work, Sam does research for pastors and churches at Docent Research Group and serves as an associate editor with Wordsmith Writing Coaches."

JOY MEDIA | JULIE-ALLYSON IERON

PO Box 413, Mt. Prospect, IL 60056

j-a@joymediaservices.com | *www.joymediaservices.com*

Contact: email

Services: back-cover copy, copyediting, discussion questions for books, manuscript evaluation, substantive/developmental editing, writing coach

Types of manuscripts: adult, articles, Bible studies, book proposals, devotionals, nonfiction books, novels

Charges: hourly rate

Credentials/experience: "Author of more than 40 Christian living books, devotionals and Bible studies, Julie-Allyson Ieron is a writing coach, editor and conference speaker. Her clients benefit from Julie's four decades in Christian publishing. She coached for the Jerry B. Jenkins Christian Writers Guild for 14 years and now works directly with first-time and established writers to prepare their works for publication."

JUDITH ROBL

PO Box 802, Lyons, KS 67554 | 620-257-3143

jrlight620@yahoo.com | *www.judithrobl.com/editing-2*

Contact: website

Services: back-cover copy, copyediting, discussion questions for books, proofreading, writing coach

Types of manuscripts: adult, Bible studies, devotionals, gift books, novels, query letters, short stories

Charges: custom

Credentials/experience: "Educated as a secondary English teacher decades ago, I've edited for people for many years. My first major accomplishment in editing was published in 2010. I use *The Chicago Manual of Style* unless another style guide is required. A sample edit lets me see if the author and I are a good fit and allows me to determine the appropriate fee. While perfection in writing is the goal, it must be done with absolute respect for the author's voice."

KAREN APPOLD

kappold@msn.com

Contact: email
Services: copyediting, ghostwriting, proofreading
Types of manuscripts: academic, articles, curriculum, devotionals
Charges: flat fee, hourly rate, word rate
Credentials/experience: "I am an award-winning journalist with a BA from Penn State University in English (Writing). I have more than 30 years of professional editorial experience. I mainly write on healthcare/medical and retail, but welcome Christian-themed work."

KARI BARLOW EDITING SERVICES

731 Cornell Ave., Pensacola, FL 32514 | 850-830-0796
www.karibarlow.com/services

Contact: website
Services: back-cover copy, copyediting, discussion questions for books, ghostwriting, manuscript evaluation, proofreading, substantive/developmental editing
Types of manuscripts: academic, adult, articles, Bible studies, curriculum, devotionals, easy readers, gift books, middle grade, nonfiction books, novels, picture books, query letters, short stories
Charges: custom, hourly rate, word rate
Credentials/experience: "Since graduating from UNC-Chapel Hill with a journalism degree, I have focused my entire career on crafting the written word. Simply put, I am at my professional best when helping individuals and organizations identify and share their best messages. I am skilled at managing projects for multiple clients simultaneously, using project management software, content management systems, and videoconferencing platforms to track progress and communication and spur collaboration. My experience includes writing new copy for rebranded websites, corporate blogging, editing manuscripts at all stages of the publishing process and writing and editing articles, op-eds, press releases, and research reports."

KATHY IDE WRITER SERVICES

Kathy@KathyIde.com | *www.KathyIde.com*

Contact: email, website

Services: copyediting, manuscript evaluation, proofreading, writing coach

Types of manuscripts: adult, Bible studies, book proposals, devotionals, gift books, nonfiction books, novels, query letters, scripts, short stories

Charges: hourly rate

Credentials/experience: "Kathy Ide is the author of *Proofreading Secrets of Best-Selling Authors, Editing Secrets of Best-Selling Authors,* and the *Capitalization Dictionary* as well as the editor/compiler of the Fiction Lover's Devotional series. She's been a professional freelance editor for 20+ years, and in 2022 started proofreading screenplays for Pinnacle Peak/PureFlix. Kathy owns Christian Editors Association, parent organization to the four divisions she founded: The Christian PEN: Proofreaders and Editors Network, The PEN Institute, PENCON, and Christian Editor Connection. CEA sponsors the Editors' Choice Award."

KATHY KUNDE

4903 Alta Camino Dr., Redding, CA 96002 | 530-701-8273

kathyjkunde@gmail.com

Contact: email

Services: copyediting, discussion questions for books, manuscript evaluation, proofreading, substantive/developmental editing

Types of manuscripts: adult, articles, Bible studies, book proposals, curriculum, devotionals, easy readers, gift books, middle grade, nonfiction books, query letters, teen/YA

Charges: custom

Credentials/experience: "As a full time English teacher then a school administrator, it was my job to represent education through proper writing. I did this by editing formal letters, informal newsletters, state reports, court queries, grants, public articles, and many many emails over years. To keep my skills sharp, I also edited informational texts as well as faith-based books for pastor friends on the side. It's a delight for me to make another's work shine. Through an author's work, I get to know a fellow artist and join in shaping and sharing his or her message. Now I am retired, but not from this passion. I eagerly look forward to my next projects as God gifts them."

KATIE PHILLIPS CREATIVE SERVICES

1500 E. Tall Tree Rd. #6206, Derby, KS 67037-6033 | 316-293-9202

katie@katiephillipscreative.com | *www.katiephillipscreative.com*

Contact: email

Services: substantive/developmental editing, writing coach

Types of manuscripts: adult, novels, teen/YA

Charges: word rate

Credentials/experience: "Katie Phillips has a Bachelor of Arts in Print Communications and over 15 years of experience content editing both fiction and non-fiction. She has worked with multiple award-winning clients, including Kara Swanson Matsumoto (Reader's Choice three consecutive years at the Realm Awards) and Emily Hayse (Book of the Year at the Realm Awards). She's the Fiction Director for the Author Conservatory. She's known for her developmental editing and coaching in adult and YA fantasy and science fiction."

KIM PETERSON

1114 Buxton Dr., Knoxville, KY 37922

petersk.ktp@gmail.com | *naturewalkwithgod.wordpress.com/about-kim*

Contact: email

Services: back-cover copy, copyediting, create brochures and newsletters, discussion questions for books, manuscript evaluation, proofreading, substantive/developmental editing, write curriculum/lesson plans, writing coach

Types of manuscripts: academic, adult, articles, Bible studies, blog posts, book proposals, curriculum, devotionals, easy readers, gift books, middle grade, nonfiction books, novels, poetry, query letters, short stories, technical material, teen/YA

Charges: hourly rate

Credentials/experience: "College writing instructor (30+ years), freelance writer (40+ years), freelance editor (15 years), conference speaker (16 years), contest judge (11 years), and former agent's fiction reader (9 years). MA in print communication."

KRISTEN STIEFFEL

kristen@kristenstieffel.com | *www.kristenstieffel.com*

Contact: email

Services: copyediting, ghostwriting, manuscript evaluation, proofreading, substantive/developmental editing, writing coach

Types of manuscripts: adult, articles, Bible studies, devotionals, middle grade, nonfiction books, novels, short stories, teen/YA
Charges: word rate
Credentials/experience: "Kristen Stieffel is an author, editor, and instructor specializing in speculative fiction: fantasy, sci-fi, steampunk, cyberpunk, and all the other -punks. She works in both the Christian submarket and the general market. In her fifteen years as a freelancer, she has edited more than one hundred books for more than ninety clients."

LEE WARREN COMMUNICATIONS
1122 Tanglewood Ct., Apt. 31, Bellevue, NE 68005
leewarrenjr@outlook.com | *www.leewarren.info/editing*

Contact: email, website
Services: copyediting, proofreading
Types of manuscripts: adult, articles, Bible studies, devotionals, gift books, nonfiction books, novels
Charges: word rate
Credentials/experience: "Lee Warren brings over twenty years of experience in the Christian publishing industry, working as a contract editor for a variety of publishers, including Barbour Publishing, Electric Moon Publishing, Bold Vision Books, and others. He also serves on the editorial staff of The Christian Communicator manuscript critique service, where he provides detailed feedback and guidance to authors seeking to refine their work."

LESLIE L. McKEE EDITING
lmckeeediting@gmail.com | *lmckeeediting.wixsite.com/lmckeeediting*

Contact: email
Services: back-cover copy, copyediting, discussion questions for books, proofreading, substantive/developmental editing
Types of manuscripts: adult, Bible studies, devotionals, easy readers, middle grade, nonfiction books, novels, poetry, short stories, teen/YA
Charges: flat fee, page rate, word rate
Credentials/experience: "Freelance editor and proofreader with various publishing houses (large and small) since 2012. I work with traditionally published and self-published/indie authors. I'm a member of The Christian PEN and American Christian Fiction Writers. See my website for details on services offered, as well as testimonials and a portfolio."

LESLIE SANTAMARIA

PO Box 195861, Winter Springs, FL 32719

www.lesliesantamaria.com

Contact: website

Services: copyediting, manuscript evaluation, proofreading, substantive/developmental editing, writing coach

Types of manuscripts: children's magazines, easy readers, middle grade, picture books, teen/YA

Charges: page rate

Credentials/experience: "Leslie Santamaria specializes in children's literature. With over 200 pieces published in periodicals, including *Highlights for Children, Pockets,* and *Spider,* and a picture book, Leslie earned a Master of Fine Arts in Creative Writing for Children from Spalding University. A longtime freelance editor for publishers, businesses, ministries, and individuals, she is a frequent contest judge and workshop presenter. Leslie has coached many writers to publication and would love to help you too."

LIBBY GONTARZ WORD SERVICES

libbygontarz@gmail.com | libbygontarz.com

Contact: email, phone

Services: copyediting, substantive/developmental editing

Types of manuscripts: adult, articles, Bible studies, curriculum, devotionals, nonfiction books

Charges: custom, page rate, word rate

Credentials/experience: "After a career of teaching and nationwide educational training, I accepted a curriculum development position at an educational publishing company. Writing lessons and assessments gradually led into editing. Since 2015, I have focused on Christian nonfiction, editing for various publishers and individuals. Earned 2022 Excellence in Editing award for copyediting winning book, *On Wings Like Eagles.* Worked on editing team for two other award-winning books—a devotional and a business book. Your project deserves professional editing!"

LIGHTNING EDITING SERVICES | DENISE LOOCK

699 Golf Course Rd., Waynesville, NC 28786 | 908-868-5854

denise@lightningeditingservices.com | www.lightningeditingservices.com

Contact: website

Services: coauthoring, copyediting, discussion questions for books,

351

ghostwriting, manuscript evaluation, proofreading, substantive/developmental editing

Types of manuscripts: adult, articles, Bible studies, book proposals, devotionals, nonfiction books, teen/YA

Charges: flat fee, hourly rate

Credentials/experience: "Former high school English teacher and college instructor Denise Loock is a general editor for Iron Stream Media and also accepts freelance projects. With thirty years of experience in the academic world coupled with ten years in the publishing industry, she helps writers produce books that attract publishers and engage readers."

LINDA RUTZEN EDITORIAL SERVICES

5735 Tradewind Pt., Colorado Springs, CO 80923 | 719-640-5703
lruthw53@gmail.com

Contact: email

Services: copyediting, ghostwriting, manuscript evaluation, proofreading, substantive/developmental editing

Types of manuscripts: adult, articles, Bible studies, devotionals, nonfiction books

Charges: hourly rate, page rate, word rate

Credentials/experience: "I bring more than 30 years of writing and editing experience to your project. I am a former editor-in-chief of USA Racquetball's national magazine, and have worked in marketing and communications in government and Christian nonprofits. My ghostwriting and editing experience brings a keen and intuitive respect for both the author and reader. My editing standards are high so that the writer's gift and message may be brought to the page in the best, clearest way possible."

LISA BARTELT

lmbartelt@gmail.com | *lisabartelt.com/the-work*

Contact: website

Services: back-cover copy, coauthoring, copyediting, manuscript evaluation, proofreading

Types of manuscripts: nonfiction books, novels

Charges: hourly rate

Credentials/experience: "20 years of experience including 8 years as a newspaper editor/reporter, 4 years as a contest judge for a well-known writing organization, ACFW contest judging, 2 co-authored books, avid reader of all kinds of books, middle school reading teacher's aide."

LISSA HALLS JOHNSON EDITORIAL

lissahallsjohnson@gmail.com | *lissahallsjohnson.com*

Contact: website

Services: copyediting, proofreading, substantive/developmental editing

Types of manuscripts: adult, novels, short stories, teen/YA

Charges: hourly rate

Credentials/experience: "I have 35+ years of writing and editing experience on both sides of the publishing desk, so I understand what a writer needs personally and editorially. I have taught conference seminars on how to write and/or edit. I have written 20 published books. Most of my written work has been in the form of novels, although I have also written (and edited) nonfiction, articles, short stories, and radio dramas as well as pre-writing chapters for other writers. Some of the books I have edited have won awards and/or starred *Publisher's Weekly* reviews."

LITTLE FOXES EDITING | LAUREN SIMONIC

13657 Canoe Ct., Jacksonville, FL 32226 | 904-477-4122

littlefoxesediting.com

Contact: phone, website

Services: manuscript evaluation, proofreading, substantive/developmental editing

Types of manuscripts: academic, adult, articles, Bible studies, curriculum, devotionals, easy readers, gift books, middle grade, nonfiction books, picture books, poetry, technical material

Charges: word rate

Credentials/experience: "I've been a freelance editor since 1996, working primarily with Christian nonfiction authors. I heard a sermon once about the 'little foxes that spoil the vines' and it seemed such a perfect analogy for what I do as an editor. Authors have the vision—a message—that they feel needs to be relayed. Oftentimes, however, all the little mistakes in their delivery—overlooked grammar issues, sluggish flow, disorganized content, pesky typographical errors, and more—end up spoiling the beauty and usefulness of a would-be vital vine. Let me help you catch all the 'little foxes' that mar your final presentation and spoil what God placed in your heart to proclaim. Let's work together to produce a product that is worthy of its calling. You have the message, let me help you clip, prune and water it until it's absolutely flourishing."

LOGOS WORD DESIGNS LLC | LINDA L. NATHAN

PO Box 735, Maple Falls, WA 98266-0735 | 360-599-3429
linda@logosword.com | *www.logosword.com*

Contact: email, website
Services: back-cover copy, manuscript evaluation
Types of manuscripts: academic, adult, articles, Bible studies, devotionals, gift books, nonfiction books, novels, query letters, short stories
Charges: custom, flat fee, hourly rate, word rate
Credentials/experience: "Owner and Managing Editor Linda Nathan has over 30 years of experience as an independent freelance writer, editor, and consultant, working with authors and institutions on a wide range of projects. She is a former Gold Member of the Christian PEN and a former freelance staff editor with Redemption Press. Linda also has a B.A. in Psychology from the University of Oregon and master's level work in that area, as well as 10 years of experience in the legal field as a paralegal, legal secretary, and notary public. She has managed Logos Word Designs since 1992."

LUCIE WINBORNE

116 Hickory Rd., Longwood, FL 2750-2708 | 321-439-7743
lwinborne704@gmail.com | *www.bluetypewriter.com*

Contact: website
Services: copyediting, proofreading
Types of manuscripts: adult, devotionals, middle grade, nonfiction books, novels, poetry, short stories, teen/YA
Charges: hourly rate
Credentials/experience: "Conversant with *Chicago Manual of Style, Merriam-Webster Collegiate Dictionary*, Google Docs and Microsoft Word, with experience in fiction, nonfiction, educational, and business documents. Demonstrated adherence to deadlines and excellent communication and organizational skills."

MEGAN RYAN EDITING

mryanediting@gmail.com | *mryanediting.wixsite.com/mryanediting*

Contact: email, website
Services: back-cover copy, copyediting, proofreading
Types of manuscripts: adult, Bible studies, children, curriculum, devotionals, gift books, middle grade, nonfiction books, novels, picture books, short stories, teen/YA
Charges: hourly rate, word rate

Credentials/experience: "Megan Ryan helps authors feel confident about sharing their writing. She is a Gold member of the Christian PEN and has edited more than 160 books for self-publishing authors and hybrid publishers since 2018. She is on staff at the Christian Editor Connection and the Well Conference for Christian Creatives. After majoring in journalism and minoring in English and anthropology, Megan was a newspaper copyeditor for three years before becoming a freelance book editor."

MEGHAN STOLL EDITING

meghanbielinski.wordpress.com

Contact: website
Services: copyediting, manuscript evaluation, substantive/developmental editing
Types of manuscripts: devotionals, nonfiction books, novels
Charges: hourly rate, word rate
Credentials/experience: "For the past six years, I've been helping independent authors bring their books to a high level of excellence. It's a great joy to aid them in producing works that are true to their vision and valuable and enjoyable to their audience. Please see my website for more information."

MG LITERARY SERVICES | MEGAN GERIG

mgliteraryservices@gmail.com | megangerig.com/editing

Contact: website
Services: copyediting, critiquing, proofreading
Types of manuscripts: middle grade, teen/YA
Charges: flat fee, word rate
Credentials/experience: "I am a proofreader for Enclave Publishing and have also performed several developmental edits for a Penguin Random House imprint. I've also worked with several incredible self-published and aspiring authors to bring their manuscripts to the next level. Client testimonials are available on my website."

MICHELLE MILLER PROOFREADING

diligentanalyzer@michellemillerproofreading.com | michellemillerproofreading.com

Contact: website
Services: proofreading
Types of manuscripts: articles, Bible studies, book proposals, devotionals, gift books, middle grade, nonfiction books, novels, query letters, short stories, teen/YA

Charges: word rate

Credentials/experience: "I am a freelance proofreader with over one year of experience working with Christian authors and clean fiction/nonfiction writers. I have proofread novels, devotionals, and self-help books for both indie authors and publishers such as Barbour Publishing. My keen eye for detail, understanding of Christian publishing standards, and ability to preserve an author's unique voice ensure manuscripts are polished and publication-ready."

MIDWEST PROOFREADING SERVICES | TRACY ADAMS

midwest-proofreading-services.com

Contact: website

Services: beta reading, copyediting, proofreading

Types of manuscripts: adult, articles, easy readers, middle grade, novels, short stories, teen/YA

Charges: word rate

Credentials/experience: "I am a passionate proofreader and copy editor, dedicated to helping authors create clean and polished manuscripts. With a keen eye for detail and a love for language, I thrive on refining written content to ensure clarity and coherence. Throughout my career, I have honed my skills in grammar, punctuation, and style, allowing me to meticulously polish texts across various genres and industries. My commitment to maintaining the author's voice while enhancing readability has earned me a reputation for delivering exceptional results. I find immense satisfaction in collaborating with writers, offering insightful suggestions and constructive feedback to bring their stories to life in the most impactful way. If you're seeking a meticulous proofreader and copy editor to elevate your work, I am eager to embark on this rewarding partnership with you."

MISSION AND MEDIA | MICHELLE RAYBURN

info@missionandmedia.com | *www.missionandmedia.com*

Contact: email

Services: copyediting, discussion questions for books, ghostwriting, proofreading, substantive/developmental editing

Types of manuscripts: Bible studies, nonfiction books

Charges: flat fee, hourly rate, word rate

Credentials/experience: "Michelle Rayburn has been a freelance writer for more than 20 years and has edited for Christian publishers as well as for indie authors. Has also worked in the marketing and public relations industry. Michelle has an MA in ministry leadership and has published hundreds of articles and Bible studies as well as five books. She specializes in Christian living, Bible study, humor, and self-help."

MOUNTAIN CREEK BOOKS | KARA STARCHER
PO Box 21, Chloe, WV 25235 | 330-705-3399
mountaincreekbooks.com

> **Contact:** website
> **Services:** copyediting, critiquing, proofreading, substantive/developmental editing
> **Types of manuscripts:** academic, adult, Bible studies, curriculum, devotionals, middle grade, nonfiction books, novels, teen/YA
> **Charges:** flat fee, word rate
> **Credentials/experience:** "BA in Publishing; 20+ years of editing and publishing experience for independent authors and small presses."

NICOLE HAYES
www.nicolehayesauthor.com/help-for-writers#editorial

> **Contact:** website
> **Services:** coauthoring, copyediting, discussion questions for books, ghostwriting, manuscript evaluation, proofreading, substantive/developmental editing, writing coach
> **Types of manuscripts:** adult, articles, curriculum, devotionals, gift books, nonfiction books, novels, poetry, short stories, technical material, teen/YA
> **Charges:** flat fee, word rate
> **Credentials/experience:** "Bachelor's degree in English; PhD in education. Although I do most writing, editing, and proofreading projects, my niche is creative nonfiction (engaging, dramatic, factual prose). I have been writing and editing for more than twenty-five years."

NOBLE CREATIVE LLC | SCOTT NOBLE
PO Box 131402, St. Paul, MN 55113 | 651-494-4169
snoble@noblecreative.com | *www.noblecreative.com*

> **Contact:** email
> **Services:** ghostwriting, proofreading, substantive/developmental editing, writing coach
> **Types of manuscripts:** adult, articles, book proposals, curriculum,

devotionals, nonfiction books, query letters

Charges: flat fee

Credentials/experience: "Nearly twenty years of experience as an award-winning journalist, writer, editor, and proofreader. More than 1,000 published articles, many of them prompting radio and television appearances. Won several awards from Evangelical Press Association. Worked with dozens of published authors and other public figures, as well as first-time authors and small businesses. Have a BA and MS from St. Cloud State University and an MA from Bethel Seminary."

NOVEL IMPROVEMENT EDITORIAL SERVICES | JEANNE MARIE LEACH

PO Box 25663, Silverthorne, CO 80498

jeanne@novelimprovement.com | *novelimprovement.com*

Contact: website

Services: ghostwriting, manuscript evaluation, substantive/developmental editing, writing coach

Types of manuscripts: book proposals, memoir, novels, query letters, short stories, teen/YA

Charges: flat fee

Credentials/experience: "Jeanne Marie Leach is a multi-published fiction author, speaker, mentor, and freelance editor specializing in fiction and memoirs. She is past coordinator and current Gold Member of The Christian PEN: Proofreaders and Editors Network and a member of the Christian Editor Connection. She has been editing for seventeen years and has edited over 160 books, of which many have gone on to win awards and make it to bestseller's lists."

OASHEIM EDITING SERVICES LLC | CATHY OASHEIM

cathy@cathyoasheim.com

Contact: email

Services: copyediting, discussion questions for books, manuscript evaluation, proofreading, substantive/developmental editing, writing coach

Types of manuscripts: academic, articles, Bible studies, curriculum, devotionals, devotions, doctoral dissertations/theses, nonfiction books, novels, query letters, short stories, technical material

Charges: custom, flat fee, hourly rate, page rate, word rate

Credentials/experience: "Cathy is a professional freelance editor since 2012, blogger, and writing coach who specializes in nonfiction, true fiction, and fiction for Indy authors. She has judged over 1,000 Indie books for the Next Generation Indie Book Awards since 2016. Her services also include academic editing and fact checking for doctoral candidates (all have passed their boards), and blogs. A BS degree in Applied Psychology from Regis University allows Cathy to 'Refine Your Masterpiece.' Earlier engineering and military experiences support highly technical work and complex storytelling to get the rough draft manuscript out of the head, to the heart, and out of the plume to a polished product for the readers.

"Organizations: Author Alliance of Independent Authors, Journal Storage, National Association of Independent Writers & Editors, Nonfiction Authors Association, Toastmasters International—Distinguished Toastmaster, and The Christian PEN Proofreaders and Editors Network—Silver Member."

PAGE & PIXEL PUBLICATIONS | SUSAN MOORE
pageandpixelpublications@gmail.com | pageandpixelpublications.com

Contact: email

Services: back-cover copy, coauthoring, copyediting, discussion questions for books, ghostwriting, indexing, manuscript evaluation, proofreading, substantive/developmental editing

Types of manuscripts: academic, adult, articles, Bible studies, book proposals, curriculum, devotionals, easy readers, gift books, middle grade, nonfiction books, novels, poetry, query letters, scripts, short stories, technical material, teen/YA

Charges: hourly rate

Credentials/experience: "Whether your project requires extensive reworking or simple proofreading, with more than 30 years of editing experience I can put that professional edge on your publication. Your full length manuscript or article can be edited for continuity and grammar to industry standards so that it's ready to submit to your publisher. If your manuscript is only in the idea stage and you can't get started . . . If you suspect you need additional assistance beyond traditional editing . . . If you have a project or assignment that you just can't get to . . . If your research is complete but you don't know where to go from there—let's talk. I am accepting freelance assignments on a variety of topics."

PENCIL SHAVINGS | CHRISTINA FENNELL
info@pencilshavingsediting.com | pencilshavingsediting.com

Contact: email

Services: copyediting, manuscript evaluation, substantive/developmental editing, writing coach

Types of manuscripts: adult, children, middle grade, nonfiction books, picture books, scripts

Charges: flat fee, word rate

Credentials/experience: "Christina Fennell has a Bachelor's in English, a certificate for Writing for Children and Teenagers, and over nine years of editorial experience. She is a published author, podcaster, and conference speaker."

PERPEDIT PUBLISHING INK LLC | REBECCA LYLES

PO Box 190246, Boise, ID 83719 | 208-562-1592

beckylyles@beckylyles.com | *www.beckylyles.com*

Contact: email

Services: back-cover copy, copyediting, discussion questions for books, ghostwriting, manuscript evaluation, proofreading, substantive/developmental editing, writing coach

Types of manuscripts: adult, articles, Bible studies, book proposals, children, devotionals, easy readers, gift books, middle grade, nonfiction books, novels, picture books, query letters, short stories, teen/YA

Charges: hourly rate, page rate

Credentials/experience: "My educational background includes a double bachelor's in Bible and Church Education plus multiple writers' conferences, classes, workshops and seminars. I have provided professional edits for clients for almost 20 years. Although I work mostly with Christian novelists, memoirists and devotional writers, I have edited business-related newsletters, magazines, articles, brochures and related documents. I have also written and published fiction and nonfiction and have helped other authors do the same."

PICKY, PICKY INK | SUE MIHOLER

1075 Willow Lake Rd. N, Salem, OR 97303 | 503-393-3356

suemiholer@comcast.net

Contact: email

Services: back-cover copy, copyediting, proofreading, substantive/developmental editing

Types of manuscripts: adult, articles, Bible studies, devotionals, nonfiction books

Charges: custom, hourly rate

Credentials/experience: "I edit to *Chicago Manual of Style* standards and have been doing so since 1998. Many of my clients are returning ones who know where to turn when they want every Bible verse checked and help structuring their manuscript."

PRATHERINK LITERARY SERVICES | VICKI PRATHER

20 Parkview Rd., Clinton, MS 39056 | 601-573-4295
pratherINK@gmail.com | pratherink.wordpress.com

Contact: email, website

Services: coauthoring, copyediting, discussion questions for books, proofreading

Types of manuscripts: academic, articles, Bible studies, curriculum, devotionals, easy readers, gift books, middle grade, nonfiction books, novels, poetry, scripts, short stories, teen/YA

Charges: custom, flat fee, hourly rate, word rate

Credentials/experience: "I've been assisting first-time and experienced authors since 2014 in taking their writing to the next level, whether that means general advice or proofreading or being by their side through publishing. My first love is Christian works of any kind. I've authored and coauthored curriculums, Bible studies, and memoirs, as well as children's books & fiction. Before transitioning into freelance work, I wrote procedures manuals in my secretarial years, then taught writing skills and study skills and Bible to middle schoolers for a decade. If I'm *not* right for your editing needs, I'll tell you!"

PROFESSIONAL PUBLISHING SERVICES | CHRISTY CALLAHAN

*professionalpublishingservices@gmail.com |
professionalpublishingservicesus.weebly.com*

Contact: website

Services: copyediting, French to English translation, French-language editing, manuscript evaluation, proofreading, substantive/developmental editing, writing coach

Types of manuscripts: academic, adult, articles, Bible studies, curriculum, devotionals, easy readers, gift books, middle grade, nonfiction books, novels, teen/YA

Charges: custom

Credentials/experience: "Christy graduated Phi Beta Kappa from Carnegie Mellon University and then earned her MA in Intercultural Studies from Fuller Seminary. A gold member of The Christian PEN: Proofreaders and Editors Network and certified by the Christian Editor Connection and Reedsy, she also completed the 40-hour Foundational Course (Christian track) with the Institute for Life Coach Training."

PS WELLS | PEGGYSUE WELLS

3419 E. 1000 N, Roanoke, IN 46783 | 260-433-2817

peggysuewells@gmail.com | *PeggySueWells.com*

> **Contact:** website
>
> **Services:** back-cover copy, coauthoring, ghostwriting, manuscript evaluation, self-publishing consulting, substantive/developmental editing, writing coach
>
> **Types of manuscripts:** adult, articles, Bible studies, book proposals, children, curriculum, devotionals, easy readers, gift books, nonfiction books, novels, picture books, query letters, short stories, teen/YA
>
> **Charges:** custom, flat fee
>
> **Credentials/experience:** "PeggySue Wells is the award-winning *USA Today* and *Wall Street Journal* bestselling author of nearly 50 books, ghostwriter for that many more, writing coach, and independent publishing strategist on mission to fill the world with fiction and nonfiction works that take people to places they've never been before."

PWC EDITING | PAUL W. CONANT

527 Bayshore Pl., Dallas, TX 75217-7755 | 214-289-3397

pwcediting@gmail.com | *PWC-editing.com*

> **Contact:** website
>
> **Services:** copyediting, proofreading, substantive/developmental editing
>
> **Types of manuscripts:** academic, adult, articles, Bible studies, business materials, devotionals, nonfiction books, novels, poetry, short stories, technical material, textbooks
>
> **Charges:** hourly rate, word rate
>
> **Credentials/experience:** "Book editor since '94; textbook editor for 1.5 years; academic editor since 2001; gold member of The Christian PEN (Proofreaders and Editors Network); copyeditor for Christian Editing & Design, Redemption Press, and Baker Books."

READ. WRITE. PRAY. CARE LLC | MARTI PIEPER

246 Maple Grove Rd., Seneca, GA 29678 | 352-409-3136

marti@martipieper.com | *www.martipieper.com*

> **Contact:** website
>
> **Services:** coauthoring, copyediting, critiquing, ghostwriting, substantive/developmental editing
>
> **Types of manuscripts:** adult, articles, book proposals, curriculum, devotionals, nonfiction books, query letters
>
> **Charges:** custom

Credentials/experience: "I have served as ghostwriter/collaborative writer for eight traditionally published books, including a CBA bestseller, and edited many more. I have written and edited for both print and digital magazines, all of these in the Christian market."

REALITY COACHING FOR WRITERS | EDDIE JONES and DIANA FLEGAL
2333 Barton Oaks Dr., Raleigh, NC 27614
writerscoach.us@gmail.com | writerscoach.us
Contact: email, website
Services: back-cover copy, book-contract evaluation, coauthoring, discussion questions for books, ghostwriting, manuscript evaluation, proofreading, substantive/developmental editing, writing coach
Types of manuscripts: adult, Bible studies, picture books, book proposals, devotionals, easy readers, gift books, middle grade, nonfiction books, novellas, query letters, scripts, short stories, teen/YA
Charges: custom, flat fee, monthly fee
Credentials/experience: "Do you need help with your novel or nonfiction project? Do you have a book idea but are not sure where to start? Book your free Introductory Coaching Session at *writerscoach. us*. With 30-plus years of experience in Christian publishing (agenting, editing, book publishing), our team can help you turn your stories, talks, sermons, life lessons, and podcasts into a book."

REBECCA LUELLA MILLER'S EDITORIAL SERVICES
rluellam@yahoo.com | rewriterewordrework.wordpress.com
Contact: email, website
Services: copyediting, critiquing, proofreading, substantive/ developmental editing, writing coach
Types of manuscripts: academic, adult, articles, devotionals, middle grade, nonfiction books, novels, query letters, short stories, teen/YA
Charges: page rate
Credentials/experience: "I became an editor as a direct result of my work as a critique partner. Behind that were the thirty years I spent as an English teacher evaluating student writing. Since 2004 I have had the privilege of working with numerous traditionally published authors, self-published authors, and aspiring authors alike."

REFINE SERVICES LLC | KATE MOTAUNG
kate@refineservices.com | www.refineservices.com
Contact: email

Services: copyediting, substantive/developmental editing

Types of manuscripts: academic, adult, articles, Bible studies, picture books, book proposals, curriculum, devotionals, easy readers, gift books, middle grade, nonfiction books, novels, poetry, query letters, scripts, short stories, teen/YA

Charges: word rate

Credentials/experience: "Kate Motaung is the owner of Refine Services LLC. She has been offering copyediting services since 2015 and enjoys serving a variety of authors. Visit *refineservices. com/reviews* to read testimonials from past clients."

REFINED PEN EDITS LLC | JESSICA BOUDREAUX

jessica@refinedpenedits.com | *www.refinedpenedits.com*

Contact: email, website

Services: copyediting, critiquing, proofreading, substantive/ developmental editing

Types of manuscripts: adult, novellas, novels, short stories, teen/YA

Charges: word rate

Credentials/experience: "10+ years studying writing. Certificates in editing courses from The PEN Institute (TPI). Continuing education with TPI, The Editorial Freelancers Association (EFA), and The Christian Writers Institute (CWI). Member of American Christian Fiction Writers (ACFW), The Christian PEN, and EFA. My goal is to create and support stories that glorify God and bring delight to his people."

REVISIONS BY RACHEL LLC | RACHEL E. BRADLEY

1512 Lynhaven Ave., Richmond, VA 23224 | 918-207-2833

editor@RevisionsbyRachel.com | *www.RevisionsbyRachel.com*

Contact: email, phone, text

Services: copyediting, indexing, manuscript evaluation, proofreading, substantive/developmental editing

Types of manuscripts: adult, Bible studies, curriculum, nonfiction books, novels, teen/YA

Charges: word rate

Credentials/experience: "Rachel holds a BS degree in Paralegal Studies from Northeastern State University in Oklahoma. She graduated *summa cum laude* in 2006 and has been awarded the Advanced Certified Paralegal designation by the National Association of Legal Assistants. She is a gold member of the Christian PEN: Proofreaders and Editors Network, is an established freelance editor with the Christian Editor Connection, is an instructor with the PEN Institute, and has served as a judge for the Excellence in Editing Award and as faculty for PENCON, the only conference for editors in the Christian market."

RICK STEELE EDITORIAL SERVICES

26 Dean Rd., Ringgold, GA 30736 | 706-937-8121

rsteelecam@gmail.com | steeleeditorialservices.myportfolio.com

Contact: website

Services: copyediting, proofreading, substantive/developmental editing, writing coach

Types of manuscripts: academic, adult, articles, Bible studies, book proposals, curriculum, devotionals, gift books, middle grade, nonfiction books, novels, query letters, scripts, short stories, technical material, teen/YA

Charges: flat fee

Credentials/experience: "Rick Steele has adeptly managed the workflow of scores of titles for two different publishing houses, working with both fledgling and experienced authors along the way. While in different editorial capacities at AMG Publishers for over twenty years, the publishing house launched five different Bible study brands plus several fiction lines along with Christian living books, study Bibles, and reference works. Rick has traveled extensively to writer's conferences all over the United States, teaching workshops and helping writers with their craft. Since 2017, Rick has been using his skills and expertise to help clients achieve their publishing objectives."

RJ THESMAN

Rebecca@RJThesman.net | RJThesman.net

Contact: email

Services: copyediting, manuscript evaluation, proofreading, writing coach

Types of manuscripts: academic, adult, articles, Bible studies, book proposals, curriculum, devotionals, gift books, middle grade, nonfiction books, novels, poetry, query letters, short stories, teen/YA

Charges: hourly rate, word rate

Credentials/experience: "RJ Thesman is the author of twenty-nine books. She is a certified Writing Coach, an Editor, a trained Biblical Counselor, a Stephen minister, and an ordained Deacon. She has published 800+ articles and/or stories in various publications. Her work is included in fourteen anthologies, and she is listed in the Who's Who of Professional Women. Thesman also holds a Bachelor of Science degree in Education. Thesman is a professional member of the National Association of Professional Women, the Kansas Authors Club, the Heart of America Christian Writer's Network, the Fellowship of Christian Writers, and the American Association of Christian Counselors. Thesman loves to help her clients birth new words and publish their books. Currently, she has helped her clients produce 38 books."

ROBIN L. REED

1857 Alcan Dr., Medford, OR 97504 | 541-301-0869
robin@robinlreed.com | robinlreed.com

> **Contact:** email
> **Services:** copyediting, proofreading
> **Types of manuscripts:** academic, adult, Bible studies, curriculum, devotionals, easy readers, middle grade, nonfiction books, novels, short stories, teen/YA
> **Charges:** word rate
> **Credentials/experience:** "I'm an experienced editor who specializes in helping independent authors get their books into print with the highest possible quality. My priority is to preserve and strengthen my clients' original writing voice and support them through the editing process. I've received training through the PEN Institute and Proofread Anywhere as well as earning a master's degree in history from UC Riverside."

SARA ELLA EDITING AND COACHING

saraellawrites@gmail.com | saraella.com/editorial-services

> **Contact:** website
> **Services:** copyediting, manuscript evaluation, proofreading, substantive/ developmental editing
> **Types of manuscripts:** adult, book proposals, middle grade, novels, teen/YA
> **Charges:** packages
> **Credentials/experience:** "Multi-published author of 6 young adult novels with Thomas Nelson/HarperCollins and Enclave Publishing. High school creative writing instructor. Three years of experience as a professional copywriter and proofreader. Experienced workshop instructor and keynote speaker for writing conferences across the country. Editor for Enclave Publishing. Freelance editor for 7+ years. Five years of experience as a social media coach and assistant."

SARA LAWSON

1509 Garfield Ave., South Pasadena, CA 91030 | 530-933-9838
sarareneelawson@gmail.com | *www.sarasbooks.com*

Contact: website
Services: copyediting, substantive/developmental editing
Types of manuscripts: academic, devotionals, middle grade, nonfiction books, novels, scripts, teen/YA
Charges: custom, word rate
Credentials/experience: "Sara Lawson has over 10 years of freelance editing experience working with fiction, nonfiction, and magazine articles of all lengths. She has also served within quite a few different Christian denominations, so she understands a variety of ministry contexts. She loves to help writers because she believes that everyone has a story to tell and no one should have to let technical writing abilities get in the way of telling that story."

SARA R. TURNQUIST

255 Alonzo Pl., Cunningham, TN 37052 | 407-288-7416
sara@saraturnquist.com | *saraturnquist.com/editing-rates*

Contact: website
Services: copyediting, proofreading, substantive/developmental editing
Types of manuscripts: adult, novels, short stories, teen/YA
Charges: word rate
Credentials/experience: "I first became an editor when I worked with Clean Reads (a medium sized publishing house out of Alabama). One of the editors on staff trained and honed my editing skills for content, developmental, line, and copy editing as well as proofing. Then I became an editor for that publishing house, editing science fiction, dystopian, contemporary romance, historical romance, historical time slip, and many other genres and subgenres. Since becoming a freelance editor, I have continued working in these genres and expanded into other subgenres of Clean and Christian Romance."

SARAH HAMAKER WRITERS COACH

sarah@sarahhamaker.com | *sarahhamakerfiction.com*

Contact: email, website
Services: coauthoring, copyediting, discussion questions for books, ghostwriting, manuscript evaluation, proofreading, writing coach
Types of manuscripts: adult, articles, Bible studies, easy readers, middle grade, nonfiction books, novels, teen/YA
Charges: custom, flat fee, hourly rate, word rate

Credentials/experience: "I specialize in helping clients finish their current work-in-progress as well as editing their final drafts. I also have a heart to encourage writers to fulfill their calling from God to write."

SARAH HAYHURST EDITORIAL LLC

1441 Haynescrest Ct., Grayson, GA 30017 | 470-825-2905
sarah@sarahhayhurst.com | www.sarahhayhurst.com/editor
 Contact: email, website
 Services: copyediting, proofreading, substantive/developmental editing, writing coach
 Types of manuscripts: articles, Bible studies, curriculum, devotionals, nonfiction books, short stories
 Charges: hourly rate, word rate
 Credentials/experience: "Sarah is a gold-level member of The Christian PEN and Christian Editor Network with whom she passed extensive testing and demonstrated expertise in the substantive editing, copyediting, and proofreading of both fiction and nonfiction manuscripts. Sarah has over ten years of editing experience and started her editorial company in 2014."

SCATTERED LIGHT BOOKS | CLAIRE KOHLER

149 Wheatfield Dr., Statesville, NC 28677 | 704-495-4194
clairekohlerbooks@yahoo.com | www.clairekohlerbooks.com/services
 Contact: email, website
 Services: back-cover copy, copyediting, proofreading
 Types of manuscripts: adult, devotionals, middle grade, novels, teen/YA
 Charges: word rate
 Credentials/experience: "I have been editing professionally for three years. I have experience with historical fiction, fantasy, romance, Christian fiction, devotionals, plays, and more. My background before I became an editor is in education."

SCRIBELANCE | VALARI WESTEREN

valari.westeren@scribelance.com
 Contact: email
 Services: copyediting, proofreading
 Types of manuscripts: academic, adult, Bible studies, nonfiction books
 Charges: word rate
 Credentials/experience: "Valari helps Christian authors and scholars become authoritative voices in their fields with meticulous copy editing that Grammarly can't provide. Her academic studies have

spanned both English and theology, and her skills have served academic Christian presses such as B&H Academic, debut authors publishing under Wipf&Stock, theology professors submitting PhD-level work, and various smaller Christian presses that publish memoirs and Bible studies. She is very knowledgeable of Scripture and double-checks all biblical references according to the chosen English translation(s)."

SCRIVEN COMMUNICATIONS | KATHIE SCRIVEN

22 Ridge Rd. #220, Greenbelt, MD 20770 | 240-542-4602
*KathieScriven@yahoo.com | www.linkedin.com/in/
    kathie-scriven-46981037*

Contact: email, phone

Services: back-cover copy, coauthoring, copyediting, discussion questions for books, ghostwriting, manuscript evaluation, proofreading, substantive/developmental editing, writing coach

Types of manuscripts: academic, adult, articles, Bible studies, book proposals, devotions, easy readers, gift books, middle grade, nonfiction books, poetry, query letters, short stories, technical material, teen/YA

Charges: custom

Credentials/experience: "I specialize in offering editing and coaching services related to self-publishing and marketing books. Have completed over 95 nonfiction Christian book-editing assignments. Former editor of three Christian publications and freelance writer for mostly secular publications. Bachelor's degree in Mass Communication (concentration in journalism) from Towson University. I'm happy to send anyone interested a document that goes over my background, credentials and the services I offer in greater detail. Discount for those in full-time ministry."

SNS EDITS | JAMIE CALLOWAY-HANAUER

snsedits@gmail.com | snsedits.com

Contact: email

Services: back-cover copy, coauthoring, copyediting, discussion questions for books, ghostwriting, manuscript evaluation, proofreading, substantive/developmental editing, writing coach

Types of manuscripts: academic, adult, articles, Bible studies, book proposals, devotionals, easy readers, gift books, middle grade, nonfiction books, novels, picture books, poetry, query letters, short stories, technical material, teen/YA

Charges: custom

Credentials/experience: "Established publishing professional with extensive experience in religious, legal, and academic writing and editing, as well as an award-winner author. Member of the Religion News Association and the Editorial Freelancers Association."

SPEAK WRITE PLAY | ETHLEEN SAWYERR

editing@speakwriteplay.com | speakwriteplay.com

Contact: email

Services: copyediting, manuscript evaluation, proofreading, substantive/developmental editing

Types of manuscripts: adult, Bible studies, children, devotionals, easy readers, middle grade, nonfiction books, novels, picture books, short stories

Charges: word rate

Credentials/experience: "We are a team of experienced manuscript editors and book translators who accompany authors and writers along the publication process. Books we've edited and/or translated have gone on to win notable awards and recognition. With years of experience and training under our proverbial belts, our aim is to help clients sharpen their craft as they release quality content to domestic and international audiences."

SUE A. FAIRCHILD, EDITOR

sueafairchild74@gmail.com | www.sueafairchild.wordpress.com

Contact: email, website

Services: copyediting, discussion questions for books, manuscript evaluation, substantive/developmental editing, writing coach

Types of manuscripts: adult, Bible studies, devotionals, gift books, middle grade, nonfiction books, novels, short stories, teen/YA

Charges: word rate

Credentials/experience: "Gold Member editor of The Christian Pen since 2014, freelance editor with Elk Lake Publishing Inc. since 2018, freelance copyeditor/proofreader for Iron Stream Media and Zeitgeist (Random House)."

SUSAN HOBBS EDITING

901 Forest Trl., Cedar Park, TX 78613 | 214-498-8328

shobbs20@gmail.com | www.susan-hobbs-editing.com

Contact: email, website

Services: copyediting, ghostwriting, manuscript evaluation, proofreading

Types of manuscripts: adult, articles, Bible studies, devotionals, nonfiction books

Charges: word rate

Credentials/experience: "As an editor, my primary goals are to preserve the author's voice and ensure the text is clear, concise, and compelling."

SUSAN KING EDITORIAL SERVICES

1113 Brookside Dr., Nashville, TN 37069 | 615-202-6019

susankingedits.com

Contact: website

Services: coauthoring, copyediting, discussion questions for books, ghostwriting, manuscript evaluation, proofreading, substantive/developmental editing, writing coach

Types of manuscripts: academic, adult, articles, Bible studies, book proposals, devotionals, gift books, nonfiction books, novels, poetry, query letters, short stories, teen/YA

Charges: hourly rate

Credentials/experience: "Of my more than 30 years in the industry, I served 24 years as an editor for *The Upper Room,* the world's premier daily devotional guide reaching 3 million subscribers in 100 countries and 35 languages. For the past 21 years, I have trained writers at over one hundred Christian writers' conferences in the U.S. and Canada. My professional life has also included teaching freshman English, American literature, and feature-writing classes at Lipscomb University, Biola University, and Abilene Christian University for a total of 27 years. I am also the compiler and editor of the Short and Sweet anthology series."

TANDEM SERVICES | JENNIFER CROSSWHITE

jennifer@tandemservicesink.com | *www.tandemservicesink.com*

Contact: website

Services: copyediting, ghostwriting, manuscript evaluation, proofreading, substantive/developmental editing, writing coach

Types of manuscripts: adult, children, devotionals, middle grade, nonfiction books, novels, short stories, teen/YA

Charges: custom, flat fee

Credentials/experience: "Many people have a story to tell but have no idea how to do it. Or if they even can. We empower influencers to increase their impact with a book through coaching, teaching, and editing. We harness the transformative power of story to spread their message, create an impact, and leave a legacy. CEO Jennifer Crosswhite has over twenty years of experience in publishing, editing, coaching, and writing. Her experience spans both sides of the publishing desk, from bestselling author to former managing editor of a HarperCollins imprint. She's worked with traditionally published, hybrid, and independently published authors to empower them to bring their writing dreams to life in both the fiction and nonfiction arenas."

THREE FATES EDITING | SARAH GRACE LIU and VALERIE DIMINO

28 Close Hollow Dr., Hamlin, NY 14464

sarah.grace@threefatesediting.com | www.threefatesediting.com

Contact: website

Services: beta reading, copyediting, manuscript evaluation, proofreading, substantive/developmental editing

Types of manuscripts: academic, adult, Bible studies, middle grade, nonfiction books, novels, poetry, short stories, teen/YA

Charges: word rate

Credentials/experience: "I have an MA in Creative Writing and have run my own editing business since 2012. My true specialization is speculative fiction. For nonfiction, I am more comfortable with progressive texts."

TINSY WINSY EDITORIAL AND DESIGN STUDIO | BRENDA WILBEE

7959 Birch Bay Dr. #2, Blaine, WA 98230 | 360-389-6895

Brenda@BrendaWilbee.com | BrendaWilbee.com

Contact: email

Services: copyediting, substantive/developmental editing

Types of manuscripts: adult, memoir, nonfiction books, novels

Charges: custom, flat fee, hourly rate, page rate, word rate

Credentials/experience: "I hold a BA in Creative Writing, an MA in Professional Writing, and a degree in Graphic Design. I've written hundreds of articles and ten books, six of which were bestsellers, selling over 700,000 copies. For 17 years I wrote devotionals for Guideposts. My background includes teaching college composition and workshops on all aspects of writing at conferences. Some of my editorial and design clients include Edirol, Habitat for Humanity, Whatcom Community College, PageMill Press, DDA Publishing, Forever Books, and writers of fiction and nonfiction—just like yourself."

TISHA MARTIN EDITORIAL

tisha@tishamartin.com | www.tishamartin.com

Contact: email, text, website

Services: back-cover copy, book coach, book-contract evaluation, copyediting, discussion questions for books, ghostwriting, manuscript evaluation, proofreading, substantive/developmental editing, writing coach

Types of manuscripts: adult, articles, book proposals, curriculum, devotionals, general study guides and resources, gift books, middle grade, nonfiction books, novelized screenplays, novels, OwnVoices, poetry, query letters, scripts, short stories, technical material, teen/YA

Charges: custom, flat fee, word rate

Credentials/experience: "Your manuscript is a fine soup. We work together for your ideal reader. A book you're proud of requires time, patience, and investment. Want a book in 9 months? We do not fit. My book editing and industry experience includes 100+ books coached and edited; 15x award-winning titles; education and curriculum background; conference and university speaker, in-person and online; professional writing bachelor's; general book marketing ideator. Fiction, Memoir, Nonfiction. Full-service assisted self-publishing packages and coaching services to help you cultivate relationships in the book industry. Let's give your book your voice. Reach out. Let's get the conversation started."

TRACIE MILES AUTHOR COACHING

3618 Walter Nelson Rd., Mint Hill, NC 28227 | 704-975-1958

tracie@traciemiles.com | traciemiles.com/services

Contact: phone, website

Services: proofreading, substantive/developmental editing, writing coach

Types of manuscripts: book proposals, devotionals, gift books, nonfiction books

Charges: flat fee

Credentials/experience: "Tracie has been the Director of COMPEL Pro Writers Training at Proverbs 31 Ministries since January 2017 where she teaches thousands of writers every month how to improve on their craft of writing, create book proposals, learn about social media and platform building, and get their book ideas published, while providing encouragement and inspiration along the way. She leads the COMPEL Pro staff and collaborates on how to deliver the best writing training and publishing opportunities in the market today.

"Tracie is a trained and certified writing coach and has served as a writing coach for multiple groups of women in Proverbs 31 Ministries' Book Proposal Boot Camp founded by Lysa TerKeurst. In these boot camps, Tracie helped dozens of authors create and prepare stellar book proposals. Several women under Tracie's guidance were awarded book contracts with major Christian publishing houses or were signed by top notch literary agents."

TRAILBLAZE EDITORIAL SERVICES | SARAH BARNUM
sarah@trail-blazes.com | trail-blazes.com

Contact: email, website

Services: coauthoring, copyediting, manuscript evaluation, substantive/developmental editing

Types of manuscripts: adult, articles, Bible studies, devotionals, gift books, nonfiction books, short stories

Charges: word rate

Credentials/experience: "Sarah Barnum is an award-winning writer and editor. She holds a bachelor's degree with highest honors and serves as the Administrative Director for the West Coast Christian Writers. Sarah's short stories have been featured in multiple anthologies, and two memoirs she coauthored earned a Selah Award and the 2022 Christian Editor Connection's Excellence in Editing award, respectively."

TURN THE PAGE CRITIQUES | CINDY THOMSON
PO Box 298, Pataskala, OH 43062 | 614-354-3904
cindyswriting@gmail.com | cindyswriting.com/index.php/critique-service

Contact: website

Services: critiquing, manuscript evaluation, proofreading

Types of manuscripts: articles, book proposals, novels, query letters

Charges: flat fee

Credentials/experience: "Published author both traditionally and independently of fiction and non-fiction, author of numerous magazine articles, and a former mentor with the Jerry B. Jenkins Christian Writers Guild, I can help you get a solid footing as you prepare to publish."

WHALIN & ASSOCIATES | W. TERRY WHALIN
PO Box 8634, Newport Beach, CA 92658 | 949-423-2188
terry@terrywhalin.com | terrywhalin.blogspot.com

Contact: email

Services: coauthoring, discussion questions for books, ghostwriting, substantive/developmental editing

Types of manuscripts: adult, book proposals, devotionals, gift books, nonfiction books

Charges: flat fee

Credentials/experience: "Terry has written more than sixty books for traditional publishers, including one book that has sold more than 100,000 copies. He has written for more than fifty publications and worked in acquisitions at three publishing houses."

WORDMELON INC. | MARGOT STARBUCK

308-B Northwood Cir., Durham, NC 27701 | 919-321-5440

wordmelon@gmail.com | www.margotstarbuck.com

Contact: email

Services: book coach, coauthoring, discussion questions for books, ghostwriting, manuscript evaluation, substantive/developmental editing, writing coach

Types of manuscripts: adult, book proposals, devotionals, nonfiction books, query letters

Charges: flat fee, word rate

Credentials/experience: "Margot, a graduate of Westmont College and Princeton Theological Seminary, has written dozens of books, including 2 *New York Times* bestsellers. She's passionate about helping writers get published."

WORDPOLISH CONSULTING SERVICES | YVONNE KANU

yvonne@wordpolish.net | www.wordpolish.net

Contact: website

Services: copyediting, proofreading, writing coach

Types of manuscripts: academic, Bible studies, devotionals, easy readers, nonfiction books, novels, short stories, teen/YA

Charges: word rate

Credentials/experience: "Over 10 years of experience in publishing, business communication, and technical writing. BA degree in English, and certificates in Editing, Publishing, and Technical Writing."

WORDPRO COMMUNICATION SERVICES | LIN JOHNSON

6525 Emerald Hill Ct., Ste. 104, Indianapolis, IN 46237-3098 | 847-296-3964

ljohnson@wordprocommunications.com | wordprocommunications.com

Contact: email

Services: back-cover copy, book-contract evaluation, copyediting, discussion questions for books, proofreading, small-group Bible study guides

Types of manuscripts: adult, Bible studies, Bible curriculum, devotionals, nonfiction books

Charges: flat fee, hourly rate

Credentials/experience: "I've worked in Christian publishing for more than four decades as an in-house and freelance Bible curriculum editor and writer; award-winning writer of more than 70 books and hundreds of articles, devotions, and reviews; former managing editor of *Christian Communicator, Advanced Christian Writer,* and *Church Libraries;* and freelance editor and proofreader for traditional and independent publishing houses, organizations, and authors. Clients have praised me for being accurate, detailed, thorough, and deadline oriented.

"In addition, I've trained thousands of writers at conferences, as an adjunct writing instructor at Taylor University, and in international settings. I have an English minor from Adrian College, a BA in Christian education from Cedarville University, a BA in Bible-theology from Moody Bible Institute, and an MS in adult and continuing education from National-Louis University."

WRITE BY LISA | LISA THOMPSON

200 Laguna Dr. S, Litchfield Park, AZ 85340 | 623-258-5258

writebylisa@gmail.com | www.writebylisa.com

Contact: website

Services: back-cover copy, copyediting, discussion questions for books, ghostwriting, manuscript evaluation, proofreading, substantive/developmental editing, writing coach

Types of manuscripts: academic, adult, articles, Bible studies, book proposals, curriculum, devotionals, easy readers, middle grade, nonfiction books, novels, picture books, query letters, short stories, teen/YA

Charges: flat fee, hourly rate, word rate

Credentials/experience: "I have a degree in elementary education and a minor in English and Spanish. I have been editing since 2009. Nearly everything I edit is Christian content. I also subcontract for a fairly large Christian publisher and several smaller indie publishers in addition to editing for many Christian leaders, pastors, and lay people."

WRITE CONCEPTS, LLC | ALICE B. CRIDER

590 Highway 105 #107, Monument, CO 80132 | 719-651-0160

editoralicecrider@gmail.com | *www.alicecrider.com*

Contact: email, website

Services: back-cover copy, coauthoring, discussion questions for books, ghostwriting, manuscript evaluation, substantive/developmental editing, writing coach

Types of manuscripts: adult, book proposals, memoir, nonfiction books

Charges: custom

Credentials/experience: "I am a freelance editor with 25+ years of experience in traditional book publishing, including eight years in a division of Random House. I have served in various editorial capacities in Christian publishing—including editor, literary agent, and director of acquisitions and development. I specialize in non-fiction, developmental, content, and line editing. I am skilled at analyzing a manuscript's strengths and weaknesses, and at suggesting improvements and revisions. I am also a certified life coach and author coach with 15+ years of experience in helping individuals and authors achieve their dreams and goals."

THE WRITE FLOURISH | TIM AND NOLA PASSMORE

nola@thewriteflourish.com.au | *www.thewriteflourish.com.au*

Contact: phone, website

Services: copyediting, manuscript evaluation, mentoring, proofreading, substantive/developmental editing

Types of manuscripts: academic, adult, articles, book proposals, devotionals, memoir, nonfiction books, novels, poetry, short stories, teen/YA

Charges: hourly rate

Credentials/experience: "Tim and Nola Passmore each have more than 20 years of experience as university academics. Nola also has a degree in creative writing. They founded The Write Flourish in 2014 and have edited a wide range of manuscripts across a variety of styles and genres. They have also had many of their own short pieces published including fiction, poetry, devotions, memoir, nonfiction and academic articles. They would love to help you add the right flourish to your manuscript."

WRITE HIS ANSWER MINISTRIES | MARLENE BAGNULL

951 Anders Rd., Lansdale, PA 19446 | 267-436-2503

mbagnull@aol.com | *writehisanswer.com/editingmentoring*

Contact: email

Services: copyediting, manuscript evaluation, proofreading, substantive/developmental editing

Types of manuscripts: adult, nonfiction books, novels, teen/YA

Charges: flat fee, hourly rate, word rate

Credentials/experience: "More than 40 years of experience in publishing, leading critique groups for over 25 years, teaching almost 50 one- and two-day writers seminars, serving on the faculty of 70 Christian writers conferences, and directing 67 Christian writers conferences. Author of 13 books plus more than 1,000 sales to over 100 different Christian periodicals. Editor of more than 30 books. Typesetter and publisher of 12 Ampelos Press books. Query with one sheet and first chapter for availability and cost."

WRITE JUSTIFIED | JUDY HAGEY

10628 Sharon Cir., Urbandale, IA 50322 | 386-562-7192

judy.hagey@gmail.com | judyhagey.com

Contact: email

Services: copyediting, proofreading

Types of manuscripts: academic, adult, Bible studies, devotionals, middle grade, nonfiction books, novels

Charges: word rate

Credentials/experience: "Freelance editor specializing in Christian nonfiction. More than a dozen years of experience editing and proofreading for Christian publishers, self-publishing/independent authors, and academics with projects ranging from dissertations to Bible studies, memoirs to devotionals, adult and middle grade novels. Nonfiction managing editor for Elk Lake Publishing, Inc. Proficient in CMOS and CWMS. Professional memberships include CPEN (Christian Professional Editors Network) and CIPA (Christian Indie Publishers Association). The relationship between an author and editor should be more duet than duel."

WRITE NOW EDITING | KARIN BEERY

PO Box 31, Elk Rapids, MI 49629 | 231-350-0226

karin@writenowedits.com | www.writenowedits.com

Contact: website

Services: copyediting, critiquing, substantive/developmental editing, writing coach

Types of manuscripts: novels

Charges: flat fee, word rate

Credentials/experience: "Turning good manuscripts into great books,

Karin is a multi-award-winning author and editor with experience in traditional and self-publishing, freelance editing, and editing for publishers. She's an active member of the Christian Editors Association, including the Christian Editor Connection, and the National Association of Independent Writers and Editors. Her book *How to Edit Your Novel: Practical Tips for Strengthening Your Story* is a 2024 Selah Award winner and Golden Scroll runner-up."

WRITE WAY COPYEDITING LLC | DIANA SCHRAMER

diana@writewaycopyediting.com | www.writewaycopyediting.com

Contact: email, website

Services: copyediting, manuscript evaluation

Types of manuscripts: Bible studies, devotionals, gift books, memoir, nonfiction books, novels

Charges: word rate

Credentials/experience: "I started my business in 2010 and have copyedited 100+ book-length manuscripts and have reviewed 200+ manuscripts. In addition, I have copyedited and reviewed front- and back-cover copy as well as business-related documents and blogs."

WRITER'S EDGE SERVICE

PO Box 310, Sisters, OR 97759

www.writersedgeservice.com

Contact: website

Services: manuscript evaluation

Types of manuscripts: academic, adult, Bible studies, book proposals, devotionals, easy readers, gift books, middle grade, nonfiction books, novels, teen/YA

Charges: $99

Credentials/experience: "Manuscripts evaluated by professional Christian editors who've worked for major publishers." If the manuscript is approved, it's referred to more than 75 traditional publishers in the monthly or bimonthly newsletter.

WRITING PURSUITS | KATHRESE McKEE

27708 Tomball Pkwy., PMB 107, Tomball, TX 77375

kmckee@writingpursuits.com | www.writingpursuits.com

Contact: website

Services: copyediting, substantive/developmental editing

Types of manuscripts: adult, middle grade, novels, short stories, teen/YA

Charges: flat fee, hourly rate

Credentials/experience: "Kathrese McKee has edited fiction professionally since 2014 in the following genres: urban and paranormal fantasy, fairytale retellings, dystopian and military science fiction, women's fiction, and contemporary and historical romance. She hosts the *Writing Pursuits* podcast and writes and produces a weekly newsletter, *Writing Pursuits Tips for Authors*."

YO PRODUCTIONS LLC | YOLONDA TONETTE SANDERS

7185 E. Main St., Unit 1543, Reynoldsburg, OH 43068 | 614-452-4920
info_4u@yoproductions.net | *www.yoproductions.net*

Contact: email, phone, website

Services: back-cover copy, copyediting, ghostwriting, manuscript evaluation, proofreading, substantive/developmental editing, writing coach

Types of manuscripts: academic, adult, articles, Bible studies, book proposals, children, curriculum, devotionals, middle grade, nonfiction books, novels, poetry, query letters, scripts, short stories, technical material, teen/YA

Charges: custom, word rate

Credentials/experience: "With over two decades of professional editing and writing experience and a Ph.D. in organizational leadership, we offer expert editorial support tailored to each client's voice, message, and goals. From developmental edits to final proofreading, we approach every project with excellence, integrity, and a passion for helping others produce their best work. Whether you're polishing a novel, refining nonfiction, or preparing devotional or biblical curriculum content, we're here to elevate your words without compromising your vision or voice."

21

PUBLICITY AND MARKETING SERVICES

THE ADAMS GROUP | GINA ADAMS
6688 Nolensville Rd. 108-149, Brentwood, TN 37027 | 615-776-1590
gina@adamsprgroup.com | *www.adamsprgroup.com*
- **Contact:** email, phone, website form
- **Services:** public relations, publicity campaigns, press releases, press-release distribution, press-kit creation, contributed content, video production
- **Books:** all genres
- **Charges:** flat fee
- **Credentials/experience:** "Honored by the prestigious Communicator Awards in 2019, 2020, and 2022, The Adams Group has represented faith-based authors for over three decades. Gina received her B.S. degree in business and marketing from Murray State University. She is a member of the National Religious Broadcasters and the Evangelical Press Association and serves on the Publicity Committee for the Arts of Southern Kentucky. Gina has also earned an Expert Rating Certification in Social Media Marketing and is a Hootsuite Certified Professional in Social Marketing."

APRICOT SERVICES | PETE FORD
PO Box 81, Belmont, MI 49306
info@apricotservices.com | *apricotservices.com*
- **Contact:** website form
- **Services:** campaign management, digital platform audit, brand consultation and website design, social-media content, digital advertising, audience engagement/launch teams, email marketing
- **Books:** nonfiction, occasional fiction and children's
- **Charges:** custom
- **Credentials/experience:** "For over a decade, we have helped

Christian authors and nonprofit organizations thrive in the digital landscape by focusing on meaningful hospitality and deeper relationships in digital communities."

BANNER CONSULTING | MIKE LOOMIS

mike@mikeloomis.co | www.mikeloomis.co

> **Contact:** email, website form
> **Services:** book-launch planning, branding, article curation and placement, web development, PR
> **Specialty:** branding and marketing strategy
> **Books:** nonfiction
> **Charges:** custom
> **Credentials/experience:** "I've worked with internationally known brands and *New York Times* bestsellers. I've helped clients get breakthrough PR, speaking engagements, and bestseller lists."

BBH LITERARY | LAURA BARDOLPH and DAVID BRATT

616-319-1641
bbhliterary.com/publicity
Laura Bardolph, laura@bbhliterary.com
David Bratt, david@bbhliterary.com

> **Contact:** email, website form
> **Services:** national media campaigns, religious media campaigns, podcast and radio campaigns, print and online media campaigns, press-kit creation
> **Books:** nonfiction
> **Charges:** flat fee
> **Credentials/experience:** "Nine years on staff in the marketing department at Eerdmans Publishing, with roles that included publicist, publicity manager, and director of marketing and publicity."

BBS PUBLISHING AND COMMUNICATIONS, LLC | PAMELA GOSSIAUX

734-846-0112
pam@pamelagossiaux.com | BestsellingBookShepherd.com

> **Contact:** website form
> **Services:** marketing, newsletters, blurbs, press kits, blogs, social media, and more
> **Specialty:** bestseller campaigns
> **Books:** fiction, nonfiction

Charges: custom, flat fee, hourly rate, package rates

Credentials/experience: "I've promoted authors to Amazon, *USA Today,* and *Wall Street Journal* bestsellers. I have dual degrees in Creative Writing and English Language and Literature from University of Michigan and am a speaker and international best-selling author."

BLUE RIDGE READER CONNECTIONS | EDIE MELSON

604 S. Almond Dr., Simpsonville, SC 29681 | 864-373-4232

ediegmelson@gmail.com | blueridgereaderconnections.com

Debb Hackett, brreaderconnection@gmail.com

Darlene Franklin, brreaderconnection@gmail.com

Heather Kreke, brreaderconnection@gmail.com

Contact: website form

Services: connecting authors to readers with an introduction to new readers with your bio, picture, and social media links; highlights of up to three of your books with Buy links; a showcase of a book trailer; a calendar note for upcoming book releases; the chance to gain more newsletter subscribers; access to our marketing resources; interaction with our readers on our Facebook group; and more

Books: all clean reads in all genres

Charges: flat fee

Credentials/experience: "We want to be . . . an author's link to their readers." BRRC was started five years ago and falls under the Blue Ridge Mountains Christian Writers Conference.

THE BLYTHE DANIEL AGENCY, INC. | BLYTHE DANIEL and STEPHANIE ALTON

PO Box 64197, Colorado Springs, CO 80962-4197

www.theblythedanielagency.com/publicity-campaigns

Blythe Daniel, blythe@theblythedanielagency.com

Stephanie Alton, stephanie@theblythedanielagency.com

Contact: website form

Services: range of publicity campaigns utilizing broadcast and print media and the Internet, including blogs, podcasts, articles, TV and radio interviews, book reviews, and book launches

Specialty: placing different genres of books with appropriate media and also with clients we represent who have media platforms; our relationships as literary agents of authors who interview guests has given us additional opportunities

Books: adult nonfiction, children's nonfiction and fiction, some adult fiction

Charges: custom

Credentials/experience: "Blythe Daniel managed the publicity for Thomas Nelson, a division of Harper Collins Christian Publishing, for seven years and led the publicity team in media relations. She has almost 30 years of experience managing relationships with traditional media and is also an author, and conducts her own publicity and marketing campaigns for clients. Stephanie Alton leads the launch teams and blog network for the agency's marketing clients."

CELEBRATE LIT PUBLICITY | SANDRA BARELA and DENISE BARELA

45459 Stockton St., Beaumont, CA 92223 | 909-520-8603

Publicityservices@celebratelit.com | *www.celebratelit.com*

Denise Barela, editor.deniseb@gmail.com

Contact: email

Services: book tours, epic book-launch promos, review blasts, coaching, social-media-building promos, sidebar ads

Specialty: book tours, book launches

Books: any Christian or clean fiction and nonfiction

Charges: flat fee

Credentials/experience: "Our ministry began in 2015. We complete between 28 and 35 promos a month and have over 700,000 views per book tour on average. Both Denise and Sandra have master's degrees in English, which include marketing classes. We have scholarships available."

CHOICE MEDIA & COMMUNICATIONS | HEATHER ADAMS

404-423-8411

hello@choicemediacommunications.com | *www.choicemediacommunications.com*

Devon Brown, publicity manager and brand strategist, Devon@ChoiceMediaCommunications.com

Morgan Sampson, digital media consultant, Morgan@ChoiceMediaCommunications.com

Katie Kronk, digital media consultant, Katie@ChoiceMediaCommunications.com

Contact: website form
Services: media relations, branding and strategy, social media, events, podcast production
Books: nonfiction
Charges: flat fee, retainer-based partnership
Credentials/experience: "Choice Media & Communications is a boutique media and communications business dedicated to providing clients with quality public relations. Choice helps authors create a clear communications plan, gain media coverage, and receive guidance they won't get anywhere else. With more than two decades of high-level professional communications experience across varying industries and with many of today's tastemakers and thought leaders, Choice founder Heather Adams created a public relations business marked with warmth and enthusiasm, strategic development, clear communication, detailed execution, and thorough reporting."

CHRISTIAN INDIE PUBLISHING ASSOCIATION | SUSAN NEAL

PO Box 481022, Charlotte, NC 28269 | 704-277-7194
cipa@christianpublishers.net | www.christianpublishers.net

Contact: email, website form
Services: resources and tools for publishing and marketing for independent authors
Specialty: marketing services
Books: all genres
Credentials/experience: "Our mission is to support, strengthen, and promote independent authors and small publishers in the Christian marketplace. We have been doing this since 2004."

CREATIVE CORNERSTONES | CAYLAH COFEEN

Huntsville, AL
creativecornerstones@gmail.com | creativecornerstones.com

Contact: phone
Services: digital marketing—social media, Facebook and Amazon advertising—media kits, brand advising
Books: fiction
Charges: flat fee, hourly rate
Credentials/experience: "Currently I work as the part-time marketing manager for Monster Ivy Publishing and have also helped multiple indie authors to reach nearly 10K followers and bring in reviews. Using Amazon ad campaigns and keyword

metrics, in just a couple months I made one author's novel rise from rank #1,484 to #283 in Religious Science Fiction and Fantasy. The Kindle deal I ran brought it to #2 in free Christian Futuristic Fiction. In the past, I've also worked as the marketing manager for The Philips Museum of Art."

EABOOKS PUBLISHING | REBECCA FORD

1136 W. Winged Foot Cir., Winter Springs, FL 32708 | 407-712-3431
rebecca.f@eabookspublishing.com | *www.eabookspublishing.com*

Contact: website form

Services: websites, Amazon optimization, social media, email marketing, book launches, blog tours, articles, book trailers, media interviews, podcasts, media pitching

Specialty: discovering authors' strengths and developing a marketing strategy for them

Books: fiction, nonfiction, children's

Charges: flat fee, package rates

Credentials/experience: "We have a team of independent contractors who specialize in each area of our marketing offerings. They are experts in their fields and each comes highly recommended and often serves on faculty at Christian writers conferences."

EPIC AGENCY | JENNIFER WILLINGHAM

117 Saundersville Rd., Henderson, TN 37075 | 615-829-6441
hello@epic.inc | *epic.inc*

Contact: email, phone, website form

Services: social-media management, email marketing, publicity campaigns, press materials, media training, platform development

Credentials/experience: Group of PR and marketing specialists with years of experience.

JESSICA BAKER

Cooperstown, NY | 607-435-2671
pjcbaker@yahoo.com | *www.abakersperspective.com/services*

Contact: email

Services: social-media management, launch-team management, newsletter formatting, website updates, administrative tasks, setting up podcast and book blog interviews, graphic creation, Amazon ads, Facebook ads, and more

Books: fiction

Charges: custom

Credentials/experience: "I have been a virtual assistant for over six years, working with authors in a variety of genres. From social-media managing, website updates, newsletter formatting, and handling launch teams to administrative tasks and more, my goal is to give you more creative time for writing."

JONES LITERARY | JASON JONES

2233 Surrey Dr., Murfreesboro, TN 37129-1043 | 512-720-2996

jason@jonesliterary.com | jonesliterary.com

Mark Breta, mark@jonesliterary.com

Marianna Gibson, marianna@jonesliterary.com

Anita Lustrea, anita@jonesliterary.com

Meg Midwood, meg@jonesliterary.com

Contact: website form

Services: publicity, PR campaigns, website buildouts, social-media management, book tours, podcast production and guest booking

Specialty: publicity for books at the intersection of faith and culture, full-service PR campaigns for traditionally published authors, DIY PR tools for self-published authors

Books: nonfiction, fiction, traditionally published, self-published

Charges: custom

Credentials/experience: "Jason led campaigns for HarperCollins Christian/Thomas Nelson's top nonfiction books, brands, and authors between 2007 and 2013. For many years since he has run one of the nation's most successful literary publicity agencies, having directed PR campaigns for over 400 books and 12 *New York Times* bestsellers. He was also host of *The Book Publicist Podcast* and is an author."

KAREN CAMPBELL MEDIA, INC. | KAREN CAMPBELL

4046 Dunes Pkwy., Norton Shores, MI 49441 | 616-309-4390

Karen@karencampbellmedia.com | www.karencampbellmedia.com

Judy McDonough, judy@karencampbellmedia.com

Jennifer Valk, jennifer@karencampbellmedia.com

Contact: website form

Services: full-service publicity, developing results-driven and detail-oriented plans to get the most media coverage; author tours; press kits; media training

Specialty: nonfiction and select fiction

Charges: custom

Credentials/experience: "After receiving her BA from Calvin College, with a focus on rhetoric and communications, Karen began her career in the publishing industry at Baker Publishing Group. From there, she moved on to Zondervan and served as their Director of Public Relations before moving on to start Karen Campbell Media, Inc. Throughout her 25 years in the publishing industry, she has had the privilege to work on 16 *New York Times* bestsellers and with dozens of top-selling authors. In 2009, Karen was awarded the WMPRSA Gold PRoof Award for her work on the publicity campaign for *Multiple Blessings* by Jon and Kate Gosselin with Beth Carson. She says there's nothing better than seeing a book receive great media coverage, succeed in sales, and change people's lives."

MEDIA CONNECT | SHARON FARNELL

301 E. 57th St., New York, NY 10022 | 212-715-1600
sharon.farnell@finnpartners.com | *www.media-connect.com*

Contact: email

Services: full-service book publicity firm with custom campaigns for each title/author, offering satellite TV tours, radio tours, media tours, as well as outreach to national and local media

Books: all types

Charges: custom, package rates

Credentials/experience: "We are a full-service book publicity agency; and for over 50 years, we've worked with publishers, authors, artists, organizations, and more."

REDEMPTION PRESS |ATHENA DEAN HOLTZ

70 S. Val Vista Dr., Ste. A3-442, Gilbert, AZ 85296 | 360-226-3488
info@redemption-press.com | *www.redemption-press.com*

Contact: email

Services: Amazon book launch, customized marketing blueprint, Christian Product Expo promotion and representation, focused media blast, and more

Books: nonfiction, fiction, children's, Bible studies

Charges: custom

Credentials/experience: "With four decades in Christian publishing, we bring unmatched credibility and proven results to author publicity and marketing. Led by veteran Athena Dean Holtz, our team has launched and promoted hundreds of books through strategic partnerships, customized marketing blueprints, Amazon bestseller campaigns, and Christian retailer events. Backed by deep industry relationships and a reputation for integrity, we blend time-tested strategies with today's most effective tools to help authors expand their reach, engage their audience, and maximize impact."

ROAR, INC. | GARY SCHNEEBERGER
1420 63rd St., Kenosha, WI 53143 | 818-309-8580
gary@weroar.la | *weroar.la*

Contact: phone, website form
Services: public relations, strategic communications, media coaching, social-media content creation
Specialty: public relations strategy and execution
Books: nonfiction
Charges: custom, package rates
Credentials/experience: "As founder and president of ROAR, Gary Schneeberger draws on his executive experience and executional acumen to help individuals and organizations engage audiences with the boldness and creative clarity that ensure they are heard. He has advised Hollywood studios (Universal, Warner Bros., 20th Century Fox), television networks (USA, History, The CW), and global nonprofits (Focus on the Family). He has counseled and created communications platforms for authors, experts, speakers, coaches, and consultants of every conceivable stripe, from some of the biggest names in movies and TV to true mom-and-pop shops. Schneeberger is the author of the bestseller *BITE THE DOG: Build a PR Strategy to Make News That Matters.*"

SIDE DOOR COMMUNICATIONS | DEBBIE LYKINS
224-234-6699
deb@sidedoorcom.net | *www.sidedoorcom.net*

Contact: website form
Services: media relations, press-kit creation, consulting, publicity-plan development
Books: primarily nonfiction, also children's and fiction but highly selective, no self-published novels, few self-published nonfiction; only projects that bring glory to God and are grounded in solid, biblical truth
Charges: custom
Credentials/experience: "Side Door Communications is a

national publicity agency that connects faith-based publishers and personalities with national and local media outlets as well as bloggers, with the goal of obtaining coverage in newspapers and magazines and on radio, television, and the Internet. Based in the Milwaukee, Wisconsin, area, founder Debbie Lykins has more than two decades of experience in marketing, publicity, and communications."

VERITAS COMMUNICATIONS | DON OTIS

318 Huppert Ln., Sandpoint, ID 83864 | 719-275-7775

don@veritasincorporated.com | *www.veritasincorporated.com*

Contact: email

Services: radio, TV, and podcast interviews; writing media materials; connecting with media; and providing training when needed

Specialty: Christian and conservative topics

Books: nonfiction, issues-driven titles

Charges: custom

Credentials/experience: "More than 30 years of experience working with Christian authors, publishers, and ministries. Former radio host, TV producer, and author of five traditionally published books. We have scheduled more than 30,000 interviews for clients."

WILDFIRE MARKETING | ROB EAGAR

3625 Chartwell Dr., Suwanee, GA 30024 | 770-887-1462

Rob@StartaWildfire.com | *www.StartaWildfire.com*

Contact: phone, website form

Services: all facets of book marketing, including book launches, author websites, email marketing, social media, and author-revenue growth

Specialty: book marketing

Books: all genres

Charges: flat fee

Credentials/experience: "Rob Eagar is the founder of Wildfire Marketing, a consulting practice that has coached more than 1,000 authors and helped books hit *The New York Times* bestseller list in three different categories: new fiction, new nonfiction, and backlist nonfiction. His company has attracted numerous best-selling authors, including Dr. Gary Chapman, Lysa TerKeurst, DeVon Franklin, Wanda Brunstetter, and Dr. John Townsend."

22

LEGAL AND ACCOUNTING SERVICES

CHASE NEELY, PC

1114 17th Ave. S, Ste. 102, Nashville, TN 37212 | 615-686-1228

chase@chaseneely.com | *chaseneely.com*

Contact: email

Services: contract review, legal

Charges: custom, flat fee, hourly rate

Credentials/experience: "For the past twelve years, I've represented authors from beginners to *New York Times* bestsellers. I'd love to help you protect your work and negotiate a fair deal."

CHRIS MORRIS, CPA, LLC

11209 N. 161st Ln., Surprise, AZ 85379 | 623-451-8182

cmorris@chrismorriscpa.com | *chrismorriscpa.com*

Contact: email, website form

Services: accounting, taxes

Charges: flat fee, hourly rate

Credentials/experience: "I have been working with creative entrepreneurs as a certified public accountant for the last decade, with about 65% of my business in the author space. Clients include publishers, agents, authors, editors, and various others related to this space. I know the tax and accounting codes related to this space because I've dedicated the last decade to it. I'm also a published author myself, so I have even more motivation to learn everything well."

TOM UMSTATTD, CPA

13276 Research Blvd., Austin, TX 78750 | 512-250-1090

tom@taxmantom.com | www.taxmantom.com

> **Contact:** phone, website form
> **Services:** accounting, consultations, tax review, taxes
> **Charges:** hourly rate
> **Credentials/experience:** More than forty years of experience in accounting and taxes.

WINTERS & KING

2448 E. 81st St., Ste. 5900, Tulsa, OK 74137 | 918-494-6868

wintersking.com/attorneys/thomas-j-winters

> **Contact:** phone, website form
> **Service:** contract negotiation
> **Credentials/experience:** "We understand that negotiating with major publishers can feel like a lopsided process, and we work hard to level the playing field. Our experience in the publishing industry allows us to negotiate comprehensive and ironclad publishing contracts based on the realities of the industry. Our goal is to help our clients tell their stories on their own terms and receive the rightful benefits of their hard work through royalties and advances."

23

SPEAKING SERVICES

ADVANCED WRITERS & SPEAKERS ASSOCIATION
See entry in "Writers Organizations and Groups."

CHRISTIAN COMMUNICATORS CONFERENCE
contact@christiancommunicators.com | *www.ChristianCommunicators.com*
Director: Pam Mitchael
Contact method: website form
Services: annual conference to educate, validate, and launch speakers to the next level for beginning or seasoned speakers; maximum 50 attendees; July 22–25 in Richardson, Texas

CHRISTIAN SPEAKER NETWORK
866 Oak Forest, Morrow, OH 45152
christianspeaker.net
Contact method: website form
Services: web page that is listed in the online database, booking requests go directly to you
Fee: $39.95 per year

CHRISTIAN SPEAKERS BOOT CAMP
PO Box 150473, Grand Rapids, MI 49505 | 616-363-4608
robyn@robyndykstra.com | *christianspeakersbootcamp.com/csbc/bootcamp*
Director: Robyn Dykstra
Contact method: phone
Services: a personalized program to catapult your speaking skills and opportunities, teaching you to craft a full-length signature talk that promotes your book, book engagements, negotiate fees, and handle contracts
Fee: custom

CHRISTIAN WOMEN SPEAKERS
4001 Marlin Dr. SE, St. Petersburg, FL 33705 | 877-774-6986
viamarnie@gmail.com | *womenspeakers.com*
   Director: Marnie Swedberg
   Contact method: website form
   Services: list speakers on the website, free and paid training available
   Fees: free; $49.99/month or $499/year for higher ranking, extra
      features and benefits; $2497/lifetime
   Qualifications/requirements: Christian woman older than 18,
      at least one public link (a home page or social-media presence),
      recommendations for your life in Christ and/or speaking ministry,
      actively involved in a local church
   Representation: nonexclusive

DECLARE
See entry in "Writers Organizations and Groups."

NEXT STEP COACHING SERVICES
amy@amycarroll.org | *amycarroll.org/coaching*
   Director: Amy Carroll
   Contact method: website form
   Services: coaching for women speakers, quarterly newsletter

NORTHWEST CHRISTIAN SPEAKERS
Bellingham, WA | 360-966-0203
Christie@freshlookthinking.com | *www.christianspeakersnw.com*
   Director: Christie Miller
   Contact method: website form
   Services: speakers bureau, not limited to the Northwest; speaker
      training
   Qualifications/requirements: attend training workshops/evaluation
      session

SPEAK UP SPEAKER SERVICES
3141 Winged Foot Dr., Lakeland, FL 33803 | 586-481-7661
gene4speakup@aol.com | *speakupspeakerservices.com*
   Director: Carol Kent
   Contact method: mail
   Services: speakers bureau, fee negotiation, contracts for services,

speech- and TV-interview coaching, SpeakUp Conference (see listing in "Writers Conferences and Seminars")

Qualifications/requirements: at least two books or CDs currently available in the Christian market and regularly speaking nationally; see list of application details to mail

Representation: exclusive, nonexclusive

24

WRITING EDUCATION RESOURCES

ANN KROEKER, WRITING COACH

annkroeker.com/podcasts

Type: podcast

Host: Ann Kroeker

Description: "These writing podcast episodes offer practical tips and motivation for writers at all stages. . . . Tune in for solutions addressing anything from self-editing and goal-setting . . . to administrative and scheduling challenges."

ANOINTED SCRIBE: CHRISTIAN AUTHOR BUSINESS, GOD'S WAY

podcasts.apple.com/us/podcast/anointed-scribe-christian-author-business-gods-way/id1779524392

Type: podcast

Host: Urcelia Teixeira

Description: "Whether you're just getting started or you've published a book or two, you'll find Spirit-led strategies, biblical encouragement, and practical tools to help you grow with clarity, joy, and Kingdom impact. . . . *Anointed Scribe* podcast equips you to align your writing career with God's call on your life so you can confidently share your message, serve your readers, and thrive with purpose."

AUTHOR CONSERVATORY

www.authorconservatory.com

Type: organization, courses

Directors: Brett Harris, Kara Swanson Matsumoto, Jaquelle Ferris

Description: "An online, college alternative focused on writing craft and entrepreneurship. Learn the writing and business skills you need to pursue publication and avoid becoming a starving artist. Download our syllabus and apply for a free consultation on our website."

BOOK MARKETING MANIA
kimstewartmarketing.com/podcast

> **Type:** podcast
> **Host:** Kim Stewart
> **Description:** "God never intended for it to feel frustrating or yucky when getting your book out there. He simply wants you to serve those He called you to, and share how you can help them. Books change lives. Wouldn't you rather spend your time writing than marketing? . . . Learn how to use the power of podcasting to build your audience, market your book, and steward your message in a way that honors God and your time."

BOOK MARKETING PRO ACADEMY (formerly Redemption Press University)
www.bookmarketingproacademy.com

> **Type:** organization, courses
> **Director:** Shelly Brown
> **Description:** "Book Marketing Pro Academy empowers Christian authors with weekly live trainings, custom courses, expert group coaching, and a supportive private community to help authors sell more books. Monthly office hours and coffee chats provide direct guidance, while ongoing encouragement and progress-tracking keep authors inspired and equipped to turn their marketing goals into lasting ministry impact."

BOOK PROPOSAL ACADEMY
bookproposalacademy.com

> **Type:** organization, courses
> **Director:** Chad R. Allen
> **Description:** "Book Proposal Academy is an online course created by publishing veteran Chad R. Allen, designed to guide writers through crafting a compelling book proposal. The course covers key components, such as concept development, chapter outlines, author bios, marketing plans, and writing samples. It also includes modules tailored for fiction and children's book writers. With access to actual contract-winning proposals and a supportive community, Book

Proposal Academy equips writers with the tools and confidence they need to craft contract-worthy book proposals."

BOOKCAMP
www.bookcamp.us

Type: organization, courses

Director: Chad R. Allen

Description: "BookCamp is an online writing community led by longtime publishing insider Chad R. Allen, designed to help writers move from idea to publication with expert support, coaching, and accountability. Members get access to live group sessions; coworking hours; editorial feedback; a private Facebook group; and a library of resources on writing, publishing, and platform building—ideal for writers seeking structure, encouragement, and practical tools."

CHRISTIAN BOOK ACADEMY
christianbookacademy.com

Type: organization

Directors: CJ and Shelley Hitz

Description: "Save time, money and the frustration of figuring it all out alone with our clear and confident self-publishing roadmap. Establish yourself as an expert, opening doors for speaking engagements and more! Develop effective marketing strategies to reach and engage readers. Connect with new writing friends in our supportive community that get you. Get tools and mentoring to help you overcome self-doubt, grow as a writer, and leave a legacy with your writing. See results in just 15 minutes a day with our monthly challenges. Make significant progress on your book in our Monthly Virtual Retreats. Reach your goals with Take Action Weeks and our Unlock Your Writing Program."

CHRISTIAN EDITORS ASSOCIATION
www.ChristianEditorsAssociation.com

Type: organization

Director: Kathy Ide

Description: "Our goal is to equip, empower, and encourage editors in the Christian market through our four divisions. Join a community of like-minded professionals at The Christian PEN. Advance your knowledge and skills through The PEN Institute. Attend the PENCON editors' conference. Once you're established, apply to join Christian Editor Connection to get more job leads. Christian Editors Association also sponsors the Editors' Choice Award, honoring beautifully written and meticulously edited recently published books."

CHRISTIAN INDIE WRITERS' PODCAST
christianindiewriters.net/category/podcast

Type: podcast
Hosts: Jenifer Carll-Tong, Christina Cattane, Rhonda Hagerman, Jamie Hershberger
Description: "We inform, encourage and support Christian indie writers on the journey toward publication."

CHRISTIAN PUBLISHING SHOW
christianpublishingshow.com

Type: podcast
Host: Thomas Umstattd, Jr.
Description: "The *Christian Publishing Show* is a podcast to help Christian authors change the world. We talk about how to improve in the craft of writing, how to get published, and how to market effectively. Get expert advice from industry insiders."

CHRISTIAN WRITERS INSTITUTE
christianwritersinstitute.com

Type: organization, courses
Director: Becky Antkowiak, CEO; Steve Laube, president emeritus
Description: "The Christian Writers Institute was created to help Christians become proficient in the skills, craft, and business of writing. To build the Kingdom of God word-by-word. It does so by providing audio and video courses taught by some of the industry's best teachers. Originally founded in 1945, it is estimated that over 30,000 students have been trained by the Christian Writers Institute. It also runs the Write-to-Publish Conference held in Wheaton, IL."

CHRISTIAN WRITERS PODCAST
kathleenguire4.podbean.com

Type: podcast
Host: Kathleen Guire
Description: "Do you want to write Christian fiction that breaks the mold? *Christian Writers Podcast* is your go-to podcast for crafting engaging, faith-filled fiction that doesn't shy away from real-world

issues. Whether you're writing cozy mysteries, middle-grade adventures, or young adult novels, you'll learn how to create relatable characters, gripping plot twists, and deep themes—all while staying true to your values."

THE COMPANY
writers.company

Type: organization

Director: Brad Pauquette

Description: "The Company is a group of Kingdom-minded writers, publishers, and creative professionals bonded together to fundamentally change the media landscape in America. This is where you gain the skills, confidence, and support you've been searching for, so that you can reach your goals as a writer. . . . We provide tools, resources, training, and essential services for writers who are serious about reaching big audiences with their work and changing the world."

THE COMPANY PODCAST
writers.company/listen

Type: podcast

Host: Brad Pauquette

Description: "Brad Pauquette and friends are talking to authors, publishing industry experts, and Kingdom-minded media producers who are doing the hard work of leveraging the media for Christ."

COMPEL PRO WRITERS TRAINING
www.compeltraining.com

Type: organization

Director: Tracie Miles

Description: "Created by writers for writers, COMPEL Pro is a biblically based training community through Proverbs 31 Ministries designed to help writers move from writer's block to penning their very best words as a content creator." Offers lessons, focus groups, critique groups, and more.

THE DAILY WRITER
www.kentsanders.net/podcast

Type: podcast

Host: Kent Sanders

Description: "*The Daily Writer* podcast helps you cultivate the mindset and habits for creative success. Each weekday, author and ghostwriter Kent Sanders brings you a short lesson on writing inspired by some of history's greatest artists, authors, and thinkers, both past and present. The weekend edition features listener Q&A, conversations with notable writers and creatives, and teaching to help you take a deeper dive as a writer." No new episodes.

FIGHTWRITE PODCAST

www.fightwrite.net/podcast

Type: podcast

Host: Carla Hoch

Description: "A writer's resource for writing believable action and fight scenes." No new episodes.

GRACEWRITERS PODCAST

gracewriters.libsyn.com

Type: podcast

Hosts: Belinda Pollard, Donita Bundy, Alison Joy

Description: "Discussions and interviews that encourage and equip Christian writers who are called to influence popular culture through books, blogs, songwriting, poetry, scriptwriting, copywriting and other forms—whether writing for Christian or mainstream audiences."

THE HABIT

thehabit.co/the-habit-podcast

Type: podcast

Host: Jonathan Rogers

Description: "Conversations with writers about writing."

INK AND IMPACT PODCAST

dalenebickel.com/ink-and-impact

Type: podcast

Host: Dalene Bickel

Description: "If you're a writer who desires to create books that counteract the worldly titles featured prominently on bookstore shelves today, takes their craft seriously, and understands that God should be glorified in all they do, then this podcast is for you. *Ink and Impact* addresses not only tips and best practices to help you improve your craft and magnify your message, but also guide you through the ENTIRE writing journey."

JERRY JENKINS

jerryjenkins.com/online-creative-writing-courses

Type: courses

Director: Jerry Jenkins

Description: Jerry Jenkins, the author of more than 200 books with sales of more than 73 million copies, including the bestselling Left Behind series and The Chosen novels, offers online courses to help you "become the best writer you can be." Most courses are recordings of live workshops, and all come with lifetime access. Plus he gives away a number of free writing guides by email.

THE JERRY JENKINS WRITERS GUILD

jerrysguild.com

Type: organization, courses

Director: Jerry Jenkins

Description: "The Writers Guild is like a writing conference you can access from anywhere 24/7. Instant access to video training on any writing topic. Additionally, several times each month Jerry answers your questions live, hosts new writing workshops, interviews industry experts, and so much more." Membership is open only periodically; email *wecare@jerryjenkins.com* for the next open period.

THE KEEP WRITING PODCAST

podcasts.apple.com/us/podcast/the-keep-writing-podcast/ id1071732977?mt=2

Type: podcast

Host: Nika Maples

Description: "Nika Maples is a writer, speaker, and lupus and stroke survivor who loves to help Christian writers conquer what's holding them back so they can finish, publish, and market their amazing books." No new podcasts.

KINGDOM WRITERS

authors.libsyn.com/podcast

Type: podcast

Hosts: CJ and Shelley Hitz

Description: "CJ and Shelley Hitz are passionate about equipping and empowering Christian writers of all genres to share their unique gifts with the world. This podcast is filled with spiritual encouragement as well as prayers to help you overcome the resistance you face as a writer. Your story matters! We believe that you have a specific role to play in the kingdom of heaven to impact lives for eternity. And because of this, we will pour out our lives encouraging writers like you to not only tell your stories but to take the courageous step of self-publishing your stories in books that will outlive you and leave behind a powerful legacy."

NOVEL MARKETING PODCAST

authormedia.com/novel-marketing

Type: podcast
Host: Thomas Umstattd Jr.
Description: "This is the show for writers who want to build their platform, sell more books, and change the world with writing worth talking about. Whether you self-publish or are with a traditional house, this podcast will make book promotion fun and easy. Thomas Umstattd Jr. interviews publishers, indie authors and bestselling traditional authors about how to get published and sell more books."

PASTOR WRITER

pastorwriter.com/episodes

Type: podcast
Host: Chase Replogle
Description: "Join me as I interview pastors, authors, and writing experts in my journey to better understand the calling and the craft of writing, reading, and living the Christian life."

THE PEN INSTITUTE

PENInstitute.com

Type: courses
Director: Pam Lagomarsino
Description: "Whether you're just beginning your editing or writing career or looking for an advanced class to update your skills, The PEN Institute has training opportunities for you. We offer online group courses with personalized feedback, one-on-one instruction, webinars, and downloadable digital curriculum options for freelance and in-house editors as well as authors. Course topics include how to set up your freelance business, proofreading basics, social media, formatting, fiction and nonfiction techniques, and more. Our instructors are all experienced industry professionals."

THE PROFITABLE WRITER COMMUNITY

www.theprofitablewriter.com

Type: organization

Director: Kent Sanders

Description: "The Profitable Writer Community is the perfect place to grow and learn alongside other writers who want to build more impact and income with their gifts. When you join the community, you'll gain access to practical teaching by Kent Sanders and other experts, as well as a vibrant group of like-minded writers who understand and support you."

THE PROFITABLE WRITER PODCAST

www.theprofitablewriter.com/podcasts/the-profitable-writer

Type: podcast

Host: Kent Sanders

Description: "*The Profitable Writer Podcast* helps you create more impact and income with a writing business. Episodes feature interviews with guest experts as well as content to help you grow your business, become more productive, and make a bigger difference in the world."

PUBLISHING DISRUPTED

podcasts.apple.com/us/podcast/publishing-disrupted/id1811616023

Type: podcast

Hosts: Mick Silva, David Morris

Description: "Exploring the ways in which book publishing is changing and how writers can best meet the challenge. A conversation between two publishing veterans and friends, editor Mick Silva and publisher and literary agent David Morris."

THE PURPOSEFUL PEN

www.amylynnsimon.com/purposeful-pen-podcast

Type: podcast

Host: Amy Lynn Simon

Description: "*The Purposeful Pen* podcast is for you if you struggle to understand how to use your writing to glorify God and serve others. We talk about all those thoughts that bounce around in your head telling you that you aren't good enough; what the Bible has to say about earning money for your work; why it's important to know who your ideal reader is and what exactly you have to offer him or her; how to think outside the box and figure out what you really want to accomplish through your writing; how to create a writing life that brings joy to you, glory to God, and benefit to others."

REFINED PEN NETWORK
refined-pen.mn.co

Type: organization
Director: Jessica Boudreaux
Description: "This community provides writers access to ask questions on the craft of writing fiction, get feedback on portions of their work, and build relationships with other writers. Benefits include professional critiques, editing advice, live Q&A sessions, word-sprint events, and a book club for reading and discussing books on the craft of writing. Members also get discounts on professional editing services through Refined Pen Edits."

ROB EAGAR MARKETING CONSULTANT
www.startawildfire.com

Type: courses
Director: Rob Eagar
Description: Offers a private Book Marketing Master Class with coaching at any time and three online video courses—Mastering Amazon for Authors, Sell Books on a Shoestring Budget, and Book Marketing for Beginners—at various times during the year.

SERIOUS WRITER
seriouswriter.com

Type: organization
Director: Cyle Young
Description: "The mission of Serious Writer is to build community, create networking opportunities, share current industry information, and provide free and affordable instruction, training, and best practices for writing, marketing, and publishing."

SERIOUS WRITER PODCAST
seriouswriterpodcast.buzzsprout.com

Type: podcast
Hosts: Cyle Young, Bethany Jett
Description: "No matter where you are in your writing journey—just starting out, working on proposals, looking for an agent, or marketing your book—we're happy you're here and we're happy to help." No new episodes.

SOUL & STORY

podcasts.apple.com/us/podcast/soul-story/id1736266695

> **Type:** podcast
>
> **Host:** Sara R. Turnquist
>
> **Description:** Sara is "a coffee lovin', word slinging, clean historical romance author whose super power is converting caffeine into novels. I love those odd tidbits of history that are stranger than fiction. That's what inspires me. Well, that and a good love story."

THE STORY BLENDER PODCAST

www.thestoryblender.com

> **Type:** podcast
>
> **Host:** Steven James
>
> **Description:** "We are passionate about well-told, impactful stories. We love to listen to them. Watch them. Create them. So, we decided to talk with premier storytellers from around the country. Hear their stories and get their insights. From novelists to comedians to film makers to artists. Stories are told through a variety of people in a variety of ways. And here they are. The secrets of great storytelling from great storytellers."

THE STORYTELLER'S MISSION WITH ZENA DELL LOWE

www.buzzsprout.com/872170

> **Type:** podcast
>
> **Host:** Zena Dell Lowe
>
> **Description:** "Zena Dell Lowe is a seasoned and engaging teacher with a passion for writers and storytellers. Her focused, concise, and practical episodes (all under 20 minutes) not only explore the nuts and bolts of the craft, but also dive deep into the inner life of the artist and the 'why' behind creativity. If you believe that story matters, you'll want to give this podcast a listen."

WRITE FOR A REASON

writeforareason.buzzsprout.com

> **Type:** podcast
>
> **Host:** Janet Wilson
>
> **Description:** "For Christians new to writing novels for kids and teens. Creative writing tips, encouragement and inspiration."

WRITE FROM THE DEEP
writefromthedeep.com/write-from-the-deep-podcast

   Type: podcast
   Hosts: Karen Ball, Erin Taylor Young
   Description: "Encouragement, refreshment, and truth from writers,
      for writers. Every writer, at some point, faces the deep places of
      crushing trials and struggles. But the deep is also a place where we
      can learn to abide in God as never before. This podcast reminds
      writers they're not alone, and equips and helps them to embrace the
      deep, to discover their truest voice and message, and to share it with
      refined craft and renewed passion." No new episodes.

THE WRITERLY LIFE
podcasts.apple.com/us/podcast/the-writerly-life/id914574328

   Type: podcast
   Host: hope*writers
   Description: "Each episode of *The Writerly Life* offers you practical
      tips and interviews with publishing pros to help you skip the long
      learning curve and put you ahead of the game. *The Writerly Life* is
      all about balancing the art of writing with the business of publishing
      so that you can hustle without losing heart. Listen in and be inspired
      to keep putting your pen to the page. We'll help you find clarity to
      take the next step in your writing journey. You have words, and your
      words matter. Let's get them out into the world!" No new episodes.

A WRITER'S DAY
podcasts.apple.com/us/podcast/a-writers-day/id1472104073

   Type: podcast
   Host: R. A. Douthitt
   Description: "A podcast to help writers learn more about the craft,
      talk with published authors, and learn more about the publishing
      industry in order to have a competitive edge. Today, it takes more
      than just a good story to become a successful writer. You must know
      about marketing strategies, publishing options, and platforms that
      will help you stand out from the millions of writers out there. This
      podcast will help you."

WRITING AT THE RED HOUSE
www.writingattheredhouse.com/podcast-2

   Type: podcast
   Host: Kathi Lipp

Description: "The podcast is for those who love God and want to share His story through writing, speaking, social media—and yes—even marketing. . . . The refreshing and honest take on the 'industry' do's and don'ts, as well as insight on what makes you stand out from the rest, will not only entertain, but will serve in helping you propel your career to the next level."

WRITING FOR YOUR LIFE
writingforyourlife.com

Type: organization
Director: Kate Rademacher
Description: "Writing for Your Life is committed to offering a wide variety of useful resources and services to support spiritual writers. We offer in-person writing conferences and online videos featuring leading spiritual writers and publishing industry experts. Authors discuss and teach about various aspects of spiritual writing. Industry experts offer advice on how to get published and how to market. We also provide a host of services and resources to support your spiritual writing. Learn to tell your own story; write for your life!"

WRITING PURSUITS
www.writingpursuits.com/podcast

Type: podcast
Host: Kathrese McKee
Description: "*Writing Pursuits* is a weekly podcast for authors who drink too much coffee, endure judgmental looks from their furry writing companions, and struggle for words. If you are a writer seeking encouragement, information, and inspiration, this podcast is for you." No new episodes.

THE YOUNG WRITER
www.theyoungwriter.com/workshop

Type: organization
Directors: Brett Harris, Jaquelle Ferris
Description: "A supportive online Christian community for young writers ages 12–25. Learn how to write more, hone your craft, and finish projects you're proud of—all while connecting with published authors and like-minded peers. Enrollment opens every January, May, and August."

YOUR BEST WRITING LIFE
www.buzzsprout.com/1127762

Type: podcast

Host: Linda Goldfarb

Description: "Christian writing industry experts share weekly content for all levels of Christian writers. Whether you're a beginner or bestseller, you receive practical information and how-to application you can use to grow your writing career as a faith-based author. Each week, Linda Goldfarb and her guests cover various topics, including the craft of writing, fiction topics, nonfiction topics, self-care for writers, and the business of writing to name a few. If you're an aspiring Christian writer, we have content to help you grow. Published writers, we have current content to make your next book proposal, manuscript editing, speaking event, and writer's conference worth your time and energy."

25

CONTESTS AND AWARDS

A listing here does not guarantee endorsement of the contest. For guidelines on evaluating contests, go to *www.sfwa.org/otherresources/for-authors/writer-beware/contests*.

Note: Dates may not be accurate since many sponsors had not posted their 2026 dates before press time.

CHILDREN AND TEENS

CORETTA SCOTT KING BOOK AWARDS
www.ala.org/awards/books-media/coretta-scott-king-book-awards
> **Description:** Sponsored by American Library Association. Annual award for children's books published the previous year by African-American authors and/or illustrators. Books must promote an understanding and appreciation of the "American Dream of a pluralistic society" and fit one of these categories: preschool to grade 4, grades 5–8, grades 9–12.
> **Deadline:** December 1
> **Entry fee:** none
> **Prizes:** $1,000 and plaque

PATTY FRIEDMANN WRITING COMPETITION
wordsandmusic.org/patty-friedmann-writing-contest
> **Description:** Sponsored by Words and Music. Categories: poetry, fiction, creative nonfiction, short story by a high-school student, and multigenre "Beyond the Bars" for incarcerated juveniles. Previously unpublished work only. Length: prose, 7,500 words maximum; poetry, five pages maximum.

Deadline: submit between July 15 and September 15
Entry fee: varies by category
Prizes: $500–1,000, depending on category, plus publication in an anthology

SOCIETY OF CHILDREN'S BOOK WRITERS AND ILLUSTRATORS

www.scbwi.org/awards-and-grants/for-writers

Description: Sponsors a variety of contests and grants.
Deadline: varies
Entry fee: none
Prizes: vary

FICTION

AMERICAN CHRISTIAN FICTION WRITERS CONTESTS

acfw.com/acfw-contests

Description: Sponsored by American Christian Fiction Writers (ACFW). Genesis Contest for unpublished Christian fiction writers in a number of categories/genres. First Impressions Contest for unpublished writers. Carol Awards for best Christian fiction published the previous year.
Deadline: Genesis Contest and Carol Awards: submit between January 2 and March 1; First Impressions Contest: submit between September 2 and October 15
Entry fee: varies by category and membership
Prizes: Genesis Contest: award and lapel pin in each category; First Impressions Contest: complementary renewal of ACFW membership for next year; Carol Awards: winners, award and lapel pin; finalists, lapel pin

THE BARD FICTION PRIZE

www.bard.edu/bfp

Description: Sponsored by Bard College. Awarded to a promising, emerging young writer of fiction, 39 years or younger and an American citizen. Entries must be previously published.
Deadline: June 1
Entry fee: none
Prize: $30,000 and appointment as writer-in-residence for one semester at Bard College, Annandale-on-Hudson, New York

THE CROWN AWARD
acfwvirginia.com/acfw-virginia-the-crown

> **Description:** Sponsored by ACFW Virginia. Gives unpublished writers the opportunity to have those all-important, first five pages of their Christian fiction manuscript evaluated by industry professionals. Requires a one-page synopsis, which is not scored. Categories: contemporary, contemporary romance, historical/historical romance/historical romantic suspense, mystery/thriller/suspense/ romantic suspense, speculative, young adult/middle grade.
>
> **Deadline:** submit between June 30 and July 28
>
> **Entry fee:** chapter members, $20; nonmembers, $25
>
> **Prizes:** badge, certificate, and crown lapel pin or tie clip for each category winner

DANUTA GLEED LITERARY AWARD
www.writersunion.ca/awards

> **Description:** Sponsored by The Writers' Union of Canada. For the best first collection of published short fiction by a Canadian writer.
>
> **Deadline:** Submit in January
>
> **Entry fee:** none
>
> **Prizes:** $10,000, two finalists $1,000 each

FAITH, HOPE, & LOVE READER'S CHOICE AWARD
fhlchristianwriters.com/fhlcw-readers-choice-award

> **Description:** Sponsored by Faith, Hope, & Love Christian Writers (FHLCW). For Christian romances or Christian novels with romantic elements in print form. FHLCW defines Christian fiction as "stories written by writers whose worldview, influenced by their faith in the God of the Bible, is woven into the fabric of the book or manuscript." Entries should not include inappropriate or gratuitous demonstration of sin, whether in language (profanity), violence, or sexual situations. Length: varies with category.
>
> **Deadline:** March 1
>
> **Entry fee:** $25 for members, $35 for nonmembers
>
> **Prizes:** winner in each category, $350 and engraved box; second place in each category, $150; finalists in each category, certificate

FLANNERY O'CONNOR AWARD FOR SHORT FICTION
www.ugapress.org/series/flannery-oconnor-award-for-short-fiction

> **Description:** Sponsored by University of Georgia Press. For collections of short fiction. Length: 40,000–75,000 words.

Deadline: submit between April 1 and May 31
Prize: $1,000 plus publication under a royalty book contract

GET PUBBED
scriveningspress.com/get-pubbed

Description: Sponsored by Scrivenings Press. Unpublished entries are divided among four broad categories: speculative, historical, contemporary, and mystery/suspense. Submit the first ten pages.
Deadline: submit between May 1 and June 30
Entry fee: $25
Prizes: grand prize: publishing contract, paid registration for annual author retreat, thorough critique of up to 25 pages of the manuscript, and $75 Amazon gift card; entry with the highest score in each genre: critique of up to 25 pages of the manuscript and $25 Amazon gift card

GRACE PALEY PRIZE FOR SHORT FICTION
www.awpwriter.org/AWP/Contests/AWP-Award-Series/Grace-Paley/Overview.aspx

Description: Sponsored by Association of Writers and Writing Programs. Short-story collections. May contain stories previously published in periodicals. Length: 150–300 pages.
Deadline: submit between January 1 and February 28
Entry fee: $25
Prize: $5,500 and publication by Ohio State University Press

HAVOK SEASONAL FLASH FICTION CONTEST
gohavok.com

Description: Sponsored by Havok Publishing. Stories accepted for monthly themed submissions are published as an ezine (no payment), and five winners per month are selected for inclusion in a seasonal anthology (currently published annually). These monthly winners earn cash prizes from $10–50, depending on funding. Seasonal Editors' Choice and Readers' Choice Award winners receive $100 prizes. Genres: mystery, thriller, humor, science fiction, and fantasy. Length: 300–1,000 words. General-market content, rated PG-13 or under.
Deadline: monthly
Entry fee: none
Prizes: varies from $10 to $100

JAMES ALAN McPHERSON PRIZE FOR THE NOVEL
www.awpwriter.org/AWP/Contests/AWP-Award-Series/
James-Alan-McPherson/Overview.aspx

Description: Sponsored by Association of Writers and Writing Programs. Open to published and unpublished authors. Length: 60,000–110,000 words.
Deadline: submit between January 1 and February 28
Entry fee: $20 for members, $30 for nonmembers
Prize: $5,500 and publication by the University of Nebraska Press

JAMES JONES FIRST NOVEL FELLOWSHIP
www.wilkes.edu/academics/graduate-programs/creative-writing-ma-mfa/ james-jones-fellowship-contest.aspx

Description: Sponsored by Wilkes University. For a first novel or novel-in-progress by a US writer who has not published a novel. Submit a two-page outline and the first 50 pages of an unpublished novel.
Deadline: submit between October 1 and March 15
Entry fee: $30 plus $3 processing fee
Prizes: first place, $12,000; first runner-up, $3,000; second runner-up, $2,000

KATHERINE ANNE PORTER PRIZE IN SHORT FICTION
untpress.unt.edu/authors/porter-prize-submissions

Description: Sponsored by University of North Texas Press. Quality unpublished fiction by emerging writers of contemporary literature. Can be a combination of short-shorts, short stories, and novellas from 100 to 200 pages (27,500–50,000 words). Material should be previously unpublished in book form.
Deadline: submit between May 1 and June 30
Entry fee: $25
Prize: $1,000 and publication by UNT Press

NOVEL STARTS
scriveningspress.com/novel-starts

Description: Sponsored by Scrivenings Press. For an unfinished novel in four genres: speculative, historical, contemporary, and mystery/suspense. Submit the first five pages.
Deadline: submit between May 1 and June 30
Entry fee: $25
Prizes: grand prize: author retreat, invitation to submit novel for consideration by Scrivenings Press once it is finished, thorough critique of up to 25 pages of the manuscript, and $75 Amazon gift

card; entry with the highest score in each genre: a critique of up to 25 pages of the manuscript and $25 Amazon gift card

REALM AWARDS

www.realmmakers.com/the-realm-awards

Description: Sponsored by The Faith and Fantasy Alliance. Speculative fiction categories: novels, short stories, audiobooks, interactive media, comics, and graphic novels. Length: novels, 60,000 words minimum; YA, 50,000 words minimum; middle grade, 20,000 words minimum; short stories, 10,000 words maximum; novellas, 10,000–50,000 words. Entries must be published in the previous year.

Deadline: submit between January 1 and 21

Entry fee: $49

Prizes: commemorative award, award stickers, promotional opportunities, and the opportunity to be carried in the Realm Makers Mobile Bookstore and Bookish bookstore

REALM MAKER'S READERS' CHOICE AWARD

www.realmmakers.com/realm-award-readers-choice-alliance-award

Description: Sponsored by The Faith and Fantasy Alliance to give readers their say in what speculative fiction novels they enjoyed most in the preceding year. Only readers may nominate books in this contest. Books may be traditionally published or self-published.

Deadline: submit between March 15 and April 15

Entry fee: none

Prize: art award

TOBIAS WOLFF AWARD FOR FICTION

www.bhreview.org/general-submissions-guidelines

Description: Sponsored by Western Washington University's *Bellingham Review*. Length: 5,000 words maximum.

Deadline: submit between December 1 and March 15

Entry fee: $20

Prize: $1,000 plus publication

ZOETROPE: ALL-STORY SHORT FICTION COMPETITION

www.all-story.com/zoetrope-all-story-short-fiction-competition

Description: Sponsored by *Zoetrope: All-Story* magazine to launch writing careers. Unpublished submissions only. Multiple entries accepted. Length: maximum 5,000 words.

Deadline: October 1

Entry fee: $30

Prize: first place, $1,000 and publication on the magazine's website; second place, $500; third place, $250; all three plus seven honorable mentions, representation by a talent agency

MULTIPLE GENRES

ANGEL BOOK AWARDS

ffbookfestival.com

Description: Sponsored by Faith & Fellowship Book Festival to promote excellent books with a Christian worldview. The awards are open to all writers whose Christian fiction or nonfiction books were originally published between January 1, 2025 and June 30, 2026. Books entered must be written from a Christian worldview. There should be no profanity, gratuitous violence, graphic sex, or other objectionable material not accepted by Christian publishing standards.

Deadline: June 30

Entry fee: $50

Prizes: certificate and logo that can be uploaded to blogs, used on memes, etc., for each winner; first-place winners also receive a display award

BLUE RIDGE MOUNTAINS CHRISTIAN WRITERS CONFERENCE CONTESTS

www.blueridgeconference.com/contest-info

Description: Sponsors two book contests for fiction or nonfiction: Foundation Awards and The Selah Awards. See the website for details.

Deadline: varies by contest

Entry fee: $35–55

Prizes: vary by contest

THE BRAUN BOOK AWARDS

wordalivepress.ca/pages/the-braun-book-awards

Description: Sponsored by Word Alive Press. For unpublished Christian books written by Canadian citizens and permanent residents in Canada. Categories: nonfiction and fiction.

Deadline: March 15

Entry fee: none

Prizes: one fiction and one nonfiction manuscript, royalty-based book publishing contract; select number of secondary winners, prizes include credit toward publishing

CASCADE WRITING CONTEST

cascadechristianwriters.org/cascade-contest

Description: Sponsored by Cascade Christian Writers. Open to anyone, with emphasis on unpublished works. All contestants receive three score sheets from the judges reviewing their work, and finalists receive an additional two score sheets.

Deadline: submit between January 15 and February 15

Entry fee: $35 for members, $45 for nonmembers

Prize: certificates to all finalists; in addition, pins to the winners

CHRISTIAN INDIE AWARDS

www.christianaward.com

Description: Sponsored by Christian Indie Publishing Association. This award is designed to promote and bring recognition to quality Christian books by small publishers and independently published authors. Books must be printed in English, be for sale in the United States, and promote the Christian faith. Awards are offered in 18 categories. Publishers and authors may nominate titles.

Deadline: October 1

Entry fee: $109

Prize: trophy and promotion

EABOOKS PUBLISHING CONTESTS

eabookspublishing.com/our-services/publishing-contest-2026

Description: To give unpublished authors writing credits and experience. Books for 2026: *Come: Knock and the Door Will Open* and *Come: All Who Are Lost—Be Found!* Types of manuscripts: articles, short stories, poems, devotions, and personal experience. May be unpublished or previously published if you own the rights. Length: 1,500 words maximum. Accepts 40 per year for onetime rights. Multiple entries accepted. Submit on website form. Judged by alignment with the theme and following all guidelines.

Deadline: June 30 and September 30, depending on the book

Entry fee: $10

Prizes: publication in an anthology, one free book and opportunity to buy copies at a discount and sell for full price

EDITORS' CHOICE AWARD
christianeditorsassociation.com/eca

Description: Sponsored by Christian Editors Association. This award celebrates the authors, editors, and publishers behind books that are superbly written, well edited, and published by a Christian publisher or self-published by a Christian author. Each year's contest is open to books published the previous calendar year. Winners announced at PENCON. Judges' notes provided on request.

Deadline: submit between June 1 and December 31

Entry fee: $70 by September 15, $85 after; $15 discount for members of The Christian PEN and Christian Editor Connection

Prizes: blog and newsletter interviews, digital emblems, certificates, select benefits from divisions of Christian Editors Association

ERIC HOFFER BOOK AWARD
www.hofferaward.com

Description: Multiple categories for books from small, academic, and independent presses, including self-published, ebooks, and older books.

Deadline: December 10

Entry fee: varies by category

Prizes: $5,000 grand prize, other prizes awarded in categories

HIGHER GOALS AWARDS
www.evangelicalpress.com/contest

Description: Sponsored by Evangelical Press Association. Awards are given in a variety of categories for periodical manuscripts published in the previous year. Although most submissions are made by publication staff members, associate EPA members may also submit their articles.

Deadline: submit between mid-November and January 24

Entry fee: $30

Prizes: certificate and critique sheet

NARRATIVE MAGAZINE CONTESTS
www.narrativemagazine.com/submit-your-work

Description: Sponsored by *Narrative* magazine. Biannual contests in a variety of categories, including short stories, essays, memoirs, poetry, and literary nonfiction. Entries must be previously unpublished. Length: varies by category.

Deadline: any time, June 15 for annual Narrative Prize

Entry fee: varies

Prizes: vary by category plus annual Narrative Prize of $5,000 for the best short story, novel excerpt, poem, or work of literary nonfiction published by a new or emerging writer in *Narrative*

NATIONAL WRITERS ASSOCIATION CONTESTS

www.nationalwriters.com/page/page/2734945.htm

Description: Sponsors five contests: novel, young writers, poetry, short story, and David Raffelock Award for Publishing Excellence.

Deadline: varies by contest

Entry fee: varies by contest

Prizes: vary by contest

NEW LETTERS EDITOR'S CHOICE AWARD

www.newletters.org/editors-choice-award

Description: Sponsored by *New Letters* magazine. For short narratives, whether they are stories, essays, poems, or hybrid forms. Length: maximum 1,000 words.

Deadline: submit between July 1 and November 10

Entry fee: $20

Prize: $1,000 and publication in magazine

NEW MILLENNIUM WRITING AWARDS

newmillenniumwritings.submittable.com/submit

Description: Sponsored by New Millennium Writings. Fiction and nonfiction, 7,499 words maximum; flash fiction, 1,000 words maximum; poetry, three poems to five pages total. No restrictions as to style or subject matter.

Deadline: August 7

Entry fee: $20, $35 for two entries, $45 for three entries, $60 for four entries, $80 for five entries

Prizes: $1,000 plus publication for each category

TENNESSEE WILLIAMS FEST CONTESTS

tennesseewilliams.net/contests

Description: Sponsored by New Orleans Literary Festival. Tennessee Williams gained some early recognition by entering a writing contest. The festival that bears his name now sponsors writing contests in poetry, fiction, very short fiction, and one-act playwriting.

Deadline: submit between May 1 and October 15

Entry fee: varies

Prizes: vary by category

THE WORD AWARDS
thewordguild.com/contests

> **Description:** Sponsored by The Word Guild. The Awards recognize the best work published in the previous year in a wide variety of categories and are open to all Canadian writers who are Christians. You do not need to be a member of The Word Guild to submit an entry, but members save money on their entry fees.
> **Deadline:** March 31
> **Entry fee:** varies according to award
> **Prizes:** vary according to award

WRITER'S DIGEST COMPETITIONS
www.writersdigest.com/writers-digest-competitions

> **Description:** Contests are available for a wide variety of genres, including inspirational, feature articles, short stories, poetry, personal essays, and self-published books.
> **Deadline:** varies according to contest
> **Entry fee:** varies
> **Prizes:** vary

NONFICTION

ANNIE DILLARD AWARD
bhreview.org/general-submissions-guidelines

> **Description:** Sponsored by Western Washington University's *Bellingham Review*. Unpublished essays on any subject. Length: 5,000 words maximum.
> **Deadline:** submit between December 1 and March 15
> **Entry fee:** $20 for first submission, $10 each additional one
> **Prize:** $1,000

BECHTEL PRIZE
teachersandwritersmagazine.org/bechtel-prize

> **Description:** Sponsored by *Teachers & Writers Magazine*. For unpublished essays describing a creative writing teaching experience, project, or activity that demonstrates innovation in creative writing instruction. Length: 2,500 words maximum.
> **Deadline:** submit between October 1 and January 10
> **Entry fee:** $20
> **Prize:** $1,000 and publication

EVENT NON-FICTION CONTEST

www.eventmagazine.ca/contest-nf

Description: Sponsored by *EVENT* magazine. Unpublished creative nonfiction. Length: 5,000 words maximum.

Deadline: submit between April 1 and October 15

Entry fee: $34.95, includes a one-year subscription to *EVENT*

Prizes: first place, $1,500; second place, $1,000; third place, $500 plus publication

INTREPID TIMES TRAVEL WRITING COMPETITION

intrepidtimes.com/competitions

Description: Sponsored by Exisle Publishing. *Intrepid Times* runs narrative, travel-writing contests that focus on stories, places, and people. Length: 2,000 words maximum.

Deadline: varies

Entry fee: free

Prizes: first place, $300, publication on website, and possible publication in anthology; runners-up, $50

RICHARD J. MARGOLIS AWARD

www.margolisaward.org

Description: Sponsored by Blue Mountain Center. Given annually to a promising young journalist or essayist whose work combines warmth, humor, wisdom, and concern with social justice. Submit two or three examples of published or unpublished work and a short biographical note, including a description of current and anticipated work. Length: 30 pages maximum.

Deadline: July 1

Entry fee: none

Prizes: first place, $10,000 plus a one-month residency at the Blue Mountain Center in Blue Mountain Lake, New York; finalists, $1,000

SHORT PROSE COMPETITION FOR EMERGING WRITERS

www.writersunion.ca/awards

Description: Sponsored by The Writers' Union of Canada. For the best piece of unpublished prose by a Canadian writer. Length: 2,500 words maximum.

Deadline: submit between December and mid to late February

Entry fee: $29 CDN

Prizes: $2,500; winner and 11 finalists, feedback and submission to three magazines for possible publication

SUE WILLIAM SILVERMAN PRIZE FOR CREATIVE NONFICTION

www.awpwriter.org/AWP/Contests/AWP-Award-Series/Sue-William/Overview.aspx

Description: Sponsored by Association of Writers and Writing Programs. Open to both published and unpublished authors. Book collection of nonfiction manuscripts.

Deadline: submit between January 1 and February 28

Entry fee: $15 for members, $30 for nonmembers

Prize: $2,500 and publication with the University of Georgia Press

PLAYS/SCRIPTS/SCREENPLAYS

ACADEMY NICHOLL FELLOWSHIPS IN SCREENWRITING

www.oscars.org/nicholl/about

Description: Sponsored by the Academy. International contest open to any writer whose total lifetime earnings for motion picture and television writing does not exceed $25,000 before the end of the competition. May submit only one script. Length: 70–160 pages. Contest closes early if 5,500 entries are received.

Deadline: submit between March 1 and May 1

Entry fee: $50–120, depending on submission date

Prizes: up to five $35,000 fellowships; recipients will be expected to complete at least one original feature-film screenplay during the fellowship year

AMERICAN ZOETROPE SCREENPLAY COMPETITION

www.all-story.com/american-zoetrope-screenplay-competition

Description: Sponsored by *Zoetrope: All-Story* magazine. To find and promote new and innovative voices in cinema. For screenplays and television pilots. No entrant may have earned more than $50,000 as a screenwriter for theatrical films or television or for the sale of, or sale of an option to, any original story, treatment, screenplay, or teleplay. Prizes, fellowships, awards, and other contest winnings are not considered earnings and are excluded from this rule. Length: film scripts, 140 pages maximum; one-hour television pilot scripts, 70 pages maximum; half-hour television scripts, 40 pages maximum.

Deadline: September 3

Entry fee: $40–50, depending on submission date

Prizes: first place, $5,000 plus consideration for film option and development; nine finalists will also get this consideration

AUSTIN FILM FESTIVAL SCREENWRITERS COMPETITION

austinfilmfestival.com/submit

> **Description:** Offers a number of contest categories, including feature film, short film, produced digital series, screenplay, teleplay, short screenplay, scripted digital series, fiction podcast, and play.
> **Deadline:** varies by type
> **Entry fee:** $35–70, varies by type and submission date
> **Prizes:** $1,000–5,000

KAIROS PRIZE FOR SPIRITUALLY UPLIFTING SCREENPLAYS

www.kairosprize.com

> **Description:** Sponsored by Timothy Plan. For unpublished, unoptioned feature-length screenplays and TV pilot shows. Judges consider not only a script's entertainment value and craftsmanship, but also whether it is uplifting, inspirational, and spiritual and if it teaches lessons in ethics and morality. Length: 87–130 pages; will accept scripts up to 150 pages (not counting the title page) for an additional $20.
> **Deadline:** submit between July 18 and October 31
> **Entry fee:** varies, depending on submission date
> **Prizes:** $15,000 each for first-time and professional screenwriters

MOONDANCE INTERNATIONAL FILM FESTIVAL COMPETITION

filmfreeway.com/MoondanceInternationalFilmFestival

> **Description:** Offers a variety of awards for films, screenplays, short stories, teleplays, librettos, and features that raise awareness about social issues.
> **Deadline:** submit between February 1 and December 31
> **Entry fee:** $25–50
> **Prize:** promotion to film companies for possible option

NEW WORKS@THE WORKS PLAYWRITING COMPETITION

playhouseonthesquare.org/newworks

> **Description:** Sponsored by Playhouse on the Square and Forest Roberts Theatre, Northern Michigan University. Unpublished, unproduced, full-length plays. Provides students and faculty members the opportunity to mount and produce an original work on stage.

Deadline: submit between January 1 and June 30
Entry fee: $15
Prizes: $1,500 and a fully mounted production; six finalists, $100 each

SCRIPTAPALOOZA SCREENPLAY COMPETITION

www.scriptapalooza.com

> **Description:** Any screenplay from any genre considered; must be the original work of the author (multiple authorship acceptable). Shorts competition: screenplays fewer than 40 pages.
> **Deadline:** April 6
> **Entry fee:** $25–45, depending on category and deadline
> **Prizes:** first place, $10,000; each genre winner, $500; plus access to 90 producers through Scriptapalooza's network

SCRIPTAPALOOZA TV COMPETITION

www.scriptapaloozatv.com

> **Description:** Scripts for television pilots, one-hour dramas, reality shows, and half-hour sitcoms. Length: pilot, 30–60 pages; one-hour drama, 50–60 pages; reality show, one- to five-page treatment; half-hour sitcom, 25–35 pages.
> **Deadline:** April and October
> **Entry fee:** $45–55, depending on deadline
> **Prizes:** first place, $500; second place, $200; third place, $100 in each category; plus six months of International Screenwriters' Association Connect Membership and access to more than 50 producers, managers, and agents through Scriptapalooza's network

POETRY

49TH PARALLEL AWARD FOR POETRY

bhreview.org/general-submissions-guidelines

> **Description:** Sponsored by Western Washington University's *Bellingham Review*. Up to three poems in any style or on any subject.
> **Deadline:** submit between December 1 and March 15
> **Entry fee:** $20; international entries, $30
> **Prize:** $1,000 and publication

ACADEMY OF AMERICAN POETS

poets.org/academy-american-poets/american-poets-prizes

> **Description:** See the website for a list of multiple contests and prizes.

BARBARA MANDIGO KELLY PEACE POETRY AWARDS

www.peacecontests.org/#poetry

> **Description:** Sponsored by Nuclear Age Peace Foundation. Awards to encourage poets to explore and illuminate positive visions of peace and the human spirit. Poems must be unpublished. May submit up to three poems for one entry fee.
> **Deadline:** July 15
> **Entry fee:** adults, $15; youth ages 13–18, $5; ages 12 and under, none
> **Prizes:** adult winner, $1,000; youth winner, $200; ages 12 and under, $200

CAVE CANEM ANGELA JACKSON PRIZE

nupress.northwestern.edu/cave-canem-angela-jackson-prize

> **Description:** Sponsored by Cave Canem Foundation. Supports the work of black poets of African descent with excellent manuscripts and who have published one book. Length: 48–75 pages.
> **Deadline:** submit between April 1 and June 12
> **Entry fee:** none
> **Prize:** $1,000 plus publication by Northwestern University Press and 15 copies of the book

THE DONALD HALL PRIZE FOR POETRY

awpwriter.org/AWP/Contests/AWP-Award-Series/Donald-Hall-Prize/Overview.aspx

> **Description:** Sponsored by Association of Writers and Writing Programs. Open to published and unpublished authors. Length: 48 pages minimum.
> **Deadline:** submit between January 1 and February 28
> **Entry fee:** $15 for members, $30 for nonmembers
> **Prize:** $5,500 and publication by University of Pittsburgh Press

HOLLIS SUMMERS POETRY PRIZE

www.ohioswallow.com/poetry_prize

> **Description:** Sponsored by Ohio University Press. For an unpublished collection of original poems, 60–95 pages. Open to both those who do not have a published book-length collection and to those who have.
> **Deadline:** submit between April 1 and December 31
> **Entry fee:** $30
> **Prize:** $1,000 plus publication in book form by Ohio University Press

JAMES LAUGHLIN AWARD

www.poets.org/academy-american-poets/james-laughlin-award-guidelines

> **Description:** Sponsored by Academy of American Poets. To recognize a second full-length print book of original poetry. Author must have

published one book of poetry in English in a standard edition (48 pages or more) in the United States or under contract and scheduled for publication during the current calendar year; publication of chapbooks (less than 48 pages) does not disqualify. Length: 48–100 pages.
Deadline: submit between July 1 and October 1
Entry fee: none
Prize: $5,000, publication, and weeklong residency at The Betsy Hotel in Miami Beach, Florida

JESSIE BRYCE NILES CHAPBOOK CONTEST
comstockreview.org

Description: Sponsored by *Comstock Review*. Submissions must be unpublished as a collection, but individual poems may have been published previously in journals. Length: 25–34 pages. Poems may run longer than one page.
Deadline: submit between August 1 and October 31
Entry fee: $30
Prize: $1,000 plus publication and author copies

KATE TUFTS DISCOVERY AWARD
arts.cgu.edu/tufts-poetry-awards

Description: Sponsored by Claremont Graduate University. For a first poetry volume published in the preceding year by a poet of genuine promise. Length: at least 48 pages.
Deadline: July 1
Entry fee: none
Prize: $10,000

KINGSLEY TUFTS POETRY AWARD
arts.cgu.edu/tufts-poetry-awards

Description: Sponsored by Claremont Graduate University. For a published book of poetry by a midcareer poet to both honor the poet and provide the resources that allow artists to continue working toward the pinnacle of their craft. Length: 48 pages minimum.
Deadline: July 1
Entry fee: none
Prize: $100,000 and one-week residence at Claremont Graduate University

MURIEL CRAFT BAILEY MEMORIAL POETRY AWARD
comstockreview.org/annual-contest

Description: Sponsored by *Comstock Review*. Unpublished poems up to

60 lines/70 characters. No limit on number of submissions.
Deadline: submit between April 1 and July 15
Entry fee: $25 plus $2.50 online fee for five poems; $5/poem if mailed
Prizes: first place, $1,000; second place, $250; third place, $100

PATRICIA CLEARY MILLER AWARD FOR POETRY
www.newletters.org/patricia-cleary-miller-award-for-poetry

Description: Sponsored by *New Letters*. A single poetry entry may contain up to six poems/30 pages, and the poems need not be related.
Deadline: submit between November 1 and May 19
Entry fee: $24 each entry, includes a one-year subscription to *New Letters*
Prize: $2,500 for best group of three to six poems

PHILIP LEVINE PRIZE FOR POETRY
cah.fresnostate.edu/english/centers-projects/levineprize/index.html

Description: Sponsored by the Creative Writing Department at California State University, Fresno. An annual book contest for original, previously unpublished, full-length poetry manuscripts. Length: 48–80 pages with no more than one poem per page.
Deadline: submit between July 1 and September 30
Entry fee: $25
Prize: $2,000, publication by Black Lawrence Press, 25 copies, public reading

POETRY SOCIETY OF VIRGINIA POETRY CONTESTS
www.poetrysocietyofvirginia.org/adult-contests

Description: More than twenty-five categories for adults and students. Form and length limit of entries vary according to the contests. All entries must be unpublished, original, and not scheduled for publication before the winners of the competition are announced.
Deadline: varies
Entry fee: $6.50 per poem
Prizes: vary by specific competition

SLIPSTREAM ANNUAL POETRY CHAPBOOK COMPETITION
www.slipstreampress.org/contest.html

Description: Sponsored by Slipstream Press. Entries may be any style, format, or theme. Length: 40 pages maximum.
Deadline: December 1
Entry fee: $25
Prize: $1,000 plus 25 published copies of chapbook

TOM HOWARD/MARGARET REID POETRY CONTEST

winningwriters.com/our-contests/tom-howard-margaret-reid-poetry-contest

Description: Sponsored by Winning Writers. Poetry in any style or genre. Published poetry accepted. Length: 250 lines maximum.

Deadline: submit between April 15 and October 1

Entry fee: $25 for up to three poems

Prizes: Tom Howard Prize, $3,500 for poem in any style or genre; Margaret Reid Prize, $3,500 for poem that rhymes or has a traditional style; $300 each for 10 honorable mentions in any style

WERGLE FLOMP HUMOR POETRY CONTEST

winningwriters.com/our-contests/wergle-flomp-humor-poetry-contest-free

Description: Sponsored by Winning Writers. Submit one published or unpublished humor poem up to 250 lines.

Deadline: submit between August 15 and April 1

Entry fee: none

Prizes: first place, $2,000; second place, $500; third place, $250; 10 honorable mentions, $100; plus the top 13 entries will be published online

RESOURCES FOR CONTESTS

These websites are sources for announcements about other contests.

DAILY WRITING TIPS

www.dailywritingtips.com/25-writing-competitions

FREELANCE WRITING

www.freelancewriting.com/writing-contests

FUNDS FOR WRITERS

fundsforwriters.com/contests

NEW PAGES

www.newpages.com/classifieds/big-list-of-writing-contests

POETS & WRITERS
www.pw.org/grants

THE WRITE LIFE
thewritelife.com/writing-contests

DENOMINATIONAL PUBLISHERS

Note: Not all of these houses and publications are owned by denominational publishing companies, and some publish for a broader audience than the denomination.

ANGLICAN
Anglican House Publishers
Anglican Journal
Forward Movement

ASSEMBLIES OF GOD
Influence
LIVE
My Healthy Church
Take 5 Plus

BAPTIST
B&H Kids
B&H Publishing
The Baptist Bulletin
Baptist Standard
The Brink
D6 Family Ministry
Forward
Fusion Family
Fusion Next
HomeLife

Judson Press
Light
Mature Living
Open Windows
ParentLife
The Secret Place
Velocity

CATHOLIC
America
The Arlington Catholic Herald
Ave Maria Press
Catholic Book Publishing Corp.
Celebrate Life Magazine
Chrism Press
Columbia
Commonweal
Creative Communications for the Parish
LEAVES
Lighthouse Publishing
Ligouri Publications

Liturgical Press
Living Faith
Living Faith Kids
Loyola Press
Our Sunday Visitor, Inc.
Paraclete Press
Pauline Books & Media
Paulist Press
Resurrection Press
St. Anthony Messenger
Twenty-third Publications
U.S. Catholic

CHARISMATIC/ PENTECOSTAL

Charisma
Charisma House
Chosen
Emanate Books
testimony/Enrich
Whitaker House

CHRISTIAN CHURCH/ CHURCH OF CHRIST

Christian Standard
College Press Publishing
Leafwood Publishers
The Pilgrim Press

CHURCH OF GOD

Beginner's Friend
Bible Advocate
Explorers
Gems of Truth
Now What?
Warner Press
Youth Compass

DISCIPLES OF CHRIST

Chalice Press

EPISCOPAL

Church Publishing Incorporated
Forward Day by Day
Forward Movement

LUTHERAN

Augsburg Fortress
Beaming Books
Broadleaf Books
Café
Canada Lutheran
The Canadian Lutheran
Christ in Our Home
Fortress Press
Gather
The Lutheran Witness
Northwestern Publishing House
Portals of Prayer
The Word in Season

MENNONITE

Canadian Mennonite
Christian Leader
The Marketplace
The Messenger
Rejoice!

MESSIANIC

The Messianic Times

METHODIST

Abingdon Press
The Upper Room
Upper Room Books

NAZARENE

The Foundry Publishing
Holiness Today
Reflecting God
Standard

ORTHODOX

Ancient Faith Publishing
Chrism Press

PRESBYTERIAN

byFaith
Flyaway Books
Paraklesis Press
Westminster John Knox Press

QUAKER/FRIENDS

Friends Journal
Fruit of the Vine
Tract Association of Friends

REFORMED

Calla Press Publishing
Christian Courier
Ignited by the Word
P&R Publishing
Reformed Free Publishing
    Association
Tulip Publishing

THE SALVATION ARMY

Caring Magazine
Faith & Friends
Just for Kids
Peer
The War Cry

SEVENTH-DAY ADVENTIST

Guide
The Journal of Adventist Education
Ministry
Our Little Friend
Pacific Press
Primary Treasure

WESLEYAN

The Foundry Publishing
Light from the Word

PUBLISHING LINGO

My first week working in a bookstore I learned a valuable lesson. I had a stack of books in my arms that I had taken from a shipment in the back room. My boss walked by; said, "Steve, please put those in the dump"; and kept walking.

I paused and thought, *Why should I throw these away? They are brand new books!* To my chagrin, I discovered that, in bookstore lingo, a dump was a cardboard display in the front of the store.

The lesson I learned is that knowing the lingo can keep you from being confused or potentially misunderstanding some instructions. Like bookstores, writing and publishing have their own lingo. The following definitions will acquaint you with some of the more important terms.

ABA: American Booksellers Association. This acronym has come to mean the general market, as opposed to CBA, the Christian market.

Advance: Money a publisher pays to an author up front, against future royalties. The amount varies greatly from publisher to publisher and is often paid in two or three installments (on signing the contract, on delivery of the manuscript, and on publication).

AE: An abbreviation for Acquisitions Editor. Not all publishing houses use this abbreviation, but they all have people who acquire in their editorial departments.

All rights: An outright sale of a manuscript. The author has no further control over any subsidiary rights or reusing the piece. You must sign a contract for this agreement to be legal.

Anecdote: A short, poignant, real-life story, usually used to illustrate a single thought. It need not be humorous.

ARC: Advance Reader Copy. An early paperback (or ebook) version of a book sent out for reviews around four to six months prior to publication.

Assignment: When an editor asks a writer to create a specific manuscript for an agreed-on price.

As-told-to story: A true story you write as a first-person account about someone else.

Audience: The people who are expected to be reading your manuscript, in terms of age, life experience, knowledge of and interest level in the story or subject. Editors want to be sure writers understand their assumed audiences well.

Audiobooks: Spoken-word books available by streaming via the Internet, on compact disc, or MP3 file.

Backlist: A publisher's previously published books that are still in print a year or more after publication.

Bible versions:
AKJV—American King James Version
AMP—Amplified Bible
ASV—American Standard Version
CB—Confraternity Bible (Catholic)
CEB—Common English Bible
CEV—Contemporary English Version
CJB—Complete Jewish Bible
CSB—Christian Standard Bible
ESV—English Standard Version
GNB—Good News Bible
GW—GOD'S WORD Translation
HCSB—Holman Christian Standard Bible (replaced by CSB)
ICB—International Children's Bible
KJV—King James Version
KJV21—21st Century King James Version
MEV—Modern English Version
MSG—The Message
NAB—New American Bible
NABRE—New American Bible Revised Edition
NASB—New American Standard Bible
NCV—New Century Version
NEB—New English Bible
NET—New English Translation

NIrV—New International Reader's Version
NIV—New International Version
NJB—New Jerusalem Bible
NKJV—New King James Version
NLT—New Living Translation
NRSV—New Revised Standard Version
NRSVue—New Revised Standard Version Updated Edition
PHILLIPS—J.B. Phillips New Testament
RSV—Revised Standard Version (replaced by NRSV)
RSV2CE—Revised Standard Version, Second Catholic Edition
TEV—Today's English Translation (aka Good News Bible)
TLB—The Living Bible
TNIV—Today's New International Version
VOICE—The Voice Bible Translation
WEB—World English Bible

Bio: Brief information about the author.

BIPOC: Black, Indigenous, and People of Color.

Bluelines: The last printer's proofs used to catch errors before a book or periodical is printed. May be physical pages or digital proofs in PDF.

BOB: Back-of-Book ad for the author's previous book(s) or a similar book released by the publisher. It uses the blank pages in the back of a book or extra pages at the end of an ebook.

Book proposal: Submission of a book idea to an agent or editor. It usually includes a hook, summary and purpose of the book, target market, uniqueness of the book compared to similar ones in the marketplace, chapter-by-chapter summaries or plot synopsis, marketing and promotion information, your credentials, and delivery date, plus one to three sample chapters, including the first one.

Byline: Author's name printed below the title of a book, article, etc.

Camera-ready copy: The text and artwork that are ready for the press.

Category romance: Novels of around 50,000–60,000 words that are published in categories and according to strict guidelines. For example, Love Inspired novels, the Christian division of Harlequin.

CBA: Christian Booksellers Association. The acronym has come to describe the Christian market as opposed to ABA, the general market. As an entity, CBA folded in 2019, but the acronym still applies when referring to the Christian publishing industry.

Chapbook: A small book or pamphlet containing poetry, etc.

Circulation: The number of copies sold or distributed of a periodical.

Clips: Copies of articles you have had published in periodicals.

Colophon: The publisher's emblem or imprint used on the title page or spine of a book or a statement at the end of a book with information about its production, such as the type of font used.

Column: A regularly appearing feature, section, or department in a periodical with the same heading. It's written by the same person or a different one each time.

Comp copies: Complimentary copies given to the author by the publisher on publication.

Comps: Shorthand for "comparable." The publisher may have comps on cover designs or titles to help position the book in the marketplace.

Concept statement: A 50- to 150-word summary of your proposed book.

Contributing editor: A freelance writer who has a regular column or writes regularly for the periodical.

Contributor's copy: Copy of an issue of a periodical sent to an author whose work appears in it.

Copyedit: The editor checks grammar, punctuation, and citations to make sure the work is accurate. More detailed than a developmental edit. Some publishers refer to this as the line edit.

Copyright: Legal protection of an author's work. A manuscript is automatically copyrighted in your name when you produce it. You don't need to register it with the Copyright Office unless you are self-publishing a book or other publication since a traditional publisher registers it for you.

Cover copy: Or "copy." The text on the back cover of a book, in the online description, or in marketing materials. For a hardcover, it can also include flap copy, the text on the inside dust-jacket flaps.

Cover letter: A letter that accompanies some article submissions. Usually it's needed only if you have to tell the editor something specific, to give your credentials for writing a manuscript of a technical nature, or to remind the editor that the manuscript was requested or expected.

Often used as the introduction to a book proposal.

Credits, list of: A listing of your previously published works.

Critique: An evaluation of a manuscript.

Defamation: A written (libel) or spoken (slander) injury to the reputation of a living person or organization. If what is said is true, it cannot be defamatory; but that does not prevent the injured party from bringing a lawsuit.

Derivative work: A work derived from another work, such as a condensation or abridgment. Contact the copyright owner for permission before doing the abridgment, and be prepared to pay that owner a fee or royalty.

Developmental edit: Usually the first round of editing done on a manuscript. The editor helps "develop" the book by shaping its content and structure. Also called a substantive edit or line edit.

Devotion: A short manuscript based on a Scripture verse or passage that shares a personal spiritual discovery, inspires to worship, challenges to commitment or action, or encourages. A book or periodical of devotions is called a devotional.

Ed board: Editorial board meeting. The editors meet to discuss the new proposals they received to determine which ones should go to the pub board.

Editorial guidelines: See "Writers guidelines."

Em dash (—): Used to create a break or set off nonessential material or extra information in a sentence instead of using commas. *The Chicago Manual of Style* calls this punctuation mark "the most versatile of the dashes."

En dash (–): An en dash is longer than a hyphen but shorter than an em dash. Often used between numbers and dates to show a range. It was called the "en" dash because in the early days of typesetting it was the same width as the capital letter N.

Endorsements: Flattering comments about a book, usually printed on the back cover or in promotional materials.

EPUB: File format used for ebooks.

Essay: A short composition expressing the author's opinion on a specific subject.

Evangelical: A person who believes that one receives God's forgiveness for sins through Jesus Christ and believes the Bible is the authoritative Word of God. This is a broad definition for a label with broad application. Often mistakenly used as a synonym for "Christian."

Exegesis: Interpretation of a Scripture passage.

Feature article: In-depth coverage of a subject, usually focusing on a person, an event, a process, an organization, a movement, a trend, or an issue. It's written to explain, encourage, help, analyze, challenge, motivate, warn, or entertain, as well as to inform.

Filler: A short item used to "fill" a page of a periodical. It could be a joke, anecdote, light verse, short humor, puzzle, game, etc.

First rights: A periodical editor buys the right to publish a manuscript that has never been published and to do so only once.

Foreign rights: Selling or giving permission to translate or reprint published material in another country.

Foreword: Opening remarks in a book to introduce the book and its author. Often misspelled as *forward*.

Freelance: Supplied by freelance writers.

Freelancer or freelance writer: A writer who is not on salary but sells his or her material to a number of different periodicals and publishers.

Galley proof: A typeset copy of a book or magazine used to detect and correct errors before printing.

General editor: Usually, the person who oversees a large work that has multiple authors writing individual chapters for a book or a series of books. This person is not an employee within a publishing house.

General market: Non-Christian market, sometimes called secular market.

Genre: Refers to a type or classification, as in fiction or poetry. For instance, westerns, romances, and mysteries are fiction genres.

Glossy: A photo with a shiny, rather than matte, finish. Also, a publication printed on such paper.

Go-ahead: When an editor tells you to write or submit your article.

Hard copy: A printed manuscript, as opposed to one sent via email.

Independent book publisher: A book publisher who charges authors to publish their books or buy a certain number of copies, as opposed to a royalty house that pays authors. Some independent publishers also pay a royalty. Sometimes called a subsidy, vanity, self, hybrid, or custom publisher.

ISBN: International Standard Book Number, an identification code needed for every version of a book.

Journal: A periodical presenting information in a particular area, often for an academic or educated audience.

Kill fee: A fee paid for a completed article done on assignment that is subsequently not published. The amount is usually 25–50 percent of the original payment.

Libel: A published false statement that is damaging to another person's reputation, a written defamation.

Line edit: See "Developmental edit" and "Copyedit." Check to see how your editor defines each process.

Little/literary: Small-circulation periodicals whose focus is providing a forum for the literary writer, rather than on making money. Often they do not pay or pay in copies.

Mainstream fiction: Other than genre fiction (such as romance, mystery, or fantasy). Stories of people and their conflicts handled on a deeper level.

Mass market: Books intended for a wide, general market; produced in a smaller format, usually with smaller type; and sold at a lower price. The expectation is that their sales will be higher.

Matte finish: A nonglossy, nonreflective finish on a book cover. Has a textured feel.

Ms: Abbreviation for manuscript.

Mss: Abbreviation for more than one manuscript.

NASR: Abbreviation for North American Serial Rights. Permission for a periodical targeting readers in the US and Canada to publish a manuscript.

New-adult fiction: A developing fiction genre with protagonists ages 18–25. In the general market, these novels often explore sexual themes considered too "adult" for the YA or teen market. They tend to be marketed to older teen readers.

Novella: A short novel, usually 20,000–35,000 words. The length varies from publisher to publisher.

On acceptance: Editor pays a writer at the time the manuscript is accepted for publication.

On publication: Publisher pays a writer when his or her manuscript is published.

On speculation/spec: Writing something for a periodical editor with the agreement that the editor will buy it only if he or she likes it.

Onetime rights: Selling the right to publish a manuscript one time to more than one periodical, primarily to nonoverlapping audiences, such as different denominations.

Over the transom: Unsolicited manuscripts sent to a book editor. Comes from the old transom, which was a window above the door in office buildings. Manuscripts could be pushed "over the transom" into the locked office.

Overrun: The extra copies of a book printed during the initial print run.

Pen name/pseudonym: A name other than your legal name used on a manuscript to protect your identity or the identities of people included or when you wish to remain anonymous. Put the pen name in the byline under the title and your real name with your contact information.

Perfect binding: When pages of a paperback are glued together (bound) on the spine and the cover is then attached.

Periodical: A magazine, journal, newsletter, or newspaper.

Permissions: Asking permission to use text or art from a copyrighted source.

Personal experience: An account based on a real-life experience.

Personality profile: A feature article that highlights a specific person's life or accomplishments.

Plagiarism: Stealing and using the ideas or writing of someone else as your own, either as is or rewriting slightly to make it sound like your own.

POD/Print-on-demand: A printing process where books are printed one at a time or in small numbers instead of in quantity. The production cost per book is higher, but no warehousing is necessary.

POV: Point-of-view. A fiction term that describes the perspective of the one telling the story, such as first person or third person.

Press kit: A compilation of promotional materials for a book or author, used to publicize a book.

Pub board: A formal meeting where people from editorial, marketing, sales, finance, and management meet to discuss whether or not to publish a book.

Public domain: Work for which copyright protection has expired. Copyright laws vary from country to country; but in the US, works published more than 97 years ago have entered the public domain. Because the US copyright law has changed several times, check with the Copyright Office (*copyright.gov*) to determine if a work is in public domain or not. Generally, since 1978, copyright endures for the author's life plus 70 years.

Query letter: A letter sent to an editor about an article or book you propose to write and asking if he or she is interested in seeing it.

Recto: The right-hand page in printing.

Reprint rights: Selling the right to reprint an article that has already been published. You must have sold only first or onetime rights originally and wait until it has been published the first time.

Response time: The number of weeks or months it takes an editor or agent to get back to you about a query, proposal, or manuscript you sent.

Review copies: Books given to reviewers or buyers for bookstore chains and online sellers.

Royalty: The percentage an author is paid by a publisher on the sale of each copy of a book.

Running head: The text at the top of each page that can show the author's name, book title, chapter, or page number.

SASE: Self-addressed, stamped envelope. Always send it with a hard-copy manuscript or query letter.

SASP: Self-addressed, stamped postcard. May be sent with a hard-copy manuscript to be returned by the editor to indicate it arrived safely. Rarely used.

Satire: Ridicule that aims at reform.

Second serial rights: See "Reprint rights."

Secular market: An outdated term for the non-Christian publishing market.

Self-publisher: See "Independent book publisher."

Serial: Refers to publication in a periodical, such as first serial rights.

Sidebar: A short feature that accompanies an article and gives additional information about the topic, such as a recommended reading list. It is often set apart by appearing within a box or border.

Signature: All books are printed in 16-page increments or signatures (occasionally in 32-page increments for large books like Bibles). A large sheet of paper is printed, then folded multiple times. Three sides are cut (top, side, and bottom). The fourth side holds eight double-sided pages. The signatures are compiled and bound into the finished book.

Simultaneous submissions: Sending the same manuscript to more than one editor at the same time. Usually this action is done with nonoverlapping periodical markets, such as denominational publications or newspapers in different cities, or when you are writing on a timely subject. Most periodical editors don't accept simultaneous submissions, but they are the norm in the book market. Be sure to state in a cover letter or on the first page that it is a simultaneous submission.

Slander: The verbal act of defamation.

Slanting: Writing an article to meet the needs of a particular market.

Slush pile: The stack of unsolicited manuscripts that arrive at an editor's desk or email inbox.

Subsidiary rights: All the rights, other than book rights, included in a book contract, such as translations, audiobooks, book clubs, and movies.

Subsidy publisher: See "Independent book publisher."

Substantive edit: See "Developmental edit."

Synopsis: A brief summary of a work, ranging from one paragraph to several pages.

Tabloid: A newspaper-format publication about half the size of a regular newspaper.

Take-home paper: A small periodical given to Sunday-school students, children through adults. These minimagazines are published with the curriculum.

Think piece: A magazine article that has an intellectual, philosophical, or provocative approach to a subject.

Trade book: Describes a 5½" x 8½" paperback book (sometimes 6" x 9"). This is a typical trim size for a paperback. Mass-market books are smaller, around 4" x 6".

Trade magazine: A magazine whose audience is in a particular business.

Trim size: The size of a book after being trimmed in the printing process. (See "Signature" for more information.)

Unsolicited manuscript: A manuscript an editor did not specifically ask to see.

Vanity publisher: See "Independent book publisher."

Verso: The left-hand page in printing.

Vignette: A short, descriptive literary sketch of a brief scene or incident.

Vita: An outline of one's personal history and experience.

Work-for-hire: A manuscript you create for an agreed payment, and you give the publisher full ownership and control of it. You must sign a contract for this agreement to be legal.

Writers guidelines: Information provided by an editor that gives specific guidance for writing for the publication or publishing house. If the information is not offered online, email or send an SASE with your request for printed guidelines.

INDEX

1517 Media 3
1DollarScan 107
49th Parallel Award for Poetry 425
540 Writers Community 277
67 Writers 306
829 Design 107

A

A Little Red Ink 313
A Writer's Day 408
AB Writing Services LLC 313
Abingdon Press 3
Above the Pages 314
Above the Sun Media 86, 108, 314
Abundance Books LLC 4
Academy Nicholl Fellowships in
  Screenwriting 423
Academy of American Poets 425
Acevedo Word Solutions LLC 315
ACFW Alabama 282
ACFW Arizona/Christian Writers of
  the West 282
ACFW Beyond the Borders 281
ACFW California 283
ACFW Central Florida 286
ACFW Charlotte 298
ACFW Chicago 292
ACFW Colorado Springs 284
ACFW Conference 269
ACFW DFW Ready Writers 272, 306
ACFW Georgia 290
ACFW Great Lakes 295
ACFW Indiana 292
ACFW Kentucky 294
ACFW KidLit 281
ACFW Knoxville 304

ACFW Louisiana 295
ACFW Memphis 304
ACFW Mid-Tennessee 305
ACFW Minnesota N.I.C.E. 296
ACFW MozArks 297
ACFW Northwest 309
ACFW NW Arkansas 283
ACFW NY/NJ 298
ACFW Ohio 300
ACFW Oklahoma City 301
ACFW South Carolina Lowcountry 303
ACFW St. Louis 297
ACFW The Woodlands/Writers on the
  Storm 306
ACFW Upstate South Carolina 303
ACFW Virginia 308
ACFW Virginia Royal Writers Virtual
  Conference 272
ACFW WI Southeast 309
The Adams Group 381
Advanced Writers & Speakers
  Association (AWSA) 277, 393
AKA Literary Management 243
Alive Literary Agency 244
Almost an Author 205
Amazon Seller Central 125
Ambassador Communications 315
Ambassador International 4
Ambassador Literary 244
America 137
American Christian Fiction Writers
  (ACFW) 278, 412
American Zoetrope Screenplay
  Competition 423
AMG Publishers 5
Ami Editing 315

Ampelos Press 86
Ancient Faith Publishing 5
Andrea Merrell 316
Aneko Press 6
Angel Book Awards 417
Angels in Our Lives 79
Angels on Earth 137
Anglican House Publishers 6
Anglican Journal 138
Ann Kroeker, Writing Coach 316, 397
Annie Dillard Award 421
Anointed Editor 317
Anointed Scribe: Christian Author
  Business, God's Way 397
Apricot Services 381
The Arlington Catholic Herald 139
Ashberry Lane 7
Asheville Christian Writers Conference
  265
Aspire Press 7
Augsburg Fortress 7
Austin Film Festival Screenwriters
  Competition 424
Author Conservatory 397
AuthorizeMe Literary Agency 244, 317
Authors Who Serve 318
Ave Maria Press 8
Avodah Editorial Services 318

B

B&H Kids 8
B&H Publishing Group 9
Baal Hamon Publishers 10
back•door DESIGN 108
Baker Academic 10
Baker Books 11
Baker Publishing Group 11
Banner Consulting 382
Banner Literary 245, 318
Banner of Truth 11
The Baptist Bulletin 139
Baptist Standard 140
Barbara Kois 319
Barbara Mandigo Kelly Peace Poetry
  Awards 426

Barbour Publishing 12, 237
The Bard Fiction Prize 412
BBH Literary 245, 319, 382
BBS Publishing and Communications
  LLC 108, 382
BCH Fulfillment & Distribution 125
Beaming Books 12, 237
Becca Wierwille Editing and Coaching
  Services 320
Bechtel Prize 421
Beginner's Friend 195
Believers Book Services 87, 109
Bestselling Book Shepherd 320
Bethany House Publishers 13
Bible Advocate 140
The Bindery 245
BK Royston Publishing 87
Blue Lake Christian Writers
  Conference 257
Blue Leaf Book Scanning 109
Blue Mountain Arts 229
Blue Ridge Christian News 141
Blue Ridge Mountains Christian
  Writers Conference 265, 417
Blue Ridge Reader Connections 383
The Blythe Daniel Agency, Inc. 246,
  383
Bold Vision Books 13
Book Edits by Jessi 320
Book Marketing Mania 398
Book Marketing Pro Academy 398
Book Proposal Academy 398
BookBaby 87
BookCamp 321, 399
BookHound Editing 321
Books & Such Literary Management
  247
Boundless 142, 187
The Braun Book Awards 417
Brazos Press 14
Breakout Editing 321
The Breakthrough Intercessor 142
Bree Rose Creative LLC 109
Brian White Design 110
Bridge Logos, Inc. 88

Brimstone Fiction 14
The Brink 188
Brio 188
Broadleaf Books 15
Broadstreet Publishing Group 15, 237
Brown Christian Press 88
Butterfield Editorial Services 110, 322
byFaith 142

C

C. S. Lakin 322
C.Y.L.E. Agency 248
Cadet Quest 189, 195
Café 143, 189
Calla Press Publishing 15
Called Writers Christian Publishing 88
Canada Lutheran 143
The Canadian Lutheran 144
Canadian Mennonite 144
Captivate Press 89
Caring Magazine 145
Carolina Christian Writers Conference 268
Cascade Books 16
Cascade Christian Writers 273, 267, 278
Cascade Writing Contest 418
Cascadia Publishing House 16
Castle Quay Books 17
Catholic Book Publishing Corp. 17
Cathy Streiner 323
Cave Canem Angela Jackson Prize 426
Cedar Falls Christian Writers Conference 263
Celebrate Life Magazine 145
Celebrate Lit Publicity 384
Celebrate Lit Publishers 18
Celebration Web Design 110
Celticfrog Editing 323
CF4K 18, 237
Chalice Press 18
Charisma 146
Charisma House 19
Chase Neely, PC 391
Cheri Fields Editing 324

Chicken Soup for the Soul 79
Choice Media & Communications 384
Chosen 19
Chris Morris, CPA LLC 391
Chrism Press 20
Christ in Our Home 213
Christian Art Gifts 229
Christian Authors Guild 290
Christian Authors Network 278
Christian Book Academy 399
The Christian Century 147
Christian Communicator Manuscript Critique Service 324
Christian Communicators Conference 393
Christian Courier 147
Christian Devotions 214
Christian Editor Connection 324
Christian Editors Association 399
Christian Faith Publishing 89
Christian Focus Publications 20
Christian Herald 148
Christian Indie Author Network 279
Christian Indie Awards 418
Christian Indie Publishing Association 385
Christian Indie Writers' Podcast 400
Christian Leader 149
Christian Literary Agent 247
The Christian PEN: Proofreaders and Editors Network 279
Christian Publishers 225
Christian Publishing Show 400
Christian Speaker Network 393
Christian Speakers Boot Camp 393
Christian Standard 149
Christian Women Speakers 394
Christian Writers Institute 400
Christian Writers Podcast 400
Christian Writers Workshop Denton 306
Christian Writers Workshop Waco 306
Christian Writers Workshop Woodway 307
ChristianBookProposals.com 325

Christianity Today 150
The Christopher Ferebee Agency 247
The Christy Award® Art of Writing
  Conference 270
Church Publishing Incorporated 21
CKN Christian Publishing 21
CLC Publications 22
CLM Publishing 89
Clovercroft Publishing Group 90
Coleman Jones Press 90
Collaborative Editorial Solutions 325
College Press Publishing 22
Collin Smith Creative 110
Columbia 151
Columbus Christian Writers
  Association 300
Commonweal 151
Communication Associates 326
The Company Podcast 401
Compel Pro Writers Training 401
Convergent Books 22
Coretta Scott King Book Awards 411
Covenant Books 90
Creation Illustrated 152, 190, 196
Creative Communications for the
  Parish 23, 237
Creative Cornerstones 111, 326, 385
Creative Editorial Solutions 327
Creative Enterprises Studio 91, 327
Creative Inspirations 153
Credo House Publishers 91
CrossLink Publishing 24
CrossRiver Media Group 24
Crossway 25
The Crown Award 413
CSS Publishing Company, Inc. 25, 225

D

D6 Family Ministry 26
The Daily Writer 401
Daily Writing Tips 429
Danuta Gleed Literary Award 413
David & Sallie 111
David C Cook 26, 235, 237

Dayton Christian Scribes 301
Declare 394
Declare Conference 271
Deep River Books LLC 91
Deeper Revelation Books 92
Delmarva Christian Writers'
  Association 286
Denica McCall Editing 327
Denise Harmer 328
Descendant Publishing 92
Desert Rain Editing 112, 328
Design Corps 112
Destiny Image Publishers 92
DevoKids 196
Devotions 214
Dicksons, Inc. 230
DiggyPOD 112
Divine Moments 80
The Donald Hall Prize for Poetry 426
Dove Christian Publishers 27
Drama Ministry 226
DTS Magazine 153
Dunamis Words 248

E

EABooks Publishing 92, 386, 418
EAH Creative 113
Ebook Conversion and Listing Services 93
Echo Creative Media 329
Edenbrooke Productions 113
Edit Resource LLC 329
Edit with Claire 329
Editing Gallery LLC 330
Editing Insiders 330
Editmore Editorial Services 331
Editor World LLC 331
Editors' Choice Award 419
Eerdmans Books for Young Readers 27
Eerdmans, Wm. B. Publishing Co. 28
Eldridge Christian Plays and Musicals
  226
Electric Moon Publishing 93
Elk Lake Publishing, Inc. 28
Ellie Claire 230

Eloquent Edits 331
Emanate Books 29
Embolden Media Group 94, 248
Enclave Publishing 29
Encourage Publishing 94
End Game Press 30
Epic Agency 386
Eric Hoffer Book Award 419
Erin Ulrich Creative 113
Evangelical Missions Quarterly 154
Evangelical Press Association Annual
  Convention 270
EVENT Non-Fiction Contest 422
Exegetica Publishing 30, 332
Expanse Books 31
Explorers 197
Extra Ink Edits 332

F

Fairway Press 95
Faith & Friends 155
Faith Editorial Services 333
Faith on Every Corner 155
Faith Today 156
Faith, Hope, & Love Christian Writers
  258, 273, 279, 413
Faithfully Magazine 157
FaithWords 31
Faithworks Editorial & Writing Inc.
  333
Fellowship of Christian Writers 302
Fellowship Tract League 233
Festival of Faith & Writing 264
Fiesta Publishing 95
FightWrite Podcast 402
Final Touch Proofreading & Editing
  LLC 334
Findley Family Video Publications 113
First Steps Publishing 32
Fistbump Media LLC 114
Flannery O'Connor Award for Short
  Fiction 413
Florida Christian Writers Conference
  260

Flyaway Books 32
Focus on the Family 33, 157
Focus on the Family Clubhouse 197
Focus on the Family Clubhouse Jr. 198
The Foreword Collective 334
Fortress Press 33
Forward 190
Forward Day by Day 214
Forward Movement 33
The Foundry Publishing 34
Frank N. Johnson 335
Freelance Writing 429
French and English Communication
  Services 335
Friends Journal 158
Fruit of the Vine 215
Full Circle Edits 336
Funds for Writers 429
Fusion Family 159
Fusion Hybrid Publishing 95
Fusion Next 159

G

Gardner Literary 249
The Gates Group 249
Gather 160
Gems of Truth 161
Get Pubbed 414
Ginny L. Yttrip's Words for Writers
  336
Golden Wheat Literary 249
The Good Book Company 34, 237
Good Books 35, 237
Good News 161
Goodwill Media Services Corp. 96
Gospel Tract Society, Inc. 233
Grace Acres Press 35
Grace Bell Publishing 35
Grace Paley Prize for Short Fiction
  414
Grace Publishing 36
Gracewriters Podcast 402
The Grammar Queen 337
Group Publishing 235

Guide 190, 199
Guideposts 36, 162

H

The Habit 402
Hanemann Editorial 337
Hannah Linder Designs 114
Harambee Press 37
Harbourlight Books 38
HarperChristian Resources 38
HarperOne 38
Harrison House 96
Harvest House Publishers 39
Havok Seasonal Flash Fiction Contest 414
Heart and Soul Writers 307
Heart of America Christian Writers Network 293
HeartBeat 163
Heartland Christian Writers 293
Heather Kleinschmidt 337
Heather Pubols 338
Hendrickson Publishers 39
Henry McLaughlin 338
Higher Goals Awards 419
Highway News 163
HisWay Graphic Design 114, 338
Holiness Today 164
Hollis Summers Poetry Prize 426
HomeLife 164
Honest Editing 339
Honeycomb House Publishing 96

I

Ignited by the Word 190, 199
Illumify Media 97
Illumify Writers Conference 259
Illuminate Literary Agency 250
Immortalise 97
Incubator Publishing 40
Index Busters LLC 339
Influence 165
Ink & Quill Quarterly 205
Ink & Willow 230
Ink and Impact Podcast 402
Inksnatcher 115
Inkspirations Online 215
The Inky Bookwyrm 340
Inscribe Christian Writers' Fellowship 311, 272
Inscript Books 97
InSite 166
Inspiration for Writers, Inc. 340
Inspirational Writers Alive! Central Houston 307
Inspirational Writers Alive! Northwest Houston 307
Inspire a Fire 166, 190
Inspire Christian Writers 280
InterVarsity Press 40
Intrepid Times Travel Writing Competition 422
Invite Press 41
Iron Stream Media 42

J

James Alan McPherson Prize for the Novel 414
James Jones First Novel Fellowship 415
James Laughlin Award 426
James Pence Editing 341
Jamie Chavez 341
Jamie Foley 115
Jami's Words 341
Jane Rubietta 342
JDLake Studios 116
Jeanette Gardner Littleton, Publication Services 342
Jeanette Hanscome 343
Jennifer Edwards Communications 116, 343
Jennifer Gott 344
Jennifer Westbrook 116
The Jerry Jenkins Writers Guild 403
Jessica Baker 386
Jessica Snell Book Services 344
Jessie Bryce Niles Chapbook Contest 427
Jesus Can Book Series 80
Joanne Creary 345
John Hinds Freelance 345

Jomaga House 98
Jones Literary 387
Jot or Tittle Editorial Services 345
The Journal of Adventist Education 167
JourneyForth 42
Joy Media 346
Joyful Living Magazine 168
Judith Robl 346
Judson Press 43
Just Between Us 168
Just for Kids 238

K

Kairos Prize for Spiritually Uplifting Screenplays 424
Karen Appold 347
Karen Campbell Media, Inc. 387
Kari Barlow Editing Services 347
Kate Tufts Discovery Award 427
Katherine Anne Porter Prize in Short Fiction 415
Kathy Ide Writer Services 348
Kathy Kunde 348
Katie Phillips Creative Services 349
The Keep Writing Podcast 403
Kellie Book Design 117
Kentucky Christian Writers Conference 263
Keys for Kids Devotional 200, 216
Kim Peterson 349
Kingdom Writers 403
Kingsley Tufts Poetry Award 427
Kregel Publications 44
Kristen Stieffel 349

L

Lake Drive Books 98
Lancaster Christian Writers 267, 302
Launch Mission Creative 117
Leading Hearts 169
Leafwood Publishers 44
LEAVES 169
Lee Warren Communications 350
Lemuel Studio 117
Leslie L. McKee Editing 350

Leslie Santamaria 351
Lexham Press 45
Libby Gontarz Word Services 351
Life Repurposed 81
Lifestone Ministries 236
Light 170
Light from the Word 216
Lighthouse Publishing 45
Lightning Editing Services 351
Liguori Publications 46
Linda Rutzen Editorial Services 352
Linda S. Glaz Literary Agency 250
Lisa Bartelt 352
LisaVDesigns LLC 118
Lissa Halls Johnson Editorial 353
Literary Management Group 251
Little Foxes Editing 353
Liturgical Press 46
Live 170
Living Faith 217
Living Faith Kids 200, 217
Living Waters 307
Logos Word Designs LLC 354
London Lane Designs 98
Love Inspired 46
Love Lines from God 218
Loyola Press 47
Lucie Winborne 354
The Lutheran Witness 171

M

MacGregor and Luedeke Collaborative LLC 251
Manitoba Christian Writers Association 311
The Marketplace 172
Martin Publishing Services 118
Mary DeMuth Literary 251
Mature Living 172
Media Connect 388
Megan Ryan Editing 354
Meghan Stoll Editing 355
The Messenger 173
The Messianic Times 174
MG Literary Services 355

Michelle Miller Proofreading 355
Mid-South Christian Writers
  Conference 270
Middletown Area Christian Writers/
  M.A.C. Writers 301
Midpoint Trade Books 125
Midwest Proofreading Services 356
Mid-South Christian Writers
  Roundtable 296
Ministry 174
Minnesota Christian Writers Guild 296
Mission and Media 118, 356
Montrose Christian Writers Conference
  268
Moody Publishers 47
Moondance International Film Festival
  Competition 424
Morgan James Publishing 99
The Mother's Heart 175
Mountain Brook Fire 48
Mountain Brook Ink 48
Mountain Creek Books LLC 119, 357
Mountainside Novelist Retreat 266
Mt Zion Ridge Press 49, 273
Muriel Craft Bailey Memorial Poetry
  Award 427
Mutuality 175
My Healthy Church 49
My Thoughts Exactly Writers 297

N

Narrative Magazine Contests 419
National Writers Association Contests
  420
Nature Friend 191, 200
NavPress 50
Nelson Books 50
New Growth Press 50
New Leaf Publishing Group 51
New Letters Editor's Choice Award
  420
New Millennium Writing Awards 420
New Pages 429
New Works® The Works Playwriting
  Competition 424

New Zealand Christian Writers 310
Next Step Coaching Services 394
Nicole Hayes 357
Noble Creative LLC 357
North Jersey Christian Writers Group
  298
Northwest Christian Speakers 394
Northwest Christian Writers Renewal
  271
Northwestern Publishing House 51
Novel Improvement Editorial Services
  358
Novel Marketing Podcast 404
Novel Starts 415
Now What? 176

O

Oasheim Editing Services LLC 358
Oklahoma Christian Fiction Writers
  Minicon 266
Olivia Kimbrell Press 52
Omega Writers 271, 311
Open Windows 218
Our Daily Bread Publishing 53
Our Little Friend 201
Our Sunday Visitor, Inc. 53
Outreach 177
Ozarks Chapter of American Christian
  Writers 297

P

P&R Publishing 54
Pacific Press 55
Page & Pixel Publications 119, 359
Pape Commons 252
Paraclete Press 55
Paraklesis Press 56
ParentLife 177
Parsons Publishing House 56
Pastor Writer 404
Pathway Book Service 125
Patricia Cleary Miller Award for Poetry
  428
Patty Friedmann Writing Competition
  411

Pauline Books & Media 57
Paulist Press 57
Peer 191
The PEN Institute 404
Pencil Shavings 359
PENCON 273
Pens of Praise Christian Writers 309
Pensacola Christian College 236
Perpedit Publishing Ink LLC 360
Philip Levine Prize for Poetry 428
Picky, Picky Ink 360
The Pilgrim Press 58
Pilgrim Tract Society 233
Poetry Society of Virginia Poetry
  Contests 428
Poets & Writers 206, 430
Portals of Prayer 218
Power for Living 178
PratherInk Literary Services 361
PrayerShop Publishing 58
Primary Treasure 202
Prism Book Group 58
Professional Publishing Services 119,
  361
The Profitable Writer 405
PS Wells 362
Publishers Storing and Shipping 126
Publishing Disrupted 405
Publishing in Color 274
Pure Amore 59
The Purposeful Pen 405
PWC Editing 362

Q

The Quiet Hour 219

R

Read. Write. Pray. Care LLC 362
Ready Writers Psalm 45:1 283
Reality Coaching for Writers 363
Realm Awards 416
Realm Makers 261, 265, 280, 416
Rebecca Luella Miller's Editorial
  Services 363
Redemption Press 99, 388
Refine Services LLC 363
Refined Pen Edits LLC 364
Refined Pen Network 406
Reflecting God 220
Reformed Free Publishing Association
  60
Rejoice! 191, 220
Relevant 179, 191
Renew—Spiritual Retreat for Writers
  and Speakers 260
Renown Publishing 100
Resource Publications 60
Resurrection Press 61
Revell 61
Revisions by Rachel LLC 364
Richard J. Margolis Award 422
Rick Steele Editorial Services 120, 365
RJ Thesman 365
Roar, Inc. 389
Roaring Lambs Publishing 100
Roaring Writers Mentoring with Frank
  Ball 308
Rob Eagar Marketing Consultant 406
Robin L. Reed 366
Rockwall Christian Writers Group 308
Rocky Mountain Christian Writers
  Conference 259
Rose Publishing 61, 238
Roseanna White Designs 120
RoseKidz 62, 238

S

Salvation Publisher and Marketing
  Group 100
Sara Ella Editing and Coaching 366
Sara Lawson 367
Sara R. Turnquist 367
Sarah Hamaker Writers Coach 367
Sarah Hayhurst Editorial LLC 368
Scattered Light Books 368
Scott La Counte 121
Scribelance 368
Scriptapalooza Screenplay & TV
  Competition 425
Scriven Communications 369

Scrivenings Press 62
The Secret Place 221
Seed and Sparrow 62
Serious Writer 406
Sermon to Book 101
The Seymour Agency 252
SFP Designs 121
Sharing: A Journal of Christian Healing 179
She Speaks Conference 266
Short Prose Competition for Emerging Writers 422
Side Door Communications 389
Slipstream Annual Poetry Chapbook Competition 428
Smyth & Helwys Books 63
SNS Edits 369
Society of Children's Book Writers and Illustrators 412
Sojourners 179
Soul & Story 407
Southern Christian Writers 258, 295
Southern Christian Writers River Parishes 295
Speak Up Conference 264
Speak Up Speaker Services 394
Speak Write Play 370
Sports Spectrum 180
Sprinkle Publishing 101
St. Anthony Messenger 180
St. Davids Christian Writers' Conference 268
Standard 181
Starlight Magazine 202
The Steve Laube Agency 252
Stone Oak Publishing 101
Stormhill Media 121
The Story Blender Podcast 407
Story Embers Summit 274
The Storyteller's Mission with Zena Dell Lowe 407
Storywrap.ca 121
Strength & Grace 221

Sue A. Fairchild, Editor 370
Sue William Silverman Prize for Creative Nonfiction 423
Suncoast Christian Writers Group 287
Susan Hobbs Editing 370
Susan King Editorial Services 371

T

Take 5 Plus 192, 222
Tandem Services 371
Taylor University Professional Writers Conference 262
Teach Services, Inc. 102
Teachers of Vision 182
Tennessee Williams Fest Contests 420
testimony/Enrich 183
Thomas Nelson and Zondervan Gift 63
Thomas Nelson Publishers 63
Thomas Nelson TNZ Fiction 63
Three Fates Editing 372
Thrilling Life Publishers 102
Time of Singing: A Journal of Christian Poetry 183
Tinnsy Winnsy Editorial and Design Studio 122, 372
Tisha Martin Editorial 373
TLC Book Design 122
TMP Books 102
Tobias Wolff Award for Fiction 416
Today's Christian Living 184
Tom Howard/Margaret Reid Poetry Contest 429
Tom Umstattd, CPA 392
Tommy Nelson 64
Too Amazing for Coincidence 82
Torchbearer Press 103
Tracie Miles Author Coaching 253, 373
Tract Association of Friends 234
Trailblaze Editorial Services 374
Trilogy Christian Publishing 103
The Trinity Foundation 64
Tulip Publishing 65
Turn the Page Critiques 374
Twenty-Third Publications 65, 238

Two Words Publishing 122
Tyndale House Publishers 66
Tyndale Kids 66, 238
Typewriter Creative Co. 123

U

U.S. Catholic 185
UMI (Urban Ministries, Inc.) 236
Unlocked 192, 222
Upper Room Books 67
The Upper Room 223

V

Vancouver Christian Writers 309
Velocity 192
Veritas Communications 390
Vision Christian Writers Conference 258
Vivid Graphics 123

W

W Publishing 67
The War Cry 185
Warner Press 68, 231, 238
Waterbrook & Multnomah 68
Watershed Books 69
The Well Conference 264
The Well Publishers 103
Wergle Flomp Humor Poetry Contest 429
West Coast Christian Writers Conference 259, 274
WestBow Press 104
Westminster John Knox Press 69
Westwood Creative Artists 254
Whalin & Associates 374
Whitaker House 69
White Rose Publishing 70
WhiteCrown Publishing 71
WhiteFire Publishing 71
WhiteSpark Publishing 72
Wild Heart Books 72
Wildfire Marketing 390
William Carey Publishing 72

William K. Jensen Literary Agency 254
Wilt and Wade Publishing 104
Winged Publications 73
Winona Christian Writers Conference 262
Winters & King 254, 392
Wipf and Stock Publishers 73
Witness Writers 308
Wolf Creek Christian Writers Network 284
Wolgemuth & Wilson 255
Word Alive Press 104
Word and Pen Christian Writers 310
The Word Awards 421
The Word Guild 311
The Word in Season 224
Word Warriors 284
Word Weavers Boone County 294
Word Weavers Brevard County 287
Word Weavers Brookhaven 290
Word Weavers Charleston 303
Word Weavers Charlotte 299
Word Weavers Clay County 287
Word Weavers Coastal Carolinas 299
Word Weavers Columbus 290
Word Weavers Conyers 291
Word Weavers Des Moines 293
Word Weavers Destin 287
Word Weavers East Central Kentucky 294
Word Weavers Gainesville 287
Word Weavers Greater Atlanta 291
Word Weavers Harrisburg 302
Word Weavers Heartland 294
Word Weavers Hendersonville 299
Word Weavers Hickory–Newton 299
Word Weavers Indy 293
Word Weavers International 280
Word Weavers Jensen Beach 288
Word Weavers Knox County 301
Word Weavers Knoxville 305
Word Weavers Lake County 288
Word Weavers Land of Lincoln 292

Word Weavers Lexington, SC 304
Word Weavers Macon–Bibb 291
Word Weavers Maggie Valley 299
Word Weavers Nashville 305
Word Weavers North Alabama 282
Word Weavers Northeast Ohio 301
Word Weavers Northern Arizona 283
Word Weavers Ocala Chapter 288
Word Weavers on the Border 292
Word Weavers Online Groups 282
Word Weavers Orlando 288
Word Weavers Pace 288
Word Weavers Pensacola 289
Word Weavers Piedmont Triad 300
Word Weavers Pikes Peak 284
Word Weavers Pittsburgh 303
Word Weavers Sanford 289
Word Weavers Sarasota 289
Word Weavers South Middle Tennessee 305
Word Weavers Southeast Arizona 283
Word Weavers St. Croix 310
Word Weavers Tampa 289
Word Weavers Treasure Coast 289
Word Weavers Valdosta 291
Word Weavers Volusia County 290
Word Weavers West Michigan Greenville 295
Word Weavers West Michigan North Grand Rapids 296
Word Weavers Western New York 298
Word Weavers Western Slope 285
Word Weavers Wilmington 300
Word Weavers Winston–Salem 300
Word Weavers Woodbridge 309
Wordcrafts Press 74, 226
WordGirls 281
Wordmelon Inc. 375
WordPolish Consulting Services 375
WordPro Communication Services 375
Words for the Way 207
WordServe Literary Group 255

WordWise Media Services 255
Wordwrights 302
Worthy Kids 74
Worthy Publishing 75
Write by Lisa 376
Write Concepts LLC 377
The Write Flourish 377
Write for a Reason 407
Write from the Deep 408
Write His Answer Conference 274
Write His Answer Critique Groups 303
Write His Answer Ministries 377
Write in the Springs 260
Write Justified 378
The Write Life 430
Write Now Editing 378
Write to Publish Conference 262
Write Way Copyediting LLC 379
Write2Ignite Master Classes 275
The Writerly Life 408
Writers on the Rock Arvada 285
Writers on the Rock Castle Rock 285
Writers on the Rock Colorado Springs 285
Writers on the Rock Highlands Ranch 285
Writers on the Rock Lakewood 286
Writers on the Rock North Metro Denver 286
Writers on the Rock Northern Colorado 286
WritersWeekly.com 208
Writer's Digest 207
Writer's Digest Competitions 421
Writer's Edge Service 379
Writing 4 Him 304
Writing at the Red House 408
Writing Corner 209
Writing for Your Life 261, 409
Writing Pursuits 379, 409

X

Xulon Press 105

Y

Yates & Yates 256
Yo Productions LLC 123, 380
The Young Writer 409
Your Best Writing Life 410
Youth Compass 193
YWAM Publishing 75

Z

Zaq Designs + D.E. West Art & Photography 124
ZoeTrope: All-Story Short Fiction Competition 416
Zonderkidz 76
Zondervan 76, 77

NOTES

WTP

WRITE TO PUBLISH

A DIVISION OF THE CHRISTIAN WRITERS INSTITUT

JUNE 9-12, 2026

WHEATON COLLEGE, WHEATON, ILLINOIS

Not a function of Wheaton College.

REGISTER ONLINE
WRITETOPUBLISH.COM

Since 1971, Write to Publish has been training, inspiring, an encouraging writers like you, connecting them with editors an publishers who are looking for good books, articles, and other type of manuscripts; with literary agents who can represent them; an with well-published authors who can help them improve their cra

WritetoPublish.com

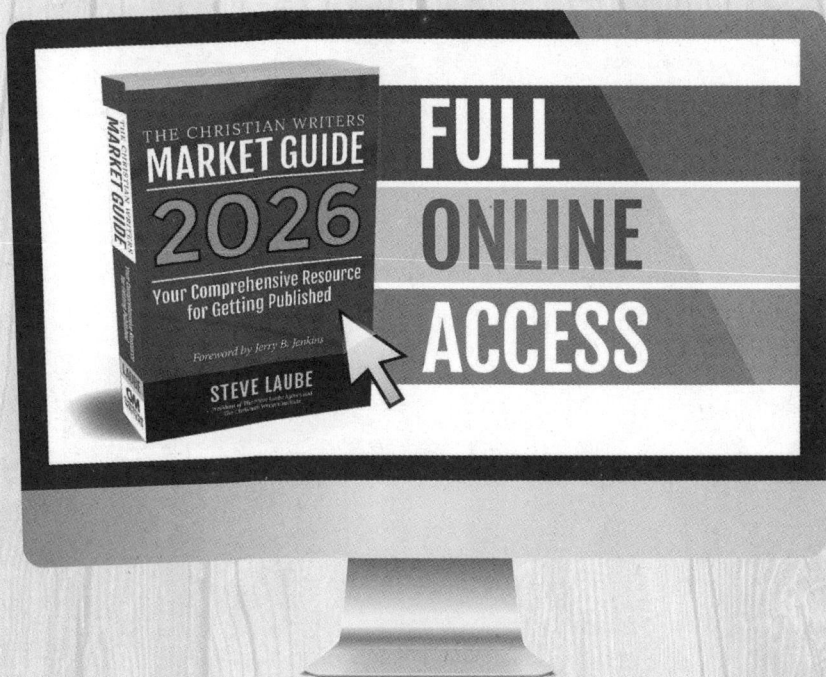